MongoDB in Action

Second Edition

KYLE BANKER
PETER BAKKUM
SHAUN VERCH
DOUGLAS GARRETT
TIM HAWKINS

MANNING

SHELTER ISLAND

Manning Publications Co.	Development editors:	Susan Conant, Jeff Bleiel
20 Baldwin Road	Technical development editors:	Brian Hanafee, Jürgen Hoffman,
PO Box 761		Wouter Thielen
Shelter Island, NY 11964	Copyeditors:	Liz Welch, Jodie Allen
	Proofreader:	Melody Dolab
	Technical proofreader:	Doug Warren
	Typesetter:	Dennis Dalinnik
	Cover designer:	Marija Tudor

ISBN: 9781617291609
Printed in the United States of America
1 2 3 4 5 6 7 8 9 10 – EBM – 21 20 19 18 17 16

MongoDB in Action

This book is dedicated to peace and human dignity
and to all those who work for these ideals

brief contents

PART 1 GETTING STARTED 1

    1 ▪ A database for the modern web 3

    2 ▪ MongoDB through the JavaScript shell 29

    3 ▪ Writing programs using MongoDB 52

PART 2 APPLICATION DEVELOPMENT IN MONGODB.................71

    4 ▪ Document-oriented data 73

    5 ▪ Constructing queries 98

    6 ▪ Aggregation 120

    7 ▪ Updates, atomic operations, and deletes 157

PART 3 MONGODB MASTERY...195

    8 ▪ Indexing and query optimization 197

    9 ▪ Text search 244

    10 ▪ WiredTiger and pluggable storage 273

    11 ▪ Replication 296

    12 ▪ Scaling your system with sharding 333

    13 ▪ Deployment and administration 376

contents

preface xvii
acknowledgments xix
about this book xxi
about the cover illustration xxiv

PART 1 GETTING STARTED..1

1 *A database for the modern web 3*

   1.1 Built for the internet 5

   1.2 MongoDB's key features 6

      Document data model 6 ▪ Ad hoc queries 10
      Indexes 10 ▪ Replication 11 ▪ Speed and durability 12
      Scaling 14

   1.3 MongoDB's core server and tools 15

      Core server 16 ▪ JavaScript shell 16 ▪ Database drivers 17
      Command-line tools 18

   1.4 Why MongoDB? 18

      MongoDB versus other databases 19 ▪ Use cases and
      production deployments 22

   1.5 Tips and limitations 24

   1.6 History of MongoDB 25

    1.7   Additional resources   27

    1.8   Summary   28

2   *MongoDB through the JavaScript shell   29*

    2.1   Diving into the MongoDB shell   30
          *Starting the shell   30 ▪ Databases, collections, and documents   31
          Inserts and queries   32 ▪ Updating documents   34
          Deleting data   38 ▪ Other shell features   38*

    2.2   Creating and querying with indexes   39
          Creating a large collection   39 ▪ Indexing and explain( )   41

    2.3   Basic administration   46
          Getting database information   46 ▪ How commands work   48

    2.4   Getting help   49

    2.5   Summary   51

3   *Writing programs using MongoDB   52*

    3.1   MongoDB through the Ruby lens   53
          *Installing and connecting   53 ▪ Inserting documents in Ruby   55
          Queries and cursors   56 ▪ Updates and deletes   57
          Database commands   58*

    3.2   How the drivers work   59
          Object ID generation   59

    3.3   Building a simple application   61
          Setting up   61 ▪ Gathering data   62 ▪ Viewing the archive   65

    3.4   Summary   69

PART 2 APPLICATION DEVELOPMENT IN MONGODB 71

4   *Document-oriented data   73*

    4.1   Principles of schema design   74

    4.2   Designing an e-commerce data model   75
          Schema basics   76 ▪ Users and orders   80 ▪ Reviews   83

    4.3   Nuts and bolts: On databases, collections,
          and documents   84
          Databases   84 ▪ Collections   87 ▪ Documents and insertion   92

    4.4   Summary   96

5 *Constructing queries   98*

   5.1 E-commerce queries   99

         Products, categories, and reviews   99 ▪ Users and orders   101

   5.2 MongoDB's query language   103

         Query criteria and selectors   103 ▪ Query options   117

   5.3 Summary   119

6 *Aggregation   120*

   6.1 Aggregation framework overview   121

   6.2 E-commerce aggregation example   123

         Products, categories, and reviews   125
         User and order   132

   6.3 Aggregation pipeline operators   135

         $project   136 ▪ $group   136 ▪ $match, $sort,
         $skip, $limit   138 ▪ $unwind   139 ▪ $out   139

   6.4 Reshaping documents   140

         String functions   141 ▪ Arithmetic functions   142
         Date functions   142 ▪ Logical functions   143
         Set Operators   144 ▪ Miscellaneous functions   145

   6.5 Understanding aggregation pipeline performance   146

         Aggregation pipeline options   147 ▪ The aggregation framework's
         explain( ) function   147 ▪ allowDiskUse option   151
         Aggregation cursor option   151

   6.6 Other aggregation capabilities   152

         .count( ) and .distinct( )   153 ▪ map-reduce   153

   6.7 Summary   156

7 *Updates, atomic operations, and deletes   157*

   7.1 A brief tour of document updates   158

         Modify by replacement   159 ▪ Modify by operator   159
         Both methods compared   160 ▪ Deciding: replacement
         vs. operators   160

   7.2 E-commerce updates   162

         Products and categories   162 ▪ Reviews   167 ▪ Orders   168

   7.3 Atomic document processing   171

         Order state transitions   172 ▪ Inventory management   174

7.4   Nuts and bolts: MongoDB updates and deletes   179

*Update types and options   179   ▪   Update operators   181
The findAndModify command   188   ▪   Deletes   189
Concurrency, atomicity, and isolation   190
Update performance notes   191*

7.5   Reviewing update operators   192

7.6   Summary   193

PART 3   MONGODB MASTERY 195

8   *Indexing and query optimization   197*

8.1   Indexing theory   198

*A thought experiment   198   ▪   Core indexing concepts   201
B-trees   205*

8.2   Indexing in practice   207

Index types   207   ▪   Index administration   211

8.3   Query optimization   216

*Identifying slow queries   217   ▪   Examining slow queries   221
Query patterns   241*

8.4   Summary   243

9   *Text search   244*

9.1   Text searches—not just pattern matching   245

*Text searches vs. pattern matching   246   ▪   Text searches vs.
web page searches   247   ▪   MongoDB text search vs. dedicated
text search engines   250*

9.2   Manning book catalog data download   253

9.3   Defining text search indexes   255

*Text index size   255   ▪   Assigning an index name and indexing
all text fields in a collection   256*

9.4   Basic text search   257

*More complex searches   259   ▪   Text search scores   261
Sorting results by text search score   262*

9.5   Aggregation framework text search   263

Where's MongoDB in Action, Second Edition?   265

9.6 Text search languages 267

Specifying language in the index 267 ▪ Specifying the language in the document 269 ▪ Specifying the language in a search 269 Available languages 271

9.7 Summary 272

10 WiredTiger and pluggable storage 273

10.1 Pluggable Storage Engine API 273

Why use different storages engines? 274

10.2 WiredTiger 275

Switching to WiredTiger 276 ▪ Migrating your database to WiredTiger 277

10.3 Comparison with MMAPv1 278

Configuration files 279 ▪ Insertion script and benchmark script 281 ▪ Insertion benchmark results 283 Read performance scripts 285 ▪ Read performance results 286 Benchmark conclusion 288

10.4 Other examples of pluggable storage engines 289

10.5 Advanced topics 290

How does a pluggable storage engine work? 290 Data structure 292 ▪ Locking 294

10.6 Summary 295

11 Replication 296

11.1 Replication overview 297

Why replication matters 297 ▪ Replication use cases and limitations 298

11.2 Replica sets 300

Setup 300 ▪ How replication works 307 Administration 314

11.3 Drivers and replication 324

Connections and failover 324 ▪ Write concern 327 Read scaling 328 ▪ Tagging 330

11.4 Summary 332

12 Scaling your system with sharding 333

12.1 Sharding overview 334

What is sharding? 334 ▪ *When should you shard? 335*

12.2 Understanding components of a sharded cluster 336

Shards: storage of application data 337 ▪ *Mongos router: router of operations 338* ▪ *Config servers: storage of metadata 338*

12.3 Distributing data in a sharded cluster 339

Ways data can be distributed in a sharded cluster 340 Distributing databases to shards 341 ▪ *Sharding within collections 341*

12.4 Building a sample shard cluster 343

Starting the mongod and mongos servers 343 ▪ *Configuring the cluster 346* ▪ *Sharding collections 347* ▪ *Writing to a sharded cluster 349*

12.5 Querying and indexing a shard cluster 355

Query routing 355 ▪ *Indexing in a sharded cluster 356 The explain() tool in a sharded cluster 357* ▪ *Aggregation in a sharded cluster 359*

12.6 Choosing a shard key 359

Imbalanced writes (hotspots) 360 ▪ *Unsplittable chunks (coarse granularity) 362* ▪ *Poor targeting (shard key not present in queries) 362* ▪ *Ideal shard keys 363* ▪ *Inherent design trade-offs (email application) 364*

12.7 Sharding in production 365

Provisioning 366 ▪ *Deployment 369* ▪ *Maintenance 370*

12.8 Summary 375

13 Deployment and administration 376

13.1 Hardware and provisioning 377

Cluster topology 377 ▪ *Deployment environment 378 Provisioning 385*

13.2 Monitoring and diagnostics 386

Logging 387 ▪ *MongoDB diagnostic commands 387 MongoDB diagnostic tools 388* ▪ *MongoDB Monitoring Service 390* ▪ *External monitoring applications 390*

13.3 Backups 391

mongodump and mongorestore 391 ▪ *Data file–based backups 392* ▪ *MMS backups 393*

13.4 Security 394

Secure environments 394 ▪ *Network encryption 395*
Authentication 397 ▪ *Replica set authentication 401*
Sharding authentication 402 ▪ *Enterprise security features 402*

13.5 Administrative tasks 402

Data imports and exports 402 ▪ *Compaction and repair 403*
Upgrading 405

13.6 Performance troubleshooting 405

Working set 406 ▪ *Performance cliff 407*
Query interactions 407 ▪ *Seek professional assistance 408*

13.7 Deployment checklist 408

13.8 Summary 410

appendix A   Installation 411
appendix B   Design patterns 421
appendix C   Binary data and GridFS 433

index 441

preface

Databases are the workhorses of the information age. Like Atlas, they go largely unnoticed in supporting the digital world we've come to inhabit. It's easy to forget that our digital interactions, from commenting and tweeting to searching and sorting, are in essence interactions with a database. Because of this fundamental yet hidden function, I always experience a certain sense of awe when thinking about databases, not unlike the awe one might feel when walking across a suspension bridge normally reserved for automobiles.

The database has taken many forms. The indexes of books and the card catalogs that once stood in libraries are both databases of a sort, as are the ad hoc structured text files of the Perl programmers of yore. Perhaps most recognizable now as databases proper are the sophisticated, fortune-making relational databases that underlie much of the world's software. These relational databases, with their idealized third-normal forms and expressive SQL interfaces, still command the respect of the old guard, and appropriately so.

But as a working web application developer a few years back, I was eager to sample the emerging alternatives to the reigning relational database. When I discovered MongoDB, the resonance was immediate. I liked the idea of using a JSON-like structure to represent data. JSON is simple, intuitive, and human-friendly. That MongoDB also based its query language on JSON lent a high degree of comfort and harmony to the usage of this new database. The interface came first. Compelling features like easy replication and sharding made the package all the more intriguing. And by the time

I'd built a few applications on MongoDB and beheld the ease of development it imparted, I'd become a convert.

Through an unlikely turn of events, I started working for 10gen, the company spearheading the development of this open source database. For two years, I've had the opportunity to improve various client drivers and work with numerous customers on their MongoDB deployments. The experience gained through this process has, I hope, been distilled faithfully into the book you're reading now.

As a piece of software and a work in progress, MongoDB is still far from perfection. But it's also successfully supporting thousands of applications atop database clusters small and large, and it's maturing daily. It's been known to bring out wonder, even happiness, in many a developer. My hope is that it can do the same for you.

This is the second edition of MongoDB in Action and I hope that you enjoy reading the book!

KYLE BANKER

acknowledgments

Thanks are due to folks at Manning for helping make this book a reality. Michael Stephens helped conceive the first edition of this book, and my development editors for this second edition, Susan Conant, Jeff Bleiel, and Maureen Spencer, pushed the book to completion while being helpful along the way. My thanks go to them.

Book writing is a time-consuming enterprise. I feel I wouldn't have found the time to finish this book had it not been for the generosity of Eliot Horowitz and Dwight Merriman. Eliot and Dwight, through their initiative and ingenuity, created MongoDB, and they trusted me to document the project. My thanks to them.

Many of the ideas in this book owe their origins to conversations I had with colleagues at 10gen. In this regard, special thanks are due to Mike Dirolf, Scott Hernandez, Alvin Richards, and Mathias Stearn. I'm especially indebted to Kristina Chowdorow, Richard Kreuter, and Aaron Staple for providing expert reviews of entire chapters for the first edition.

The following reviewers read the manuscript of the first edition at various stages during its development: Kevin Jackson, Hardy Ferentschik, David Sinclair, Chris Chandler, John Nunemaker, Robert Hanson, Alberto Lerner, Rick Wagner, Ryan Cox, Andy Brudtkuhl, Daniel Bretoi, Greg Donald, Sean Reilly, Curtis Miller, Sanchet Dighe, Philip Hallstrom, and Andy Dingley. And I am also indebted to all the reviewers who read the second edition, including Agustin Treceno, Basheeruddin Ahmed, Gavin Whyte, George Girton, Gregor Zurowski, Hardy Ferentschik, Hernan Garcia, Jeet Marwah, Johan Mattisson, Jonathan Thoms, Julia Varigina, Jürgen Hoffmann, Mike Frey, Phlippie Smith, Scott Lyons, and Steve Johnson. Special thanks go to Wouter Thielen for his work on chapter 10, technical editor Mihalis Tsoukalos, who devoted many hours to whipping the second edition into shape, and to Doug Warren for his thorough technical review of the second edition shortly before it went to press.

My amazing wife, Dominika, offered her patience and support, through the writing of both editions of this book, and to my wonderful son, Oliver, just for being awesome.

KYLE BANKER

about this book

This book is for application developers and DBAs wanting to learn MongoDB from the ground up. If you're new to MongoDB, you'll find in this book a tutorial that moves at a comfortable pace. If you're already a user, the more detailed reference sections in the book will come in handy and should fill any gaps in your knowledge. In terms of depth, the material should be suitable for all but the most advanced users. Although the book is about the latest MongoDB version, which at the time of writing is 3.0.x, it also covers the previous stable MongoDB version that is 2.6.

The code examples are written in JavaScript, the language of the MongoDB shell, and Ruby, a popular scripting language. Every effort has been made to provide simple but useful examples, and only the plainest features of the JavaScript and Ruby languages are used. The main goal is to present the MongoDB API in the most accessible way possible. If you have experience with other programming languages, you should find the examples easy to follow.

One more note about languages. If you're wondering, "Why couldn't this book use language X?" you can take heart. The officially supported MongoDB drivers feature consistent and analogous APIs. This means that once you learn the basic API for one driver, you can pick up the others fairly easily.

How to use this book

This book is part tutorial, part reference. If you're brand-new to MongoDB, then reading through the book in order makes a lot of sense. There are numerous code examples that you can run on your own to help solidify the concepts. At minimum, you'll need to install MongoDB and optionally the Ruby driver. Instructions for these installations can be found in appendix A.

If you've already used MongoDB, then you may be more interested in particular topics. Chapters 8 to 13 and all of the appendixes stand on their own and can safely be read in any order. Additionally, chapters 4 to 7 contain the so-called "nuts and bolts" sections, which focus on fundamentals. These also can be read outside the flow of the surrounding text.

Roadmap

This book is divided into three parts.

Part 1 is an end-to-end introduction to MongoDB. Chapter 1 gives an overview of MongoDB's history, features, and use cases. Chapter 2 teaches the database's core concepts through a tutorial on the MongoDB command shell. Chapter 3 walks through the design of a simple application that uses MongoDB on the back end.

Part 2 is an elaboration on the MongoDB API presented in part 1. With a specific focus on application development, the four chapters in part 2 progressively describe a schema and its operations for an e-commerce app. Chapter 4 delves into documents, the smallest unit of data in MongoDB, and puts forth a basic e-commerce schema design. Chapters 5, 6, and 7 then teach you how to work with this schema by covering queries and updates. To augment the presentation, each of the chapters in part 2 contains a detailed breakdown of its subject matter.

Part 3 focuses on MongoDB mastery. Chapter 8 is a thorough study of indexing and query optimization. The subject of Chapter 9 is text searching inside MongoDB. Chapter 10, which is totally new in this edition, is about the WiredTiger storage engine and pluggable storage, which are unique features of MongoDB v3. Chapter 11 concentrates on replication, with strategies for deploying MongoDB for high availability and read scaling. Chapter 12 describes sharding, MongoDB's path to horizontal scalability. And chapter 13 provides a series of best practices for deploying, administering, and troubleshooting MongoDB installations.

The book ends with three appendixes. Appendix A covers installation of MongoDB and Ruby (for the driver examples) on Linux, Mac OS X, and Windows. Appendix B presents a series of schema and application design patterns, and it also includes a list of anti-patterns. Appendix C shows how to work with binary data in MongoDB and how to use GridFS, a spec implemented by all the drivers, to store especially large files in the database.

Code conventions and downloads

All source code in the listings and in the text is presented in a `fixed-width font`, which separates it from ordinary text.

Code annotations accompany some of the listings, highlighting important concepts. In some cases, numbered bullets link to explanations that follow in the text.

As an open source project, 10gen keeps MongoDB's bug tracker open to the community at large. At several points in the book, particularly in the footnotes, you'll see references to bug reports and planned improvements. For example, the ticket for adding full-text search to the database is SERVER-380. To view the status of any such ticket, point your browser to http://jira.mongodb.org, and enter the ticket ID in the search box.

You can download the book's source code, with some sample data, from the book's site at http://mongodb-book.com as well as from the publisher's website at http://manning.com/MongoDBinAction.

Software requirements

To get the most out of this book, you'll need to have MongoDB installed on your system. Instructions for installing MongoDB can be found in appendix A and also on the official MongoDB website (http://mongodb.org).

If you want to run the Ruby driver examples, you'll also need to install Ruby. Again, consult appendix A for instructions on this.

Author Online

The purchase of *MongoDB in Action, Second Edition* includes free access to a private forum run by Manning Publications where you can make comments about the book, ask technical questions, and receive help from the author and other users. To access and subscribe to the forum, point your browser to www.manning.com/MongoDBinAction. This page provides information on how to get on the forum once you are registered, what kind of help is available, and the rules of conduct in the forum.

Manning's commitment to our readers is to provide a venue where a meaningful dialogue between individual readers and between readers and the author can take place. It's not a commitment to any specific amount of participation on the part of the author, whose contribution to the book's forum remains voluntary (and unpaid). We suggest you try asking him some challenging questions, lest his interest stray!

The Author Online forum and the archives of previous discussions will be accessible from the publisher's website as long as the book is in print.

about the cover illustration

The figure on the cover of MongoDB in Action is captioned "Le Bourginion," or a resident of the Burgundy region in northeastern France. The illustration is taken from a nineteenth-century collection of works by many artists, edited by Louis Curmer and published in Paris in 1841. The title of the collection is *Les Français peints par eux-mêmes*, which translates as *The French People Painted by Themselves*. Each illustration is finely drawn and colored by hand, and the rich variety of drawings in the collection reminds us vividly of how culturally apart the world's regions, towns, villages, and neighborhoods were just 200 years ago. Isolated from each other, people spoke different dialects and languages. In the streets or in the countryside, it was easy to identify where they lived and what their trade or station in life was just by their dress.

Dress codes have changed since then and the diversity by region, so rich at the time, has faded away. It is now hard to tell apart the inhabitants of different continents, let alone different towns or regions. Perhaps we have traded cultural diversity for a more varied personal life—certainly for a more varied and fast-paced technological life.

At a time when it is hard to tell one computer book from another, Manning celebrates the inventiveness and initiative of the computer business with book covers based on the rich diversity of regional life of two centuries ago, brought back to life by pictures from collections such as this one.

Part 1

Getting started

Part 1 of this book provides a broad, practical introduction to MongoDB. It also introduces the JavaScript shell and the Ruby driver, both of which are used in examples throughout the book.

We've written this book with developers in mind, but it should be useful even if you're a casual user of MongoDB. Some programming experience will prove helpful in understanding the examples, though we focus most on MongoDB itself. If you've worked with relational databases in the past, great! We compare these to MongoDB often.

MongoDB version 3.0.x is the most recent MongoDB version at the time of writing, but most of the discussion applies to previous versions of MongoDB (and presumably later versions). We usually mention it when a particular feature wasn't available in previous versions.

You'll use JavaScript for most examples because MongoDB's JavaScript shell makes it easy for you to experiment with these queries. Ruby is a popular language among MongoDB users, and our examples show how the use of Ruby in real-world applications can take advantage of MongoDB. Rest assured, even if you're not a Ruby developer you can access MongoDB in much the same way as in other languages.

In chapter 1, you'll look at MongoDB's history, design goals, and application use cases. You'll also see what makes MongoDB unique as you compare it with other databases emerging in the "NoSQL" space.

In chapter 2, you'll become conversant in the language of MongoDB's shell. You'll learn the basics of MongoDB's query language, and you'll practice by creating, querying, updating, and deleting documents. The chapter also features some advanced shell tricks and MongoDB commands.

Chapter 3 introduces the MongoDB drivers and MongoDB's data format, BSON. Here you'll learn how to talk to the database through the Ruby programming language, and you'll build a simple application in Ruby demonstrating MongoDB's flexibility and query power.

To get the most out of this book, follow along and try out the examples. If you don't have MongoDB installed yet, appendix A can help you get it running on your machine.

A database
for the modern web

This chapter covers

- MongoDB's history, design goals, and key features
- A brief introduction to the shell and drivers
- Use cases and limitations
- Recent changes in MongoDB

If you've built web applications in recent years, you've probably used a relational database as the primary data store. If you're familiar with SQL, you might appreciate the usefulness of a well-normalized[1] data model, the necessity of transactions, and the assurances provided by a durable storage engine. Simply put, the relational database is mature and well-known. When developers start advocating alternative datastores, questions about the viability and utility of these new technologies arise. Are these new datastores replacements for relational database systems? Who's using them in production, and why? What trade-offs are involved in moving

---

[1] When we mention normalization we're usually talking about reducing redundancy when you store data. For example, in a SQL database you can split parts of your data, such as users and orders, into their own tables to reduce redundant storage of usernames.

to a nonrelational database? The answers to those questions rest on the answer to this one: why are developers interested in MongoDB?

MongoDB is a database management system designed to rapidly develop web applications and internet infrastructure. The data model and persistence strategies are built for high read-and-write throughput and the ability to scale easily with automatic failover. Whether an application requires just one database node or dozens of them, MongoDB can provide surprisingly good performance. If you've experienced difficulties scaling relational databases, this may be great news. But not everyone needs to operate at scale. Maybe all you've ever needed is a single database server. Why would you use MongoDB?

Perhaps the biggest reason developers use MongoDB isn't because of its scaling strategy, but because of its intuitive data model. MongoDB stores its information in documents rather than rows. What's a document? Here's an example:

```
{
  _id: 10,
  username: 'peter',
  email: 'pbbakkum@gmail.com'
}
```

This is a pretty simple document; it's storing a few fields of information about a user (he sounds cool). What's the advantage of this model? Consider the case where you'd like to store multiple emails for each user. In the relational world, you might create a separate table of email addresses and the users to which they're associated. MongoDB gives you another way to store these:

```
{
  _id: 10,
  username: 'peter',
  email: [
    'pbbakkum@gmail.com',
    'pbb7c@virginia.edu'
  ]
}
```

And just like that, you've created an array of email addresses and solved your problem. As a developer, you'll find it extremely useful to be able to store a structured document like this in your database without worrying about fitting a schema or adding more tables when your data changes.

MongoDB's document format is based on JSON, a popular scheme for storing arbitrary data structures. JSON is an acronym for *JavaScript Object Notation*. As you just saw, JSON structures consist of keys and values, and they can nest arbitrarily deep. They're analogous to the dictionaries and hash maps of other programming languages.

A document-based data model can represent rich, hierarchical data structures. It's often possible to do without the multitable joins common to relational databases. For example, suppose you're modeling products for an e-commerce site. With a fully normalized relational data model, the information for any one product might be divided among dozens of tables. If you want to get a product representation from the database shell, you'll need to write a SQL query full of joins.

With a document model, by contrast, most of a product's information can be represented within a single document. When you open the MongoDB JavaScript shell, you can easily get a comprehensible representation of your product with all its information hierarchically organized in a JSON-like structure. You can also query for it and manipulate it. MongoDB's query capabilities are designed specifically for manipulating structured documents, so users switching from relational databases experience a similar level of query power. In addition, most developers now work with object-oriented languages, and they want a data store that better maps to objects. With MongoDB, an object defined in the programming language can often be persisted as is, removing some of the complexity of object mappers. If you're experienced with relational databases, it can be helpful to approach MongoDB from the perspective of transitioning your existing skills into this new database.

If the distinction between a tabular and object representation of data is new to you, you probably have a lot of questions. Rest assured that by the end of this chapter you'll have a thorough overview of MongoDB's features and design goals. You'll learn the history of MongoDB and take a tour of the database's main features. Next, you'll explore some alternative database solutions in the NoSQL[2] category and see how MongoDB fits in. Finally, you'll learn where MongoDB works best and where an alternative datastore might be preferable given some of MongoDB's limitations.

MongoDB has been criticized on several fronts, sometimes fairly and sometimes unfairly. Our view is that it's a tool in the developer's toolbox, like any other database, and you should know its limitations and strengths. Some workloads demand relational joins and different memory management than MongoDB provides. On the other hand, the document-based model fits particularly well with some workloads, and the lack of a schema means that MongoDB can be one of the best tools for quickly developing and iterating on an application. Our goal is to give you the information you need to decide if MongoDB is right for you and explain how to use it effectively.

1.1 Built for the internet

The history of MongoDB is brief but worth recounting, for it was born out of a much more ambitious project. In mid-2007, a startup in New York City called 10gen began work on a platform-as-a-service (PaaS), composed of an application server and a database, that would host web applications and scale them as needed. Like Google's App Engine, 10gen's platform was designed to handle the scaling and management of hardware and software infrastructure automatically, freeing developers to focus solely on their application code. 10gen ultimately discovered that most developers didn't feel comfortable giving up so much control over their technology stacks, but users did

---

[2] The umbrella term NoSQL was coined in 2009 to lump together the many nonrelational databases gaining in popularity at the time, one of their commonalities being that they use a query language other than SQL.

want 10gen's new database technology. This led 10gen to concentrate its efforts solely on the database that became MongoDB.

10gen has since changed its name to MongoDB, Inc. and continues to sponsor the database's development as an open source project. The code is publicly available and free to modify and use, subject to the terms of its license, and the community at large is encouraged to file bug reports and submit patches. Still, most of MongoDB's core developers are either founders or employees of MongoDB, Inc., and the project's roadmap continues to be determined by the needs of its user community and the overarching goal of creating a database that combines the best features of relational databases and distributed key-value stores. Thus, MongoDB, Inc.'s business model isn't unlike that of other well-known open source companies: support the development of an open source product and provide subscription services to end users.

The most important thing to remember from its history is that MongoDB was intended to be an extremely simple, yet flexible, part of a web-application stack. These kinds of use cases have driven the choices made in MongoDB's development and help explain its features.

1.2   MongoDB's key features

A database is defined in large part by its data model. In this section, you'll look at the document data model, and then you'll see the features of MongoDB that allow you to operate effectively on that model. This section also explores operations, focusing on MongoDB's flavor of replication and its strategy for scaling horizontally.

1.2.1   Document data model

MongoDB's data model is document-oriented. If you're not familiar with documents in the context of databases, the concept can be most easily demonstrated by an example. A JSON document needs double quotes everywhere except for numeric values. The following listing shows the JavaScript version of a JSON document where double quotes aren't necessary.

Listing 1.1   A document representing an entry on a social news site

```
{
  _id: ObjectID('4bd9e8e17cefd644108961bb'),        ◁─── _id field,
  title: 'Adventures in Databases',                       primary key
  url: 'http://example.com/databases.txt',
  author: 'msmith',
  vote_count: 20,
  tags: ['databases', 'mongodb', 'indexing'],       ◁───  Tags stored
  image: {                                        ◁─           as array of
    url: 'http://example.com/db.jpg',                    ❶ strings
    caption: 'A database.',
    type: 'jpg',                                         Attribute pointing to
    size: 75381,                                     ❷ another document
    data: 'Binary'
  },
```

```
  comments: [                                ◁──┐   Comments stored
    {                                            │   as array of
      user: 'bjones',                          ❸   comment objects
      text: 'Interesting article.'
    },
    {
      user: 'sverch',
      text: 'Color me skeptical!'
    }
  ]
}
```

This listing shows a JSON document representing an article on a social news site (think Reddit or Twitter). As you can see, a *document* is essentially a set of property names and their values. The values can be simple data types, such as strings, numbers, and dates. But these values can also be arrays and even other JSON documents ❷. These latter constructs permit documents to represent a variety of rich data structures. You'll see that the sample document has a property, `tags` ❶, which stores the article's tags in an array. But even more interesting is the `comments` property ❸, which is an array of comment documents.

Internally, MongoDB stores documents in a format called Binary JSON, or BSON. BSON has a similar structure but is intended for storing many documents. When you query MongoDB and get results back, these will be translated into an easy-to-read data structure. The MongoDB shell uses JavaScript and gets documents in JSON, which is what we'll use for most of our examples. We'll discuss the BSON format extensively in later chapters.

Where relational databases have tables, MongoDB has *collections*. In other words, MySQL (a popular relational database) keeps its data in tables of rows, while MongoDB keeps its data in collections of documents, which you can think of as a group of documents. Collections are an important concept in MongoDB. The data in a collection is stored to disk, and most queries require you to specify which collection you'd like to target.

Let's take a moment to compare MongoDB collections to a standard relational database representation of the same data. Figure 1.1 shows a likely relational analog. Because tables are essentially flat, representing the various one-to-many relationships in your post document requires multiple tables. You start with a posts table containing the core information for each post. Then you create three other tables, each of which includes a field, `post_id`, referencing the original post. The technique of separating an object's data into multiple tables like this is known as *normalization*. A normalized data set, among other things, ensures that each unit of data is represented in one place only.

But strict normalization isn't without its costs. Notably, some assembly is required. To display the post you just referenced, you'll need to perform a join between the post and comments tables. Ultimately, the question of whether strict normalization is required depends on the kind of data you're modeling, and chapter 4 will have much more to say about the topic. What's important to note here is that a document-oriented data model naturally represents data in an aggregate form, allowing you to work with an object holistically: all the data representing a post, from comments to tags, can be fitted into a single database object.

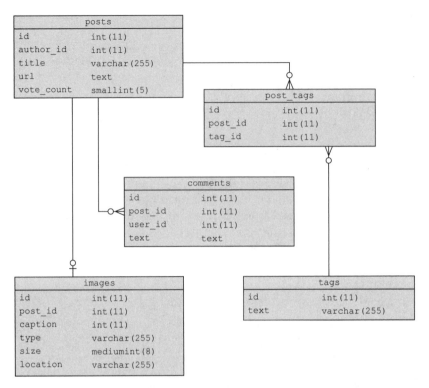

Figure 1.1   A basic relational data model for entries on a social news site. The line terminator that looks like a cross represents a one-to-one relationship, so there's only one row from the images table associated with a row from the posts table. The line terminator that branches apart represents a one-to-many relationship, so there can be many rows in the comments table associated with a row from the posts table.

You've probably noticed that in addition to providing a richness of structure, documents needn't conform to a prespecified schema. With a relational database, you store rows in a table. Each table has a strictly defined schema specifying which columns and types are permitted. If any row in a table needs an extra field, you have to alter the table explicitly. MongoDB groups documents into collections, containers that don't impose any sort of schema. In theory, each document in a collection can have a completely different structure; in practice, a collection's document will be relatively uniform. For instance, every document in the posts collection will have fields for the title, tags, comments, and so forth.

SCHEMA-LESS MODEL ADVANTAGES

This lack of imposed schema confers some advantages. First, your application code, and not the database, enforces the data's structure. This can speed up initial application development when the schema is changing frequently.

Second, and more significantly, a schema-less model allows you to represent data with truly variable properties. For example, imagine you're building an e-commerce

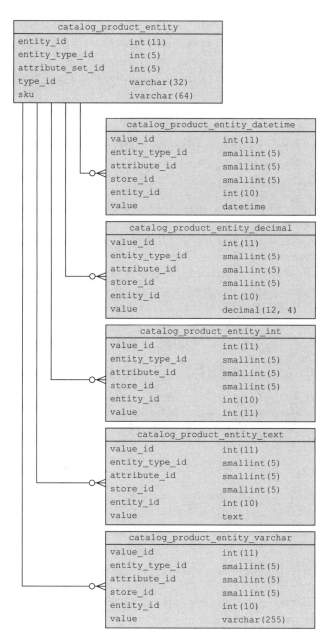

Figure 1.2 A portion of the schema for an e-commerce application. These tables facilitate dynamic attribute creation for products.

product catalog. There's no way of knowing in advance what attributes a product will have, so the application will need to account for that variability. The traditional way of handling this in a fixed-schema database is to use the entity-attribute-value pattern,[3] shown in figure 1.2.

---

[3] For more information see http://en.wikipedia.org/wiki/Entity-attribute-value_model.

What you're seeing is one section of the data model for an e-commerce framework. Note the series of tables that are all essentially the same, except for a single attribute, value, that varies only by data type. This structure allows an administrator to define additional product types and their attributes, but the result is significant complexity. Think about firing up the MySQL shell to examine or update a product modeled in this way; the SQL joins required to assemble the product would be enormously complex. Modeled as a document, no join is required, and new attributes can be added dynamically. Not all relational models are this complex, but the point is that when you're developing a MongoDB application you don't need to worry as much about what data fields you'll need in the future.

1.2.2   Ad hoc queries

To say that a system supports *ad hoc queries* is to say that it isn't necessary to define in advance what sorts of queries the system will accept. Relational databases have this property; they'll faithfully execute any well-formed SQL query with any number of conditions. Ad hoc queries are easy to take for granted if the only databases you've ever used have been relational. But not all databases support dynamic queries. For instance, key-value stores are queryable on one axis only: the value's key. Like many other systems, key-value stores sacrifice rich query power in exchange for a simple scalability model. One of MongoDB's design goals is to preserve most of the query power that's been so fundamental to the relational database world.

To see how MongoDB's query language works, let's take a simple example involving posts and comments. Suppose you want to find all posts tagged with the term *politics* having more than 10 votes. A SQL query would look like this:

```
SELECT * FROM posts
  INNER JOIN posts_tags ON posts.id = posts_tags.post_id
  INNER JOIN tags ON posts_tags.tag_id == tags.id
  WHERE tags.text = 'politics' AND posts.vote_count > 10;
```

The equivalent query in MongoDB is specified using a document as a matcher. The special $gt key indicates the greater-than condition:

```
db.posts.find({'tags': 'politics', 'vote_count': {'$gt': 10}});
```

Note that the two queries assume a different data model. The SQL query relies on a strictly normalized model, where posts and tags are stored in distinct tables, whereas the MongoDB query assumes that tags are stored within each post document. But both queries demonstrate an ability to query on arbitrary combinations of attributes, which is the essence of ad hoc query ability.

1.2.3   Indexes

A critical element of ad hoc queries is that they search for values that you don't know when you create the database. As you add more and more documents to your database, searching for a value becomes increasingly expensive; it's a needle in an ever-expanding haystack. Thus, you need a way to efficiently search through your data. The solution to this is an index.

The best way to understand database indexes is by analogy: many books have indexes matching keywords to page numbers. Suppose you have a cookbook and want to find all recipes calling for pears (maybe you have a lot of pears and don't want them to go bad). The time-consuming approach would be to page through every recipe, checking each ingredient list for pears. Most people would prefer to check the book's index for the pears entry, which would give a list of all the recipes containing pears. Database indexes are data structures that provide this same service.

Indexes in MongoDB are implemented as a *B-tree* data structure. B-tree indexes, also used in many relational databases, are optimized for a variety of queries, including range scans and queries with sort clauses. But WiredTiger has support for log-structured merge-trees (LSM) that's expected to be available in the MongoDB 3.2 production release.

Most databases give each document or row a *primary key*, a unique identifier for that datum. The primary key is generally indexed automatically so that each datum can be efficiently accessed using its unique key, and MongoDB is no different. But not every database allows you to also index the data inside that row or document. These are called *secondary indexes*. Many NoSQL databases, such as HBase, are considered *key-value stores* because they don't allow any secondary indexes. This is a significant feature in MongoDB; by permitting multiple secondary indexes MongoDB allows users to optimize for a wide variety of queries.

With MongoDB, you can create up to 64 indexes per collection. The kinds of indexes supported include all the ones you'd find in an RDMBS; ascending, descending, unique, compound-key, hashed, text, and even geospatial indexes[4] are supported. Because MongoDB and most RDBMSs use the same data structure for their indexes, advice for managing indexes in both of these systems is similar. You'll begin looking at indexes in the next chapter, and because an understanding of indexing is so crucial to efficiently operating a database, chapter 8 is devoted to the topic.

1.2.4 Replication

MongoDB provides database replication via a topology known as a replica set. *Replica sets* distribute data across two or more machines for redundancy and automate failover in the event of server and network outages. Additionally, replication is used to scale database reads. If you have a read-intensive application, as is commonly the case on the web, it's possible to spread database reads across machines in the replica set cluster.

---

[4] Geospatial indexes allow you to efficiently query for latitude and longitude points; they're discussed later in this book.

Replica sets consist of many MongoDB servers, usually with each server on a separate physical machine; we'll call these nodes. At any given time, one node serves as the replica set primary node and one or more nodes serve as secondaries. Like the master-slave replication that you may be familiar with from other databases, a replica set's primary node can accept both reads and writes, but the secondary nodes are read-only. What makes replica sets unique is their support for automated failover: if the primary node fails, the cluster will pick a secondary node and automatically promote it to primary. When the former primary comes back online, it'll do so as a secondary. An illustration of this process is provided in figure 1.3.

Replication is one of MongoDB's most useful features and we'll cover it in depth later in the book.

1.2.5   *Speed and durability*

To understand MongoDB's approach to durability, it pays to consider a few ideas first. In the realm of database systems there exists an inverse relationship between write speed and durability. *Write speed* can be understood as the volume of inserts, updates, and deletes that a database can process in a given time frame. *Durability* refers to level of assurance that these write operations have been made permanent.

For instance, suppose you write 100 records of 50 KB each to a database and then immediately cut the power on the server. Will those records be recoverable when you bring the machine back online? The answer depends on your database system, its configuration, and the hardware hosting it. Most databases enable good durability by default, so you're safe if this happens. For some applications, like storing log lines, it might make more sense to have faster writes, even if you risk data loss. The problem is that writing to a magnetic hard drive is orders of magnitude slower than writing to RAM. Certain databases, such as Memcached, write exclusively to RAM, which makes them extremely fast but completely volatile. On the other hand, few databases write exclusively to disk because the low performance of such an operation is unacceptable. Therefore, database designers often need to make compromises to provide the best balance of speed and durability.

1. A working replica set

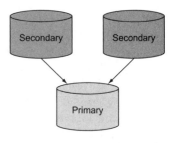

2. Original primary node fails and a secondary is promoted to primary.

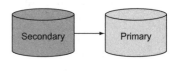

3. Original primary comes back online as a secondary.

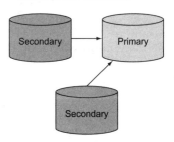

Figure 1.3   Automated failover with a replica set

Transaction logging

One compromise between speed and durability can be seen in MySQL's InnoDB. InnoDB is a transactional storage engine, which by definition must guarantee durability. It accomplishes this by writing its updates in two places: once to a transaction log and again to an in-memory buffer pool. The transaction log is synced to disk immediately, whereas the buffer pool is only eventually synced by a background thread. The reason for this dual write is because generally speaking, random I/O is much slower than sequential I/O. Because writes to the main data files constitute random I/O, it's faster to write these changes to RAM first, allowing the sync to disk to happen later. But some sort of write to disk is necessary to guarantee durability and it's important that the write be sequential, and thus fast; this is what the transaction log provides. In the event of an unclean shutdown, InnoDB can replay its transaction log and update the main data files accordingly. This provides an acceptable level of performance while guaranteeing a high level of durability.

In MongoDB's case, users control the speed and durability trade-off by choosing write semantics and deciding whether to enable journaling. Journaling is enabled by default since MongoDB v2.0. In the drivers released after November 2012 MongoDB safely guarantees that a write has been written to RAM before returning to the user, though this characteristic is configurable. You can configure MongoDB to *fire-and-forget*, sending off a write to the server without waiting for an acknowledgment. You can also configure MongoDB to guarantee that a write has gone to multiple replicas before considering it committed. For high-volume, low-value data (like clickstreams and logs), fire-and-forget-style writes can be ideal. For important data, a safe mode setting is necessary. It's important to know that in MongoDB versions older than 2.0, the unsafe fire-and-forget strategy was set as the default, because when 10gen started the development of MongoDB, it was focusing solely on that data tier and it was believed that the application tier would handle such errors. But as MongoDB was used for more and more use cases and not solely for the web tier, it was deemed that it was too unsafe for any data you didn't want to lose.

Since MongoDB v2.0, journaling is enabled by default. With *journaling*, every write is flushed to the journal file every 100 ms. If the server is ever shut down uncleanly (say, in a power outage), the journal will be used to ensure that MongoDB's data files are restored to a consistent state when you restart the server. This is the safest way to run MongoDB.

It's possible to run the server without journaling as a way of increasing performance for some write loads. The downside is that the data files may be corrupted after an unclean shutdown. As a consequence, anyone planning to disable journaling should run with replication, preferably to a second datacenter, to increase the likelihood that a pristine copy of the data will still exist even if there's a failure.

MongoDB was designed to give you options in the speed-durability tradeoff, but we highly recommend safe settings for essential data. The topics of replication and durability are vast; you'll see a detailed exploration of them in chapter 11.

1.2.6   *Scaling*

The easiest way to scale most databases is to upgrade the hardware. If your application is running on a single node, it's usually possible to add some combination of faster disks, more memory, and a beefier CPU to ease any database bottlenecks. The technique of augmenting a single node's hardware for scale is known as *vertical scaling*, or *scaling up*. Vertical scaling has the advantages of being simple, reliable, and cost-effective up to a certain point, but eventually you reach a point where it's no longer feasible to move to a better machine.

It then makes sense to consider scaling *horizontally*, or *scaling out* (see figure 1.4). Instead of beefing up a single node, scaling horizontally means distributing the database across multiple machines. A horizontally scaled architecture can run on many smaller, less expensive machines, often reducing your hosting costs. What's more, the distribution of data across machines mitigates the consequences of failure. Machines will unavoidably fail from time to time. If you've scaled vertically and the machine fails, then you need to deal with the failure of a machine on which most of your system depends. This may not be an issue if a copy of the data exists on a replicated slave, but it's still the case that only a single server need fail to bring down the entire system. Contrast that with failure inside a horizontally scaled architecture. This may be less catastrophic because a single machine represents a much smaller percentage of the system as a whole.

MongoDB was designed to make horizontal scaling manageable. It does so via a range-based partitioning mechanism, known as *sharding*, which automatically manages

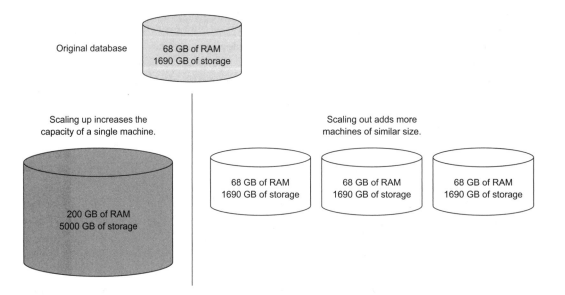

Figure 1.4   Horizontal versus vertical scaling

the distribution of data across nodes. There's also a hash- and tag-based sharding mechanism, but it's just another form of the range-based sharding mechanism.

The sharding system handles the addition of shard nodes, and it also facilitates automatic failover. Individual shards are made up of a replica set consisting of at least two nodes, ensuring automatic recovery with no single point of failure. All this means that no application code has to handle these logistics; your application code communicates with a sharded cluster just as it speaks to a single node. Chapter 12 explores sharding in detail.

You've seen a lot of MongoDB's most compelling features; in chapter 2, you'll begin to see how some of them work in practice. But at this point, let's take a more pragmatic look at the database. In the next section, you'll look at MongoDB in its environment, the tools that ship with the core server, and a few ways of getting data in and out.

1.3 MongoDB's core server and tools

MongoDB is written in C++ and actively developed by MongoDB, Inc. The project compiles on all major operating systems, including Mac OS X, Windows, Solaris, and most flavors of Linux. Precompiled binaries are available for each of these platforms at http://mongodb.org. MongoDB is open source and licensed under the GNU-Affero General Public License (AGPL). The source code is freely available on GitHub, and contributions from the community are frequently accepted. But the project is guided by the MongoDB, Inc. core server team, and the overwhelming majority of commits come from this group.

> **About the GNU-AGPL**
>
> The GNU-AGPL is the subject of some controversy. In practice, this licensing means that the source code is freely available and that contributions from the community are encouraged. But GNU-AGPL requires that any modifications made to the source code must be published publicly for the benefit of the community. This can be a concern for companies that want to modify MongoDB but don't want to publish these changes to others. For companies wanting to safeguard their core server enhancements, MongoDB, Inc. provides special commercial licenses.

MongoDB v1.0 was released in November 2009. Major releases appear approximately once every three months, with even point numbers for stable branches and odd numbers for development. As of this writing, the latest stable release is v3.0.[5]

What follows is an overview of the components that ship with MongoDB along with a high-level description of the tools and language drivers for developing applications with the database.

---

[5] You should always use the latest stable point release; for example, v3.0.6. Check out the complete installation instructions in appendix A.

1.3.1 *Core server*

The core database server runs via an executable called `mongod` (`mongodb.exe` on Windows). The `mongod` server process receives commands over a network socket using a custom binary protocol. All the data files for a `mongod` process are stored by default in /data/db on Unix-like systems and in c:\data\db on Windows. Some of the examples in this text may be more Linux-oriented. Most of our MongoDB production servers are run on Linux because of its reliability, wide adoption, and excellent tools.

`mongod` can be run in several modes, such as a standalone server or a member of a replica set. Replication is recommended when you're running MongoDB in production, and you generally see replica set configurations consisting of two replicas plus a `mongod` running in arbiter mode. When you use MongoDB's sharding feature, you'll also run `mongod` in config server mode. Finally, a separate routing server exists called `mongos`, which is used to send requests to the appropriate shard in this kind of setup. Don't worry too much about all these options yet; we'll describe each in detail in the replication (11) and sharding (12) chapters.

Configuring a `mongod` process is relatively simple; it can be accomplished both with command-line arguments and with a text configuration file. Some common configurations to change are setting the port that `mongod` listens on and setting the directory where it stores its data. To see these configurations, you can run `mongod --help`.

1.3.2 *JavaScript shell*

The MongoDB command shell is a JavaScript[6]-based tool for administering the database and manipulating data. The `mongo` executable loads the shell and connects to a specified `mongod` process, or one running locally by default. The shell was developed to be similar to the MySQL shell; the biggest differences are that it's based on JavaScript and SQL isn't used. For instance, you can pick your database and then insert a simple document into the `users` collection like this:

```
> use my_database
> db.users.insert({name: "Kyle"})
```

The first command, indicating which database you want to use, will be familiar to users of MySQL. The second command is a JavaScript expression that inserts a simple document. To see the results of your insert, you can issue a simple query:

```
> db.users.find()
{ _id: ObjectId("4ba667b0a90578631c9caea0"), name: "Kyle" }
```

---

[6] If you'd like an introduction or refresher to JavaScript, a good resource is http://eloquentjavascript.net. JavaScript has a syntax similar to languages like C or Java. If you're familiar with either of those, you should be able to understand most of the JavaScript examples.

The find method returns the inserted document, with an object ID added. All documents require a primary key stored in the _id field. You're allowed to enter a custom _id as long as you can guarantee its uniqueness. But if you omit the _id altogether, a MongoDB object ID will be inserted automatically.

In addition to allowing you to insert and query for data, the shell permits you to run administrative commands. Some examples include viewing the current database operation, checking the status of replication to a secondary node, and configuring a collection for sharding. As you'll see, the MongoDB shell is indeed a powerful tool that's worth getting to know well.

All that said, the bulk of your work with MongoDB will be done through an application written in a given programming language. To see how that's done, we must say a few things about MongoDB's language drivers.

1.3.3 Database drivers

If the notion of a database driver conjures up nightmares of low-level device hacking, don't fret; the MongoDB drivers are easy to use. The driver is the code used in an application to communicate with a MongoDB server. All drivers have functionality to query, retrieve results, write data, and run database commands. Every effort has been made to provide an API that matches the idioms of the given language while also maintaining relatively uniform interfaces across languages. For instance, all of the drivers implement similar methods for saving a document to a collection, but the representation of the document itself will usually be whatever is most natural to each language. In Ruby, that means using a Ruby hash. In Python, a dictionary is appropriate. And in Java, which lacks any analogous language primitive, you usually represent documents as a Map object or something similar. Some developers like using an object-relational mapper to help manage representing their data this way, but in practice, the MongoDB drivers are complete enough that this isn't required.

> **Language drivers**
>
> As of this writing, MongoDB, Inc. officially supports drivers for C, C++, C#, Erlang, Java, Node.js, JavaScript, Perl, PHP, Python, Scala, and Ruby—and the list is always growing. If you need support for another language, there are probably community-supported drivers for it, developed by MongoDB users but not officially managed by MongoDB, Inc., most of which are pretty good. If no community-supported driver exists for your language, specifications for building a new driver are documented at http://mongodb.org. Because all of the officially supported drivers are used heavily in production and provided under the Apache license, plenty of good examples are freely available for would-be driver authors.

Beginning in chapter 3, we describe how the drivers work and how to use them to write programs.

1.3.4   *Command-line tools*

MongoDB is bundled with several command-line utilities:

- mongodump and mongorestore—Standard utilities for backing up and restoring a database. mongodump saves the database's data in its native BSON format and thus is best used for backups only; this tool has the advantage of being usable for hot backups, which can easily be restored with mongorestore.

- mongoexport and mongoimport—Export and import JSON, CSV, and TSV[7] data; this is useful if you need your data in widely supported formats. mongoimport can also be good for initial imports of large data sets, although before importing, it's often desirable to adjust the data model to take best advantage of MongoDB. In such cases, it's easier to import the data through one of the drivers using a custom script.

- mongosniff—A wire-sniffing tool for viewing operations sent to the database. It essentially translates the BSON going over the wire to human-readable shell statements.

- mongostat—Similar to iostat, this utility constantly polls MongoDB and the system to provide helpful stats, including the number of operations per second (inserts, queries, updates, deletes, and so on), the amount of virtual memory allocated, and the number of connections to the server.

- mongotop—Similar to top, this utility polls MongoDB and shows the amount of time it spends reading and writing data in each collection.

- mongoperf—Helps you understand the disk operations happening in a running MongoDB instance.

- mongooplog—Shows what's happening in the MongoDB oplog.

- Bsondump—Converts BSON files into human-readable formats including JSON. We'll cover BSON in much more detail in chapter 2.

1.4   *Why MongoDB?*

You've seen a few reasons why MongoDB might be a good choice for your projects. Here, we'll make this more explicit, first by considering the overall design objectives of the MongoDB project. According to its creators, MongoDB was designed to combine the best features of key-value stores and relational databases. Because of their simplicity, key-value stores are extremely fast and relatively easy to scale. Relational databases are more difficult to scale, at least horizontally, but have a rich data model and a powerful query language. MongoDB is intended to be a compromise between these two designs, with useful aspects of both. The end goal is for it to be a database that scales easily, stores rich data structures, and provides sophisticated query mechanisms.

---

[7]   CSV stands for Comma-Separated Values, meaning data split into multiple fields, which are separated by commas. This is a popular format for representing tabular data, since column names and many rows of values can be listed in a readable file. TSV stands for Tab-Separated Values—the same format with tabs used instead of commas.

In terms of use cases, MongoDB is well-suited as a primary datastore for web applications, analytics and logging applications, and any application requiring a medium-grade cache. In addition, because it easily stores schema-less data, MongoDB is also good for capturing data whose structure can't be known in advance.

The preceding claims are bold. To substantiate them, we're going to take a broad look at the varieties of databases currently in use and contrast them with MongoDB. Next, you'll see some specific MongoDB use cases as well as examples of them in production. Then, we'll discuss some important practical considerations for using MongoDB.

1.4.1 *MongoDB versus other databases*

The number of available databases has exploded, and weighing one against another can be difficult. Fortunately, most of these databases fall under one of a few categories. In table 1.1, and in the sections that follow, we describe simple and sophisticated key-value stores, relational databases, and document databases, and show how these compare with MongoDB.

Table 1.1 Database families

	Examples	Data model	Scalability model	Use cases
Simple key-value stores	Memcached	Key-value, where the value is a binary blob.	Variable. Memcached can scale across nodes, converting all available RAM into a single, monolithic datastore.	Caching. Web ops.
Sophisticated key-value stores	HBase, Cassandra, Riak KV, Redis, CouchDB	Variable. Cassandra uses a key-value structure known as a *column*. HBase and Redis store binary blobs. CouchDB stores JSON documents.	Eventually consistent, multinode distribution for high availability and easy failover.	High-throughput verticals (activity feeds, message queues). Caching. Web ops.
Relational databases	Oracle Database, IBM DB2, Microsoft SQL Server, MySQL, PostgreSQL	Tables.	Vertical scaling. Limited support for clustering and manual partitioning.	System requiring transactions (banking, finance) or SQL. Normalized data model.

SIMPLE KEY-VALUE STORES

Simple key-value stores do what their name implies: they index values based on a supplied key. A common use case is caching. For instance, suppose you needed to cache an HTML page rendered by your app. The key in this case might be the page's URL, and the value would be the rendered HTML itself. Note that as far as a key-value store is concerned, the value is an opaque byte array. There's no enforced schema, as you'd find in a relational database, nor is there any concept of data types. This naturally limits the operations permitted by key-value stores: you can insert a new value and then use its key either to retrieve that value or delete it. Systems with such simplicity are generally fast and scalable.

The best-known simple key-value store is *Memcached*, which stores its data in memory only, so it trades durability for speed. It's also distributed; Memcached nodes running across multiple servers can act as a single datastore, eliminating the complexity of maintaining cache state across machines.

Compared with MongoDB, a simple key-value store like Memcached will often allow for faster reads and writes. But unlike MongoDB, these systems can rarely act as primary datastores. Simple key-value stores are best used as adjuncts, either as caching layers atop a more traditional database or as simple persistence layers for ephemeral services like job queues.

SOPHISTICATED KEY-VALUE STORES

It's possible to refine the simple key-value model to handle complicated read/write schemes or to provide a richer data model. In these cases, you end up with what we'll term a sophisticated key-value store. One example is Amazon's Dynamo, described in a widely studied white paper titled "Dynamo: Amazon's Highly Available Key-Value Store" (http://allthingsdistributed.com/files/amazon-dynamo-sosp2007.pdf). The aim of Dynamo is to be a database robust enough to continue functioning in the face of network failures, datacenter outages, and similar disruptions. This requires that the system always be read from and written to, which essentially requires that data be automatically replicated across multiple nodes. If a node fails, a user of the system—perhaps in this case a customer with an Amazon shopping cart—won't experience any interruptions in service. Dynamo provides ways of resolving the inevitable conflicts that arise when a system allows the same data to be written to multiple nodes. At the same time, Dynamo is easily scaled. Because it's masterless—all nodes are equal—it's easy to understand the system as a whole, and nodes can be added easily. Although Dynamo is a proprietary system, the ideas used to build it have inspired many systems falling under the NoSQL umbrella, including Cassandra, HBase, and Riak KV.

By looking at who developed these sophisticated key-value stores, and how they've been used in practice, you can see where these systems shine. Let's take Cassandra, which implements many of Dynamo's scaling properties while providing a column-oriented data model inspired by Google's BigTable. Cassandra is an open source version of a datastore built by Facebook for its inbox search feature. The system scales horizontally to index more than 50 TB of inbox data, allowing for searches on inbox keywords and recipients. Data is indexed by user ID, where each record consists of an array of search terms for keyword searches and an array of recipient IDs for recipient searches.[8]

---

[8]   See "Cassandra: A Decentralized Structured Storage System," at http://mng.bz/5321.

These sophisticated key-value stores were developed by major internet companies such as Amazon, Google, and Facebook to manage cross-sections of systems with extraordinarily large amounts of data. In other words, sophisticated key-value stores manage a relatively self-contained domain that demands significant storage and availability. Because of their masterless architecture, these systems scale easily with the addition of nodes. They opt for eventual consistency, which means that reads don't necessarily reflect the latest write. But what users get in exchange for weaker consistency is the ability to write in the face of any one node's failure.

This contrasts with MongoDB, which provides strong consistency, a rich data model, and secondary indexes. The last two of these attributes go hand in hand; key-value stores can generally store any data structure in the value, but the database is unable to query them unless these values can be indexed. You can fetch them with the primary key, or perhaps scan across all of the keys, but the database is useless for querying these without secondary indexes.

RELATIONAL DATABASES

Much has already been said of relational databases in this introduction, so in the interest of brevity, we need only discuss what RDBMSs (Relational Database Management Systems) have in common with MongoDB and where they diverge. Popular relational databases include MySQL, PostgreSQL, Microsoft SQL Server, Oracle Database, IBM DB2, and so on; some are open-source and some are proprietary. MongoDB and relational databases are both capable of representing a rich data model. Where relational databases use fixed-schema tables, MongoDB has schema-free documents. Most relational databases support secondary indexes and aggregations.

Perhaps the biggest defining feature of relational databases from the user's perspective is the use of SQL as a query language. SQL is a powerful tool for working with data; it's not perfect for every job, but in some cases it's more expressive and easier to work with than MongoDB's query language. Additionally, SQL is fairly portable between databases, though each implementation has its own quirks. One way to think about it is that SQL may be easier for a data scientist or full-time analyst who writes queries to explore data. MongoDB's query language is aimed more at developers, who write a query once to embed it in their application. Both models have their strengths and weaknesses, and sometimes it comes down to personal preference.

There are also many relational databases intended for analytics (or as a "data warehouse") rather than as an application database. Usually data is imported in bulk to these platforms and then queried by analysts to answer business-intelligence questions. This area is dominated by enterprise vendors with HP Vertica or Teradata Database, which both offer horizontally scalable SQL databases.

There is also growing interest in running SQL queries over data stored in Hadoop. Apache Hive is a widely used tool that translates a SQL query into a Map-Reduce job, which offers a scalable way of querying large data sets. These queries use the relational model, but are intended only for slower analytics queries, not for use inside an application.

DOCUMENT DATABASES

Few databases identify themselves as document databases. As of this writing, the closest open-source database comparable to MongoDB is Apache's CouchDB. CouchDB's document model is similar, although data is stored in plain text as JSON, whereas MongoDB uses the BSON binary format. Like MongoDB, CouchDB supports secondary indexes; the difference is that the indexes in CouchDB are defined by writing mapreduce functions, a process that's more involved than using the declarative syntax used by MySQL and MongoDB. They also scale differently. CouchDB doesn't partition data across machines; rather, each CouchDB node is a complete replica of every other.

1.4.2 *Use cases and production deployments*

Let's be honest. You're not going to choose a database solely on the basis of its features. You need to know that real businesses are using it successfully. Let's look at a few broadly defined use cases for MongoDB and some examples of its use in production.[9]

WEB APPLICATIONS

MongoDB is well-suited as a primary datastore for web applications. Even a simple web application will require numerous data models for managing users, sessions, app-specific data, uploads, and permissions, to say nothing of the overarching domain. Just as this aligns well with the tabular approach provided by relational databases, so too it benefits from MongoDB's collection and document model. And because documents can represent rich data structures, the number of collections needed will usually be less than the number of tables required to model the same data using a fully normalized relational model. In addition, dynamic queries and secondary indexes allow for the easy implementation of most queries familiar to SQL developers. Finally, as a web application grows, MongoDB provides a clear path for scale.

MongoDB can be a useful tool for powering a high-traffic website. This is the case with *The Business Insider (TBI)*, which has used MongoDB as its primary datastore since January 2008. TBI is a news site, although it gets substantial traffic, serving more than a million unique page views per day. What's interesting in this case is that in addition to handling the site's main content (posts, comments, users, and so on), MongoDB processes and stores real-time analytics data. These analytics are used by TBI to generate dynamic heat maps indicating click-through rates for the various news stories.

AGILE DEVELOPMENT

Regardless of what you may think about the agile development movement, it's hard to deny the desirability of building an application quickly. A number of development teams, including those from Shutterfly and The New York Times, have chosen MongoDB in part because they can develop applications much more quickly on it than on relational databases. One obvious reason for this is that MongoDB has no fixed schema, so all the time spent committing, communicating, and applying schema changes is saved.

---

[9] For an up-to-date list of MongoDB production deployments, see http://mng.bz/z2CH.

In addition, less time need be spent shoehorning the relational representation of data into an object-oriented data model or dealing with the vagaries and optimizing the SQL produced by object-relational mapping (ORM) technology. Thus, MongoDB often complements projects with shorter development cycles and agile, mid-sized teams.

ANALYTICS AND LOGGING

We alluded earlier to the idea that MongoDB works well for analytics and logging, and the number of applications using MongoDB for these is growing. Often, a well-established company will begin its forays into the MongoDB world with special apps dedicated to analytics. Some of these companies include GitHub, Disqus, Justin.tv, and Gilt Groupe, among others.

MongoDB's relevance to analytics derives from its speed and from two key features: targeted atomic updates and capped collections. Atomic updates let clients efficiently increment counters and push values onto arrays. Capped collections are useful for logging because they store only the most recent documents. Storing logging data in a database, as compared with the filesystem, provides easier organization and greater query power. Now, instead of using `grep` or a custom log search utility, users can employ the MongoDB query language to examine log output.

CACHING

Many web-applications use a layer of caching to help deliver content faster. A data model that allows for a more holistic representation of objects (it's easy to shove a document into MongoDB without worrying much about the structure), combined with faster average query speeds, frequently allows MongoDB to be run as a cache with richer query capabilities, or to do away with the caching layer all together. The Business Insider, for example, was able to dispense with Memcached, serving page requests directly from MongoDB.

VARIABLE SCHEMAS

You can get some sample JSON data from https://dev.twitter.com/rest/tools/console, provided that you know how to use it. After getting the data and saving it as sample.json, you can import it to MongoDB as follows:

```
$ cat sample.json | mongoimport -c tweets
2015-08-28T11:48:27.584+0300        connected to: localhost
2015-08-28T11:48:27.660+0300        imported 1 document
```

Here you're pulling down a small sample of a Twitter stream and piping that directly into a MongoDB collection. Because the stream produces JSON documents, there's no need to alter the data before sending it to the database. The `mongoimport` tool directly translates the data to BSON. This means that each tweet is stored with its structure intact, as a separate document in the collection. This makes it easy to index and query its content with no need to declare the structure of the data in advance.

If your application needs to consume a JSON API, then having a system that so easily translates JSON is invaluable. It's difficult to know the structure of your data before you store it, and MongoDB's lack of schema constraints may simplify your data model.

1.5   *Tips and limitations*

For all these good features, it's worth keeping in mind a system's trade-offs and limitations. We'd like to note some limitations before you start building a real-world application on MongoDB and running it in production. Many of these are consequences of how MongoDB manages data and moves it between disk and memory in memory-mapped files.

First, MongoDB should usually be run on 64-bit machines. The processes in a 32-bit system are only capable of addressing 4 GB of memory. This means that as soon as your data set, including metadata and storage overhead, hits 4 GB, MongoDB will no longer be able to store additional data. Most production systems will require more than this, so a 64-bit system will be necessary.[10]

A second consequence of using virtual memory mapping is that memory for the data will be allocated automatically, as needed. This makes it trickier to run the database in a shared environment. As with database servers in general, MongoDB is best run on a dedicated server.

Perhaps the most important thing to know about MongoDB's use of memory-mapped files is how it affects data sets that exceed the size of available RAM. When you query such a data set, it often requires a disk access for data that has been swapped out of memory. The consequence is that many users report excellent MongoDB performance until the working set of their data exceeds memory and queries slow significantly. This problem isn't exclusive to MongoDB, but it's a common pitfall and something to watch.

A related problem is that the data structures MongoDB uses to store its collections and documents aren't terribly efficient from a data-size perspective. For example, MongoDB stores the document keys in each document. This means that every document with a field named 'username' will use 8 bytes to store the name of the field.

An oft-cited pain-point with MongoDB from SQL developers is that its query language isn't as familiar or easy as writing SQL queries, and this is certainly true in some cases. MongoDB has been more explicitly targeted at developers—not analysts—than most databases. Its philosophy is that a query is something you write once and embed in your application. As you'll see, MongoDB queries are generally composed of JSON objects rather than text strings as in SQL. This makes them simpler to create and parse programmatically, which can be an important consideration, but may be more difficult to change for ad-hoc queries. If you're an analyst who writes queries all day, you'll probably prefer working with SQL.

Finally, it's worth mentioning that although MongoDB is one of the simplest databases to run locally as a single node, there's a maintenance cost to running a large cluster. This is true of most distributed databases, but it's acute with MongoDB because it requires a cluster of three configuration nodes and handles replication separately

---

[10] 64-bit architectures can theoretically address up to 16 exabytes of memory, which is for all intents and purposes unlimited.

with sharding. In some databases, such as HBase, data is grouped into shards that can be replicated on any machine of the cluster. MongoDB instead allows shards of replica sets, meaning that a piece of data is replicated only within its replica set. Keeping sharding and replication as separate concepts has certain advantages, but also means that each must be configured and managed when you set up a MongoDB cluster.

Let's have a quick look at the other changes that have happened in MongoDB.

1.6 History of MongoDB

When the first edition of *MongoDB in Action* was released, MongoDB 1.8.x was the most recent stable version, with version 2.0.0 just around the corner. With this second edition, 3.0.x is the latest stable version.[11]

A list of the biggest changes in each of the official versions is shown below. You should always use the most recent version available, if possible, in which case this list isn't particularly useful. If not, this list may help you determine how your version differs from the content of this book. This is by no means an exhaustive list, and because of space constraints, we've listed only the top four or five items for each release.

VERSION 1.8.X (NO LONGER OFFICIALLY SUPPORTED)

- *Sharding*—Sharding was moved from "experimental" to production-ready status.
- *Replica sets*—Replica sets were made production-ready.
- *Replica pairs deprecated*—Replica set pairs are no longer supported by MongoDB, Inc.
- *Geo search*—Two-dimensional geo-indexing with coordinate pairs (2D indexes) was introduced.

VERSION 2.0.X (NO LONGER OFFICIALLY SUPPORTED)

- *Journaling enabled by default*—This version changed the default for new databases to enable journaling. Journaling is an important function that prevents data corruption.
- *$and queries*—This version added the $and query operator to complement the $or operator.
- *Sparse indexes*—Previous versions of MongoDB included nodes in an index for every document, even if the document didn't contain any of the fields being tracked by the index. Sparse indexing adds only document nodes that have relevant fields. This feature significantly reduces index size. In some cases this can improve performance because smaller indexes can result in more efficient use of memory.
- *Replica set priorities*—This version allows "weighting" of replica set members to ensure that your best servers get priority when electing a new primary server.
- *Collection level compact/repair*—Previously you could perform compact/repair only on a database; this enhancement extends it to individual collections.

---

[11] MongoDB actually had a version jump from 2.6 straight to 3.0, skipping 2.8. See http://www.mongodb.com/blog/post/announcing-mongodb-30 for more details about v3.0.

VERSION 2.2.X (NO LONGER OFFICIALLY SUPPORTED)

- *Aggregation framework*—This version features the first iteration of a facility to make analysis and transformation of data much easier and more efficient. In many respects this facility takes over where map/reduce leaves off; it's built on a pipeline paradigm, instead of the map/reduce model (which some find difficult to grasp).

- *TTL collections*—Collections in which the documents have a time-limited lifespan are introduced to allow you to create caching models such as those provided by Memcached.

- *DB level locking*—This version adds database level locking to take the place of the global lock, which improves the write concurrency by allowing multiple operations to happen simultaneously on different databases.

- *Tag-aware sharding*—This version allows nodes to be tagged with IDs that reflect their physical location. In this way, applications can control where data is stored in clusters, thus increasing efficiency (read-only nodes reside in the same data center) and reducing legal jurisdiction issues (you store data required to remain in a specific country only on servers in that country).

VERSION 2.4.X (OLDEST STABLE RELEASE)

- *Enterprise version*—The first subscriber-only edition of MongoDB, the Enterprise version of MongoDB includes an additional authentication module that allows the use of Kerberos authentication systems to manage database login data. The free version has all the other features of the Enterprise version.

- *Aggregation framework performance*—Improvements are made in the performance of the aggregation framework to support real-time analytics; chapter 6 explores the Aggregation framework.

- *Text search*—An enterprise-class search solution is integrated as an experimental feature in MongoDB; chapter 9 explores the new text search features.

- *Enhancements to geospatial indexing*—This version includes support for polygon intersection queries and GeoJSON, and features an improved spherical model supporting ellipsoids.

- *V8 JavaScript engine*—MongoDB has switched from the Spider Monkey JavaScript engine to the Google V8 Engine; this move improves multithreaded operation and opens up future performance gains in MongoDB's JavaScript-based map/reduce system.

VERSION 2.6.X (STABLE RELEASE)

- *$text queries*—This version added the $text query operator to support text search in normal find queries.

- *Aggregation improvements*—Aggregation has various improvements in this version. It can stream data over cursors, it can output to collections, and it has many new supported operators and pipeline stages, among many other features and performance improvements.

- *Improved wire protocol for writes*—Now bulk writes will receive more granular and detailed responses regarding the success or failure of individual writes in a batch, thanks to improvements in the way errors are returned over the network for write operations.
- *New update operators*—New operators have been added for update operations, such as $mul, which multiplies the field value by the given amount.
- *Sharding improvements*—Improvements have been made in sharding to better handle certain edge cases. Contiguous chunks can now be merged, and duplicate data that was left behind after a chunk migration can be cleaned up automatically.
- *Security improvements*—Collection-level access control is supported in this version, as well as user-defined roles. Improvements have also been made in SSL and x509 support.
- *Query system improvements*—Much of the query system has been refactored. This improves performance and predictability of queries.
- *Enterprise module*—The MongoDB Enterprise module has improvements and extensions of existing features, as well as support for auditing.

VERSION 3.0.X (NEWEST STABLE RELEASE)

- The MMAPv1 storage engine now has support for collection-level locking.
- Replica sets can now have up to 50 members.
- Support for the WiredTiger storage engine; WiredTiger is only available in the 64-bit versions of MongoDB 3.0.
- The 3.0 WiredTiger storage engine provides document-level locking and compression.
- Pluggable storage engine API that allows third parties to develop storage engines for MongoDB.
- Improved explain functionality.
- SCRAM-SHA-1 authentication mechanism.
- The `ensureIndex()` function has been replaced by the `createIndex()` function and should no longer be used.

1.7 Additional resources

This text is intended to be both a tutorial and a reference, so much of the language is intended to introduce readers to new subjects and then describe these subjects in more detail. If you're looking for a pure reference, the best resource is the MongoDB user's manual, available at http://docs.mongodb.org/manual. This is an in-depth guide to the database, which will be useful if you need to review a subject, and we highly recommend it.

If you have a specific problem or question about MongoDB, it's likely that someone else has as well. A simple web-search will usually return results about it from resources like blog posts or from Stack Overflow (http://stackoverflow.com), a tech-oriented question and answer site. These are invaluable when you get stuck, but double-check that the answer applies to your version of MongoDB.

You can also get help in places like the MongoDB IRC chat or user forums. MongoDB, Inc. also offers consulting services intended to help make MongoDB easy to use in an enterprise environment. Many cities have their own MongoDB user groups, organized through sites like http://meetup.com. These are often a good way to meet folks knowledgeable about MongoDB and learn about how others are using the database. Finally, you can contact us (the authors) directly at the Manning forums, which have a space specifically for MongoDB in Action at http://manning-sandbox.com/forum.jspa?forumID=677. This is a space to ask in-depth questions that might not be covered in the text and point out omissions or errata. Please don't hesitate to post a question!

1.8   *Summary*

We've covered a lot. To summarize, MongoDB is an open source, document-based database management system. Designed for the data and scalability requirements of modern internet applications, MongoDB features dynamic queries and secondary indexes, fast atomic updates and complex aggregations, and support for replication with automatic failover and sharding for scaling horizontally.

That's a mouthful, but if you've read this far, you should have a good feel for all these capabilities. You're probably itching to code. It's one thing to talk about a database's features, but another to use the database in practice. Fortunately, that's what you'll do in the next two chapters. First, you'll get acquainted with the MongoDB JavaScript shell, which is incredibly useful for interacting with the database. Then, in chapter 3 you'll start experimenting with the driver and build a simple MongoDB-based application in Ruby.

MongoDB through
the JavaScript shell

This chapter covers

- Using CRUD operations in the MongoDB shell
- Building indexes and using `explain()`
- Understanding basic administration
- Getting help

The previous chapter hinted at the experience of running MongoDB. If you're ready for a more hands-on introduction, this is it. Using the MongoDB shell, this chapter teaches the database's basic concepts through a series of exercises. You'll learn how to create, read, update, and delete (CRUD) documents and, in the process, get to know MongoDB's query language. In addition, we'll take a preliminary look at database indexes and how they're used to optimize queries. Then we'll explore some basic administrative commands and suggest a few ways of getting help as you continue working with MongoDB's shell. Think of this chapter as both an elaboration of the concepts already introduced and as a practical tour of the most common tasks performed from the MongoDB shell.

The MongoDB shell is the go-to tool for experimenting with the database, running ad-hoc queries, and administering running MongoDB instances. When you're writing an application that uses MongoDB, you'll use a language driver (like

MongoDB's Ruby gem) rather than the shell, but the shell is likely where you'll test and refine these queries. Any and all MongoDB queries can be run from the shell.

If you're completely new to MongoDB's shell, know that it provides all the features that you'd expect of such a tool; it allows you to examine and manipulate data and administer the database server itself. MongoDB's shell differs from others, however, in its query language. Instead of employing a standardized query language such as SQL, you interact with the server using the JavaScript programming language and a simple API. This means that you can write JavaScript scripts in the shell that interact with a MongoDB database. If you're not familiar with JavaScript, rest assured that only a superficial knowledge of the language is necessary to take advantage of the shell, and all examples in this chapter will be explained thoroughly. The MongoDB API in the shell is similar to most of the language drivers, so it's easy to take queries you write in the shell and run them from your application.

You'll benefit most from this chapter if you follow along with the examples, but to do that, you'll need to have MongoDB installed on your system. You'll find installation instructions in appendix A.

2.1   Diving into the MongoDB shell

MongoDB's JavaScript shell makes it easy to play with data and get a tangible sense of documents, collections, and the database's particular query language. Think of the following walkthrough as a practical introduction to MongoDB.

You'll begin by getting the shell up and running. Then you'll see how JavaScript represents documents, and you'll learn how to insert these documents into a MongoDB collection. To verify these inserts, you'll practice querying the collection. Then it's on to updates. Finally, we'll finish out the CRUD operations by learning to remove data and drop collections.

2.1.1   Starting the shell

Follow the instructions in appendix A and you should quickly have a working MongoDB installation on your computer, as well as a running mongod instance. Once you do, start the MongoDB shell by running the mongo executable:

```
mongo
```

If the shell program starts successfully, your screen will look like figure 2.1. The shell heading displays the version of MongoDB you're running, along with some additional information about the currently selected database.

Figure 2.1   MongoDB JavaScript shell on startup

If you know some JavaScript, you can start entering code and exploring the shell right away. In either case, read on to see how to run your first operations against MongoDB.

2.1.2 *Databases, collections, and documents*

As you probably know by now, MongoDB stores its information in documents, which can be printed out in JSON (JavaScript Object Notation) format. You'd probably like to store different types of documents, like users and orders, in separate places. This means that MongoDB needs a way to group documents, similar to a table in an RDBMS. In MongoDB, this is called a *collection*.

MongoDB divides collections into separate *databases*. Unlike the usual overhead that databases produce in the SQL world, databases in MongoDB are just namespaces to distinguish between collections. To query MongoDB, you'll need to know the database (or namespace) and collection you want to query for documents. If no other database is specified on startup, the shell selects a default database called test. As a way of keeping all the subsequent tutorial exercises under the same namespace, let's start by switching to the tutorial database:

```
> use tutorial
switched to db tutorial
```

You'll see a message verifying that you've switched databases.

Why does MongoDB have both databases and collections? The answer lies in how MongoDB writes its data out to disk. All collections in a database are grouped in the same files, so it makes sense, from a memory perspective, to keep related collections in the same database. You might also want to have different applications access the same collections (multitenancy) and, it's also useful to keep your data organized so you're prepared for future requirements.

> **On creating databases and collections**
>
> You may be wondering how you can switch to the tutorial database without explicitly creating it. In fact, creating the database isn't required. Databases and collections are created only when documents are first inserted. This behavior is consistent with MongoDB's dynamic approach to data; just as the structure of documents needn't be defined in advance, individual collections and databases can be created at runtime. This can lead to a simplified and accelerated development process. That said, if you're concerned about databases or collections being created accidentally, most of the drivers let you enable a *strict mode* to prevent such careless errors.

It's time to create your first document. Because you're using a JavaScript shell, your documents will be specified in JSON. For instance, a simple document describing a user might look like this:

```
{username: "smith"}
```

The document contains a single key and value for storing Smith's username.

2.1.3 *Inserts and queries*

To save this document, you need to choose a collection to save it to. Appropriately enough, you'll save it to the users collection. Here's how:

```
> db.users.insert({username: "smith"})
WriteResult({ "nInserted" : 1 })
```

> **NOTE** Note that in our examples, we'll preface MongoDB shell commands with a > so that you can tell the difference between the command and its output.

You may notice a slight delay after entering this code. At this point, neither the tutorial database nor the users collection has been created on disk. The delay is caused by the allocation of the initial data files for both.

If the insert succeeds, you've just saved your first document. In the default MongoDB configuration, this data is now guaranteed to be inserted even if you kill the shell or suddenly restart your machine. You can issue a query to see the new document:

```
> db.users.find()
```

Since the data is now part of the users collection, reopening the shell and running the query will show the same result. The response will look something like this:

```
{ "_id" : ObjectId("552e458158cd52bcb257c324"), "username" : "smith" }
```

_ID FIELDS IN MONGODB

Note that an _id field has been added to the document. You can think of the _id value as the document's primary key. Every MongoDB document requires an _id, and if one isn't present when the document is created, a special MongoDB ObjectID will be generated and added to the document at that time. The ObjectID that appears in your console won't be the same as the one in the code listing, but it will be unique among all _id values in the collection, which is the only requirement for the field. You can set your own _id by setting it in the document you insert, the ObjectID is just MongoDB's default.

We'll have more to say about ObjectIDs in the next chapter. Let's continue for now by adding a second user to the collection:

```
> db.users.insert({username: "jones"})
WriteResult({ "nInserted" : 1 })
```

There should now be two documents in the collection. Go ahead and verify this by running the count command:

```
> db.users.count()
2
```

PASS A QUERY PREDICATE

Now that you have more than one document in the collection, let's look at some slightly more sophisticated queries. As before, you can still query for all the documents in the collection:

```
> db.users.find()
{ "_id" : ObjectId("552e458158cd52bcb257c324"), "username" : "smith" }
{ "_id" : ObjectId("552e542a58cd52bcb257c325"), "username" : "jones" }
```

You can also pass a simple query selector to the find method. A query selector is a document that's used to match against all documents in the collection. To query for all documents where the username is jones, you pass a simple document that acts as your query selector like this:

```
> db.users.find({username: "jones"})
{ "_id" : ObjectId("552e542a58cd52bcb257c325"), "username" : "jones" }
```

The query predicate {username: "jones"} returns all documents where the username is jones—it literally matches against the existing documents.

Note that calling the find method without any argument is equivalent to passing in an empty predicate; db.users.find() is the same as db.users.find({}).

You can also specify multiple fields in the query predicate, which creates an implicit AND among the fields. For example, you query with the following selector:

```
> db.users.find({
... _id: ObjectId("552e458158cd52bcb257c324"),
... username: "smith"
... })
{ "_id" : ObjectId("552e458158cd52bcb257c324"), "username" : "smith" }
```

The three dots after the first line of the query are added by the MongoDB shell to indicate that the command takes more than one line.

The query predicate is identical to the returned document. The predicate ANDs the fields, so this query searches for a document that matches on both the _id and username fields.

You can also use MongoDB's $and operator explicitly. The previous query is identical to

```
> db.users.find({ $and: [
... { _id: ObjectId("552e458158cd52bcb257c324") },
... { username: "smith" }
... ] })
{ "_id" : ObjectId("552e458158cd52bcb257c324"), "username" : "smith" }
```

Selecting documents with an OR is similar: just use the $or operator. Consider the following query:

```
> db.users.find({ $or: [
... { username: "smith" },
```

```
... { username: "jones" }
... ]})
{ "_id" : ObjectId("552e458158cd52bcb257c324"), "username" : "smith" }
{ "_id" : ObjectId("552e542a58cd52bcb257c325"), "username" : "jones" }
```

The query returns both the smith and jones documents, because we asked for either a username of smith or a username of jones.

This example is different than previous ones, because it doesn't just insert or search for a specific document. Rather, the query itself is a document. The idea of representing commands as documents is used often in MongoDB and may come as a surprise if you're used to relational databases. One advantage of this interface is that it's easier to build queries programmatically in your application because they're documents rather than a long SQL string.

We've presented the basics of creating and reading data. Now it's time to look at how to update that data.

2.1.4   *Updating documents*

All updates require at least two arguments. The first specifies which documents to update, and the second defines how the selected documents should be modified. The first few examples demonstrate modifying a single document, but the same operations can be applied to many documents, even an entire collection, as we show at the end of this section. But keep in mind that by default the update() method updates a single document.

There are two general types of updates, with different properties and use cases. One type of update involves applying modification operations to a document or documents, and the other type involves replacing the old document with a new one.

For the following examples, we'll look at this sample document:

```
> db.users.find({username: "smith"})
{ "_id" : ObjectId("552e458158cd52bcb257c324"), "username" : "smith" }
```

OPERATOR UPDATE

The first type of update involves passing a document with some kind of operator description as the second argument to the update function. In this section, you'll see an example of how to use the $set operator, which sets a single field to the specified value.

Suppose that user Smith decides to add her country of residence. You can record this with the following update:

```
> db.users.update({username: "smith"}, {$set: {country: "Canada"}})
WriteResult({ "nMatched" : 1, "nUpserted" : 0, "nModified" : 1 })
```

This update tells MongoDB to find a document where the username is smith, and then to set the value of the country property to Canada. You see the change reflected in the message that gets sent back by the server. If you now issue a query, you'll see that the document has been updated accordingly:

```
> db.users.find({username: "smith"})
{ "_id" : ObjectId("552e458158cd52bcb257c324"), "username" : "smith",
    "country" : "Canada" }
```

REPLACEMENT UPDATE

Another way to update a document is to replace it rather than just set a field. This is sometimes mistakenly used when an operator update with a $set was intended. Consider a slightly different update command:

```
> db.users.update({username: "smith"}, {country: "Canada"})
WriteResult({ "nMatched" : 1, "nUpserted" : 0, "nModified" : 1 })
```

In this case, the document is replaced with one that only contains the country field, and the username field is removed because the first document is used only for matching and the second document is used for replacing the document that was previously matched. You should be careful when you use this kind of update. A query for the document yields the following:

```
> db.users.find({country: "Canada"})
{ "_id" : ObjectId("552e458158cd52bcb257c324"), "country" : "Canada" }
```

The _id is the same, yet data has been *replaced* in the update. Be sure to use the $set operator if you intend to add or set fields rather than to replace the entire document. Add the username back to the record:

```
> db.users.update({country: "Canada"}, {$set: {username: "smith"}})
WriteResult({ "nMatched" : 1, "nUpserted" : 0, "nModified" : 1 })
> db.users.find({country: "Canada"})
{ "_id" : ObjectId("552e458158cd52bcb257c324"), "country" : "Canada",
    "username" : "smith" }
```

If you later decide that the country stored in the profile is no longer needed, the value can be removed as easily using the $unset operator:

```
> db.users.update({username: "smith"}, {$unset: {country: 1}})
WriteResult({ "nMatched" : 1, "nUpserted" : 0, "nModified" : 1 })
> db.users.find({username: "smith"})
{ "_id" : ObjectId("552e458158cd52bcb257c324"), "username" : "smith" }
```

UPDATING COMPLEX DATA

Let's enrich this example. You're representing your data with documents, which, as you saw in chapter 1, can contain complex data structures. Let's suppose that, in addition to storing profile information, your users can store lists of their favorite things. A good document representation might look something like this:

```
{
  username: "smith",
  favorites: {
```

```
        cities: ["Chicago", "Cheyenne"],
        movies: ["Casablanca", "For a Few Dollars More", "The Sting"]
    }
}
```

The favorites key points to an object containing two other keys, which point to lists of favorite cities and movies. Given what you know already, can you think of a way to modify the original smith document to look like this? The $set operator should come to mind:

```
> db.users.update( {username: "smith"},
...   {
...       $set: {
...         favorites: {
...             cities: ["Chicago", "Cheyenne"],
...             movies: ["Casablanca", "For a Few Dollars More", "The Sting"]
...         }
...       }
...   })
WriteResult({ "nMatched" : 1, "nUpserted" : 0, "nModified" : 1 })
```

Please note that the use of spacing for indenting isn't mandatory, but it helps avoid errors as the document is more readable this way.

Let's modify jones similarly, but in this case you'll only add a couple of favorite movies:

```
> db.users.update( {username: "jones"},
...   {
...       $set: {
...         favorites: {
...             movies: ["Casablanca", "Rocky"]
...         }
...       }
...   })
WriteResult({ "nMatched" : 1, "nUpserted" : 0, "nModified" : 1 })
```

If you make a typo, you can use the up arrow key to recall the last shell statement.

Now query the users collection to make sure that both updates succeeded:

```
> > db.users.find().pretty()
{
    "_id" : ObjectId("552e458158cd52bcb257c324"),
    "username" : "smith",
    "favorites" : {
        "cities" : [
            "Chicago",
            "Cheyenne"
        ],
        "movies" : [
            "Casablanca",
            "For a Few Dollars More",
            "The Sting"
        ]
    }
}
```

```
{
    "_id" : ObjectId("552e542a58cd52bcb257c325"),
    "username" : "jones",
    "favorites" : {
        "movies" : [
            "Casablanca",
            "Rocky"
        ]
    }
}
```

Strictly speaking, the find() command returns a *cursor* to the returning documents. Therefore, to access the documents you'll need to iterate the cursor. The find() command automatically returns 20 documents—if they're available—after iterating the cursor 20 times.

With a couple of example documents at your fingertips, you can now begin to see the power of MongoDB's query language. In particular, the query engine's ability to reach into nested inner objects and match against array elements proves useful in this situation. Notice how we appended the pretty operation to the find operation to get nicely formatted results returned by the server. Strictly speaking, pretty() is actually cursor.pretty(), which is a way of configuring a cursor to display results in an easy-to-read format.

You can see an example of both of these concepts demonstrated in this query to find all users who like the movie *Casablanca*:

```
> db.users.find({"favorites.movies": "Casablanca"})
```

The dot between favorites and movies instructs the query engine to look for a key named favorites that points to an object with an inner key named movies and then to match the value of the inner key. Thus, this query will return both user documents because queries on arrays will match if any element in the array matches the original query.

To see a more involved example, suppose you know that any user who likes *Casablanca* also likes *The Maltese Falcon* and that you want to update your database to reflect this fact. How would you represent this as a MongoDB update?

MORE ADVANCED UPDATES

You could conceivably use the $set operator again, but doing so would require you to rewrite and send the entire array of movies. Because all you want to do is to add an element to the list, you're better off using either $push or $addToSet. Both operators add an item to an array, but the second does so uniquely, preventing a duplicate addition. This is the update you're looking for:

```
> db.users.update( {"favorites.movies": "Casablanca"},
...       {$addToSet: {"favorites.movies": "The Maltese Falcon"} },
...            false,
...            true )
WriteResult({ "nMatched" : 2, "nUpserted" : 0, "nModified" : 2 })
```

Most of this should be decipherable by now. The first argument is a query predicate that matches against users who have *Casablanca* in their movies list. The second argument adds *The Maltese Falcon* to that list using the $addToSet operator.

The third argument, `false`, controls whether an upsert is allowed. This tells the update operation whether it should insert a document if it doesn't already exist, which has different behavior depending on whether the update is an operator update or a replacement update.

The fourth argument, `true`, indicates that this is a multi-update. By default, a MongoDB update operation will apply only to the first document matched by the query selector. If you want the operation to apply to all documents matched, you must be explicit about that. You want your update to apply to both `smith` and `jones`, so the multi-update is necessary.

We'll cover updates in more detail later, but try these examples before moving on.

2.1.5 Deleting data

Now you know the basics of creating, reading, and updating data through the MongoDB shell. We've saved the simplest operation, removing data, for last.

If given no parameters, a remove operation will clear a collection of all its documents. To get rid of, say, a foo collection's contents, you enter:

```
> db.foo.remove()
```

You often need to remove only a certain subset of a collection's documents, and for that, you can pass a query selector to the `remove()` method. If you want to remove all users whose favorite city is Cheyenne, the expression is straightforward:

```
> db.users.remove({"favorites.cities": "Cheyenne"})
WriteResult({ "nRemoved" : 1 })
```

Note that the `remove()` operation doesn't actually delete the collection; it merely removes documents from a collection. You can think of it as being analogous to SQL's `DELETE` command.

If your intent is to delete the collection along with all of its indexes, use the `drop()` method:

```
> db.users.drop()
```

Creating, reading, updating, and deleting are the basic operations of any database; if you've followed along, you should be in a position to continue practicing basic CRUD operations in MongoDB. In the next section, you'll learn how to enhance your queries, updates, and deletes by taking a brief look at secondary indexes.

2.1.6 Other shell features

You may have noticed this already, but the shell does a lot of things to make working with MongoDB easier. You can revisit earlier commands by using the up and down arrows, and use autocomplete for certain inputs, like collection names. The autocomplete feature uses the tab key to autocomplete or to list the completion possibilities.[1] You can also discover more information in the shell by typing this:

```
> help
```

A lot of functions print pretty help messages that explain them as well. Try it out:

```
> db.help()
DB methods:
    db.adminCommand(nameOrDocument) - switches to 'admin' db, and runs
      command [ just calls db.runCommand(...) ]
    db.auth(username, password)
    db.cloneDatabase(fromhost)
    db.commandHelp(name) returns the help for the command
    db.copyDatabase(fromdb, todb, fromhost)
...
```

Help on queries is provided through a different function called `explain`, which we'll investigate in later sections. There are also a number of options you can use when starting the MongoDB shell. To display a list of these, add the help flag when you start the MongoDB shell:

```
$ mongo --help
```

You don't need to worry about all these features, and we're not done working with the shell yet, but it's worth knowing where you can find more information when you need it.

2.2 Creating and querying with indexes

It's common to create indexes to enhance query performance. Fortunately, MongoDB's indexes can be created easily from the shell. If you're new to database indexes, this section should make the need for them clear; if you already have indexing experience, you'll see how easy it is to create indexes and then profile queries against them using the `explain()` method.

2.2.1 Creating a large collection

An indexing example makes sense only if you have a collection with many documents. So you'll add 20,000 simple documents to a `numbers` collection. Because the MongoDB shell is also a JavaScript interpreter, the code to accomplish this is simple:

```
> for(i = 0; i < 20000; i++) {
    db.numbers.save({num: i});
  }
WriteResult({ "nInserted" : 1 })
```

---

[1] For the full list of keyboard shortcuts, please visit http://docs.mongodb.org/v3.0/reference/program/mongo/#mongo-keyboard-shortcuts.

That's a lot of documents, so don't be surprised if the insert takes a few seconds to complete. Once it returns, you can run a couple of queries to verify that all the documents are present:

```
> db.numbers.count()
20000
> db.numbers.find()
{ "_id": ObjectId("4bfbf132dba1aa7c30ac830a"), "num": 0 }
{ "_id": ObjectId("4bfbf132dba1aa7c30ac830b"), "num": 1 }
{ "_id": ObjectId("4bfbf132dba1aa7c30ac830c"), "num": 2 }
{ "_id": ObjectId("4bfbf132dba1aa7c30ac830d"), "num": 3 }
{ "_id": ObjectId("4bfbf132dba1aa7c30ac830e"), "num": 4 }
{ "_id": ObjectId("4bfbf132dba1aa7c30ac830f"), "num": 5 }
{ "_id": ObjectId("4bfbf132dba1aa7c30ac8310"), "num": 6 }
{ "_id": ObjectId("4bfbf132dba1aa7c30ac8311"), "num": 7 }
{ "_id": ObjectId("4bfbf132dba1aa7c30ac8312"), "num": 8 }
{ "_id": ObjectId("4bfbf132dba1aa7c30ac8313"), "num": 9 }
{ "_id": ObjectId("4bfbf132dba1aa7c30ac8314"), "num": 10 }
{ "_id": ObjectId("4bfbf132dba1aa7c30ac8315"), "num": 11 }
{ "_id": ObjectId("4bfbf132dba1aa7c30ac8316"), "num": 12 }
{ "_id": ObjectId("4bfbf132dba1aa7c30ac8317"), "num": 13 }
{ "_id": ObjectId("4bfbf132dba1aa7c30ac8318"), "num": 14 }
{ "_id": ObjectId("4bfbf132dba1aa7c30ac8319"), "num": 15 }
{ "_id": ObjectId("4bfbf132dba1aa7c30ac831a"), "num": 16 }
{ "_id": ObjectId("4bfbf132dba1aa7c30ac831b"), "num": 17 }
{ "_id": ObjectId("4bfbf132dba1aa7c30ac831c"), "num": 18 }
{ "_id": ObjectId("4bfbf132dba1aa7c30ac831d"), "num": 19 }
Type "it" for more
```

The count() command shows that you've inserted 20,000 documents. The subsequent query displays the first 20 results (this number may be different in your shell). You can display additional results with the it command:

```
> it
{ "_id": ObjectId("4bfbf132dba1aa7c30ac831e"), "num": 20 }
{ "_id": ObjectId("4bfbf132dba1aa7c30ac831f"), "num": 21 }
{ "_id": ObjectId("4bfbf132dba1aa7c30ac8320"), "num": 22 }
...
```

The it command instructs the shell to return the next result set.[2]

With a sizable set of documents available, let's try a couple queries. Given what you know about MongoDB's query engine, a simple query matching a document on its num attribute makes sense:

```
> db.numbers.find({num: 500})
{ "_id" : ObjectId("4bfbf132dba1aa7c30ac84fe"), "num" : 500 }
```

---

[2] You may be wondering what's happening behind the scenes here. All queries create a cursor, which allows for iteration over a result set. This is somewhat hidden when using the shell, so it isn't necessary to discuss in detail at the moment. If you can't wait to learn more about cursors and their idiosyncrasies, see chapters 3 and 4.

RANGE QUERIES

More interestingly, you can also issue range queries using the special $gt and $lt operators. They stand for greater than and less than, respectively. Here's how you query for all documents with a num value greater than 199,995:

```
> db.numbers.find( {num: {"$gt": 19995 }} )
{ "_id" : ObjectId("552e660b58cd52bcb2581142"), "num" : 19996 }
{ "_id" : ObjectId("552e660b58cd52bcb2581143"), "num" : 19997 }
{ "_id" : ObjectId("552e660b58cd52bcb2581144"), "num" : 19998 }
{ "_id" : ObjectId("552e660b58cd52bcb2581145"), "num" : 19999 }
```

You can also combine the two operators to specify upper and lower boundaries:

```
> db.numbers.find( {num: {"$gt": 20, "$lt": 25 }} )
{ "_id" : ObjectId("552e660558cd52bcb257c33b"), "num" : 21 }
{ "_id" : ObjectId("552e660558cd52bcb257c33c"), "num" : 22 }
{ "_id" : ObjectId("552e660558cd52bcb257c33d"), "num" : 23 }
{ "_id" : ObjectId("552e660558cd52bcb257c33e"), "num" : 24 }
```

You can see that by using a simple JSON document, you're able to specify a range query in much the same way you might in SQL. $gt and $lt are only two of a host of operators that comprise the MongoDB query language. Others include $gte for greater than or equal to, $lte for (you guessed it) less than or equal to, and $ne for not equal to. You'll see other operators and many more example queries in later chapters.

Of course, queries like this are of little value unless they're also efficient. In the next section, we'll start thinking about query efficiency by exploring MongoDB's indexing features.

2.2.2 *Indexing and explain( )*

If you've spent time working with relational databases, you're probably familiar with SQL's EXPLAIN, an invaluable tool for debugging or optimizing a query. When any database receives a query, it must plan out how to execute it; this is called a query plan. EXPLAIN describes query paths and allows developers to diagnose slow operations by determining which indexes a query has used. Often a query can be executed in multiple ways, and sometimes this results in behavior you might not expect. EXPLAIN explains. MongoDB has its own version of EXPLAIN that provides the same service. To get an idea of how it works, let's apply it to one of the queries you just issued. Try running the following on your system:

```
> db.numbers.find({num: {"$gt": 19995}}).explain("executionStats")
```

The result should look something like what you see in the next listing. The "execution-Stats" keyword is new to MongoDB 3.0 and requests a different mode that gives more detailed output.

Listing 2.1   Typical `explain("executionStats")` output for an unindexed query

```
{
    "queryPlanner" : {
        "plannerVersion" : 1,
        "namespace" : "tutorial.numbers",
        "indexFilterSet" : false,
        "parsedQuery" : {
            "num" : {
                    "$gt" : 19995
            }
        },
        "winningPlan" : {
            "stage" : "COLLSCAN",
            "filter" : {
                "num" : {
                        "$gt" : 19995
                }
            },
            "direction" : "forward"
        },
        "rejectedPlans" : [ ]
    },
    "executionStats" : {
        "executionSuccess" : true,
        "nReturned" : 4,
        "executionTimeMillis" : 8,
        "totalKeysExamined" : 0,
        "totalDocsExamined" : 20000,
        "executionStages" : {
            "stage" : "COLLSCAN",
            "filter" : {
                "num" : {
                        "$gt" : 19995
                }
            },
            "nReturned" : 4,
            "executionTimeMillisEstimate" : 0,
            "works" : 20002,
            "advanced" : 4,
            "needTime" : 19997,
            "needFetch" : 0,
            "saveState" : 156,
            "restoreState" : 156,
            "isEOF" : 1,
            "invalidates" : 0,
            "direction" : "forward",
            "docsExamined" : 20000
        }
    },
    "serverInfo" : {
        "host" : "rMacBook.local",
        "port" : 27017,
        "version" : "3.0.6",
```

```
        "gitVersion" : "nogitversion"
    },
    "ok" : 1
}
```

Upon examining the `explain()` output,[3] you may be surprised to see that the query engine has to scan the entire collection, all 20,000 documents (docsExamined), to return only four results (nReturned). The value of the `totalKeysExamined` field shows the number of index entries scanned, which is zero. Such a large difference between the number of documents scanned and the number returned marks this as an inefficient query. In a real-world situation, where the collection and the documents themselves would likely be larger, the time needed to process the query would be substantially greater than the eight milliseconds (`millis`) noted here (this may be different on your machine).

What this collection needs is an index. You can create an index for the num key within the documents using the `createIndex()` method. Try entering the following index creation code:

```
> db.numbers.createIndex({num: 1})
{
    "createdCollectionAutomatically" : false,
    "numIndexesBefore" : 1,
    "numIndexesAfter" : 2,
    "ok" : 1
}
```

The `createIndex()` method replaces the `ensureIndex()` method in MongoDB 3. If you're using an older MongoDB version, you should use `ensureIndex()` instead of `createIndex()`. In MongoDB 3, `ensureIndex()` is still valid as it's an alias for `createIndex()`, but you should stop using it.

As with other MongoDB operations, such as queries and updates, you pass a document to the `createIndex()` method to define the index's keys. In this case, the `{num: 1}` document indicates that an ascending index should be built on the num key for all documents in the numbers collection.

You can verify that the index has been created by calling the `getIndexes()` method:

```
> db.numbers.getIndexes()
[
    {
        "v" : 1,
        "key" : {
            "_id" : 1
        },
```

---

[3] In these examples we're inserting "hostname" as the machine's hostname. On your platform this may appear as `localhost`, your machine's name, or its name plus `.local`. Don't worry if your output looks a little different than ours'; it can vary based on your platform and your exact version of MongoDB.

```
        "name" : "_id_",
        "ns" : "tutorial.numbers"
    },
    {

        "v" : 1,
        "key" : {
            "num" : 1
        },
        "name" : "num_1",
        "ns" : "tutorial.numbers"
    }
]
```

The collection now has two indexes. The first is the standard _id index that's automatically built for every collection; the second is the index you created on num. The indexes for those fields are called _id_ and num_1, respectively. If you don't provide a name, MongoDB sets hopefully meaningful names automatically.

If you run your query with the explain() method, you'll now see the dramatic difference in query response time, as shown in the following listing.

Listing 2.2 explain() output for an indexed query

```
> db.numbers.find({num: {"$gt": 19995 }}).explain("executionStats")
{
    "queryPlanner" : {
        "plannerVersion" : 1,
        "namespace" : "tutorial.numbers",
        "indexFilterSet" : false,
        "parsedQuery" : {
            "num" : {
                "$gt" : 19995
            }
        },
        "winningPlan" : {
            "stage" : "FETCH",
            "inputStage" : {
                "stage" : "IXSCAN",
                "keyPattern" : {
                    "num" : 1
                },
                "indexName" : "num_1",              ◁──── Using the
                "isMultiKey" : false,                      num_1 index
                "direction" : "forward",
                "indexBounds" : {
                    "num" : [
                        "(19995.0, inf.0]"
                    ]
                }
            }
        },
        "rejectedPlans" : [ ]
    },
```

Four documents returned

Only four documents scanned

Much faster!

Using the num_1 index

```
"executionStats" : {
    "executionSuccess" : true,
    "nReturned" : 4,
    "executionTimeMillis" : 0,
    "totalKeysExamined" : 4,
    "totalDocsExamined" : 4,
    "executionStages" : {
        "stage" : "FETCH",
        "nReturned" : 4,
        "executionTimeMillisEstimate" : 0,
        "works" : 5,
        "advanced" : 4,
        "needTime" : 0,
        "needFetch" : 0,
        "saveState" : 0,
        "restoreState" : 0,
        "isEOF" : 1,
        "invalidates" : 0,
        "docsExamined" : 4,
        "alreadyHasObj" : 0,
        "inputStage" : {
            "stage" : "IXSCAN",
            "nReturned" : 4,
            "executionTimeMillisEstimate" : 0,
            "works" : 4,
            "advanced" : 4,
            "needTime" : 0,
            "needFetch" : 0,
            "saveState" : 0,
            "restoreState" : 0,
            "isEOF" : 1,
            "invalidates" : 0,
            "keyPattern" : {
                "num" : 1
            },
            "indexName" : "num_1",
            "isMultiKey" : false,
            "direction" : "forward",
            "indexBounds" : {
                "num" : [
                    "(19995.0, inf.0]"
                ]
            },
            "keysExamined" : 4,
            "dupsTested" : 0,
            "dupsDropped" : 0,
            "seenInvalidated" : 0,
            "matchTested" : 0
        }
    }
},
"serverInfo" : {
    "host" : "rMacBook.local",
    "port" : 27017,
    "version" : "3.0.6",
```

```
        "gitVersion" : "nogitversion"
    },
    "ok" : 1
}
```

Now that the query utilizes the index num_1 on num, it scans only the four documents pertaining to the query. This reduces the total time to serve the query from 8 ms to 0 ms!

Indexes don't come free; they take up some space and can make your inserts slightly more expensive, but they're an essential tool for query optimization. If this example intrigues you, be sure to check out chapter 8, which is devoted to indexing and query optimization. Next you'll look at the basic administrative commands required to get information about your MongoDB instance. You'll also learn techniques for getting help from the shell, which will aid in mastering the various shell commands.

2.3 *Basic administration*

This chapter promised to be an introduction to MongoDB via the JavaScript shell. You've already learned the basics of data manipulation and indexing. Here, we'll present techniques for getting information about your mongod process. For instance, you'll probably want to know how much space your various collections are taking up, or how many indexes you've defined on a given collection. The commands detailed here can take you a long way in helping to diagnose performance issues and keep tabs on your data.

We'll also look at MongoDB's command interface. Most of the special, non-CRUD operations that can be performed on a MongoDB instance, from server status checks to data file integrity verification, are implemented using database commands. We'll explain what commands are in the MongoDB context and show how easy they are to use. Finally, it's always good to know where to look for help. To that end, we'll point out places in the shell where you can turn for help to further your exploration of MongoDB.

2.3.1 *Getting database information*

You'll often want to know which collections and databases exist on a given installation. Fortunately, the MongoDB shell provides a number of commands, along with some syntactic sugar, for getting information about the system.

show dbs prints a list of all the databases on the system:

```
> show dbs
admin     (empty)
local     0.078GB
tutorial  0.078GB
```

show collections displays a list of all the collections defined on the current database.[4] If the tutorial database is still selected, you'll see a list of the collections you worked with in the preceding tutorial:

```
> show collections
numbers
system.indexes
users
```

The one collection that you may not recognize is system.indexes. This is a special collection that exists for every database. Each entry in system.indexes defines an index for the database, which you can view using the getIndexes() method, as you saw earlier. But MongoDB 3.0 deprecates direct access to the system.indexes collections; you should use createIndexes and listIndexes instead. The getIndexes() JavaScript method can be replaced by the db.runCommand({"listIndexes": "numbers"}) shell command.

For lower-level insight into databases and collections, the stats() method proves useful. When you run it on a database object, you'll get the following output:

```
> db.stats()
{
    "db" : "tutorial",
    "collections" : 4,
    "objects" : 20010,
    "avgObjSize" : 48.0223888055972,
    "dataSize" : 960928,
    "storageSize" : 2818048,
    "numExtents" : 8,
    "indexes" : 3,
    "indexSize" : 1177344,
    "fileSize" : 67108864,
    "nsSizeMB" : 16,
    "extentFreeList" : {
        "num" : 0,
        "totalSize" : 0
    },
    "dataFileVersion" : {
        "major" : 4,
        "minor" : 5
    },
    "ok" : 1
}
```

You can also run the stats() command on an individual collection:

```
> db.numbers.stats()
{
    "ns" : "tutorial.numbers",
    "count" : 20000,
```

---

[4] You can also enter the more succinct show tables.

```
    "size" : 960064,
    "avgObjSize" : 48,
    "storageSize" : 2793472,
    "numExtents" : 5,
    "nindexes" : 2,
    "lastExtentSize" : 2097152,
    "paddingFactor" : 1,
    "paddingFactorNote" : "paddingFactor is unused and unmaintained in 3.0.
     It remains hard coded to 1.0 for compatibility only.",
    "systemFlags" : 1,
    "userFlags" : 1,
    "totalIndexSize" : 1169168,
    "indexSizes" : {
        "_id_" : 654080,
        "num_1" : 515088
    },
    "ok" : 1
}
```

Some of the values provided in these result documents are useful only in complicated debugging or tuning situations. But at the very least, you'll be able to find out how much space a given collection and its indexes are occupying.

2.3.2   *How commands work*

A certain set of MongoDB operations—distinct from the insert, update, remove, and query operations described so far in this chapter—are known as database commands. Database commands are generally administrative, as with the stats() methods just presented, but they may also control core MongoDB features, such as updating data.

Regardless of the functionality they provide, what all database commands have in common is their implementation as queries on a special virtual collection called $cmd. To show what this means, let's take a quick example. Recall how you invoked the stats() database command:

```
> db.stats()
```

The stats() method is a helper that wraps the shell's command invocation method. Try entering the following equivalent operation:

```
> db.runCommand( {dbstats: 1} )
```

The results are identical to what's provided by the stats() method. Note that the command is defined by the document {dbstats: 1}. In general, you can run any available command by passing its document definition to the runCommand() method. Here's how you'd run the collection stats command:

```
> db.runCommand( {collstats: "numbers"} )
```

The output should look familiar.

But to get to the heart of database commands, you need to see how the `run-Command()` method works. That's not hard to find out because the MongoDB shell will print the implementation of any method whose executing parentheses are omitted. Instead of running the command like this

```
> db.runCommand()
```

you can execute the parentheses-less version and see the internals:

```
> db.runCommand
  function ( obj, extra ){
    if ( typeof( obj ) == "string" ){
        var n = {};
        n[obj] = 1;
        obj = n;
        if ( extra && typeof( extra ) == "object" ) {
            for ( var x in extra ) {
                n[x] = extra[x];
            }
        }
    }
    return this.getCollection( "$cmd" ).findOne( obj );
}
```

The last line in the function is nothing more than a query on the `$cmd` collection. To define it properly, then, a database command is a query on a special collection, `$cmd`, where the query selector defines the command itself. That's all there is to it. Can you think of a way to run the collection stats command manually? It's this simple:

```
> db.$cmd.findOne( {collstats: "numbers"} );
```

Using the `runCommand` helper is easier but it's always good to know what's going on beneath the surface.

2.4 *Getting help*

By now, the value of the MongoDB shell as a testing ground for experimenting with data and administering the database should be evident. But because you'll likely spend a lot of time in the shell, it's worth knowing how to get help.

The built-in help commands are the first place to look. `db.help()` prints a list of commonly used methods for operating on databases. You'll find a similar list of methods for operating on collections by running `db.numbers.help()`.

There's also built-in tab completion. Start typing the first characters of any method and then press the Tab key twice. You'll see a list of all matching methods. Here's the tab completion for collection methods beginning with `get`:

```
> db.numbers.get
db.numbers.getCollection(           db.numbers.getIndexes(
db.numbers.getShardDistribution(
```

```
db.numbers.getDB(                    db.numbers.getIndices(
db.numbers.getShardVersion(
db.numbers.getDiskStorageStats(      db.numbers.getMongo(
db.numbers.getSlaveOk(
db.numbers.getFullName(              db.numbers.getName(
db.numbers.getSplitKeysForChunks(
db.numbers.getIndexKeys(             db.numbers.getPagesInRAM(
db.numbers.getWriteConcern(
db.numbers.getIndexSpecs(            db.numbers.getPlanCache(
db.numbers.getIndexStats(            db.numbers.getQueryOptions(
```

The official MongoDB manual is an invaluable resource and can be found at http://
docs.mongodb.org. It has both tutorials and reference material, and it's kept up-to-
date with new releases of MongoDB. The manual also includes documentation for
each language-specific MongoDB driver implementation, such as the Ruby driver,
which is necessary when accessing MongoDB from an application.

   If you're more ambitious, and are comfortable with JavaScript, the shell makes it
easy to examine the implementation of any given method. For instance, suppose
you'd like to know exactly how the save() method works. Sure, you could go trolling
through the MongoDB source code, but there's an easier way: enter the method name
without the executing parentheses. Here's how you'd normally execute save():

```
> db.numbers.save({num: 123123123});
```

And this is how you can check the implementation:

```
> db.numbers.save
function ( obj , opts ){
    if ( obj == null )
        throw "can't save a null";

    if ( typeof( obj ) == "number" || typeof( obj) == "string" )
        throw "can't save a number or string"

    if ( typeof( obj._id ) == "undefined" ){
        obj._id = new ObjectId();
        return this.insert( obj , opts );
    }
    else {
        return this.update( { _id : obj._id } , obj , Object.merge({
     upsert:true }, opts));
    }
}
```

Read the function definition closely, and you'll see that save() is merely a wrapper for
insert() and update(). After checking the type of the obj argument, if the object
you're trying to save doesn't have an _id field, then the field is added, and insert() is
invoked. Otherwise an update is performed.

   This trick for examining the shell's methods comes in handy. Keep this technique
in mind as you continue exploring the MongoDB shell.

2.5   *Summary*

You've now seen the document data model in practice, and we've demonstrated a variety of common MongoDB operations on that data model. You've learned how to create indexes and have seen an example of index-based performance improvements through the use of explain(). In addition, you should be able to extract information about the collections and databases on your system, you now know all about the clever $cmd collection, and if you ever need help, you've picked up a few tricks for finding your way around.

You can learn a lot by working in the MongoDB shell, but there's no substitute for the experience of building a real application. That's why we're going from a carefree data playground to a real-world data workshop in the next chapter. You'll see how the drivers work, and then, using the Ruby driver, you'll build a simple application, hitting MongoDB with some real, live data.

Writing programs using MongoDB

This chapter covers

- Introducing the MongoDB API through Ruby
- Understanding how the drivers work
- Using the BSON format and MongoDB network protocol
- Building a complete sample application

It's time to get practical. Though there's much to learn from experimenting with the MongoDB shell, you can see the real value of this database only after you've built something with it. That means jumping into programming and taking a first look at the MongoDB drivers. As mentioned before, MongoDB, Inc. provides officially supported, Apache-licensed MongoDB drivers for all of the most popular programming languages. The driver examples in the book use Ruby, but the principles we'll illustrate are universal and easily transferable to other drivers. Throughout the book we'll illustrate most commands with the JavaScript shell, but examples of using MongoDB from within an application will be in Ruby.

We're going to explore programming in MongoDB in three stages. First, you'll install the MongoDB Ruby driver and we'll introduce the basic CRUD (create, read, update, delete) operations. This process should go quickly and feel familiar because the driver API is similar to that of the shell. Next, we're going to delve deeper into the driver, explaining how it interfaces with MongoDB. Without getting too low-level, this section will show you what's going on behind the scenes with the drivers in general. Finally, you'll develop a simple Ruby application for monitoring Twitter. Working with a real-world data set, you'll begin to see how MongoDB works in the wild. This final section will also lay the groundwork for the more in-depth examples presented in part 2 of the book.

New to Ruby?

Ruby is a popular and readable scripting language. The code examples have been designed to be as explicit as possible so that even programmers unfamiliar with Ruby can benefit. Any Ruby idioms that may be hard to understand will be explained in the book. If you'd like to spend a few minutes getting up to speed with Ruby, start with the official 20-minute tutorial at http://mng.bz/THR3.

3.1 MongoDB through the Ruby lens

Normally when you think of drivers, what comes to mind are low-level bit manipulations and obtuse interfaces. Thankfully, the MongoDB language drivers are nothing like that; instead, they've been designed with intuitive, language-sensitive APIs so that many applications can sanely use a MongoDB driver as the sole interface to the database. The driver APIs are also fairly consistent across languages, which means that developers can easily move between languages as needed; anything you can do in the JavaScript API, you can do in the Ruby API. If you're an application developer, you can expect to find yourself comfortable and productive with any of the MongoDB drivers without having to concern yourself with low-level implementation details.

In this first section, you'll install the MongoDB Ruby driver, connect to the database, and learn how to perform basic CRUD operations. This will lay the groundwork for the application you'll build at the end of the chapter.

3.1.1 Installing and connecting

You can install the MongoDB Ruby driver using RubyGems, Ruby's package management system.

Many newer operating systems come with Ruby already installed. You can check if you already have Ruby installed by running `ruby --version` from your shell. If you don't have Ruby installed on your system, you can find detailed installation instructions at www.ruby-lang.org/en/downloads.

You'll also need Ruby's package manager, RubyGems. You may already have this as well; check by running `gem --version`. Instructions for installing RubyGems can be found at http://docs.rubygems.org/read/chapter/3. Once you have RubyGems installed, run:

```
gem install mongo
```

This should install both the `mongo` and `bson`[1] gems. You should see output like the following (the version numbers will likely be newer than what's shown here):

```
Fetching: bson-3.2.1.gem (100%)
Building native extensions.  This could take a while...
Successfully installed bson-3.2.1
Fetching: mongo-2.0.6.gem (100%)
Successfully installed mongo-2.0.6
2 gems installed
```

We also recommend you install the `bson_ext` gem, though this is optional. `bson_ext` is an official gem that contains a C implementation of BSON, enabling more efficient handling of BSON in the MongoDB driver. This gem isn't installed by default because installation requires a compiler. Rest assured, if you're unable to install `bson_ext`, your programs will still work as intended.

You'll start by connecting to MongoDB. First, make sure that `mongod` is running by running the `mongo` shell to ensure you can connect. Next, create a file called connect.rb and enter the following code:

```ruby
require 'rubygems'
require 'mongo'

$client = Mongo::Client.new([ '127.0.0.1:27017' ], :database => 'tutorial')
Mongo::Logger.logger.level = ::Logger::ERROR
$users = $client[:users]
puts 'connected!'
```

The first two `require` statements ensure that you've loaded the driver. The next three lines instantiate the client to localhost and connect to the tutorial database, store a reference to the users collection in the $users variable, and print the string `connected!`. We place a $ in front of each variable to make it global so that it'll be accessible outside of the connect.rb script. Save the file and run it:

```
$ ruby connect.rb
D, [2015-06-05T12:32:38.843933 #33946] DEBUG -- : MONGODB | Adding
    127.0.0.1:27017 to the cluster. | runtime: 0.0031ms
D, [2015-06-05T12:32:38.847534 #33946] DEBUG -- : MONGODB | COMMAND |
    namespace=admin.$cmd selector={:ismaster=>1} flags=[] limit=-1 skip=0
    project=nil | runtime: 3.4170ms
connected!
```

If no exceptions are raised, you've successfully connected to MongoDB from Ruby and you should see `connected!` printed to your shell. That may not seem glamorous, but connecting is the first step in using MongoDB from any language. Next, you'll use that connection to insert some documents.

---

[1] BSON, explained in the next section, is the JSON-inspired binary format that MongoDB uses to represent documents. The `bson` Ruby gem serializes Ruby objects to and from BSON.

3.1.2   *Inserting documents in Ruby*

To run interesting MongoDB queries you first need some data, so let's create some (this is the C in CRUD). All of the MongoDB drivers are designed to use the most natural document representation for their language. In JavaScript, JSON objects are the obvious choice, because JSON is a document data structure; in Ruby, the hash data structure makes the most sense. The native Ruby hash differs from a JSON object in only a couple of small ways; most notably, where JSON separates keys and values with a colon, Ruby uses a hash rocket (=>).[2]

If you're following along, you can continue adding code to the connect.rb file. Alternatively, a nice approach is to use Ruby's interactive shell, irb. irb is a REPL (Read, Evaluate, Print Loop) console, in which you can type Ruby code to have it dynamically executed, making it ideal for experimentation. Anything you write in irb can be put in a script, so we recommend using it to learn new things, then copying your commands when you'd like them executed in a program. You can launch irb and require connect.rb so that you'll immediately have access to the connection, database, and collection objects initialized therein. You can then run Ruby code and receive immediate feedback. Here's an example:

```
$ irb -r ./connect.rb
irb(main):017:0> id = $users.insert_one({"last_name" => "mtsouk"})
=> #<Mongo::Operation::Result:70275279152800 documents=[{"ok"=>1, "n"=>1}]>
irb(main):014:0> $users.find().each do |user|
irb(main):015:1* puts user
irb(main):016:1> end
{"_id"=>BSON::ObjectId('55e3ee1c5ae119511d000000'), "last_name"=>"knuth"}
{"_id"=>BSON::ObjectId('55e3f13d5ae119516a000000'), "last_name"=>"mtsouk"}
=> #<Enumerator: #<Mongo::Cursor:0x70275279317980
@view=#<Mongo::Collection::View:0x70275279322740 namespace='tutorial.users
@selector={} @options={}>>:each>
```

irb gives you a command line shell with a prompt followed by > (this may look a little different on your machine). The prompt allows you to type in commands, and in the previous code we've highlighted the user input in bold. When you run a command in irb it will print out the value returned by the command, if there is one; that's what is shown after => above.

Let's build some documents for your users' collection. You'll create two documents representing two users, Smith and Jones. Each document, expressed as a Ruby hash, is assigned to a variable:

```
smith = {"last_name" => "smith", "age" => 30}
jones = {"last_name" => "jones", "age" => 40}
```

---

[2] In Ruby 1.9, you may optionally use a colon as the key-value separator, like hash = {foo: 'bar'}, but we'll stick with the hash rocket in the interest of backward compatibility.

To save the documents, you'll pass them to the collection's insert method. Each call to insert returns a unique ID, which you'll store in a variable to simplify later retrieval:

```
smith_id = $users.insert_one(smith)
jones_id = $users.insert_one(jones)
```

You can verify that the documents have been saved with some simple queries, so you can query with the user collection's find() method like this:

```
irb(main):013:0> $users.find("age" => {"$gt" => 20}).each.to_a do |row|
irb(main):014:1* puts row
irb(main):015:1> end
=> [{"_id"=>BSON::ObjectId('55e3f7dd5ae119516a000002'), "last_name"=>"smith",
     "age"=>30}, {"_id"=>BSON::ObjectId('55e3f7e25ae119516a000003'),
     "last_name"=>"jones", "age"=>40}]
```

The return values for these queries will appear at the prompt if run in irb. If the code is being run from a Ruby file, prepend Ruby's p method to print the output to the screen:

```
p $users.find( :age => {"$gt" => 20}).to_a
```

You've successfully inserted two documents from Ruby. Let's now take a closer look at queries.

3.1.3 *Queries and cursors*

Now that you've created documents, it's on to the read operations (the R in CRUD) provided by MongoDB. The Ruby driver defines a rich interface for accessing data and handles most of the details for you. The queries we show in this section are fairly simple selections, but keep in mind that MongoDB allows more complex queries, such as text searches and aggregations, which are described in later chapters.

You'll see how this is so by looking at the standard find method. Here are two possible find operations on your data set:

```
$users.find({"last_name" => "smith"}).to_a
$users.find({"age" => {"$gt" => 30}}).to_a
```

The first query searches for all user documents where the last_name is smith and that the second query matches all documents where age is greater than 30. Try entering the second query in irb:

```
2.1.4 :020 > $users.find({"age" => {"$gt" => 30}})
 => #<Mongo::Collection::View:0x70210212601420 namespace='tutorial.users'
@selector={"age"=>{"$gt"=>30}} @options={}>
```

The results are returned in a Mongo::Collection::View object, which extends Iterable and makes it easy to iterate through the results. We'll discuss cursors in

more detail in Section 3.2.3. In the meantime, you can fetch the results of the
$gt query:

```
cursor = $users.find({"age" => {"$gt" => 30}})
cursor.each do |doc|
  puts doc["last_name"]
end
```

Here you use Ruby's each iterator, which passes each result to a code block. The
last_name attribute is then printed to the console. The $gt used in the query is a
MongoDB operator; the $ character has no relation to the $ placed before global Ruby
variables like $users. Also, if there are any documents in the collection without
last_name, you might notice that nil (Ruby's null value) is printed out; this indicates
the lack of a value and it's normal to see this.

The fact that you even have to think about cursors here may come as a surprise
given the shell examples from the previous chapter. But the shell uses cursors the
same way every driver does; the difference is that the shell automatically iterates over
the first 20 cursor results when you call find(). To get the remaining results, you can
continue iterating manually by entering the it command.

3.1.4 Updates and deletes

Recall from chapter 2 that *updates* require at least two arguments: a query selector and
an update document. Here's a simple example using the Ruby driver:

```
$users.find({"last_name" => "smith"}).update_one({"$set" => {"city" =>
"Chicago"}})
```

This update finds the first user with a last_name of smith and, if found, sets the value
of city to Chicago. This update uses the $set operator. You can run a query to show
the change:

```
$users.find({"last_name" => "smith"}).to_a
```

The view allows you to decide whether you only want to update one document or all
documents matching the query. In the preceding example, even if you had several
users with the last name of smith, only one document would be updated. To apply the
update to a particular smith, you'd need to add more conditions to your query selector. But if you actually want to apply the update to all smith documents, you must
replace the update_one with the update_many method:

```
$users.find({"last_name" => "smith"}).update_many({"$set" => {"city" =>
"Chicago"}})
```

Deleting data is much simpler. We've discussed how it works in the MongoDB shell and
the Ruby driver is no different. To review: you simply use the remove method. This
method takes an optional query selector that will remove only those documents
matching the selector. If no selector is provided, all documents in the collection will

be removed. Here, you're removing all user documents where the age attribute is greater than or equal to 40:

```
$users.find({"age" => {"$gte" => 40}}).delete_one
```

This will only delete the first one matching the matching criteria. If you want to delete all documents matching the criteria, you'd have to run this:

```
$users.find({"age" => {"$gte" => 40}}).delete_many
```

With no arguments, the drop method deletes all remaining documents:

```
$users.drop
```

3.1.5   *Database commands*

In the previous chapter you saw the centrality of database commands. There, we looked at the two stats commands. Here, we'll look at how you can run commands from the driver using the listDatabases command as an example. This is one of a number of commands that must be run on the admin database, which is treated specially when authentication is enabled. For details on the authentication and the admin database, see chapter 10.

First, you instantiate a Ruby database object referencing the admin database. You then pass the command's query specification to the command method:

```
$admin_db = $client.use('admin')
$admin_db.command({"listDatabases" => 1})
```

Note that this code still depends on what we put in the connect.rb script above because it expects the MongoDB connection to be in $client. The response is a Ruby hash listing all the existing databases and their sizes on disk:

```
#<Mongo::Operation::Result:70112905054200 documents=[{"databases"=>[
{
    "name"=>"local",
    "sizeOnDisk"=>83886080.0,
    "empty"=>false
},
{
    "name"=>"tutorial",
"sizeOnDisk"=>83886080.0,
"empty"=>false
},
{
    "name"=>"admin",
    "sizeOnDisk"=>1.0, "empty"=>true
}], "totalSize"=>167772160.0, "ok"=>1.0}]>
 => nil
```

This may look a little different with your version of irb and the MongoDB driver, but it should still be easy to access. Once you get used to representing documents as Ruby hashes, the transition from the shell API is almost seamless.

Most drivers provide you convenient functionality that wraps database commands. You may recall from the previous chapter that remove doesn't actually drop the collection. To drop a collection and all its indexes, use the drop_collection method:

```
db = $client.use('tutorial')
db['users'].drop
```

It's okay if you're still feeling shaky about using MongoDB with Ruby; you'll get more practice in section 3.3. But for now, we're going to take a brief intermission to see how the MongoDB drivers work. This will shed more light on some of MongoDB's design and prepare you to use the drivers effectively.

3.2   *How the drivers work*

At this point it's natural to wonder what's going on behind the scenes when you issue commands through a driver or via the MongoDB shell. In this section, you'll see how the drivers serialize data and communicate it to the database.

All MongoDB drivers perform three major functions. First, they generate MongoDB object IDs. These are the default values stored in the _id field of all documents. Next, the drivers convert any language-specific representation of documents to and from BSON, the binary data format used by MongoDB. In the previous examples, the driver serializes all the Ruby hashes into BSON and then deserializes the BSON that's returned from the database back to Ruby hashes.

The drivers' final function is to communicate with the database over a TCP socket using the MongoDB wire protocol. The details of the protocol are beyond the scope of this discussion. But the style of socket communication, in particular whether writes on the socket wait for a response, is important, and we'll explore the topic in this section.

3.2.1   *Object ID generation*

Every MongoDB document requires a primary key. That key, which must be unique for all documents in each collection, is stored in the document's _id field. Developers are free to use their own custom values as the _id, but when not provided, a MongoDB object ID will be used. Before sending a document to the server, the driver checks whether the _id field is present. If the field is missing, an object ID will be generated and stored as _id.

MongoDB object IDs are designed to be globally unique, meaning they're guaranteed to be unique within a certain context. How can this be guaranteed? Let's examine this in more detail.

You've probably seen object IDs in the wild if you've inserted documents into MongoDB, and at first glance they appear to be a string of mostly random text, like 4c291856238d3b19b2000001. You may not have realized that this text is the hex

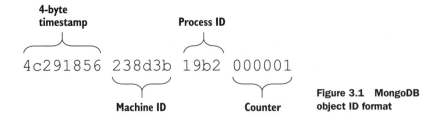

Figure 3.1 MongoDB object ID format

representation of 12 bytes, and actually stores some useful information. These bytes have a specific structure, as illustrated in figure 3.1.

The most significant four bytes carry a standard Unix (epoch) timestamp[3]. The next three bytes store the machine ID, which is followed by a two-byte process ID. The final three bytes store a process-local counter that's incremented each time an object ID is generated. The counter means that ids generated in the same process and second won't be duplicated.

Why does the object ID have this format? It's important to understand that these IDs are generated in the driver, not on the server. This is different than many RDBMSs, which increment a primary key on the server, thus creating a bottleneck for the server generating the key. If more than one driver is generating IDs and inserting documents, they need a way of creating unique identifiers without talking to each other. Thus, the timestamp, machine ID, and process ID are included in the identifier itself to make it extremely unlikely that IDs will overlap.

You may already be considering the odds of this happening. In practice, you would encounter other limits before inserting documents at the rate required to overflow the counter for a given second (2^{24} million per second). It's slightly more conceivable (though still unlikely) to imagine that if you had many drivers distributed across many machines, two machines could have the same machine ID. For example, the Ruby driver uses the following:

```
@@machine_id = Digest::MD5.digest(Socket.gethostname)[0, 3]
```

For this to be a problem, they would still have to have started the MongoDB driver's process with the same process ID, and have the same counter value in a given second. In practice, don't worry about duplication; it's extremely unlikely.

One of the incidental benefits of using MongoDB object IDs is that they include a timestamp. Most of the drivers allow you to extract the timestamp, thus providing the document creation time, with resolution to the nearest second, for free. Using the Ruby

---

[3] Many Unix machines (we're including Linux when we say Unix machine) store time values in a format called Unix Time or POSIX time; they just count up the number of seconds since 00:00 on January 1st, 1970, called the epoch. This means that a timestamp can be stored as an integer. For example, 2010-06-28 21:47:02 is represented as 1277761622 (or 0x4c291856 in hexadecimal), the number of seconds since the epoch.

driver, you can call an object ID's `generation_time` method to get that ID's creation time as a Ruby `Time` object:

```
irb> require 'mongo'
irb> id = BSON::ObjectId.from_string('4c291856238d3b19b2000001')
=> BSON::ObjectId('4c291856238d3b19b2000001')
irb> id.generation_time
=> 2010-06-28 21:47:02 UTC
```

Naturally, you can also use object IDs to issue range queries on object creation time. For instance, if you wanted to query for all documents created during June 2013, you could create two object IDs whose timestamps encode those dates and then issue a range query on `_id`. Because Ruby provides methods for generating object IDs from any `Time` object, the code for doing this is trivial:[4]

```
jun_id = BSON::ObjectId.from_time(Time.utc(2013, 6, 1))
jul_id = BSON::ObjectId.from_time(Time.utc(2013, 7, 1))
@users.find({'_id' => {'$gte' => jun_id, '$lt' => jul_id}})
```

As mentioned before, you can also set your own value for `_id`. This might make sense in cases where one of the document's fields is important and always unique. For instance, in a collection of users you could store the username in `_id` rather than on object ID. There are advantages to both ways, and it comes down to your preference as a developer.

3.3 Building a simple application

Next you'll build a simple application for archiving and displaying Tweets. You can imagine this being a component in a larger application that allows users to keep tabs on search terms relevant to their businesses. This example will demonstrate how easy it is to consume JSON from an API like Twitter's and convert that to MongoDB documents. If you were doing this with a relational database, you'd have to devise a schema in advance, probably consisting of multiple tables, and then declare those tables. Here, none of that's required, yet you'll still preserve the rich structure of the Tweet documents, and you'll be able to query them effectively.

Let's call the app TweetArchiver. TweetArchiver will consist of two components: the archiver and the viewer. The archiver will call the Twitter search API and store the relevant Tweets, and the viewer will display the results in a web browser.

3.3.1 Setting up

This application requires four Ruby libraries. The source code repository for this chapter includes a file called Gemfile, which lists these gems. Change your working directory

---

[4] This example will actually not work; it's meant as a thoughtful exercise. By now you should have enough knowledge to create meaningful data for the query to return something. Why not take the time and try it out?

to chapter3 and make sure an `ls` command shows the Gemfile. You can then install them from your system command line like this:

```
gem install bundler
bundle install
```

This will ensure the `bundler` gem is installed. Next, install the other gems using Bundler's package management tools. This is a widely used Ruby tool for ensuring that the gems you use match some predetermined versions: the versions that match our code examples.

Our Gemfile lists the `mongo`, `twitter`, `bson` and `sinatra` gems, so these will be installed. The `mongo` gem we've used already, but we include it to be sure we have the right version. The `twitter` gem is useful for communicating with the Twitter API. The `sinatra` gem is a framework for running a simple web server in Ruby, and we discuss it in more detail in section 3.3.3.

We provide the source code for this example separately, but introduce it gradually to help you understand it. We recommend you experiment and try new things to get the most out of the example.

It'll be useful to have a configuration file that you can share between the archiver and viewer scripts. Create a file called config.rb (or copy it from the source code) that looks like this:

```
DATABASE_HOST    = 'localhost'
DATABASE_PORT    = 27017
DATABASE_NAME    = "twitter-archive"
COLLECTION_NAME  = "tweets"
TAGS = ["#MongoDB", "#Mongo"]

CONSUMER_KEY     = "replace me"
CONSUMER_SECRET  = "replace me"
TOKEN            = "replace me"
TOKEN_SECRET     = "replace me"
```

First you specify the names of the database and collection you'll use for your application. Then you define an array of search terms, which you'll send to the Twitter API.

Twitter requires that you register a free account and an application for accessing the API, which can be accomplished at http://apps.twitter.com. Once you've registered an application, you should see a page with its authentication information, perhaps on the API keys tab. You will also have to click the button that creates your access token. Use the values shown to fill in the consumer and API keys and secrets.

3.3.2 *Gathering data*

The next step is to write the archiver script. You start with a `TweetArchiver` class. You'll instantiate the class with a search term. Then you'll call the `update` method on the `TweetArchiver` instance, which issues a Twitter API call, and save the results to a MongoDB collection.

Let's start with the class's constructor:

```
def initialize(tag)
  connection = Mongo::Connection.new(DATABASE_HOST, DATABASE_PORT)
  db         = connection[DATABASE_NAME]
  @tweets    = db[COLLECTION_NAME]
  @tweets.ensure_index([['tags', 1], ['id', -1]])
  @tag = tag
  @tweets_found = 0

  @client = Twitter::REST::Client.new do |config|
    config.consumer_key        = API_KEY
    config.consumer_secret     = API_SECRET
    config.access_token        = ACCESS_TOKEN
    config.access_token_secret = ACCESS_TOKEN_SECRET
  end
end
```

The `initialize` method instantiates a connection, a database object, and the collection object you'll use to store the Tweets.

You're creating a compound index on `tags` ascending and `id` descending. Because you're going to want to query for a particular tag and show the results from newest to oldest, an index with `tags` ascending and `id` descending will make that query use the index both for filtering results and for sorting them. As you can see here, you indicate index direction with `1` for *ascending* and `-1` for *descending*. Don't worry if this doesn't make sense now—we discuss indexes with much greater depth in chapter 8.

You're also configuring the Twitter client with the authentication information from config.rb. This step hands these values to the Twitter gem, which will use them when calling the Twitter API. Ruby has somewhat unique syntax often used for this sort of configuration; the `config` variable is passed to a Ruby block, in which you set its values.

MongoDB allows you to insert data regardless of its structure. With a relational database, each table needs a well-defined schema, which requires planning out which values you would like to store. In the future, Twitter may change its API so that different values are returned, which will likely require a schema change if you want to store these additional values. Not so with MongoDB. Its schema-less design allows you to save the document you get from the Twitter API without worrying about the exact format.

The Ruby Twitter library returns Ruby hashes, so you can pass these directly to your MongoDB collection object. Within your `TweetArchiver`, you add the following instance method:

```
def save_tweets_for(term)
  @client.search(term).each do |tweet|
    @tweets_found += 1
    tweet_doc = tweet.to_h
    tweet_doc[:tags] = term
    tweet_doc[:_id] = tweet_doc[:id]
    @tweets.insert_one(tweet_doc)
  end
end
```

Before saving each Tweet document, make two small modifications. To simplify later queries, add the search term to a `tags` attribute. You also set the `_id` field to the ID of the Tweet, replacing the primary key of your collection and ensuring that each Tweet is added only once. Then you pass the modified document to the `save` method.

To use this code in a class, you need some additional code. First, you must configure the MongoDB driver so that it connects to the correct `mongod` and uses the desired database and collection. This is simple code that you'll replicate often as you use MongoDB. Next, you must configure the Twitter gem with your developer credentials. This step is necessary because Twitter restricts its API to registered developers. The next listing also provides an `update` method, which gives the user feedback and calls `save_tweets_for`.

Listing 3.1   archiver.rb—A class for fetching Tweets and archiving them in MongoDB

```
$LOAD_PATH << File.dirname(__FILE__)
require 'rubygems'
require 'mongo'
require 'twitter'
require 'config'

class TweetArchiver

def initialize(tag)
    client =
     Mongo::Client.new(["#{DATABASE_HOST}:#{DATABASE_PORT}"],:database =>
     "#{DATABASE_NAME}")
    @tweets    = client["#{COLLECTION_NAME}"]
    @tweets.indexes.drop_all
    @tweets.indexes.create_many([
      { :key => { tags: 1 }},
      { :key => { id: -1 }}
      ])
    @tag = tag
    @tweets_found = 0

    @client = Twitter::REST::Client.new do |config|
      config.consumer_key        = "#{API_KEY}"
      config.consumer_secret     = "#{API_SECRET}"
      config.access_token        = "#{ACCESS_TOKEN}"
      config.access_token_secret = "#{ACCESS_TOKEN_SECRET}"
    end
  end

  def update
    puts "Starting Twitter search for '#{@tag}'..."
    save_tweets_for(@tag)
    print "#{@tweets_found} Tweets saved.\n\n"
  end

  private
```

Create a new instance of Tweet-Archive.

Configure the Twitter client using the values found in config.rb.

A user facing method to wrap save_tweets_for

```
def save_tweets_for(term)
  @client.search(term).each do |tweet|
    @tweets_found += 1
    tweet_doc = tweet.to_h
    tweet_doc[:tags] = term
    tweet_doc[:_id] = tweet_doc[:id]
    @tweets.insert_one(tweet_doc)
  end
end
end
```

Search with the Twitter client and save the results to Mongo.

All that remains is to write a script to run the `TweetArchiver` code against each of the search terms. Create a file called update.rb (or copy it from the provided code) containing the following:

```
$LOAD_PATH << File.dirname(__FILE__)
require 'config'
require 'archiver'

TAGS.each do |tag|
  archive = TweetArchiver.new(tag)
  archive.update
end
```

Next, run the update script:

```
ruby update.rb
```

You'll see some status messages indicating that Tweets have been found and saved. You can verify that the script works by opening the MongoDB shell and querying the collection directly:

```
> use twitter-archive
switched to db twitter-archive
> db.tweets.count()
30
```

What's important here is that you've managed to store Tweets from Twitter searches in only a few lines of code.[5] Next comes the task of displaying the results.

3.3.3 *Viewing the archive*

You'll use Ruby's Sinatra web framework to build a simple app to display the results. Sinatra allows you to define the endpoints for a web application and directly specify the response. Its power lies in its simplicity. For example, the content of the index page for your application can be specified with the following:

```
get '/' do
  "response"
end
```

---

[5] It's possible to accomplish this in far fewer lines of code. Doing so is left as an exercise to the reader.

This code specifies that GET requests to the / endpoint of your application return the value of response to the client. Using this format, you can write full web applications with many endpoints, each of which can execute arbitrary Ruby code before returning a response. You can find more information, including Sinatra's full documentation, at http://sinatrarb.com.

We'll now introduce a file called viewer.rb and place it in the same directory as the other scripts. Next, make a subdirectory called views, and place a file there called tweets.erb. After these steps, the project's file structure should look like this:

```
- config.rb
- archiver.rb
- update.rb
- viewer.rb
- /views
   - tweets.erb
```

Again, feel free to create these files yourself or copy them from the code examples. Now edit viewer.rb with the code in the following listing.

Listing 3.2   viewer.rb—Sinatra application for displaying the Tweet archive

```
$LOAD_PATH << File.dirname(__FILE__)
require 'rubygems'
require 'mongo'                            ❶ Required
require 'sinatra'                             libraries
require 'config'
require 'open-uri'

configure do
  client = Mongo::Client.new(["#{DATABASE_HOST}:#{DATABASE_PORT}"], :database
    => "#{DATABASE_NAME}")
  TWEETS = client["#{COLLECTION_NAME}"]     ❷ Instantiate collection
end                                             for tweets

get '/' do
  if params['tag']                          ❸ Dynamically build
    selector = {:tags => params['tag']}        query selector...
  else
    selector = {}                           ...or use
  end                                       ❹ blank selector

  @tweets = TWEETS.find(selector).sort(["id", -1])  ❺ Issue query
  erb :tweets                               ❻ Render view
end
```

The first lines require the necessary libraries along with your config file ❶. Next there's a configuration block that creates a connection to MongoDB and stores a reference to your tweets collection in the constant TWEETS ❷.

The real meat of the application is in the lines beginning with get '/' do. The code in this block handles requests to the application's root URL. First, you build your query selector. If a `tags` URL parameter has been provided, you create a query selector that restricts the result set to the given tags ❸. Otherwise, you create a blank selector, which returns all documents in the collection ❹. You then issue the query ❺. By now, you should know that what gets assigned to the `@tweets` variable isn't a result set but a cursor. You'll iterate over that cursor in your view.

The last line ❻ renders the view file tweets.erb (see the next listing).

Listing 3.3   tweets.erb—HTML with embedded Ruby for rendering the Tweets

```
<!DOCTYPE html>
<html>
<head>
  <meta http-equiv="Content-Type" content="text/html; charset=UTF-8"/>
  <style>
    body {
      width: 1000px;
      margin: 50px auto;
      font-family: Palatino, serif;
      background-color: #dbd4c2;
      color: #555050;
    }
    h2 {
      margin-top: 2em;
      font-family: Arial, sans-serif;
      font-weight: 100;
    }
  </style>
</head>
<body>
<h1>Tweet Archive</h1>
<% TAGS.each do |tag| %>
  <a href="/?tag=<%= URI::encode(tag) %>"><%= tag %></a>
<% end %>
<% @tweets.each do |tweet| %>
  <h2><%= tweet['text'] %></h2>
  <p>
    <a href="http://twitter.com/<%= tweet['user']['screen_name'] %>">
      <%= tweet['user']['screen_name'] %>
    </a>
    on <%= tweet['created_at'] %>
  </p>
  <img src="<%= tweet['user']['profile_image_url'] %>" width="48" />
<% end %>
</body>
</html>
```

Most of the code is just HTML with some ERB (embedded Ruby) mixed in. The Sinatra app runs the `tweets.erb` file through an ERB processor and evaluates any Ruby code between `<%` and `%>` in the context of the application.

The important parts come near the end, with the two iterators. The first of these cycles through the list of tags to display links for restricting the result set to a given tag.

The second iterator, beginning with the @tweets.each code, cycles through each Tweet to display the Tweet's text, creation date, and user profile image. You can see results by running the application:

```
$ ruby viewer.rb
```

If the application starts without error, you'll see the standard Sinatra startup message that looks something like this:

```
$ ruby viewer.rb
[2013-07-05 18:30:19] INFO  WEBrick 1.3.1
[2013-07-05 18:30:19] INFO  ruby 1.9.3 (2012-04-20) [x86_64-darwin10.8.0]
== Sinatra/1.4.3 has taken the stage on 4567 for development with backup from
    WEBrick
[2013-07-05 18:30:19] INFO  WEBrick::HTTPServer#start: pid=18465 port=4567
```

You can then point your web browser to http://localhost:4567. The page should look something like the screenshot in figure 3.2. Try clicking on the links at the top of the screen to narrow the results to a particular tag.

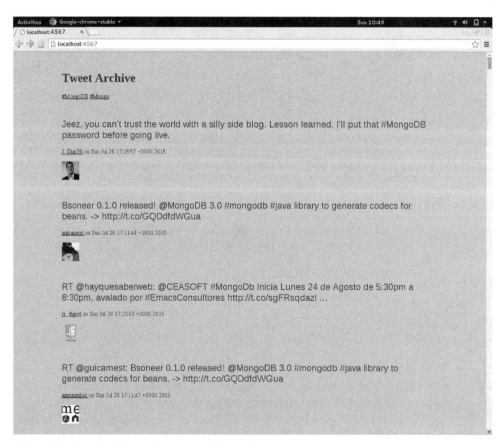

Figure 3.2 Tweet Archiver output rendered in a web browser

That's the extent of the application. It's admittedly simple, but it demonstrates some of the ease of using MongoDB. You didn't have to define your schema in advance, you took advantage of secondary indexes to make your queries fast and prevent duplicate inserts, and you had a relatively simple integration with your programming language.

3.4 Summary

You've just learned the basics of talking to MongoDB through the Ruby programming language. You saw how easy it is to represent documents in Ruby, and how similar Ruby's CRUD API is to that of the MongoDB shell. We dove into some internals, exploring how the drivers in general are built and looking in detail at object IDs, BSON, and the MongoDB network protocol. Finally, you built a simple application to show the use of MongoDB with real data. Though using MongoDB in the real world often requires more complexity, the prospect of writing applications with the database should be in reach.

Beginning with chapter 4, we're going to take everything you've learned so far and drill down. Specifically, you'll investigate how you might build an e-commerce application in MongoDB. That would be an enormous project, so we'll focus solely on a few sections on the back end. We'll present some data models for that domain, and you'll see how to insert and query that kind of data.

Part 2

Application development in MongoDB

Part 2 of this book is a deep exploration of MongoDB's document data model, query language, and CRUD (create, read, update, and delete) operations.

We'll make these topics concrete by progressively designing an e-commerce data model and the CRUD operations necessary for managing such data. Each chapter will present its subject matter in a top-down fashion, first by presenting examples within the sample e-commerce application's domain, and then by systematically filling in the details. On your first reading, you may want to read the e-commerce examples only and save the detailed material for later, or vice versa.

In chapter 4, you'll learn some schema design principles and then construct a basic e-commerce data model for products, categories, users, orders, and product reviews. Then you'll learn how MongoDB organizes data on the database, collection, and document levels. This chapter includes a summary of BSON's core data types.

Chapter 5 covers MongoDB's query language. You'll learn how to issue common queries against the data model developed in the previous chapter. Then, in the nuts and bolts sections, you'll see the semantics of query operators presented in detail.

Chapter 6 is all about aggregations. We'll show you how to do some simple groupings, and also go in depth into MongoDB's aggregation framework.

In presenting MongoDB's update and delete operations, chapter 7 brings us full circle by showing the rationale for the e-commerce data model. You'll learn how to maintain the category hierarchy and how to manage inventory transactionally. In addition, the update operators will be covered in detail along with the powerful find-AndModify command.

Document-oriented data

This chapter covers
- Schema design
- Data models for e-commerce
- Nuts and bolts of databases, collections, and documents

This chapter takes a close look at document-oriented data modeling and how data is organized at the database, collection, and document levels in MongoDB. We'll start with a brief, general discussion of how to design schemas to use with MongoDB. Remember, MongoDB itself doesn't enforce a schema, but every application needs some basic internal standards about how its data is stored. This exploration of principles sets the stage for the second part of the chapter, where we examine the design of an e-commerce schema in MongoDB. Along the way, you'll see how this schema differs from an equivalent RDBMS schema, and you'll learn how the typical relationships between entities, such as one-to-many and many-to-many, are represented in MongoDB. The e-commerce schema presented here will also serve as a basis for our discussions of queries, aggregation, and updates in subsequent chapters.

Because documents are the raw materials of MongoDB, we'll devote the final portion of this chapter to some of the many details you might encounter when thinking through your own schemas. This involves a more detailed discussion of databases, collections, and documents than you've seen up to this point. But if you read to the end, you'll be familiar with most of the obscure features and limitations of document data in MongoDB. You may also find yourself returning to this final section of the chapter later on, as it contains many of the "gotchas" you'll encounter when using MongoDB in the wild.

4.1   *Principles of schema design*

Database schema design is the process of choosing the best representation for a data set, given the features of the database system, the nature of the data, and the application requirements. The principles of schema design for relational database systems are well established. With RDBMSs, you're encouraged to shoot for a normalized data model,[1] which helps to ensure generic query ability and avoid updates to data that might result in inconsistencies. Moreover, the established patterns prevent developers from wondering how to model, say, one-to-many and many-to-many relationships. But schema design is never an exact science, even with relational databases. Application functionality and performance is the ultimate master in schema design, so every "rule" has exceptions.

If you're coming from the RDBMS world, you may be troubled by MongoDB's lack of hard schema design rules. Good practices have emerged, but there's still usually more than one good way to model a given data set. The premise of this section is that principles can drive schema design, but the reality is that those principles are pliable. To get you thinking, here are a few questions you can bring to the table when modeling data with any database system:

■ *What are your application access patterns?* You need to pin down the needs of your application, and this should inform not only your schema design but also which database you choose. Remember, MongoDB isn't right for every application. Understanding your application access patterns is by far the most important aspect of schema design.

The idiosyncrasies of an application can easily demand a schema that goes against firmly held data modeling principles. The upshot is that you must ask numerous questions about the application before you can determine the ideal data model. What's the read/write ratio? Will queries be simple, such as looking up a key, or more complex? Will aggregations be necessary? How much data will be stored?

■ *What's the basic unit of data?* In an RDBMS, you have tables with columns and rows. In a key-value store, you have keys pointing to amorphous values. In MongoDB, the basic unit of data is the BSON document.

---

[1] A simple way to think about a "normalized data model" is that information is never stored more than once. Thus, a one-to-many relationship between entities will always be split into at least two tables.

■ *What are the capabilities of your database?* Once you understand the basic data type, you need to know how to manipulate it. RDBMSs feature ad hoc queries and joins, usually written in SQL while simple key-value stores permit fetching values only by a single key. MongoDB also allows ad hoc queries, but joins aren't supported.

Databases also diverge in the kinds of updates they permit. With an RDBMS, you can update records in sophisticated ways using SQL and wrap multiple updates in a transaction to get atomicity and rollback. MongoDB doesn't support transactions in the traditional sense, but it does support a variety of atomic update operations that can work on the internal structures of a complex document. With simple key-value stores, you might be able to update a value, but every update will usually mean replacing the value completely.

■ *What makes a good unique id or primary key for a record?* There are exceptions, but many schemas, regardless of the database system, have some unique key for each record. Choosing this key carefully can make a big difference in how you access your data and how it's stored. If you're designing a user's collection, for example, should you use an arbitrary value, a legal name, a username, or a social security number as the primary key? It turns out that neither legal names nor social security numbers are unique or even applicable to all users within a given dataset.

In MongoDB choosing a primary key means picking what should go in the _id field. The automatic object ids are good defaults, but not ideal in every case. This is particularly important if you shard your data across multiple machines because it determines where a certain record will go. We'll discuss this in much greater detail in chapter 12.

The best schema designs are always the product of deep knowledge of the database you're using, good judgment about the requirements of the application at hand, and plain old experience. A good schema often requires experimentation and iteration, such as when an application scales and performance considerations change. Don't be afraid to alter your schema when you learn new things; only rarely is it possible to fully plan an application before its implementation. The examples in this chapter have been designed to help you develop a good sense of schema design in MongoDB. Having studied these examples, you'll be well-prepared to design the best schemas for your own applications.

4.2   *Designing an e-commerce data model*

The Twitter example application provided in chapter 3 demonstrated the basic MongoDB features, but didn't require much thought about its schema design. That's why, in this and in subsequent chapters, we'll look at the much richer domain of e-commerce. E-commerce has the advantage of including a large number of familiar data modeling patterns. Plus, it's not hard to imagine how products, categories, product reviews, and orders are typically modeled in an RDBMS. This should make the upcoming examples more instructive because you'll be able to compare them to your preconceived notions of schema design.

E-commerce has typically been done with RDBMSs for a couple of reasons. The first is that e-commerce sites generally require transactions, and transactions are an RDBMS staple. The second is that, until recently, domains that require rich data models and sophisticated queries have been assumed to fit best within the realm of the RDBMS. The following examples call into question this second assumption.

Building an entire e-commerce back end isn't practical within the space of this book. Instead, we'll pick out a handful of common and useful e-commerce entities, such as products and customer reviews, and show how they might be modeled in MongoDB. In particular, we'll look at products and categories, users and orders, and product reviews. For each entity, we'll show an example document. Then, we'll show some of the database features that complement the document's structure.

For many developers, *data model* goes hand in hand with *object mapping*, and for that purpose you may have used an object-relational mapping library, such as Java's Hibernate framework or Ruby's ActiveRecord. Such libraries can be useful for efficiently building applications with a RDBMS, but they're less necessary with MongoDB. This is due in part to the fact that a document is already an object-like representation. It's also partly due to the MongoDB drivers, which already provide a fairly high-level interface to MongoDB. Without question, you can build applications on MongoDB using the driver interface alone.

Object mappers can provide value by helping with validations, type checking, and associations between models, and come standard in frameworks like Ruby on Rails. Object mappers also introduce an additional layer of complexity between the programmer and the database that can obscure important query characteristics. You should evaluate this tradeoff when deciding if your application should use an object mapper; there are plenty of excellent applications written both with and without one.[2] We don't use an object mapper in any this book's examples, and we recommend you first learn about MongoDB without one.

4.2.1   Schema basics

Products and categories are the mainstays of any e-commerce site. Products, in a normalized RDBMS model, tend to require a large number of tables. There's a table for basic product information, such as the name and SKU, but there will be other tables to relate shipping information and pricing histories. This multitable schema will be facilitated by the RDBMS's ability to join tables.

Modeling a product in MongoDB should be less complicated. Because collections don't enforce a schema, any product document will have room for whichever dynamic attributes the product needs. By using arrays in your document, you can typically condense a multitable RDBMS representation into a single MongoDB collection.

---

[2] To find out which object mappers are most current for your language of choice, consult the recommendations at mongodb.org.

More concretely, listing 4.1 shows a sample product from a gardening store. It's advisable to assign this document to a variable before inserting it to the database using `db.products.insert(yourVariable)` to be able to run the queries discussed over the next several pages.

Listing 4.1   A sample product document

```
{
  _id: ObjectId("4c4b1476238d3b4dd5003981"),        ←──① Unique object ID
  slug: "wheelbarrow-9092",                          ←─┐
  sku: "9092",                                         ② Unique slug
  name: "Extra Large Wheelbarrow",
  description: "Heavy duty wheelbarrow...",
  details: {                                         ←─┐  Nested
    weight: 47,                                        ③ document
    weight_units: "lbs",
    model_num: 4039283402,
    manufacturer: "Acme",
    color: "Green"
  },
  total_reviews: 4,
  average_review: 4.5,
  pricing: {
    retail: 589700,
    sale: 489700,
  },
  price_history: [                                   ←─┐
    {
      retail: 529700,
      sale: 429700,
      start: new Date(2010, 4, 1),
      end: new Date(2010, 4, 8)
    },
    {                                                  ④ One-to-many
      retail: 529700,                                    relationship
      sale: 529700,
      start: new Date(2010, 4, 9),
      end: new Date(2010, 4, 16)
    },
  ],
  primary_category: ObjectId("6a5b1476238d3b4dd5000048"),  ←─┘
  category_ids: [                                    ←─┐
    ObjectId("6a5b1476238d3b4dd5000048"),
    ObjectId("6a5b1476238d3b4dd5000049")
  ],                                                   ⑤ Many-to-many
  main_cat_id: ObjectId("6a5b1476238d3b4dd5000048"),    relationship
  tags: ["tools", "gardening", "soil"],
}
```

The document contains the basic `name`, `sku`, and `description` fields. There's also the standard MongoDB object ID ① stored in the `_id` field. We discuss other aspects of this document in the next section.

UNIQUE SLUG

In addition, you've defined a slug ❷, wheelbarrow-9092, to provide a meaningful URL. MongoDB users sometimes complain about the ugliness of object IDs in URLs. Naturally, you don't want URLs that look like this:

```
http://mygardensite.org/products/4c4b1476238d3b4dd5003981
```

Meaningful IDs are so much better:

```
http://mygardensite.org/products/wheelbarrow-9092
```

These user-friendly permalinks are often called slugs. We generally recommend building a slug field if a URL will be generated for the document. Such a field should have a unique index on it so that the value has fast query access and is guaranteed to be unique. You could also store the slug in _id and use it as a primary key. We've chosen not to in this case to demonstrate unique indexes; either way is acceptable. Assuming you're storing this document in the products collection, you can create the unique index like this:

```
db.products.createIndex({slug: 1}, {unique: true})
```

If you have a unique index on slug, an exception will be thrown if you try to insert a duplicate value. That way, you can retry with a different slug if necessary. Imagine your gardening store has multiple wheelbarrows for sale. When you start selling a new wheelbarrow, your code will need to generate a unique slug for the new product. Here's how you'd perform the insert from Ruby:

```ruby
@products.insert_one({
  :name => "Extra Large Wheelbarrow",
  :sku  => "9092",
  :slug => "wheelbarrow-9092"})
```

Unless you specify otherwise, the driver automatically ensures that no errors were raised. If the insert succeeds without raising an exception, you know you've chosen a unique slug. But if an exception is raised, your code will need to retry with a new value for the slug. You can see an example of catching and gracefully handling an exception in section 7.3.2.

NESTED DOCUMENTS

Say you have a key, details ❸, that points to a subdocument containing various product details. This key is totally different from the _id field because it allows you to find things inside an existing document. You've specified the weight, weight units, and the manufacturer's model number. You might store other ad hoc attributes here as well. For instance, if you were selling seeds, you might include attributes for the expected yield and time to harvest, and if you were selling lawnmowers, you could include horsepower, fuel type, and mulching options. The details attribute provides a nice container for these kinds of dynamic attributes.

You can also store the product's current and past prices in the same document. The pricing key points to an object containing retail and sale prices. price_history, by contrast, references a whole array of pricing options. Storing copies of documents like this is a common versioning technique.

Next, there's an array of tag names for the product. You saw a similar tagging example in chapter 1. Because you can index array keys, this is the simplest and best way of storing relevant tags on an item while at the same time assuring efficient queryability.

ONE-TO-MANY RELATIONSHIPS

What about relationships? You often need to relate to documents in other collections. To start, you'll relate products to a category structure ❹. You probably want to define a taxonomy of categories distinct from your products themselves. Assuming a separate categories collection, you then need a relationship between a product and its primary category ❺. This is a one-to-many relationship, since a product only has one primary category, but a category can be the primary for many products.

MANY-TO-MANY RELATIONSHIPS

You also want to associate each product with a list of relevant categories other than the primary category. This relationship is many-to-many, since each product can belong to more than one category and each category can contain multiple products. In an RDMBS, you'd use a join table to represent a many-to-many relationship like this one. Join tables store all the relationship references between two tables in a single table. Using a SQL join, it's then possible to issue a single query to retrieve a product with all its categories, and vice versa.

MongoDB doesn't support joins, so you need a different many-to-many strategy. We've defined a field called category_ids ❺ containing an array of object IDs. Each object ID acts as a pointer to the _id field of some category document.

A RELATIONSHIP STRUCTURE

The next listing shows a sample category document. You can assign it to a new variable and insert it into the categories collection using db.categories.insert(newCategory). This will help you using it in forthcoming queries without having to type it again.

Listing 4.2 A category document

```
{
  _id: ObjectId("6a5b1476238d3b4dd5000048"),
  slug: "gardening-tools",
  name: "Gardening Tools",
  description: "Gardening gadgets galore!",
  parent_id: ObjectId("55804822812cb336b78728f9"),
    ancestors: [
        {
          name: "Home",
          _id: ObjectId("558048f0812cb336b78728fa"),
          slug: "home"
        },
```

```
    {
      name: "Outdoors",
      _id: ObjectId("55804822812cb336b78728f9"),
      slug: "outdoors"
    }
  ]
}
```

If you go back to the product document and look carefully at the object IDs in its category_ids field, you'll see that the product is related to the Gardening Tools category just shown. Having the category_ids array key in the product document enables all the kinds of queries you might issue on a many-to-many relationship. For instance, to query for all products in the Gardening Tools category, the code is simple:

```
db.products.find({category_ids: ObjectId('6a5b1476238d3b4dd5000048')})
```

To query for all categories from a given product, you use the $in operator:

```
db.categories.find({_id: {$in: product['category_ids']}})
```

The previous command assumes the product variable is already defined with a command similar to the following:

```
product = db.products.findOne({"slug": "wheelbarrow-9092"})
```

You'll notice the standard _id, slug, name, and description fields in the category document. These are straightforward, but the array of parent documents may not be. Why are you redundantly storing such a large percentage of each of the document's ancestor categories?

Categories are almost always conceived of as a hierarchy, and there are many ways of representing this in a database. For this example, assume that "Home" is the category of products, "Outdoors" a subcategory of that, and "Gardening Tools" a subcategory of that. MongoDB doesn't support joins, so we've elected to denormalize the parent category names in each child document, which means they're duplicated. This way, when querying for the Gardening Products category, there's no need to perform additional queries to get the names and URLs of the parent categories, Outdoors and Home.

Some developers would consider this level of denormalization unacceptable. But for the moment, try to be open to the possibility that the schema is best determined by the demands of the application, and not necessarily the dictates of theory. When you see more examples of querying and updating this structure in the next two chapters, the rationale will become clearer.

4.2.2 *Users and orders*

If you look at how you model users and orders, you'll see another common relationship: one-to-many. That is, every user has many orders. In an RDBMS, you'd use a foreign key in your orders table; here, the convention is similar. See the following listing.

Listing 4.3 An e-commerce order, with line items, pricing, and a shipping address

```
{
  _id: ObjectId("6a5b1476238d3b4dd5000048"),
  user_id: ObjectId("4c4b1476238d3b4dd5000001"),
  state: "CART",
  line_items: [                                    ◄─┐  Denormalized
    {                                                 │  product
      _id: ObjectId("4c4b1476238d3b4dd5003981"),      │  information
      sku: "9092",
      name: "Extra Large Wheelbarrow",
      quantity: 1,
      pricing: {
        retail: 5897,
        sale: 4897,
      }
    },
    {
      _id: ObjectId("4c4b1476238d3b4dd5003982"),
      sku: "10027",
      name: "Rubberized Work Glove, Black",
      quantity: 2,
      pricing: {
        retail: 1499,
        sale: 1299
      }
    }
  ],
  shipping_address: {
    street: "588 5th Street",
    city: "Brooklyn",
    state: "NY",
    zip: 11215                         Denormalized
  },                                   sum of sale
  sub_total: 6196      ◄─┘             prices
}
```

The second order attribute, `user_id`, stores a given user's `_id`. It's effectively a pointer to the sample user, which will be discussed in listing 4.4. This arrangement makes it easy to query either side of the relationship. Finding all orders for a given user is simple:

```
db.orders.find({user_id: user['_id']})
```

The query for getting the user for a particular order is equally simple:

```
db.users.findOne({_id: order['user_id']})
```

Using an object ID as a reference in this way, it's easy to build a one-to-many relationship between orders and users.

THINKING WITH DOCUMENTS

We'll now look at some other salient aspects of the order document. In general, you're using the rich representation afforded by the document data model. Order documents include both the line items and the shipping address. These attributes, in a normalized relational model, would be located in separate tables. Here, the line items are an array of subdocuments, each describing a product in the shopping cart. The shipping address attribute points to a single object containing address fields.

This representation has several advantages. First, there's a win for the human mind. Your entire concept of an order, including line items, shipping address, and eventual payment information, can be encapsulated in a single entity. When querying the database, you can return the entire order object with one simple query. What's more, the products, as they appeared when purchased, are effectively frozen within your order document. Finally, as you'll see in the next two chapters, you can easily query and modify this order document.

The user document (shown in listing 4.4) presents similar patterns, because it stores a list of address documents along with a list of payment method documents. In addition, at the top level of the document, you find the basic attributes common to any user model. As with the slug field on your product, it's smart to keep a unique index on the username field.

Listing 4.4   A user document, with addresses and payment methods

```
{
  _id: ObjectId("4c4b1476238d3b4dd5000001"),
  username: "kbanker",
  email: "kylebanker@gmail.com",
  first_name: "Kyle",
  last_name: "Banker",
  hashed_password: "bd1cfa194c3a603e7186780824b04419",
  addresses: [
    {
      name: "home",
      street: "588 5th Street",
      city: "Brooklyn",
      state: "NY",
      zip: 11215
    },
    {
      name: "work",
      street: "1 E. 23rd Street",
      city: "New York",
      state: "NY",
      zip: 10010
    }
  ],
  payment_methods: [
    {
      name: "VISA",
      payment_token: "43f6ba1dfda6b8106dc7"
    }
  ]
}
```

4.2.3 Reviews

We'll close the sample data model with product reviews, shown in the following listing. Each product can have many reviews, and you create this relationship by storing a product_id in each review.

Listing 4.5 A document representing a product review

```
{
  _id: ObjectId("4c4b1476238d3b4dd5000041"),
  product_id: ObjectId("4c4b1476238d3b4dd5003981"),
  date: new Date(2010, 5, 7),
  title: "Amazing",
  text: "Has a squeaky wheel, but still a darn good wheelbarrow.",
  rating: 4,
  user_id: ObjectId("4c4b1476238d3b4dd5000042"),
  username: "dgreenthumb",
  helpful_votes: 3,
  voter_ids: [
    ObjectId("4c4b1476238d3b4dd5000033"),
    ObjectId("7a4f0376238d3b4dd5000003"),
    ObjectId("92c21476238d3b4dd5000032")
  ]
}
```

Most of the remaining attributes are self-explanatory. You store the review's date, title, and text; the rating provided by the user; and the user's ID. But it may come as a surprise that you store the username as well. If this were an RDBMS, you'd be able to pull in the username with a join on the users table. Because you don't have the join option with MongoDB, you can proceed in one of two ways: either query against the user collection for each review or accept some denormalization. Issuing a query for every review might be unnecessarily costly when username is extremely unlikely to change, so here we've chosen to optimize for query speed rather than normalization.

Also noteworthy is the decision to store votes in the review document itself. It's common for users to be able to vote on reviews. Here, you store the object ID of each voting user in an array of voter IDs. This allows you to prevent users from voting on a review more than once, and it also gives you the ability to query for all the reviews a user has voted on. You cache the total number of helpful votes, which among other things allows you to sort reviews based on helpfulness. Caching is useful because MongoDB doesn't allow you to query the size of an array within a document. A query to sort reviews by helpful votes, for example, is much easier if the size of the voting array is cached in the helpful_votes field.

At this point, we've covered a basic e-commerce data model. We've seen the basics of a schema with subdocuments, arrays, one-to-many and many-to-many relationships, and how to use denormalization as a tool to make your queries simpler. If this is your first time looking at a MongoDB data model, contemplating the utility of this model may require a leap of faith. Rest assured that the mechanics of all of this—from adding votes uniquely, to modifying orders, to querying products intelligently—will be explored and explained in the next few chapters.

4.3 Nuts and bolts: On databases, collections, and documents

We're going to take a break from the e-commerce example to look at some of the core details of using databases, collections, and documents. Much of this involves definitions, special features, and edge cases. If you've ever wondered how MongoDB allocates data files, which data types are strictly permitted within a document, or what the benefits of using capped collections are, read on.

4.3.1 Databases

A database is a namespace and physical grouping of collections and their indexes. In this section, we'll discuss the details of creating and deleting databases. We'll also jump down a level to see how MongoDB allocates space for individual databases on the filesystem.

MANAGING DATABASES

There's no explicit way to create a database in MongoDB. Instead, a database is created automatically once you write to a collection in that database. Have a look at this Ruby code:

```
connection = Mongo::Client.new( [ '127.0.0.1:27017' ], :database => 'garden' )
db = connection.database
```

Recall that the JavaScript shell performs this connection when you start it, and then allows you to select a database like this:

```
use garden
```

Assuming that the database doesn't exist already, the database has yet to be created on disk even after executing this code. All you've done is instantiate an instance of the class Mongo::DB, which represents a MongoDB database. Only when you write to a collection are the data files created. Continuing on in Ruby,

```
products = db['products']
products.insert_one({:name => "Extra Large Wheelbarrow"})
```

When you call insert_one on the products collection, the driver tells MongoDB to insert the product document into the garden.products collection. If that collection doesn't exist, it's created; part of this involves allocating the garden database on disk.

You can delete all the data in this collection by calling:

```
products.find({}).delete_many
```

This removes all documents which match the filter { }, which is all documents in the collection. This command doesn't remove the collection itself; it only empties it. To remove a collection entirely, you use the drop method, like this:

```
products.drop
```

To delete a database, which means dropping all its collections, you issue a special command. You can drop the garden database from Ruby like so:

```
db.drop
```

From the MongoDB shell, run the dropDatabase() method using JavaScript:

```
use garden
db.dropDatabase();
```

Be careful when dropping databases; there's no way to undo this operation since it erases the associated files from disk. Let's look in more detail at how databases store their data.

DATA FILES AND ALLOCATION

When you create a database, MongoDB allocates a set of data files on disk. All collections, indexes, and other metadata for the database are stored in these files. The data files reside in whichever directory you designated as the dbpath when starting mongod. When left unspecified, mongod stores all its files in /data/db.[3] Let's see how this directory looks after creating the garden database:

```
$ cd /data/db
$ ls -lah
drwxr-xr-x  81 pbakkum  admin   2.7K Jul  1 10:42 .
drwxr-xr-x   5 root     admin   170B Sep 19 2012 ..
-rw-------   1 pbakkum  admin    64M Jul  1 10:43 garden.0
-rw-------   1 pbakkum  admin   128M Jul  1 10:42 garden.1
-rw-------   1 pbakkum  admin    16M Jul  1 10:43 garden.ns
-rwxr-xr-x   1 pbakkum  admin     3B Jul  1 08:31 mongod.lock
```

These files depend on the databases you've created and database configuration, so they will likely look different on your machine. First note the mongod.lock file, which stores the server's process ID. Never delete or alter the lock file unless you're recovering from an unclean shutdown. If you start mongod and get an error message about the lock file, there's a good chance that you've shut down uncleanly, and you may have to initiate a recovery process. We discuss this further in chapter 11.

The database files themselves are all named after the database they belong to. garden.ns is the first file to be generated. The file's extension, ns, stands for namespaces. The metadata for each collection and index in a database gets its own namespace file,

---

[3] On Windows, it's c:\data\db. If you install MongoDB with a package manager, it may store the files elsewhere. For example using Homebrew on OS X places your data files in /usr/local/var/mongodb.

which is organized as a hash table. By default, the .ns file is fixed to 16 MB, which lets it store approximately 26,000 entries, given the size of their metadata. This means that the sum of the number of indexes and collections in your database can't exceed 26,000. There's usually no good reason to have this many indexes and collections, but if you do need more than this, you can make the file larger by using the `--nssize` option when starting `mongod`.

In addition to creating the namespace file, MongoDB allocates space for the collections and indexes in files ending with incrementing integers starting with 0. Study the directory listing and you'll see two core data files, the 64 MB `garden.0` and the 128 MB `garden.1`. The initial size of these files often comes as a shock to new users. But MongoDB favors this preallocation to ensure that as much data as possible will be stored contiguously. This way, when you query and update the data, those operations are more likely to occur in proximity rather than being spread across the disk.

As you add data to your database, MongoDB continues to allocate more data files. Each new data file gets twice the space of the previously allocated file until the largest preallocated size of 2 GB is reached. At that point, subsequent files will all be 2 GB. Thus, garden.2 will be 256 MB, garden.3 will use 512 MB, and so forth. The assumption here is that if the total data size is growing at a constant rate, the data files should be allocated increasingly, which is a common allocation strategy. Certainly one consequence is that the difference between allocated space and actual space used can be high.[4]

You can always check the amount of space used versus the amount allocated by using the `stats` command in the JavaScript shell:

```
> db.stats()
{
  "db" : "garden",
  "collections" : 3,
  "objects" : 5,
  "avgObjSize" : 49.6,
  "dataSize" : 248,
  "storageSize" : 12288,
  "numExtents" : 3,
  "indexes" : 1,
  "indexSize" : 8176,
  "fileSize" : 201326592,
  "nsSizeMB" : 16,
  "dataFileVersion" : {
    "major" : 4,
    "minor" : 5
  },
  "ok" : 1
}
```

---

[4] This may present a problem in deployments where space is at a premium. For those situations, you may use some combination of the `--noprealloc` and `--smallfiles` server options.

In this example, the `fileSize` field indicates the total size of files allocated for this database. This is simply the sum of the sizes of the garden database's two data files, `garden.0` and `garden.1`. The difference between `dataSize` and `storageSize` is trickier. The former is the actual size of the BSON objects in the database; the latter includes extra space reserved for collection growth and also unallocated deleted space.[5] Finally, the `indexSize` value shows the total size of indexes for this database.

It's important to keep an eye on total index size; database performance will be best when all utilized indexes can fit in RAM. We'll elaborate on this in chapters 8 and 12 when presenting techniques for troubleshooting performance issues.

What does this all mean when you plan a MongoDB deployment? In practical terms, you should use this information to help plan how much disk space and RAM you'll need to run MongoDB. You should have enough disk space for your expected data size, plus a comfortable margin for the overhead of MongoDB storage, indexes, and room to grow, plus other files stored on the machine, such as log files. Disk space is generally cheap, so it's usually best to allocate more space than you think you'll need.

Estimating how much RAM you'll need is a little trickier. You'll want enough RAM to comfortably fit your "working set" in memory. The working set is the data you touch regularly in running your application. In the e-commerce example, you'll probably access the collections we covered, such products and categories collections, frequently while your application is running. These collections, plus their overhead and the size of their indexes, should fit into memory; otherwise there will be frequent disk accesses and performance will suffer. This is perhaps the most common MongoDB performance issue. We may have other collections, however, that we only need to access infrequently, such as during an audit, which we can exclude from the working set. In general, plan ahead for enough memory to fit the collections necessary for normal application operation.

4.3.2 Collections

Collections are containers for structurally or conceptually similar documents. Here, we'll describe creating and deleting collections in more detail. Then we'll present MongoDB's special capped collections, and we'll look at examples of how the core server uses collections internally.

MANAGING COLLECTIONS

As you saw in the previous section, you create collections implicitly by inserting documents into a particular namespace. But because more than one collection type exists, MongoDB also provides a command for creating collections. It provides this command from the JavaScript shell:

```
db.createCollection("users")
```

---

[5] Technically, collections are allocated space inside each data file in chunks called *extents*. The `storageSize` is the total space allocated for collection extents.

When creating a standard collection, you have the option of preallocating a specific number of bytes. This usually isn't necessary but can be done like this in the Java-Script shell:

```
db.createCollection("users", {size: 20000})
```

Collection names may contain numbers, letters, or . characters, but must begin with a letter or number. Internally, a collection name is identified by its namespace name, which includes the name of the database it belongs to. Thus, the products collection is technically referred to as garden.products when referenced in a message to or from the core server. This fully qualified collection name can't be longer than 128 characters.

It's sometimes useful to include the . character in collection names to provide a kind of virtual namespacing. For instance, you can imagine a series of collections with titles like the following:

```
products.categories
products.images
products.reviews
```

Keep in mind that this is only an organizational principle; the database treats collections named with a . like any other collection.

Collections can also be renamed. As an example, you can rename the products collection with the shell's renameCollection method:

```
db.products.renameCollection("store_products")
```

CAPPED COLLECTIONS

In addition to the standard collections you've created so far, it's possible to create what's known as a capped collection. Capped collections are originally designed for high-performance logging scenarios. They're distinguished from standard collections by their fixed size. This means that once a capped collection reaches its maximum size, subsequent inserts will overwrite the least-recently-inserted documents in the collection. This design prevents users from having to prune the collection manually when only recent data may be of value.

To understand how you might use a capped collection, imagine you want to keep track of users' actions on your site. Such actions might include viewing a product, adding to the cart, checking out, and purchasing. You can write a script to simulate logging these user actions to a capped collection. In the process, you'll see some of these collections' interesting properties. The next listing presents a simple demonstration.

Listing 4.6 Simulating the logging of user actions to a capped collection

```
require 'mongo'

VIEW_PRODUCT = 0       # action type constants      ◁┐  Action
ADD_TO_CART  = 1                                    ①  types
CHECKOUT     = 2
PURCHASE     = 3

client = Mongo::Client.new([ '127.0.0.1:27017' ], :database => 'garden')
client[:user_actions].drop
actions = client[:user_actions, :capped => true, :size => 16384]   ◁┤ garden.user
actions.create                                                        _actions
                                                                      collection

500.times do |n|                  # loop 500 times, using n as the iterator
  doc = {                                                         ◁┐
    :username => "kbanker",                                         │
    :action_code => rand(4), # random value between 0 and 3, inclusive
    :time => Time.now.utc,                                          │
    :n => n                                       Sample           │
  }                                               document         │
  actions.insert_one(doc)
end
```

First, you create a 16 KB capped collection called `user_actions` using `client`.[6] Next, you insert 500 sample log documents ①. Each document contains a username, an action code (represented as a random integer from 0 through 3), and a timestamp. You've included an incrementing integer, n, so that you can identify which documents have aged out. Now you'll query the collection from the shell:

```
> use garden
> db.user_actions.count();
160
```

Even though you've inserted 500 documents, only 160 documents exist in the collection.[7] If you query the collection, you'll see why:

```
db.user_actions.find().pretty();
{
    "_id" : ObjectId("51d1c69878b10e1a0e000040"),
    "username" : "kbanker",
    "action_code" : 3,
    "time" : ISODate("2013-07-01T18:12:40.443Z"),
    "n" : 340
}
```

---

[6] The equivalent creation command from the shell would be `db.createCollection("user_actions", {capped: true, size: 16384})`.

[7] This number may vary depending on your version of MongoDB; the notable part is that it's less than the number of documents inserted.

```
{
    "_id" : ObjectId("51d1c69878b10e1a0e000041"),
    "username" : "kbanker",
    "action_code" : 2,
    "time" : ISODate("2013-07-01T18:12:40.444Z"),
    "n" : 341
}
{
    "_id" : ObjectId("51d1c69878b10e1a0e000042"),
    "username" : "kbanker",
    "action_code" : 2,
    "time" : ISODate("2013-07-01T18:12:40.445Z"),
    "n" : 342
}
...
```

The documents are returned in order of insertion. If you look at the n values, it's clear that the oldest document in the collection is the collection where n is 340, which means that documents 0 through 339 have already aged out. Because this capped collection has a maximum size of 16,384 bytes and contains only 160 documents, you can conclude that each document is about 102 bytes in length. You'll see how to confirm this assumption in the next subsection. Try adding a field to the example to observe how the number of documents stored decreases as the average document size increases.

In addition to the size limit, MongoDB allows you to specify a maximum number of documents for a capped collection with the max parameter. This is useful because it allows finer-grained control over the number of documents stored. Bear in mind that the size configuration has precedence. Creating a collection this way might look like this:

```
> db.createCollection("users.actions",
    {capped: true, size: 16384, max: 100})
```

Capped collections don't allow all operations available for a normal collection. For one, you can't delete individual documents from a capped collection, nor can you perform any update that will increase the size of a document. Capped collections were originally designed for logging, so there was no need to implement the deletion or updating of documents.

TTL COLLECTIONS

MongoDB also allows you to expire documents from a collection after a certain amount of time has passed. These are sometimes called time-to-live (TTL) collections, though this functionality is actually implemented using a special kind of index. Here's how you would create such a TTL index:

```
> db.reviews.createIndex({time_field: 1}, {expireAfterSeconds: 3600})
```

This command will create an index on time_field. This field will be periodically checked for a timestamp value, which is compared to the current time. If the difference between `time_field` and the current time is greater than your `expireAfterSeconds` setting, then the document will be removed automatically. In this example, review documents will be deleted after an hour.

Using a TTL index in this way assumes that you store a timestamp in time_field. Here's an example of how to do this:

```
> db.reviews.insert({
    time_field: new Date(),
    ...
  })
```

This insertion sets `time_field` to the time at insertion. You can also insert other time-stamp values, such as a value in the future. Remember, TTL indexes just measure the difference between the indexed value and the current time, to compare to `expire-AfterSeconds`. Thus, if you put a future timestamp in this field, it won't be deleted until that timestamp plus the `expireAfterSeconds` value. This functionality can be used to carefully manage the lifecycle of your documents.

TTL indexes have several restrictions. You can't have a TTL index on `_id`, or on a field used in another index. You also can't use TTL indexes with capped collections because they don't support removing individual documents. Finally, you can't have com-pound TTL indexes, though you can have an array of timestamps in the indexed field. In that case, the TTL property will be applied to the earliest timestamp in the collection.

In practice, you may never find yourself using TTL collections, but they can be a valuable tool in some cases, so it's good to keep them in mind.

SYSTEM COLLECTIONS

Part of MongoDB's design lies in its own internal use of collections. Two of these spe-cial system collections are `system.namespaces` and `system.indexes`. You can query the former to see all the namespaces defined for the current database:

```
> db.system.namespaces.find();
{ "name" : "garden.system.indexes" }
{ "name" : "garden.products.$_id_" }
{ "name" : "garden.products" }
{ "name" : "garden.user_actions.$_id_" }
{ "name" : "garden.user_actions", "options" : { "create" : "user_actions",
"capped" : true, "size" : 1024 } }
```

The first collection, `system.indexes`, stores each index definition for the current database. To see a list of indexes you've defined for the garden database, query the collection:

```
> db.system.indexes.find();
{ "v" : 1, "key" : { "_id" : 1 }, "ns" : "garden.products", "name" : "_id_" }
{ "v" : 1, "key" : { "_id" : 1 }, "ns" : "garden.user_actions", "name" :
"_id_" }
{ "v" : 1, "key" : { "time_field" : 1 }, "name" : "time_field_1", "ns" :
"garden.reviews", "expireAfterSeconds" : 3600 }
```

system.namespaces and system.indexes are both standard collections, and accessing them is a useful feature for debugging. MongoDB also uses capped collections for replication, a feature that keeps two or more mongod servers in sync with each other. Each member of a replica set logs all its writes to a special capped collection called oplog.rs. Secondary nodes then read from this collection sequentially and apply new operations to themselves. We'll discuss replication in more detail in chapter 10.

4.3.3 *Documents and insertion*

We'll round out this chapter with some details on documents and their insertion.

DOCUMENT SERIALIZATION, TYPES, AND LIMITS

All documents are serialized to BSON before being sent to MongoDB; they're later deserialized from BSON. The driver handles this process and translates it from and to the appropriate data types in its programming language. Most of the drivers provide a simple interface for serializing from and to BSON; this happens automatically when reading and writing documents. You don't need to worry about this normally, but we'll demonstrate it explicitly for educational purposes.

In the previous capped collections example, it was reasonable to assume that the sample document size was roughly 102 bytes. You can check this assumption by using the Ruby driver's BSON serializer:

```
doc = {
  :_id => BSON::ObjectId.new,
  :username => "kbanker",
  :action_code => rand(5),
  :time => Time.now.utc,
  :n => 1
}
bson = doc.to_bson
puts "Document #{doc.inspect} takes up #{bson.length} bytes as BSON"
```

The serialize method returns a byte array. If you run this code, you'll get a BSON object 82 bytes long, which isn't far from the estimate. The difference between the 82-byte document size and the 102-byte estimate is due to normal collection and document overhead. MongoDB allocates a certain amount of space for a collection, but must also store metadata. Additionally, in a normal (uncapped) collection, updating a document can make it outgrow its current space, necessitating a move to a new location and leaving an empty space in the collection's memory.[8] Characteristics like these create a difference in the size of your data and the size MongoDB uses on disk.

---

[8] For more details take a look at the padding factor configuration directive. The padding factor ensures that there's some room for the document to grow before it has to be relocated. The padding factor starts at 1, so in the case of the first insertion, there's no additional space allocated.

Deserializing BSON is as straightforward with a little help from the `StringIO` class. Try running this Ruby code to verify that it works:

```
string_io = StringIO.new(bson)
deserialized_doc = String.from_bson(string_io)
puts "Here's our document deserialized from BSON:"
puts deserialized_doc.inspect
```

Note that you can't serialize just any hash data structure. To serialize without error, the key names must be valid, and each of the values must be convertible into a BSON type. A valid key name consists of a string with a maximum length of 255 bytes. The string may consist of any combination of ASCII characters, with three exceptions: it can't begin with a $, it must not contain any . characters, and it must not contain the null byte, except in the final position. When programming in Ruby, you may use symbols as hash keys, but they'll be converted into their string equivalents when serialized.

It may seem odd, but the key names you choose affect your data size because key names are stored in the documents themselves. This contrasts with an RDBMS, where column names are always kept separate from the rows they refer to. When using BSON, if you can live with dob in place of date_of_birth as a key name, you'll save 10 bytes per document. That may not sound like much, but once you have a billion such documents, you'll save nearly 10 GB of data size by using a shorter key name. This doesn't mean you should go to unreasonable lengths to ensure small key names; be sensible. But if you expect massive amounts of data, economizing on key names will save space.

In addition to valid key names, documents must contain values that can be serialized into BSON. You can view a table of BSON types, with examples and notes, at http://bsonspec.org. Here, we'll only point out some of the highlights and gotchas.

STRINGS

All string values must be encoded as UTF-8. Though UTF-8 is quickly becoming the standard for character encoding, there are plenty of situations when an older encoding is still used. Users typically encounter issues with this when importing data generated by legacy systems into MongoDB. The solution usually involves either converting to UTF-8 before inserting, or, bearing that, storing the text as the BSON binary type.[9]

NUMBERS

BSON specifies three numeric types: double, int, and long. This means that BSON can encode any IEEE floating-point value and any signed integer up to 8 bytes in length. When serializing integers in dynamic languages, such as Ruby and Python, the driver will automatically determine whether to encode as an int or a long. In fact, there's only one common situation where a number's type must be made explicit: when you're inserting numeric data via the JavaScript shell. JavaScript, unhappily, natively

---

[9] Incidentally, if you're new to character encodings, you owe it to yourself to read Joel Spolsky's well-known introduction (http://mng.bz/LVO6).

supports only a single numeric type called Number, which is equivalent to an IEEE 754 Double. Consequently, if you want to save a numeric value from the shell as an integer, you need to be explicit, using either `NumberLong()` or `NumberInt()`. Try this example:

```
db.numbers.save({n: 5});
db.numbers.save({n: NumberLong(5)});
```

You've saved two documents to the `numbers` collection, and though their values are equal, the first is saved as a double and the second as a long integer. Querying for all documents where n is 5 will return both documents:

```
> db.numbers.find({n: 5});
{ "_id" : ObjectId("4c581c98d5bbeb2365a838f9"), "n" : 5 }
{ "_id" : ObjectId("4c581c9bd5bbeb2365a838fa"), "n" : NumberLong( 5 ) }
```

You can see that the second value is marked as a long integer. Another way to see this is to query by BSON type using the special `$type` operator. Each BSON type is identified by an integer, beginning with 1. If you consult the BSON spec at http://bsonspec.org, you'll see that doubles are type 1 and 64-bit integers are type 18. Thus, you can query the collection for values by type:

```
> db.numbers.find({n: {$type: 1}});
{ "_id" : ObjectId("4c581c98d5bbeb2365a838f9"), "n" : 5 }
> db.numbers.find({n: {$type: 18}});
{ "_id" : ObjectId("4c581c9bd5bbeb2365a838fa"), "n" : NumberLong( 5 ) }
```

This verifies the difference in storage. You might never use the `$type` operator in production, but as seen here, it's a great tool for debugging.

The only other issue that commonly arises with BSON numeric types is the lack of decimal support. This means that if you're planning on storing currency values in MongoDB, you need to use an integer type and keep the values in cents.

DATETIMES

The BSON datetime type is used to store temporal values. Time values are represented using a signed 64-bit integer marking milliseconds since the Unix epoch. A negative value marks milliseconds prior to the epoch.[10]

A couple usage notes follow. First, if you're creating dates in JavaScript, keep in mind that months in JavaScript dates are 0-based. This means that `new Date(2011, 5, 11)` will create a date object representing June 11, 2011. Next, if you're using the Ruby driver to store temporal data, the BSON serializer expects a Ruby `Time` object in UTC. Consequently, you can't use date classes that maintain a time zone because a BSON datetime can't encode that data.

---

[10] The Unix epoch is defined as midnight, January 1, 1970, coordinated universal time (UTC). We discuss epoch time briefly in section 3.2.1.

VIRTUAL TYPES

What if you must store your times with their time zones? Sometimes the basic BSON types don't suffice. Though there's no way to create a custom BSON type, you can compose the various primitive BSON values to create your own virtual type in a sub-document. For instance, if you wanted to store times with zone, you might use a document structure like this, in Ruby:

```
{
  time_with_zone: {
    time: new Date(),
    zone: "EST"
  }
}
```

It's not difficult to write an application so that it transparently handles these composite representations. This is usually how it's done in the real world. For example, Mongo-Mapper, an object mapper for MongoDB written in Ruby, allows you to define to_mongo and from_mongo methods for any object to accommodate these sorts of custom composite types.

LIMITS ON DOCUMENTS

BSON documents in MongoDB v2.0 and later are limited to 16 MB in size.[11] The limit exists for two related reasons. First, it's there to prevent developers from creating ungainly data models. Though poor data models are still possible with this limit, the 16 MB limit helps discourage schemas with oversized documents. If you find yourself needing to store documents greater than 16 MB, consider whether your schema should split data into smaller documents, or whether a MongoDB document is even the right place to store such information—it may be better managed as a file.

The second reason for the 16 MB limit is performance-related. On the server side, querying a large document requires that the document be copied into a buffer before being sent to the client. This copying can get expensive, especially (as is often the case) when the client doesn't need the entire document.[12] In addition, once sent, there's the work of transporting the document across the network and then deserializing it on the driver side. This can become especially costly if large batches of multi-megabyte documents are being requested at once.

MongoDB documents are also limited to a maximum nesting depth of 100. Nesting occurs whenever you store a document within a document. Using deeply nested documents—for example, if you wanted to serialize a tree data structure to a MongoDB

---

[11] The number has varied by server version and is continually increasing. To see the limit for your server version, run db.isMaster() in the shell and examine the maxBsonObjectSize field. If you can't find this field, then the limit is 4 MB (and you're using a very old version of MongoDB). You can find more on limits like this at http://docs.mongodb.org/manual/reference/limits.

[12] As you'll see in the next chapter, you can always specify which fields of a document to return in a query to limit response size. If you're doing this frequently, it may be worth reevaluating your data model.

document—results in documents that are difficult to query and can cause problems during access. These types of data structures are usually accessed through recursive function calls, which can outgrow their stack for especially deeply nested documents.

If you find yourself with documents hitting the size or nesting limits, you're probably better off splitting them up, modifying your data model, or using an extra collection or two. If you're storing large binary objects, like images or videos, that's a slightly different case. See appendix C for techniques on handling large binary objects.

BULK INSERTS

As soon as you have valid documents, the process of inserting them is straightforward. Most of the relevant details about inserting documents, including object ID generation, how inserts work on the network layer, and checking for exceptions, were covered in chapter 3. But one final feature, bulk inserts, is worth discussing here.

All of the drivers make it possible to insert multiple documents at once. This can be extremely handy if you're inserting lots of data, as in an initial bulk import or a migration from another database system. Here's a simple Ruby example of this feature:

```
docs = [                            # define an array of documents
  { :username => 'kbanker' },
  { :username => 'pbakkum' },
  { :username => 'sverch' }
]
@col = @db['test_bulk_insert']
@ids = @col.insert_many(docs)        # pass the entire array to insert
puts "Here are the ids from the bulk insert: #{@ids.inspect}"
```

Instead of returning a single object ID, a bulk insert returns an array with the object IDs of all documents inserted. This is standard for MongoDB drivers.

Bulk inserts are useful mostly for performance. Inserting this way means only a single roundtrip of communication to the server, rather than three separate roundtrips. This method has a limit, however, so if you want to insert a million documents, you'll have to split this into multiple bulk inserts of a group of documents.[13]

Users commonly ask what the ideal bulk insert size is, but the answer to this is dependent on too many factors to respond concretely, and the ideal number can range from 10 to 200. Benchmarking will be the best counsel in this case. The only limitation imposed by the database here is a 16 MB cap on any one insert operation. Experience shows that the most efficient bulk inserts will fall well below this limit.

4.4   Summary

We've covered a lot of ground in this chapter; congratulations for making it this far!

We began with a theoretical discussion of schema design and then proceeded to outline the data model for an e-commerce application. This gave you a chance to see

---

[13] The limit for bulk inserts is 16 MB.

what documents might look like in a production system, and it should have started you thinking in a more concrete way about the differences between schemas in RDMBSs and MongoDB.

We ended the chapter with a harder look at databases, documents, and collections; you may return to this section later on for reference. We've explained the rudiments of MongoDB, but we haven't started moving data around. That will all change in the next chapter, where you'll explore the power of ad hoc queries.

Constructing queries

This chapter covers

- Querying an e-commerce data model
- The MongoDB query language in detail
- Query selectors and options

MongoDB doesn't use SQL. It instead features its own JSON-like query language. You've explored this language throughout the book, but now let's turn to some meatier, real-world examples. You'll revisit the e-commerce data model introduced in the previous chapter and present a variety of queries against it. Among the queries you'll practice are _id lookups, ranges, ordering, and projections. This chapter then surveys the MongoDB query language as a whole, looking at each available query operator in detail.

Keep in mind as you're reading this chapter that MongoDB's query language and aggregation functions (which chapter 6 covers) are still works in progress, and refinements are being added with each release. As it stands, mastering queries and aggregations in MongoDB isn't so much a matter of mapping out every nook as it is finding the best ways to accomplish everyday tasks. Through the examples in this chapter, you'll learn the clearest routes to take. By the end of the chapter, you should have a good intuitive understanding of queries in MongoDB, and you'll be ready to apply these tools to the design of application schemas.

5.1   *E-commerce queries*

This section continues our exploration of the e-commerce data model sketched out in the previous chapter. You've defined a document structure for products, categories, users, orders, and product reviews. Now, with that structure in mind, we'll show you how you might query these entities in a typical e-commerce application. Some of these queries are simple. For instance, _id lookups shouldn't be a mystery at this point. But we'll also show you a few more sophisticated patterns, including querying for and displaying a category hierarchy, as well as providing filtered views of product listings. In addition, we'll keep efficiency in mind by looking at possible indexes for some of these queries.

5.1.1   *Products, categories, and reviews*

Most e-commerce applications provide at least two basic views of products and categories. First is the product home page, which highlights a given product, displays reviews, and gives some sense of the product's categories. Second is the product listing page, which allows users to browse the category hierarchy and view thumbnails of all the products within a selected category. Let's begin with the product home page, in many ways the simpler of the two.

Imagine that your product page URLs are keyed on a product slug (you learned about these user-friendly permalinks in chapter 4). In that case, you can get all the data you need for your product page with the following three queries:

```
product = db.products.findOne({'slug': 'wheel-barrow-9092'})
db.categories.findOne({'_id': product['main_cat_id']})
db.reviews.find({'product_id': product['_id']})
```

The first query finds the product with the slug wheel-barrow-9092. Once you have your product, you query for its category information with a simple _id query on the categories collection. Finally, you issue another simple lookup that gets all the reviews associated with the product.

FINDONE VS. FIND QUERIES

You'll notice that the first two queries use the findOne method but the last uses find instead. All of the MongoDB drivers provide these two methods, so it's worth reviewing the difference between them. As discussed in chapter 3, find returns a cursor object, whereas findOne returns a document. The findOne method is similar to the following, though a cursor is returned even when you apply a limit:

```
db.products.find({'slug': 'wheel-barrow-9092'}).limit(1)
```

If you're expecting a single document, findOne will return that document if it exists. If you need to return multiple documents, use find. You'll then need to iterate over that cursor somewhere in your application.

If your findOne query matches multiple items in the database, it'll return the first item in the natural sort order of the documents in the collection. In most cases (but not always) this is the same order that the documents were inserted into the collection, and for capped collections, it's always the case. If you expect multiple result documents, you should almost always use a `find` query or explicitly sort the results.

Now look again at the product page queries. See anything unsettling? If the query for reviews seems a bit liberal, you're right. This query says to return all reviews for the given product, but doing so wouldn't be prudent in cases where a product had hundreds of reviews.

SKIP, LIMIT, AND SORT QUERY OPTIONS
Most applications paginate reviews, and for enabling this MongoDB provides `skip` and `limit` options. You can use these options to paginate the review document like this:

```
db.reviews.find({'product_id': product['_id']}).skip(0).limit(12)
```

Notice how you set these options by calling the `skip` and `limit` methods on the returned value of `find`. This can be confusing because it's a different pattern than you usually see, even in other MongoDB drivers. They appear to be called after the query, but the sorting and limiting parameters are sent with the query and handled by the MongoDB server. This syntax pattern, called *method chaining*, is intended to make it easier to build queries.

You also want to display reviews in a consistent order, which means you have to sort your query results. If you want to sort by the number of helpful votes received by each review, you can specify that easily:

```
db.reviews.find({'product_id': product['_id']}).
                sort({'helpful_votes': -1}).
                limit(12)
```

In short, this query tells MongoDB to return the first 12 reviews sorted by the total number of helpful votes in descending order. Now, with skip, limit, and sort in place, you need to decide whether to paginate in the first place. For this, you can issue a count query. You then use the results of the count in combination with the page of reviews you want. Your queries for the product page are complete:

```
page_number = 1
product  = db.products.findOne({'slug': 'wheel-barrow-9092'})
category = db.categories.findOne({'_id': product['main_cat_id']})
reviews_count = db.reviews.count({'product_id': product['_id']})
reviews = db.reviews.find({'product_id': product['_id']}).
                    skip((page_number - 1) * 12).
                    limit(12).
                    sort({'helpful_votes': -1})
```

The order in which you call skip, limit, and sort in the JavaScript shell doesn't matter.

These lookups should use indexes. You've already seen that slugs should have a unique index on them because they serve as alternate primary keys, and you know that all _id fields will automatically have a unique index for standard collections. But it's also important that you have an index on any fields acting as references. In this case, that would include the `user_id` and `product_id` fields on the reviews collection.

PRODUCT LISTING PAGE

With the queries for the product home pages in place, you can now turn to the product listing page. Such a page will display a given category with a browsable listing of products. Links to parent and sibling categories will also appear on the page.

A product listing page is defined by its category; thus, requests for the page will use the category's slug:

```
page_number = 1
category = db.categories.findOne({'slug': 'gardening-tools'})
siblings = db.categories.find({'parent_id': category['_id']})
products = db.products.find({'category_id': category['_id']})
                     .skip((page_number - 1) * 12)
                     .limit(12)
                     .sort({'helpful_votes': -1})
```

Siblings are any other categories with the same parent ID, so the query for siblings is straightforward. Because products all contain an array of category IDs, the query for finding all products in a given category is also trivial. You can imagine providing alternative sort methods (by name, price, and so forth). For those cases, you change the sort field.

It's important to consider whether these sorts will be efficient. You may choose to rely on your index to handle sorting for you, but as you add more sort options, the number of indexes grows, and the cost of maintaining those indexes may not be reasonable because each index makes writes slightly more expensive. We'll discuss this further in chapter 8, but start thinking about these trade-offs now.

The product listing page has a base case, where you're viewing the root-level categories but no products. A query against the categories collection for a `null` parent ID is all that's required to get these root-level categories:

```
categories = db.categories.find({'parent_id': null})
```

5.1.2 Users and orders

The queries in the previous section were generally limited to `_id` lookups and sorts. In looking at users and orders, we'll dig deeper because you'll want to generate basic reports on orders. The example queries search documents that look like those from chapter 4, listing 4.1 (products) and listing 4.4 (users).

Let's start with something simpler: user authentication. Users log in to the application by providing a username and password. Thus, you'd expect to see the following query frequently:

```
db.users.findOne({
    'username': 'kbanker',
    'hashed_password': 'bd1cfa194c3a603e7186780824b04419'})
```

If the user exists and the password is correct, you'll get back an entire user document; otherwise, the query will return nothing. This query is acceptable, but why should you return the entire user document if you only want to check that the user exists? You can limit the fields returned using a projection:

```
db.users.findOne({
  'username': 'kbanker',
  'hashed_password': 'bd1cfa194c3a603e7186780824b04419'},
  {'_id': 1})
```

In the JavaScript shell you do a projection by passing in an additional argument: a hash of the fields you want with their values set to 1. We discuss projections more in section 5.2.2. If you're already familiar with SQL and RDBMS, this is the difference between SELECT * and SELECT ID. The response now consists exclusively of the document's _id field:

```
{ "_id": ObjectId("4c4b1476238d3b4dd5000001") }
```

PARTIAL MATCH QUERIES IN USERS

You might want to query the users collection in a few other ways, such as searching by name. Often you'll want to perform a lookup on a single field, such as last_name:

```
db.users.find({'last_name': 'Banker'})
```

This approach works, but there are limits to searching for an exact match. For one, you might not know how to spell a given user's name. In this case, you'll want some way of querying for a partial match. Suppose you know that the user's last name starts with Ba. MongoDB allows you to query using regular expressions:

```
db.users.find({'last_name': /^Ba/})
```

The regular expression /^Ba/ can be read as "the beginning of the line followed by a *B* followed by an a." A prefix search like this one can take advantage of an index, but not all regular expression queries can use an index.

QUERYING SPECIFIC RANGES

When it comes to marketing to your users, you'll most likely want to target ranges of users. For instance, if you want to query for all users residing in Upper Manhattan, you issue this range query on a user's zip code:

```
db.users.find({'addresses.zip': {'$gt': 10019, '$lt': 10040}})
```

Recall that each user document contains an array of one or more addresses. This query will match a user document if any zip code among those addresses falls within the given range. You can use the $gte (greater than) and $lt (less than) operators to define this range. To make this query efficient, you'll want an index defined on addresses.zip.

You'll see more examples of querying this data in the next chapter, and later on, you'll learn how to get insight from the data using MongoDB's aggregation functions.

But with this introduction under your belt, we'll now look at MongoDB's query language in some depth, explaining the syntax in general and each operator in particular.

5.2 MongoDB's query language

It's time we explore MongoDB's query language in all its glory. We've already walked through some real-world query examples; this section is intended as a more comprehensive reference of MongoDB query capabilities. If you're learning about MongoDB queries for the first time, it may be easier to skim this section and revisit it when you need to write more advanced queries for your application.

5.2.1 Query criteria and selectors

Query criteria allow you to use one or more query selectors to specify the query's results. MongoDB gives you many possible selectors. This section provides an overview.

SELECTOR MATCHING

The simplest way to specify a query is with a selector whose key-value pairs literally match against the document you're looking for. Here are a couple of examples:

```
db.users.find({'last_name': "Banker"})
db.users.find({'first_name': "Smith", birth_year: 1975})
```

The second query reads, "Find me all users such that the `first_name` is Smith and was born in 1975." Note that whenever you pass more than one key-value pair, both must match; the query conditions function as a Boolean AND. If you want to express a Boolean OR, see the upcoming section on Boolean operators.

In MongoDB all text string matches are case sensitive. If you need to perform case-insensitive matches, consider using a regex term (explained later in this chapter, when we discuss the use of the `i` regex flag) or investigate the use of text search introduced in chapter 9.

RANGES

You frequently need to query for documents the values of which span a certain range. In most languages, you use <, <=, >, and >=. With MongoDB, you get the analogous set of operators `$lt`, `$lte`, `$gt`, and `$gte`. You've used these operators throughout the book, and they work as you'd expect. Table 5.1 shows the range query operators most commonly used in MongoDB.

Table 5.1 Summary of range query operators

Operator	Description
$lt	Less than
$gt	Greater than
$lte	Less than or equal
$gte	Greater than or equal

Beginners sometimes struggle with combining these operators. A common mistake is to repeat the search key:

```
db.users.find({'birth_year': {'$gte': 1985}, 'birth_year': {'$lte': 2015}})
```

The aforementioned query only takes into account the last condition. You can properly express this query as follows:

```
db.users.find({'birth_year': {'$gte': 1985, '$lte': 2015}})
```

You should also know how these work with different data types. Range queries will match values only if they have the same type as the value to be compared against.[1] For example, suppose you have a collection with the following documents:

```
{ "_id" : ObjectId("4caf82011b0978483ea29ada"), "value" : 97 }
{ "_id" : ObjectId("4caf82031b0978483ea29adb"), "value" : 98 }
{ "_id" : ObjectId("4caf82051b0978483ea29adc"), "value" : 99 }
{ "_id" : ObjectId("4caf820d1b0978483ea29ade"), "value" : "a" }
{ "_id" : ObjectId("4caf820f1b0978483ea29adf"), "value" : "b" }
{ "_id" : ObjectId("4caf82101b0978483ea29ae0"), "value" : "c" }
```

You then issue the following query:

```
db.items.find({'value': {'$gte': 97}})
```

You may think that this query should return all six documents because the strings are numerically equivalent to the integers 97, 98, and 99. But this isn't the case. As MongoDB is schemaless, this query returns the integer results only because the criteria supplied was an integer itself. If you want the string results, you must query with a string instead:

```
db.items.find({'value': {'$gte': "a"}})
```

You won't need to worry about this type restriction as long as you never store multiple types for the same key within the same collection. This is a good general practice, and you should abide by it.

SET OPERATORS
Three query operators—$in, $all, and $nin—take a list of one or more values as their predicate, so these are called set operators. $in returns a document if any of the given values matches the search key. You might use this operator to return all products belonging to some discrete set of categories. Table 5.2 shows these set query operators.

---

[1] Note that the numeric types—integer, long integer, and double—have type equivalence for these queries.

Table 5.2 Summary of set operators

Operator	Description
$in	Matches if any of the arguments are in the referenced set
$all	Matches if all of the arguments are in the referenced set and is used in documents that contain arrays
$nin	Matches if none of the arguments are in the referenced set

If the following list of category IDs

```
[
  ObjectId("6a5b1476238d3b4dd5000048"),
  ObjectId("6a5b1476238d3b4dd5000051"),
  ObjectId("6a5b1476238d3b4dd5000057")
]
```

corresponds to the lawnmowers, hand tools, and work clothing categories, the query to find all products belonging to these categories looks like this:

```
db.products.find({
    'main_cat_id': {
      '$in': [
        ObjectId("6a5b1476238d3b4dd5000048"),
        ObjectId("6a5b1476238d3b4dd5000051"),
        ObjectId("6a5b1476238d3b4dd5000057")
      ]
    }
  })
```

Another way of thinking about the $in operator is as a kind of Boolean inclusive OR against a single attribute. Expressed this way, the previous query might be read, "Find me all products of which the category is lawnmowers or hand tools or work clothing." Note that if you need a Boolean OR over multiple attributes, you'll want to use the $or operator, described in the next section:

- $in is frequently used with lists of IDs.
- $nin (not in)) returns a document only when none of the given elements matches. You might use $nin to find all products that are neither black nor blue:

  ```
  db.products.find({'details.color': {'$nin': ["black", "blue"]}})
  ```

- $all matches if every given element matches the search key. If you wanted to find all products tagged as gift and garden, $all would be a good choice:

  ```
  db.products.find({'tags': {'$all': ["gift", "garden"]}})
  ```

Naturally, this query makes sense only if the tags attribute stores an array of terms, like this:

```
{
  'name': "Bird Feeder",
  'tags': [ "gift", "birds", "garden" ]
}
```

Selectivity is the ability of a query to narrow results using the index. The problem is that both $ne and $nin operators aren't selective. Therefore, when using the set operators, keep in mind that $in and $all can take advantage of indexes, but $nin can't and thus requires a collection scan. If you use $nin, try to use it in combination with another query term that does use an index. Better yet, find a different way to express the query. You may, for instance, be able to store an attribute whose presence indicates a condition equivalent to your $nin query. For example, if you commonly issue a query for {timeframe: {$nin: ['morning', 'afternoon']}}, you may be able to express this more directly as {timeframe: 'evening'}.

BOOLEAN OPERATORS

MongoDB's Boolean operators include $ne, $not, $or, $and, $nor, and $exists. Table 5.3 summarizes the Boolean operators.

Table 5.3 Summary of Boolean operators

Operator	Description
$ne	Matches if the argument is not equal to the element
$not	Inverts the result of a match
$or	Matches if any of the supplied set of query terms is true
$nor	Matches if none of the supplied set of query terms are true
$and	Matches if all of the supplied set of query terms are true
$exists	Matches if the element exists in the document.

$ne, the *not equal to* operator, works as you'd expect. In practice, it's best used in combination with at least one other operator; otherwise, it's likely to be inefficient because it can't take advantage of indexes. For example, you might use $ne to find all products manufactured by Acme that aren't tagged with *gardening*:

```
db.products.find({'details.manufacturer': 'Acme', tags: {$ne: "gardening"} })
```

$ne works on keys pointing to single values and to arrays, as shown in the example where you match against the tags array.

Whereas $ne matches the negation of a specified value, $not negates the result of another MongoDB operator or regular expression query. Most query operators already have a negated form ($in and $nin, $gt and $lte, and so on); $not is useful because it includes documents that aren't evaluated by the given expression. Consider the following example:

```
db.users.find({'age': {'$not': {'$lte': 30}}})
```

As you'd expect, this query returns documents where age is greater than 30. It also returns documents with no age field, which makes it distinct from using the $gt operator in this case.

$or expresses the logical disjunction of two values for two different keys. This is an important point: if the possible values are scoped to the same key, use $in instead. Trivially, finding all products that are either blue or green looks like this:

```
db.products.find({'details.color': {$in: ['blue', 'Green']}})
```

But finding all products that are either blue or made by Acme requires $or:

```
db.products.find({
    '$or': [
      {'details.color': 'blue'},
      {'details.manufacturer': 'Acme'}
    ]
  })
```

$or takes an array of query selectors, where each selector can be arbitrarily complex and may itself contain other query operators. $nor works much the same as $or but is logically true only when none of its query selectors are true.

Like $or, the $and operator takes an array of query selectors. Because MongoDB interprets all query selectors containing more than one key by ANDing the conditions, you should use $and only when you can't express an AND in a simpler way. For example, suppose you want to find all products that are tagged with *gift* or *holiday* and either *gardening* or *landscaping*. The only way to express this query is with the conjunction of two $in queries:

```
db.products.find({
    $and: [
      {
        tags: {$in: ['gift', 'holiday']}
      },
      {
        tags: {$in: ['gardening', 'landscaping']}
      }
    ]
  })
```

QUERYING FOR A DOCUMENT WITH A SPECIFIC KEY

The final operator we'll discuss in this section is $exists. This operator is necessary because collections don't enforce a fixed schema, so you occasionally need a way to query for documents containing a particular key. Recall that you'd planned to use each product's `details` attribute to store custom fields. You might, for instance, store a color field inside the `details` attribute. But if only a subset of all products specify a set of colors, then you can query for the ones that don't like this:

```
db.products.find({'details.color': {$exists: false}})
```

The opposite query is also possible:

```
db.products.find({'details.color': {$exists: true}})
```

Here you're checking whether the field exists in a document at all. Even if a field exists, it can still be set to `null`. Depending on your data and query, you may want to filter those values as well.

MATCHING SUBDOCUMENTS

Some of the entities in this book's e-commerce data model have keys that point to a single embedded object. The product's `details` attribute is one good example. Here's part of the relevant document, expressed as JSON:

```
{
  _id:  ObjectId("4c4b1476238d3b4dd5003981"),
  slug: "wheel-barrow-9092",
  sku:  "9092",
  details: {
    model_num: 4039283402,
    manufacturer: "Acme",
    manufacturer_id: 432,
    color:  "Green"
  }
}
```

You can query such objects by separating the relevant keys with a . (dot). For instance, if you want to find all products manufactured by Acme, you can use this query:

```
db.products.find({'details.manufacturer': "Acme"});
```

Such queries can be specified arbitrarily deep. Supposing you had the following slightly modified representation

```
{
  _id: ObjectId("4c4b1476238d3b4dd5003981"),
  slug: "wheel-barrow-9092",
  sku: "9092",
  details: {
    model_num: 4039283402,
    manufacturer: {
      name: "Acme",
      id: 432
    },
    color:  "Green"
  }
}
```

the key in the query selector would contain two dots:

```
db.products.find({'details.manufacturer.id': 432});
```

But in addition to matching against an individual subdocument attribute, you can match an object as a whole. For example, imagine you're using MongoDB to store stock market positions. To save space, you forgo the standard object ID and replace it with a compound key consisting of a stock symbol and a timestamp. Here's how a representative document might look:[2]

```
{
  _id: {
    sym: 'GOOG',
    date: 20101005
  }
  open:  40.23,
  high:  45.50,
  low:   38.81,
  close: 41.22
}
```

You could then find the summary of GOOG for October 5, 2010 with the following `_id` query:

```
db.ticks.find({'_id': {'sym': 'GOOG', 'date': 20101005}})
```

It's important to realize that a query matching an entire object like this will perform a strict byte-by-byte comparison, which means that the order of the keys matters. The following query isn't equivalent and won't match the sample document:

```
db.ticks.find({'_id': {'date': 20101005, 'sym': 'GOOG'}})
```

Though the order of keys will be preserved in JSON documents entered via the shell, this isn't necessarily true for other programming languages, and it's safer to assume that order won't be preserved. For example, hashes in Ruby 1.8 aren't order-preserving. To preserve key order in Ruby 1.8, you must use an object of class `BSON::OrderedHash` instead:

```
doc = BSON::OrderedHash.new
doc['sym']  = 'GOOG'
doc['date'] = 20101005
@ticks.find(doc)
```

Be sure to check whether the language you're using supports ordered dictionaries; if not, the language's MongoDB driver will always provide an ordered alternative.

---

[2] In a potential high-throughput scenario, you'd want to limit document size as much as possible. You could accomplish this in part by using short key names. Thus you might use the key name *o* in place of *open*.

ARRAYS

Arrays give the document model much of its power. As you've seen in the e-commerce example, arrays are used to store lists of strings, object IDs, and even other documents. Arrays afford rich yet comprehensible documents; it stands to reason that MongoDB would let you query and index the array type with ease. And it's true: the simplest array queries look like queries on any other document type, as you can see in table 5.4.

Table 5.4   Summary of array operators

Operator	Description
`$elemMatch`	Matches if all supplied terms are in the same subdocument
`$size`	Matches if the size of the array subdocument is the same as the supplied literal value

Let's look at these arrays in action. Take product tags again. These tags are represented as a simple list of strings:

```
{
  _id:  ObjectId("4c4b1476238d3b4dd5003981"),
  slug: "wheel-barrow-9092",
  sku:  "9092",
  tags: ["tools", "equipment", "soil"]
}
```

Querying for products with the tag `"soil"` is trivial and uses the same syntax as querying a single document value:

```
db.products.find({tags: "soil"})
```

Importantly, this query can take advantage of an index on the `tags` field. If you build the required index and run your query with `explain()`, you'll see that a B-tree cursor[3] is used:

```
db.products.ensureIndex({tags: 1})
db.products.find({tags: "soil"}).explain()
```

When you need more control over your array queries, you can use dot notation to query for a value at a particular position within the array. Here's how you'd restrict the previous query to the first of a product's tags:

```
db.products.find({'tags.0': "soil"})
```

---

[3] The WiredTiger storage engine can support additional data structures for indexing. You can find more information about it in chapter 10.

It might not make much sense to query tags in this way, but imagine you're dealing with user addresses. You might represent these with an array of subdocuments:

```
{
  _id: ObjectId("4c4b1476238d3b4dd5000001"),
  username: "kbanker",
  addresses: [
    {
      name:    "home",
      street:  "588 5th Street",
      city:    "Brooklyn",
      state:   "NY",
      zip:     11215
    },
    {
      name:    "work",
      street:  "1 E. 23rd Street",
      city:    "New York",
      state    "NY",
      zip      10010
    },
  ]
}
```

You might stipulate that the zeroth element of the array always be the user's primary shipping address. Thus, to find all users whose primary shipping address is in New York, you could again specify the zeroth position and combine that with a dot to target the state field:

```
db.users.find({'addresses.0.state': "NY"})
```

As you can easily understand, you shouldn't stipulate when writing production code.

You can just as easily omit the position and specify a field alone. The following query will return a user document if any of the addresses in the list is in New York:

```
db.users.find({'addresses.state': "NY"})
```

As before, you'll want to index this dotted field:

```
db.users.ensureIndex({'addresses.state': 1})
```

Note that you use the same dot notation regardless of whether a field points to a sub-document or to an array of subdocuments. The dot notation is powerful, and the consistency is reassuring. But ambiguity can arise when querying against more than one attribute within an array of subobjects. For example, suppose you want to fetch a list of all users whose home address is in New York. Can you think of a way to express this query?

```
db.users.find({'addresses.name': 'home', 'addresses.state': 'NY'})
```

The problem with this query is that the field references aren't restricted to a single address. In other words, this query will match as long as one of the addresses is designated as "home" and one is in New York, but what you want is for both attributes to apply to the same address. Fortunately, there's a query operator for this. To restrict multiple conditions to the same subdocument, you use the `$elemMatch` operator. You can properly satisfy the query like this:

```
db.users.find({
    'addresses': {
      '$elemMatch': {
        'name': 'home',
        'state': 'NY'
      }
    }
  })
```

Logically, use `$elemMatch` only when you need to match two or more attributes in a subdocument.

QUERYING FOR AN ARRAY BY SIZE

The only array operator left to discuss is the `$size` operator. This operator allows you to query for an array by its size. For example, if you want to find all users with exactly three addresses, you can use the `$size` operator like this:

```
db.users.find({'addresses': {$size: 3}})
```

As of this writing, the `$size` operator doesn't use an index and is limited to exact matches (you can't specify a range of sizes).[4] Therefore, if you need to perform queries based on the size of an array, you should cache the size in its own attribute within the document and update it manually as the array changes. For instance, you might consider adding an `address_length` field to your user document. You could then build an index on this field and issue all the range and exact match queries you require. A possible solution is to use the aggregation framework, which is described in chapter 6.

JAVASCRIPT QUERY OPERATORS

If you can't express your query with the tools described thus far, you may need to write some JavaScript. You can use the special `$where` operator to pass a JavaScript expression to any query, as summarized here:

- `$where`   Execute some arbitrary JavaScript to select a document

Within a JavaScript context, the keyword `this` refers to the current document. Let's take a contrived example:

```
db.reviews.find({
    '$where': "function() { return this.helpful_votes > 3; }"
  })
```

---

[4] See https://jira.mongodb.org/browse/SERVER-478 for updates on this issue.

There's also an abbreviated form for simple expressions like this one:

```
db.reviews.find({'$where': "this.helpful_votes > 3"})
```

This query works, but you'd never want to use it because you can easily express it using other query operators. The problem is that JavaScript expressions can't use an index, and they incur substantial overhead because they must be evaluated within a JavaScript interpreter context and are single-threaded. For these reasons, you should issue JavaScript queries only when you can't express your query using other query operators. If you do need JavaScript, try to combine the JavaScript expression with at least one other query operator. The other query operator will pare down the result set, reducing the number of documents that must be loaded into a JavaScript context. Let's look at a quick example to see how this might make sense.

Imagine that for each user, you've calculated a rating reliability factor. This is essentially an integer that, when multiplied by the user's rating, results in a more normalized rating. Also suppose that you want to query a particular user's reviews and return only a normalized rating greater than 3. Here's how that query would look:

```
db.reviews.find({
    'user_id': ObjectId("4c4b1476238d3b4dd5000001"),
    '$where': "(this.rating * .92) > 3"
  })
```

This query meets both recommendations: it uses a standard query on a presumably indexed user_id field, and it employs a JavaScript expression that's absolutely beyond the capabilities of other query operators. Keep in mind that sometimes using the Aggregation framework can make your life easier.

In addition to recognizing the attendant performance penalties, it's good to be aware of the possibility of JavaScript *injection attacks*. An injection attack becomes possible whenever a user is allowed to enter code directly into a JavaScript query. An example is when the user submits a web form and the values are used directly in this sort of query. If the user sets the values of attribute or value, this query is unsafe:

```
@users.find({'$where' => "this.#{attribute} == #{value}"})
```

In this case, the values of attribute and value are inserted into a string, which is then evaluated to JavaScript. This approach is dangerous because users could potentially include JavaScript code in the values they send, giving them access to other data in the collection. This would result in a serious security breach if a malicious user was able to see data about other users. In general, you should always assume that your users can and will send you malicious data and plan accordingly.

REGULAR EXPRESSIONS

You saw near the beginning of the chapter that you can use a regular expression within a query. In that example, you used a prefix expression, /^Ba/, to find last names beginning with Ba, and I pointed out that this query would use an index. In fact, much more is possible. MongoDB is compiled with Perl Compatible Regular Expressions (PCRE; http://mng.bz/hxmh), which supports a huge gamut of regular expressions. The $regex operator is summarized here:

- $regex   Match the element against the supplied regex term

With the exception of the prefix-style query just described, regular expressions queries can't use an index and take longer to execute than most selectors. We recommend using them sparingly. Here's how you might query a given user's reviews for text containing the words *best* or *worst*. Note that you use the i regex flag[5] to indicate case-insensitivity:

```
db.reviews.find({
    'user_id': ObjectId("4c4b1476238d3b4dd5000001"),
    'text': /best|worst/i
})
```

Using the case-insensitive flag has penalties; it excludes the use of any indexes, which in MongoDB are always case-sensitive. If you want to use case-insensitive searches on large numbers of documents, you should use the new text search capability supplied in version 2.4 or later, or integrate an external text search engine. See chapter 9 for an explanation of MongoDB's searching capabilities.

If the language you're using has a native regex type, you can use a native regex object to perform the query. You can express an identical query in Ruby like this:

```
@reviews.find({
    :user_id => BSON::ObjectId("4c4b1476238d3b4dd5000001"),
    :text => /best|worst/i
})
```

Even though the regex is defined locally, it's evaluated on the MongoDB server.

If you're querying from an environment that doesn't support a native regex type, you can use the special $regex and $options operators. Using these operators from the shell, you can express the query in yet another way:

```
db.reviews.find({
    'user_id': ObjectId("4c4b1476238d3b4dd5000001"),
    'text': {
      '$regex': "best|worst",
      '$options': "i"}
})
```

---

[5] The case-insensitive option will always prevent an index from being used to serve the query, even in the case of a prefix match.

MongoDB is a case-sensitive system, and when using a regex, unless you use the `/i` modifier (that is, `/best|worst/i`), the search will have to exactly match the case of the fields being searched. But one caveat is that if you do use `/i`, it will disable the use of indexes. If you want to do indexed case-insensitive search of the contents of string fields in documents, consider either storing a duplicate field with the contents forced to lowercase specifically for searching or using MongoDB's text search capabilities, which can be combined with other queries and does provide an indexed case-insensitive search.

MISCELLANEOUS QUERY OPERATORS

Two more query operators aren't easily categorized and thus deserve their own section. The first is `$mod`, which allows you to query documents matching a given modulo operation, and the second is `$type`, which matches values by their BSON type. Both are detailed in table 5.5.

Table 5.5　Summary of miscellaneous operators

Operator	Description
`$mod [(quotient),(result)]`	Matches if the element matches the result when divided by the quotient
`$type`	Matches if the element type matches a specified BSON type
`$text`	Allows you to performs a text search on the content of the fields indexed with a text index

For instance, `$mod` allows you to find all order subtotals that are evenly divisible by 3 using the following query:

```
db.orders.find({subtotal: {$mod: [3, 0]}})
```

You can see that the `$mod` operator takes an array having two values. The first is the divisor and the second is the expected remainder. This query technically reads, "Find all documents with subtotals that return a remainder of 0 when divided by 3." This is a contrived example, but it demonstrates the idea. If you end up using the `$mod` operator, keep in mind that it won't use an index.

The second miscellaneous operator, `$type`, matches values by their BSON type. I don't recommend storing multiple types for the same field within a collection, but if the situation ever arises, you have a query operator that lets you test against type.

Table 5.6 shows the type numbers associated with each element type used in MongoDB. The example shown is how a member of that type would appear in the JavaScript console. For example, other MongoDB drivers may have a different way of storing the equivalent of an `ISODate` object.

Table 5.6 BSON types

BSON type	`$type` number	Example
Double	1	123.456
String (UTF-8)	2	"Now is the time"
Object	3	`{ name:"Tim",age:"myob" }`
Array	4	`[123,2345,"string"]`
Binary	5	`BinData(2,"DgAAAEltIHNvbWUgYmluYXJ5")`
`ObjectId`	7	`ObjectId("4e1bdda65025ea6601560b50")`
Boolean	8	`true`
Date	9	`ISODate("2011-02-24T21:26:00Z")`
Null	10	`null`
Regex	11	`/test/i`
JavaScript	13	`function() {return false;}`
Symbol	14	Not used; deprecated in the standard
Scoped JavaScript	15	`function (){return false;}`
32-bit integer	16	10

Timestamp	17	`{  "t" : 1371429067,`
		`  "i" : 0`
		`}`

64-bit integer	18	`NumberLong(10)`
`Maxkey`	127	`{"$maxKey": 1}`
`Minkey`	255	`{ "$minKey" : 1}`
`Maxkey`	128	`{"maxkey" : { "$maxKey" : 1 }}`

There are a couple of elements in table 5.6 worth mentioning. `maxkey` and `minkey` are used to insert a "virtual" value that's the same as the maximum or minimum value in the index. This means that it can be used to force the document to be sorted out as the first or last item when using a sort index. Gone are the days of adding a field with "aardvark" in it to the collection to force a document to sort to the front. Most of the language drivers have a means for adding a `minkey` or `maxkey` type.

Scoped JavaScript and JavaScript look identical in the table, but this is only because the console doesn't display the scope, which is a dictionary of key-value pairs supplied with the JavaScript code fragment. Scope means the context under which the function is executed. In other words, the function will be able to see the variables defined in the scope dictionary and use them during execution.

Finally, the symbol type has no representation. That's because in most languages it's not used—it's only used where the language has a distinct type for "keys." For instance, in Ruby there's a difference between `"foo"` and `:foo`—the latter is a symbol. The Ruby driver will store any key as a symbol.

> **BSON symbol types**
>
> As far as querying is concerned, the MongoDB server will treat a BSON symbol type in the same way it treats a string; it's only when the document is retrieved that a distinct symbol type mapping to the language key type is done. Note also that the symbol type is deprecated in the latest BSON spec (http://bsonspec.org) and may disappear at any moment. Regardless of the language you write your data with, you'll be able to retrieve it in any other language with a BSON implementation.

5.2.2 *Query options*

All queries require a query selector. Even if empty, the query selector essentially defines the query. But when issuing a query, you have a variety of query options to choose from that allow you to further constrain the result set. Let's look at those options next.

PROJECTIONS

You can use a projection to select a subset of fields to return from each document in a query result set. Especially in cases where you have large documents, using a projection will minimize the costs of network latency and deserialization. The only operator, `$slice`, is summarized here:

- `$slice`   Select a subset of a document to be returned

Projections are most commonly defined as a set of fields to return:

```
db.users.find({}, {'username': 1})
```

This query returns user documents excluding all but two fields: the `username` and the `_id` field, which is a special case and always included by default.

In some situations you may want to specify fields to exclude instead. For instance, this book's user document contains shipping addresses and payment methods, but you don't usually need these. To exclude them, add those fields to the projection with a value of `0`:

```
db.users.find({}, {'addresses': 0, 'payment_methods': 0})
```

In your projection you should either do inclusions or exclusions, though the `_id` field is a special case. You can exclude the `_id` field in the same way, by setting the value to `0` in the projection document.

In addition to including and excluding fields, you can return a range of values stored in an array. For example, you might want to store product reviews within the product document itself. In this case, you'd still want to be able to paginate those reviews, and for that you could use the $slice operator. To return the first 12 reviews, or the last 5, you'd use $slice like this:

```
db.products.find({}, {'reviews': {$slice: 12}})
db.products.find({}, {'reviews': {$slice: -5}})
```

$slice can also take a two-element array the values of which represent numbers to skip and limit, respectively. Here's how to skip the first 24 reviews and limit the number of reviews to 12:

```
db.products.find({}, {'reviews': {$slice: [24, 12]}})
```

Finally, note that using $slice won't prevent other fields from being returned. If you want to limit the other fields in the document, you must do so explicitly. For example, here's how you can modify the previous query to return only the reviews and the review rating :

```
db.products.find({}, {'reviews': {'$slice': [24, 12]}, 'reviews.rating': 1})
```

SORTING

As we touched on early in this chapter, you can sort any query result by one or more fields in ascending or descending order. A simple sort of reviews by rating, descending from highest to lowest, looks like this:

```
db.reviews.find({}).sort({'rating': -1})
```

Naturally, it might be more useful to sort by helpfulness and then by rating:

```
db.reviews.find({}).sort({'helpful_votes':-1, 'rating': -1})
```

In compound sorts like this, the order does matter. As noted elsewhere, JSON entered via the shell is ordered. Because Ruby hashes aren't ordered, you indicate sort order in Ruby with an array of arrays, which is ordered:

```
@reviews.find({}).sort([['helpful_votes', -1], ['rating', -1]])
```

The way you specify sorts in MongoDB is straightforward; understanding how indices can help improve sorting speeds is critical to using them well. We'll get to that in chapter 8, but feel free to skip ahead if you're using sorts heavily now.

SKIP AND LIMIT

There's nothing mysterious about the semantics of skip and limit. These query options should always work as you expect. But you should beware of passing large values (say, values greater than 10,000) for skip because serving such queries requires scanning over a number of documents equal to the skip value. For example, imagine you're paginating a million documents sorted by date, descending, with 10 results per page. This means that the query to display the 50,000th page will include a skip value of 500,000, which is incredibly inefficient. A better strategy is to omit the `skip` altogether and instead add a range condition to the query that indicates where the next result set begins. Thus, this query

```
db.docs.find({}).skip(500000).limit(10).sort({date: -1})
```

becomes this:

```
previous_page_date = new Date(2013, 05, 05)
db.docs.find({'date': {'$gt': previous_page_date}}).limit(10).sort({'date': -1})
```

This second query will scan far fewer items than the first. The only potential problem is that if date isn't unique for each document, the same document may be displayed more than once. There are many strategies for dealing with this, but the solutions are left as exercises for the reader.

There's another set of query types that you can perform on MongoDB data: geospatial queries, which are used to index and retrieve geographical or geometric data and are typically used for mapping and location-aware applications.

5.3 Summary

Queries make up a critical corner of the MongoDB interface. Once you've skimmed this chapter's material, you're encouraged to put the query mechanisms to the test. If you're ever unsure of how a particular combination of query operators will serve you, the shell is always a ready test bed.

MongoDB also supports query modifiers that are meta-operators that let you modify the output or behavior of a query. You can find more about them at http://docs.mongodb.org/manual/reference/operator/query-modifier/.

You'll use MongoDB queries consistently from now on, and the next two chapters are a good reminder of that. You'll tackle aggregation, document updates, and deletes. Because queries play a key role in most updates, you can look forward to yet more exploration of the query language.

Aggregation

6

This chapter covers
- Aggregation on the e-commerce data model
- Aggregation framework details
- Performance and limitations
- Other aggregation capabilities

In the previous chapter, you saw how to use MongoDB's JSON-like query language to perform common query operations, such as lookup by ID, lookup by name, and sorting. In this chapter, we'll extend that topic to include more complex queries using the MongoDB aggregation framework. The *aggregation framework* is MongoDB's advanced query language, and it allows you to transform and combine data from multiple documents to generate new information not available in any single document. For example, you might use the aggregation framework to determine sales by month, sales by product, or order totals by user. For those familiar with relational databases, you can think of the aggregation framework as MongoDB's equivalent to the SQL GROUP BY clause. Although you could have calculated this information previously using MongoDB's map reduce capabilities or within program code, the aggregation framework makes this task much easier as well as more efficient by allowing you to define a series of document operations and then send them as an array to MongoDB in a single call.

In this chapter, we'll show you a number of examples using the e-commerce data model that's used in the rest of the book and then provide a detailed look at all the aggregation framework operators and various options for each operator. By the end of this chapter, we'll have examples for the key aspects of the aggregation framework, along with examples of how to use them on the e-commerce data model. We won't cover even a fraction of the types of aggregations you might want to build for an e-commerce data model, but that's the idea of the aggregation framework: it provides you with the flexibility to examine your data in more ways than you could have ever foreseen.

Up to now, you've designed your data model and database queries to support fast and responsive website performance. The aggregation framework can also help with real-time information summarization that may be needed for an e-commerce website, but it can do much more: providing answers to a wide variety of questions you might want to answer from your data but that may require crunching large amounts of data.

> ### Aggregation in MongoDB v2.6 and v3.0
> The MongoDB aggregation framework, first introduced in MongoDB v2.2, has continued to evolve over subsequent releases. This chapter covers the capabilities included in MongoDB v2.6, first available in April 2014; MongoDB v3.0 uses the same aggregation framework as the 2.6 version of MongoDB. Version 2.6 incorporates a number of important enhancements and new operators that improve the capabilities of the aggregation framework significantly. If you're running an earlier version of MongoDB, you should upgrade to v2.6 or later in order to run the examples from this chapter.

6.1   Aggregation framework overview

A call to the aggregation framework defines a pipeline (figure 6.1), the *aggregation pipeline*, where the output from each step in the pipeline provides input to the next step. Each step executes a single operation on the input documents to transform the input and generate output documents.

Aggregation pipeline operations include the following:

- $project—Specify fields to be placed in the output document (projected).
- $match—Select documents to be processed, similar to find().

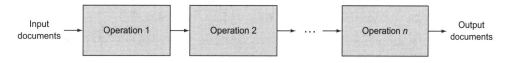

Figure 6.1   Aggregation pipeline: the output of each operation is input to the next operation.

- $limit—Limit the number of documents to be passed to the next step.
- $skip—Skip a specified number of documents.
- $unwind—Expand an array, generating one output document for each array entry.
- $group—Group documents by a specified key.
- $sort—Sort documents.
- $geoNear—Select documents near a geospatial location.
- $out—Write the results of the pipeline to a collection (new in v2.6).
- $redact—Control access to certain data (new in v2.6).

Most of these operators will look familiar if you've read the previous chapter on constructing MongoDB queries. Because most of the aggregation framework operators work similarly to a function used for MongoDB queries, you should make sure you have a good understanding of section 5.2 on the MongoDB query language before continuing.

This code example defines an aggregation framework pipeline that consists of a match, a group, and then a sort:

```
db.products.aggregate([ {$match: …}, {$group: …}, {$sort: …} ] )
```

This series of operations is illustrated in figure 6.2.

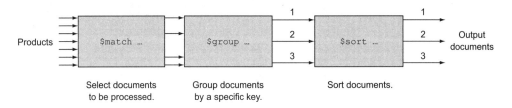

Figure 6.2   Example aggregation framework pipeline

As the figure illustrates, the code defines a pipeline where

- The entire products collection is passed to the $match operation, which then selects only certain documents from the input collection.
- The output from $match is passed to the $group operator, which then groups the output by a specific key to provide new information such as sums and averages.
- The output from the $group operator is then passed to a final $sort operator to be sorted before being returned as the final result.

If you're familiar with the SQL GROUP BY clause, you know that it's used to provide summary information similar to the summaries outlined here. Table 6.1 provides a detailed comparison of SQL commands to the aggregation framework operators.

Table 6.1 SQL versus aggregation framework comparison

SQL command	Aggregation framework operator
SELECT	`$project`
	`$group` functions: `$sum`, `$min`, `$avg`, etc.
FROM	`db.collectionName.aggregate(...)`
JOIN	`$unwind`
WHERE	`$match`
GROUP BY	`$group`
HAVING	`$match`

In the next section, we'll take a close look at how the aggregation framework might be used on the e-commerce data model. First, you'll see how to use the aggregation framework to provide summary information for the product web page. You'll then see how the aggregation framework can be used outside the web page application to crunch large amounts of data and provide interesting information, such as finding the highest-spending Upper Manhattan customers.

6.2   *E-commerce aggregation example*

In this section you'll produce a few example queries for your e-commerce database, illustrating how to answer a few of the many questions you may want to answer from your data using aggregation. Before we continue, let's revisit the e-commerce data model.

Figure 6.3 shows a data model diagram of our e-commerce data model. Each large box represents one of the collections in our data model: products, reviews, categories, orders, and users. Within each collection we show the document structure, indicating any arrays as separate objects. For example, the products collection in the upper left of the figure contains product information. For each product there may be many price_history objects, many `category_id` objects, and many tags.

The line between products and reviews in the center of the figure shows that a product may have many reviews and that a review is for one product. You can also see that a review may have many `voter_id` objects related to it, showing who has voted that the review is helpful.

A model such as this becomes especially helpful as the data model grows and it becomes difficult to remember all the implied relationships between collections, or even the details of what the structure is for each collection. It can also be useful in helping you determine what types of questions you might want to answer from your data.

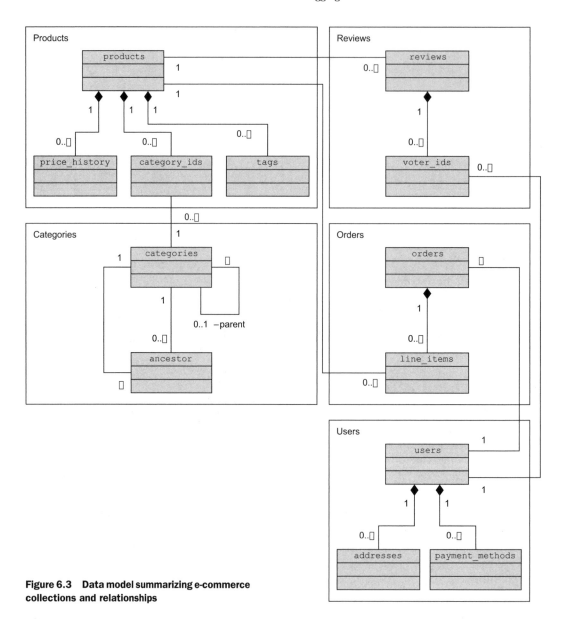

Figure 6.3   Data model summarizing e-commerce collections and relationships

6.2.1 *Products, categories, and reviews*

Now let's look at a simple example of how the aggregation framework can be used to summarize information about a product. Chapter 5 showed an example of counting the number of reviews for a given product using this query:

```
product     = db.products.findOne({'slug': 'wheelbarrow-9092'})
reviews_count = db.reviews.count({'product_id': product['_id']})
```

Let's see how to do this using the aggregation framework. First, we'll look at a query that will calculate the total number of reviews for all products:

```
db.reviews.aggregate([                          Group the input
  {$group : { _id:'$product_id',                documents by product_id.
            count:{$sum:1} }}                   Count the number of
]);                                             reviews for each product.
```

This single operator pipeline returns one document for each product in your database that has a review, as illustrated here:

```
{ "_id" : ObjectId("4c4b1476238d3b4dd5003982"), "count" : 2 }    Outputs one
{ "_id" : ObjectId("4c4b1476238d3b4dd5003981"), "count" : 3 }    document for
                                                                 each product
```

In this example, you'll have many documents as input to the $group operator but only one output document for each unique _id value—each unique product_id in this case. The $group operator will add the number 1 for each input document for a product, in effect counting the number of input documents for each product_id. The result is then placed in the count field of the output document.

An important point to note is that, in general, input document fields are specified by preceding them with a dollar sign ($). In this example, when you defined the value of the _id field you used $product_id to specify that you wanted to use the value of the input document's product_id field.

This example also uses the $sum function to count the number of input documents for each product by adding 1 to the count field for each input document for a given product_id. The $group operator supports a number of functions that can calculate various aggregated results, including average, minimum, and maximum as well as sum. These functions are covered in more detail in section 6.3.2 on the $group operator.

Next, add one more operator to your pipeline so that you select only the one product you want to get a count for:

```
product     = db.products.findOne({'slug': 'wheelbarrow-9092'})

ratingSummary = db.reviews.aggregate([                    Select only a
  {$match : { product_id: product['_id']} },              single product.
  {$group : { _id:'$product_id',
            count:{$sum:1} }}                Return the first
]).next();                                   document in the results.
```

This example returns the one product you're interested in and assigns it to the variable `ratingSummary`. Note that the result from the aggregation pipeline is a *cursor*, a pointer to your results that allows you to process results of almost any size, one document at a time. To retrieve the single document in the result, you use the `next()` function to return the first document from the cursor:

```
{ "_id" : ObjectId("4c4b1476238d3b4dd5003981"), "count" : 3 }
```

> ### Aggregation cursors: New in MongoDB v2.6
> Prior to MongoDB v2.6, the result from the aggregation pipeline was a single document with a maximum size of 16 MB. Starting with MongoDB v2.6, you can process results of any size using the cursor. Returning a cursor is the default when you're running shell commands. But to avoid breaking existing programs, the default for programs is still a single 16 MB limited document. To use cursors in a program, you override this default explicitly to specify that you want a cursor. See "Aggregation cursor option" in section 6.5 to learn more and to see other functions available on the cursor returned from the aggregation pipeline.

The parameters passed to the `$match` operator, `{'product_id': product['_id']}`, should look familiar. They're the same as those used for the query taken from chapter 5 to calculate the count of reviews for a product:

```
db.reviews.count({'product_id': product['_id']})
```

These parameters were covered in detail in the previous chapter in section 5.1.1. Most query operators we covered there are also available in the `$match` operator.

It's important to have `$match` before `$group`. You could've reversed the order, putting `$match` after `$group`, and the query would've returned the same results. But doing so would've made MongoDB calculate the count of reviews for all products and then throw away all but one result. By putting `$match` first, you greatly reduce how many documents have to be processed by the `$group` operator.

Now that you have the total number of reviews for a product, let's see how to calculate the average review for a product. This topic takes you beyond the capabilities of the query language covered in chapter 5.

CALCULATING THE AVERAGE REVIEW
To calculate the average review for a product, you use the same pipeline as in the previous example and add one more field:

```
product   = db.products.findOne({'slug': 'wheelbarrow-9092'})

ratingSummary = db.reviews.aggregate([
    {$match : {'product_id': product['_id']}},      Calculate the
    {$group : { _id:'$product_id',                  average rating
        average:{$avg:'$rating'},                   for a product.
        count: {$sum:1}}}
]).next();
```

The previous example returns a single document and assigns it to the variable rating-Summary with the content shown here:

```
{
    "_id" : ObjectId("4c4b1476238d3b4dd5003981"),
    "average" : 4.333333333333333,
    "count" : 3
}
```

This example uses the $avg function to calculate the average rating for the product. Notice also that the field being averaged, rating, is specified using '$rating' in the $avg function. This is the same convention used for specifying the field for the $group _id value, where you used this:

```
_id:'$product_id'.
```

COUNTING REVIEWS BY RATING

Next let's extend the product summary further and show a breakdown of review counts for each rating. This is probably something you've seen before when shopping online and is illustrated in figure 6.4. You can see that five reviewers have rated the product a 5, two have rated it a 4, and one has rated it a 3.

Using the aggregation framework, you can calculate this summary using a single command. In this case, you first use $match to select only reviews for the product being displayed, as we did in the previous example. Next, you group the $match results by rating and count the number of reviews for each rating. Here's the aggregation command needed to do this:

Figure 6.4 Reviews summary

```
countsByRating = db.reviews.aggregate([
    {$match : {'product_id': product['_id']}},
    {$group : { _id:'$rating',
                count:{$sum:1}}}
]).toArray();
```

- ← Select product
- ← Group by value of rating: '$rating'
- ← Count number of reviews for each rating
- ← Convert resulting cursor to an array

As shown in this snippet, you've once again produced a count using the $sum function; this time you counted the number of reviews for each rating. Also note that the result of this aggregation call is a cursor that you've converted to an array and assigned to the variable countsByRating.

> ### SQL query
> For those familiar with SQL, the equivalent SQL query would look something like this:
>
> ```
> SELECT RATING, COUNT(*) AS COUNT
>   FROM REVIEWS
>   WHERE PRODUCT_ID = '4c4b1476238d3b4dd5003981'
>   GROUP BY RATING
> ```

This aggregation call would produce an array similar to this:

```
[ { "_id" : 5, "count" : 5 },
  { "_id" : 4, "count" : 2 },
  { "_id" : 3, "count" : 1 } ]
```

JOINING COLLECTIONS

Next, suppose you want to examine the contents of your database and count the number of products for each main category. Recall that a product has only one main category. The aggregation command looks like this:

```
db.products.aggregate([
    {$group : { _id:'$main_cat_id',
             count:{$sum:1}}}
]);
```

This command would produce a list of output documents. Here's an example:

```
{ "_id" : ObjectId("6a5b1476238d3b4dd5000048"), "count" : 2 }
```

This result alone may not be very helpful, because you'd be unlikely to know what category is represented by `ObjectId("6a5b1476238d3b4dd5000048")`. One of the limitations of MongoDB is that it doesn't allow joins between collections. You usually overcome this by *denormalizing* your data model—making it contain, through grouping or redundancy, attributes that your e-commerce application might normally be expected to display. For example, in your order collection, each line item also contains the product name, so you don't have to make another call to read the product name for each line item when you display an order.

But keep in mind that the aggregation framework will often be used to produce ad hoc summary reports that you may not always be aware of ahead of time. You may also want to limit how much you denormalize your data so you don't end up replicating too much data, which can increase the amount of space used by your database and complicate updates (because it may require updating the same information in multiple documents).

Although MongoDB doesn't allow automatic joins, starting with MongoDB 2.6, there are a couple of options you can use to provide the equivalent of a SQL join. One option is to use the forEach function to process the cursor returned from the aggregation command and add the name using a pseudo-join. Here's an example:

```
db.mainCategorySummary.remove({});          ◁─┐ Remove existing documents
                                               │ from mainCategorySummary
db.products.aggregate([                        │ collection
    {$group : { _id:'$main_cat_id',
                count:{$sum:1}}}
                                                         Read category
]).forEach(function(doc){                              ─┘ for a result
    var category = db.categories.findOne({_id:doc._id});  ◁
    if (category !== null) {              ◁
        doc.category_name = category.name;
    }                                       You aren't guaranteed the
    else {                                  category actually exists!
        doc.category_name = 'not found';
    }                                       Insert combined
    db.mainCategorySummary.insert(doc);  ◁─ result into your
})                                          summary collection
```

In this code, you first remove any existing documents from the existing mainCategory-Summary collection, just in case it already existed. To perform your pseudo-join, you process every result document and execute a findOne() call to read the category name. After adding the category name to the aggregation output document, you then insert the result into a collection named mainCategorySummary. Don't worry too much about the insert function; we'll cover it in the next chapter.

A find() on the collection mainCategorySummary then will provide you with a result for each category. The following findOne() command shows the attributes of the first result:

```
> db.mainCategorySummary.findOne();
{
        "_id" : ObjectId("6a5b1476238d3b4dd5000048"),
        "count" : 2,
        "category_name" : "Gardening Tools"
}
```

> ### Caution: Pseudo-joins can be slow
> As mentioned earlier, starting with MongoDB v2.6 the aggregation pipeline can return a cursor. But be careful when using a cursor to perform this type of pseudo-join. Although you can process almost any number of output documents, running the find-One() command for each document, as you did here to read the category name, can still be time consuming if done millions of times.

$OUT AND $PROJECT
In a moment you'll see a much faster option for doing joins using the $unwind operator, but first you should understand two other operators: $out and $project. In the

previous example, you saved the results of your aggregation pipeline into a collection named `mainCategorySummary` using program code to process each output document. You then saved the document using the following:

```
db.mainCategorySummary.insert(doc);
```

With the `$out` operator, you can automatically save the output from a pipeline into a collection. The `$out` operator will create the collection if it doesn't exist, or it'll replace the collection completely if it does exist. In addition, if the creation of the new collection fails for some reason, MongoDB leaves the previous collection unchanged. For example, the following would save the pipeline results to a collection named `mainCategorySummary`:

```
db.products.aggregate([
    {$group : { _id:'$main_cat_id',
               count:{$sum:1}}},
    {$out : 'mainCategorySummary'}
])
```

> **Save pipeline results to collection mainCategorySummary**

The `$project` operator allows you to filter which fields will be passed to the next stage of the pipeline. Although `$match` allows you to limit how much data is passed to the next stage by limiting the number of documents passed, `$project` can be used to limit the size of each document passed to the next stage. Limiting the size of each document can improve performance if you are processing large documents and only need part of each document. The following is an example of a `$project` operator that limits the output documents to just the list of category IDs used for each product:

```
> db.products.aggregate([
... {$project : {category_ids:1}}
... ]);
{ "_id" : ObjectId("4c4b1476238d3b4dd5003981"),
  "category_ids" : [ ObjectId("6a5b1476238d3b4dd5000048"),
                     ObjectId("6a5b1476238d3b4dd5000049") ] }
{ "_id" : ObjectId("4c4b1476238d3b4dd5003982"),
  "category_ids" : [ ObjectId("6a5b1476238d3b4dd5000048"),
                     ObjectId("6a5b1476238d3b4dd5000049") ] }
```

Now let's see how to use these operators with the `$unwind` operator to perform faster joins.

FASTER JOINS WITH $UNWIND

Next we'll look at another powerful feature of the aggregation framework, the `$unwind` operation. This operator allows you to expand an array, generating one output document for every input document array entry. In effect, it provides another type of MongoDB join, where you can join a document with each occurrence of a subdocument.

Earlier you counted the number of products for each main category, where a product had only one main category. But suppose you want to calculate the number of products for each category regardless of whether it was the main category. Recall in the data model shown at the beginning of the chapter (figure 6.4) that each product can have an array of `category_ids`. The $unwind operator will then allow you to join each product with each entry in the array, producing one document for each product and `category_id`. You can then summarize that result by the `category_id`. The aggregation command for this is shown in the next listing.

Listing 6.1 $unwind, which joins each product with its `category id` array

```
db.products.aggregate([
    {$project : {category_ids:1}},
    {$unwind : '$category_ids'},
    {$group : { _id:'$category_ids',
                count:{$sum:1}}},
    {$out : 'countsByCategory'}
]);
```

Pass only the array of category IDs to the next step. The _id attribute is passed by default.

Create an output document for every array entry in category_ids.

$out writes aggregation results to the named collection countsByCategory.

The first operator in your aggregation pipeline, $project, limits attributes that will be passed to the next step in the pipeline and is often important for pipelines with the $unwind operator. Because $unwind will produce one output document for each entry in the array, you want to limit how much data is being output. If the rest of the document is large and the array includes a large number of entries, you'll end up with a huge result being passed on to the next step in the pipeline. Before MongoDB v2.6, this could cause your command to fail, but even with MongoDB v2.6 and later, large documents will slow down your pipeline. If a stage requires more than 100 MB of RAM, you'll also have to use a disk to store the stage output, further slowing down the pipeline.

The last operator in the pipeline, $out, saves the results to the collection named countsByCategory. Here's an example of the output saved in countsByCategory:

```
> db.countsByCategory.findOne()
{ "_id" : ObjectId("6a5b1476238d3b4dd5000049"), "count" : 2 }
```

Once you've loaded this new collection, countsByCategory, you can then process each row in the collection to add the category name if needed. The next chapter will show you how to update a collection.

You've seen how you can use the aggregation framework to produce various summaries based on products and categories. The previous section also introduced two key operators for the aggregation pipeline: $group and $unwind. You've also seen the $out operator, which can be used to save the results of your aggregation. Now, let's take a look at a few summaries that might be useful for analyzing information about users and orders. We'll also introduce a few more aggregation capabilities and show you examples.

6.2.2   *User and order*

When the first edition of this book was written, the aggregation framework, first introduced in MongoDB v2.2, hadn't yet been released. The first edition used the MongoDB map-reduce function in two examples, grouping reviews by users and summarizing sales by month. The example grouping reviews by user showed how many reviews each reviewer had and how many helpful votes each reviewer had on average. Here's what this looks like in the aggregation framework, which provides a much simpler and more intuitive approach:

```
db.reviews.aggregate([
    {$group :
        {_id : '$user_id',
         count : {$sum : 1},
         avg_helpful : {$avg : '$helpful_votes'}}
    }
])
```

The result from this call looks like this:

```
{ "_id" : ObjectId("4c4b1476238d3b4dd5000003"),
    "count" : 1, "avg_helpful" : 10 }
{ "_id" : ObjectId("4c4b1476238d3b4dd5000002"),
    "count" : 2, "avg_helpful" : 4 }
{ "_id" : ObjectId("4c4b1476238d3b4dd5000001"),
    "count" : 2, "avg_helpful" : 5 }
```

SUMMARIZING SALES BY YEAR AND MONTH

The following is an example that summarizes orders by month and year for orders beginning in 2010. You can see what this looks like using MongoDB map-reduce in section 6.6.2, which requires 18 lines of code to generate the same summary. Here's how it looks in the aggregation framework:

```
db.orders.aggregate([
    {$match: {purchase_data: {$gte: new Date(2010, 0, 1)}}},
    {$group: {
        _id: {year : {$year :'$purchase_data'},
              month: {$month :'$purchase_data'}},
        count: {$sum:1},
        total: {$sum:'$sub_total'}}},
    {$sort: {_id:-1}}
]);
```

Running this command, you'd see something like the results shown here:

```
{ "_id" : { "year" : 2014, "month" : 11 },
    "count" : 1, "total" : 4897 }
{ "_id" : { "year" : 2014, "month" : 10 },
    "count" : 2, "total" : 11093 }
{ "_id" : { "year" : 2014, "month" : 9 },
    "count" : 1, "total" : 4897 }
```

In this example, you're using the $match operator to select only orders on or after January 1, 2010. Note that in JavaScript, January is month 0, and your match therefore looks for dates on or after Date(2010,0,1). The matching function $gte should look familiar, as it was introduced in the previous chapter, in section 5.1.2.

For the $group operator, you're using a compound key to group the orders by year and month. Although compound keys are less frequently used in a typical collection, they often become useful in the aggregation framework. In this case, the compound key is composed of two attributes: year and month. You've also used the $year and $month functions to extract the year and month from your purchase date. You're counting the number of orders, $sum:1, as well as summing the order totals, $sum: $sub_total.

The final operation in the pipeline then sorts the result from most recent to oldest month. The values passed to the $sort operation should also look familiar to you: they're the same ones used in the MongoDB query sort() function. Note that the order of the fields in the compound key field, _id does matter. If you'd placed the month before the year within the group for _id, the sort would've sorted first by month, and then by year, which would've looked very strange, unless you were trying to determine trends by month across years.

Now that you're familiar with the basics of the aggregation framework, let's take a look at an even more complex query.

FINDING BEST MANHATTAN CUSTOMERS

In section 5.1.2, you found all customers in Upper Manhattan. Now let's extend that query to find the highest spenders in Upper Manhattan. This pipeline is summarized in figure 6.5. Notice that the $match is the first step in the pipeline, greatly reducing the number of documents your pipeline has to process.

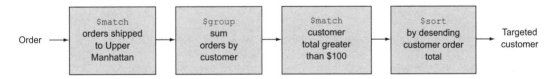

Figure 6.5 Selecting targeted customers

The query includes these steps:

- $match—Find orders shipped to Upper Manhattan.
- $group—Sum the order amounts for each customer.
- $match—Select those customers with order totals greater than $100.
- $sort—Sort the result by descending customer order total.

Let's develop this pipeline using an approach that may make it easy to develop and test our pipelines in general. First we'll define the parameters for each of the steps:

```
upperManhattanOrders = {'shipping_address.zip': {$gte: 10019, $lt: 10040}};

sumByUserId = {_id: '$user_id',
               total: {$sum:'$sub_total'}, };

orderTotalLarge = {total: {$gt:10000}};

sortTotalDesc = {total: -1};
```

These commands define the parameters you'll be passing to each of the steps of the aggregation pipeline. This makes the overall pipeline easier to understand, because an array of nested JSON objects can be difficult to decipher. Given these definitions, the entire pipeline call would appear as shown here:

```
db.orders.aggregate([
    {$match: upperManhattanOrders},
    {$group: sumByUserId},
    {$match: orderTotalLarge},
    {$sort: sortTotalDesc}
]);
```

You can now easily test the individual steps in this process by including one or more of the steps to verify that they run as expected. For example, let's run just the part of the pipeline that summed all customers:

```
db.orders.aggregate([
    {$group: sumByUserId},
    {$match: orderTotalLarge},
    {$limit: 10}
]);
```

This code would show you a list of 10 users using the following format:

```
{ "_id" : ObjectId("4c4b1476238d3b4dd5000002"), "total" : 19588 }
```

Let's say you decide to keep the count of the number of orders. To do so, modify the sumByuserId value:

```
sumByUserId = {_id: '$user_id',
               total: {$sum:'$sub_total'},
               count: {$sum: 1}};
```

Rerunning the previous aggregate command, you'll see the following:

```
{ "_id" : ObjectId("4c4b1476238d3b4dd5000002"),
    "total" : 19588, "count" : 4 }
```

Building an aggregation pipeline this way allows you to easily develop, iterate, and test your pipeline and also makes it much easier to understand. Once you're satisfied with the result, you can add the $out operator to save the results to a new collection and thus make the results easily accessible by various applications:

```
db.orders.aggregate([
    {$match: upperManhattanOrders},
    {$group: sumByUserId},
    {$match: orderTotalLarge},
    {$sort: sortTotalDesc},
    {$out: 'targetedCustomers'}
]);
```

You've now seen how the aggregation framework can take you far beyond the limits of your original database design and allow you to extend what you learned in the previous chapter on queries to explore and aggregate your data. You've learned about the aggregation pipeline and the key operators in that pipeline, including $group and $unwind. Next we'll look in detail at each of the aggregation operators and explain how to use them. As we mentioned earlier, much of this will be familiar if you've read the previous chapter.

6.3 Aggregation pipeline operators

The aggregation framework supports 10 operators:

- $project—Specify document fields to be processed.
- $group—Group documents by a specified key.
- $match—Select documents to be processed, similar to find(…).
- $limit—Limit the number of documents passed to the next step.
- $skip—Skip a specified number of documents and don't pass them to the next step.
- $unwind—Expand an array, generating one output document for each array entry.
- $sort—Sort documents.
- $geoNear—Select documents near a geospatial location.
- $out—Write the results of the pipeline to a collection (new in v2.6).
- $redact—Control access to certain data (new in v2.6).

The following sections describe using these operators in detail. Two of the operators, $geoNear and $redact, are used less often by most applications and won't be covered in this chapter. You can read more about them here: http://docs.mongodb.org/manual/reference/operator/aggregation/.

6.3.1   *$project*

The $project operator contains all of the functionality available in the query projec-
tion option covered in chapter 5 and more. The following is a query based on the
example in section 5.1.2 for reading the user's first and last name:

```
db.users.findOne(
   {username: 'kbanker',
    hashed_password: 'bd1cfa194c3a603e7186780824b04419'},
   {first_name:1, last_name:1}
)
```

**Projection object
that returns first
name and last name**

You can code the previous query as shown here using the same find criteria and projection objects as in the previous example:

```
db.users.aggregate([
   {$match: {username: 'kbanker',
            hashed_password: 'bd1cfa194c3a603e7186780824b04419'}},
   {$project: {first_name:1, last_name:1}}
])
```

**Project pipeline operator
that returns first name
and last name**

In addition to using the same features as those previously covered for the query projection option, you can use a large number of document reshaping functions. Because
there are so many of these, and they can also be used for defining the _id of a $group
operator, they're covered in a section 6.4, which focuses on reshaping documents.

6.3.2   *$group*

The $group operator is the main operator used by most aggregation pipelines. This is
the operator that handles the aggregation of data from multiple documents, providing you with summary statistics using functions such as min, max, and average. For
those familiar with SQL, the $group function is equivalent to the SQL GROUP BY clause.
The complete list of $group aggregation functions is shown in table 6.2.

  You tell the $group operator how to group documents by defining the _id field.
The $group operator then groups the input documents by the specified _id field, pro-
viding aggregated information for each group of documents. The following example
was shown in 6.2.2, where you summarized sales by month and year:

```
> db.orders.aggregate([
...    {$match: {purchase_data: {$gte: new Date(2010, 0, 1)}}},
...    {$group: {
...      _id: {year : {$year  :'$purchase_data'},
...            month: {$month :'$purchase_data'}},
...      count: {$sum:1},
...      total: {$sum:'$sub_total'}}},
...    {$sort: {_id:-1}}
... ]);
{ "_id" : { "year" : 2014, "month" : 11 },
  "count" : 1, "total" : 4897 }
```

```
{ "_id" : { "year" : 2014, "month" : 8 },
  "count" : 2, "total" : 11093 }
{ "_id" : { "year" : 2014, "month" : 4 },
  "count" : 1, "total" : 4897 }
```

When defining the _id field for the group, you can use one or more existing fields, or you can use one of the document reshaping functions covered in section 6.4. This example illustrates the use of two reshaping functions: $year and $month. Only the _id field definition can use reshaping functions. The remaining fields in the $group output documents are limited to being defined using the $group functions shown in table 6.2.

Table 6.2 $group **functions**

$group functions	
$addToSet	Creates an array of unique values for the group.
$first	The first value in a group. Makes sense only if preceded by a $sort.
$last	Last value in a group. Makes sense only if preceded by a $sort.
$max	Maximum value of a field for a group.
$min	Minimum value of a field for a group.
$avg	Average value for a field.
$push	Returns an array of all values for the group. Doesn't eliminate duplicate values.
$sum	Sum of all values in a group.

Although most of the functions are self-explanatory, two are less obvious: $push and $addToSet. The following example creates a list of customers, each with an array of products ordered by that customer. The array of products is created using the $push function:

```
db.orders.aggregate([
    {$project: {user_id:1, line_items:1}},
    {$unwind: '$line_items'},
    {$group: {_id: {user_id:'$user_id'},
            purchasedItems: {$push: '$line_items'}}}
]).toArray();
```
$push function adds object to purchasedItems array

The previous example would create something like the output shown here:

```
[
    {
        "_id" : {
            "user_id" : ObjectId("4c4b1476238d3b4dd5000002")
        },
```

```
"purchasedItems" : [
    {
        "_id" : ObjectId("4c4b1476238d3b4dd5003981"),
        "sku" : "9092",
        "name" : "Extra Large Wheel Barrow",
        "quantity" : 1,
        "pricing" : {
            "retail" : 5897,
            "sale" : 4897
        }
    },
    {
        "_id" : ObjectId("4c4b1476238d3b4dd5003981"),
        "sku" : "9092",
        "name" : "Extra Large Wheel Barrow",
        "quantity" : 1,
        "pricing" : {
            "retail" : 5897,
            "sale" : 4897
        }
    },
    ...
```

$addToSet VS. $push
Looking at the group functions, you may wonder about the difference between
$addToSet and $push. The elements in a set are guaranteed to be unique. A given
value doesn't appear twice in the set, and this is enforced by $addToSet. An array
like one created by the $push operator doesn't require each element to be unique.
Therefore, the same element may appear more than once in an array created
by $push.

Let's continue with some operators that should look more familiar.

6.3.3 *$match, $sort, $skip, $limit*

These four pipeline operators are covered together because they work identically to
the query functions covered in chapter 5. With these operators, you can select certain
documents, sort the documents, skip a specified number of documents, and limit the
size of the number of documents processed.

Comparing these operators to the query language covered in chapter 5, you'll see
that the parameters are almost identical. Here's an example based on the paging
query shown in section 5.1.1:

```
page_number = 1
product = db.products.findOne({'slug': 'wheelbarrow-9092'})

reviews = db.reviews.find({'product_id': product['_id']}).
                skip((page_number - 1) * 12).
                limit(12).
                sort({'helpful_votes': -1})
```

The identical query in the aggregation framework would look like this:

```
reviews2 = db.reviews.aggregate([
    {$match: {'product_id': product['_id']}},
    {$skip : (page_number - 1) * 12},
    {$limit: 12},
    {$sort:  {'helpful_votes': -1}}
]).toArray();
```

As you can see, functionality and input parameters for the two versions are identical. One exception to this is the find() $where function, which allows you to select documents using a JavaScript expression. The $where can't be used with the aggregation framework $match operator.

6.3.4 *$unwind*

You saw the $unwind operator in section 6.2.1 when we discussed faster joins. This operator expands an array by generating one output document for every entry in an array. The fields from the main document, as well as the fields from each array entry, are put into the output document. This example shows the categories for a product before and after a $unwind:

```
> db.products.findOne({},{category_ids:1})
{
    "_id" : ObjectId("4c4b1476238d3b4dd5003981"),
    "category_ids" : [
        ObjectId("6a5b1476238d3b4dd5000048"),
        ObjectId("6a5b1476238d3b4dd5000049")
    ]
}
> db.products.aggregate([
...      {$project : {category_ids:1}},
...      {$unwind : '$category_ids'},
...      {$limit : 2}
... ]);
{ "_id" : ObjectId("4c4b1476238d3b4dd5003981"),
  "category_ids" : ObjectId("6a5b1476238d3b4dd5000048") }
{ "_id" : ObjectId("4c4b1476238d3b4dd5003981"),
  "category_ids" : ObjectId("6a5b1476238d3b4dd5000049") }
```

Now let's look at an operator new in MongoDB v2.6: $out.

6.3.5 *$out*

In section 6.2.2 you created a pipeline to find the best Manhattan customers. We'll use that example again here, but this time the final output of the pipeline is saved in the collection targetedCustomers using the $out operator. The $out operator must be the last operator in your pipeline:

```
db.orders.aggregate([
    {$match: upperManhattanOrders},
    {$group: sumByUserId},
```

```
    {$match: orderTotalLarge},
    {$sort: sortTotalDesc},
    {$out: 'targetedCustomers'}
]);
```

The result of the pipeline creates a new collection or, if the collection already exists, completely replaces the contents of the collection, targetedCustomers in this case, keeping any existing indexes. Be careful what name you use for the $out operation or you could inadvertently wipe out an existing collection. For example, what would happen if by mistake you used the name users for the $out collection name?

The loaded results must comply with any constraints the collection has. For example, all collection documents must have a unique _id. If for some reason the pipeline fails, either before or during the $out operation, the existing collection remains unchanged. Keep this in mind if you're using this approach to produce the equivalent of a SQL materialized view.

Materialized views MongoDB style

Most relational databases provide a capability known as a *materialized view*. Materialized views are a way of providing pregenerated results in an efficient and easy-to-use manner. By pregenerating this information, you save the time and overhead that would be required to produce the result. You also make it easier for other applications to use this preprocessed information. The failsafe nature of the $out operation is critical if you use it to generate the equivalent of a materialized view. If the regeneration of the new collection fails for any reason, you leave the previous version intact, an important characteristic if you expect a number of other applications to be dependent on this information. It's better that the collection be a bit out of date than missing entirely.

You've now seen all of the main aggregation pipeline operators. Let's return to a previously mentioned subject: reshaping documents.

6.4   *Reshaping documents*

The MongoDB aggregation pipeline contains a number of functions you can use to reshape a document and thus produce an output document that contains fields not in the original input document. You'll typically use these functions with the $project operator, but you can also use them when defining the _id for the $group operator.

The simplest reshaping function is renaming a field to create a new field, but you can also reshape a document by altering or creating a new structure. For example, going back to a prior example where you read a user's first and last name, if you wanted to create a subobject called name with two fields, first and last, you could use this code:

```
db.users.aggregate([
    {$match: {username: 'kbanker'}},
    {$project: {name: {first:'$first_name',
                       last:'$last_name'}}
    }
])
```

The results from running this code look like this:

```
{ "_id" : ObjectId("4c4b1476238d3b4dd5000001"),
    "name" : { "first" : "Kyle",
               "last" : "Banker" }
}
```

In addition to renaming or restructuring existing document fields, you can create new fields using a variety of reshaping functions. The reshaping function descriptions are divided into groups based on the type of function they perform: string, arithmetic, date, logical, sets, and a few others that have been grouped into a miscellaneous category. Next, we'll take a closer look at each group of functions, starting with those that perform string manipulations.

> ### Aggregation framework reshaping functions
>
> There are a number of functions—more in each release, it seems—that allow you to perform a variety of operations on the input document fields to produce new fields. In this section we'll provide an overview of the various types of operators, along with an idea of what some of the more complex functions can accomplish. For the latest list of available functions, see the MongoDB documentation at http://docs.mongodb .org/manual/reference/operator/aggregation/group/.

6.4.1 String functions

The string functions shown in table 6.3 allow you to manipulate strings.

Table 6.3 String functions

Strings	
`$concat`	Concatenates two or more strings into a single string
`$strcasecmp`	Case-insensitive string comparison that returns a number
`$substr`	Creates a substring of a string
`$toLower`	Converts a string to all lowercase
`$toUpper`	Converts a string to all uppercase

This example uses three functions, $concat, $substr, and $toUpper:

```
db.users.aggregate([
    {$match: {username: 'kbanker'}},
    {$project:
        {name: {$concat:['$first_name', ' ', '$last_name']},
         firstInitial: {$substr: ['$first_name',0,1]},
         usernameUpperCase: {$toUpper: '$username'}
        }
    }
])
```

Concatenate first and last name with a space in between

Set firstInitial to the first character in the first name.

Change the username to uppercase.

The results from running this code look like this:

```
{ "_id" : ObjectId("4c4b1476238d3b4dd5000001"),
  "name" : "Kyle Banker",
  "firstInitial" : "K",
  "usernameUpperCase" : "KBANKER"
}
```

Most of the string functions should look familiar.

Next we'll take a look at the arithmetic-related functions.

6.4.2   *Arithmetic functions*

Arithmetic functions include the standard list of arithmetic operators shown in table 6.4.

Table 6.4   Arithmetic functions

Arithmetic	
$add	Adds array numbers
$divide	Divides the first number by the second number
$mod	Divides remainder of the first number by the second number
$multiply	Multiplies an array of numbers
$subtract	Subtracts the second number from the first number

In general, arithmetic functions allow you to perform basic arithmetic on numbers, such as add, subtract, divide, and multiply.

Next let's take a look at some of the date-related functions.

6.4.3   *Date functions*

The date functions shown in table 6.5 create a new field by extracting part of an existing date time field, or by calculating another aspect of a date such as day of year, day of month, or day of week.

Table 6.5   Date functions

Dates	
$dayOfYear	The day of the year, 1 to 366
$dayOfMonth	The day of month, 1 to 31
$dayOfWeek	The day of week, 1 to 7, where 1 is Sunday
$year	The year portion of a date
$month	The month portion of a date, 1 to 12
$week	The week of the year, 0 to 53
$hour	The hours portion of a date, 0 to 23
$minute	The minutes portion of a date, 0 to 59
$second	The seconds portion of a date, 0 to 59 (60 for leap seconds)
$millisecond	The milliseconds portion of a date, 0 to 999

You already saw one example of using $year and $month in section 6.2.2 that dealt with summarizing sales by month and year.

The rest of the date functions are straightforward, so let's move on to a detailed look at the logical functions.

6.4.4   Logical functions

The logical functions, shown in table 6.6, should look familiar. Most are similar to the find query operators summarized in chapter 5, section 5.2.

Table 6.6   Logical functions

Logical	
$and	`true` if all of the values in an array are true.
$cmp	Returns a number from the comparison of two values, 0 if they're equal.
$cond	`if… then… else` conditional logic.
$eq	Are two values equal?
$gt	Is value 1 greater than value 2?
$gte	Is value 1 greater than or equal value 2?
$ifNull	Converts a `null` value/expression to a specified value.
$lt	Is value 1 less than value 2?
$lte	Is value 1 less than or equal value 2?

Table 6.6   Logical functions *(continued)*

Logical	
`$ne`	Is value 1 not equal to value 2?
`$not`	Returns opposite condition of value: `false` if value is `true`, `true` if value is `false`.
`$or`	`true` if any of the values in an array are true.

The `$cond` function is different from most of the functions you've seen and allows complex if, then, else conditional logic. It's similar to the ternary operator (?) found in many languages. For example x ? y : z, which, given a condition x, will evaluate to the value y if the condition x is true and otherwise evaluate to the value z.

Next up are set functions, which allow you to compare sets of values with each other in various ways.

6.4.5   *Set Operators*

Set operators, summarized in table 6.7, allow you to compare the contents of two arrays. With set operators, you can compare two arrays to see if they're exactly the same, what elements they have in common, or what elements are in one but not the other. If you need to use any of these functions, the easiest way to see how they work is to visit the MongoDB documentation at http://docs.mongodb.org/manual/reference/operator/aggregation-set/.

Table 6.7   Set functions

Sets	
`$setEquals`	`true` if two sets have exactly the same elements
`$setIntersection`	Returns an array with the common elements in two sets
`$setDifference`	Returns elements of the first set that aren't in the second set
`$setUnion`	Returns a set that's the combination of two sets
`$setIsSubset`	`true` if the second set is a subset of the first set: all elements in the second are also in the first
`$anyElementTrue`	`true` if any element of a set is true
`$allElementsTrue`	`true` if all elements of a set are true

Here's one example using the `$setUnion` function. Given that you have the following products:

```
{ "_id" : ObjectId("4c4b1476238d3b4dd5003981"),
  "productName" : "Extra Large Wheel Barrow",
  "tags" : [ "tools", "gardening", "soil" ]}
```

```
{ "_id" : ObjectId("4c4b1476238d3b4dd5003982"),
  "productName" : "Rubberized Work Glove, Black",
  "tags" : [ "gardening" ]}
```

If you union the `tags` in these products, you'll get the array named `testSet1` as shown here:

```
testSet1 = ['tools']

db.products.aggregate([
  {$project:
    {productName: '$name',
     tags:1,
     setUnion: {$setUnion:['$tags',testSet1]},
   }
  }
])
```

The results will contain tags as shown here:

```
{    "_id" : ObjectId("4c4b1476238d3b4dd5003981"),
  "productName" : "Extra Large Wheel Barrow",
  "tags" : ["tools", "gardening", "soil"],
  "setUnion" : ["gardening","tools","soil"]       ◁──┘  Union of tools and
}                                                       gardening, tools, soil

{    "_id" : ObjectId("4c4b1476238d3b4dd5003982"),
  "productName" : "Rubberized Work Glove, Black",
  "tags" : ["gardening"],                                Union of tools
  "setUnion" : ["tools", "gardening"]             ◁──┘   and gardening
}
```

We're almost done with the various document reshaping functions, but there's still one more category to cover: the infamous "miscellaneous" category, where we group everything that didn't fit a previous category.

6.4.6 *Miscellaneous functions*

The last group, miscellaneous functions, are summarized in table 6.8. These functions perform a variety of functions, so we'll cover them one at a time. The `$meta` function relates to text searches and won't be covered in this chapter. You can read more about text searches in chapter 9.

Table 6.8 Miscellaneous functions

Miscellaneous	
`$meta`	Accesses text search–related information. See chapter 9 on text search
`$size`	Returns the size of an array
`$map`	Applies an expression to each member of an array
`$let`	Defines variables used within the scope of an expression
`$literal`	Returns the value of an expression without evaluating it

The $size function returns the size of an array. This function can be useful if, for example, you want to see whether an array contains any elements or is empty. The $literal function allows you to avoid problems with initializing field values to 0, 1, or $.

The $let function allows you to use temporarily defined variables without having to use multiple $project stages. This function can be useful if you have a complex series of functions or calculations you need to perform.

The $map function lets you process an array and generate a new array by performing one or more functions on each element in the array. $map can be useful if you want to reshape the contents of an array without using the $unwind to first flatten the array.

That wraps up our overview of reshaping documents. Next, we'll cover some performance considerations.

6.5   *Understanding aggregation pipeline performance*

In this section you'll see how to improve the performance of your pipeline, understand why a pipeline might be slow, and also learn how to overcome some of the limits on intermediate and final output size, constraints that have been removed starting with MongoDB v2.6.

Here are some key considerations that can have a major impact on the performance of your aggregation pipeline:

- Try to reduce the number and size of documents as early as possible in your pipeline.
- Indexes can only be used by $match and $sort operations and can greatly speed up these operations.
- You can't use an index after your pipeline uses an operator other than $match or $sort.
- If you use sharding (a common practice for extremely large collections), the $match and $project operators will be run on individual shards. Once you use any other operator, the remaining pipeline will be run on the primary shard.

Throughout this book you've been encouraged to use indexes as much as possible. In chapter 8 "Indexing and Query Optimization," you'll cover this topic in detail. But of these four key performance points, two of them mention indexes, so hopefully you now have the idea that indexes can greatly speed up selective searching and sorting of large collections.

There are still cases, especially when using the aggregation framework, where you're going to have to crunch through huge amounts of data, and indexing may not be an option. An example of this was when you calculated sales by year and month in section 6.2.2. Processing large amounts of data is fine, as long as a user isn't left waiting for a web page to display while you're crunching the data. When you do have to show summarized data—on a web page, for example—you always have the option to pre-generate the data during off hours and save it to a collection using $out.

That said, let's move on to learning how to tell if your query is in fact using an index via the aggregation framework's version of the explain() function.

6.5.1 Aggregation pipeline options

Until now, we've only shown the aggregate() function when it's passed an array of pipeline operations. Starting with MongoDB v2.6, there's a second parameter you can pass to the aggregate() function that you can use to specify options for the aggregation call. The options available include the following:

- explain()—Runs the pipeline and returns only pipeline process details
- allowDiskUse—Uses disk for intermediate results
- cursor—Specifies initial batch size

The options are passed using this format

```
db.collection.aggregate(pipeline,additionalOptions)
```

where pipeline is the array of pipeline operations you've seen in previous examples and additionalOptions is an optional JSON object you can pass to the aggregate() function. The format of the additionalOptions parameter is as follows:

```
{explain:true, allowDiskUse:true, cursor: {batchSize: n} }
```

Let's take a closer look at each of the options one at a time, starting with the explain() function.

6.5.2 The aggregation framework's explain( ) function

The MongoDB explain() function, similar to the EXPLAIN function you might have seen in SQL, describes query paths and allows developers to diagnose slow operations by determining indexes that a query has used. You were first introduced to the explain() function when we discussed the find() query function in chapter 2. We've duplicated listing 2.2 in the next listing, which demonstrates how an index can improve the performance of a find() query function.

Listing 6.2 explain() output for an indexed query

```
> db.numbers.find({num: {"$gt": 19995 }}).explain("executionStats")
{
    "queryPlanner" : {
        "plannerVersion" : 1,
        "namespace" : "tutorial.numbers",
        "indexFilterSet" : false,
        "parsedQuery" : {
            "num" : {
                "$gt" : 19995
            }
        },
```

```
        "winningPlan" : {
            "stage" : "FETCH",
            "inputStage" : {
                "stage" : "IXSCAN",
                "keyPattern" : {
                    "num" : 1
                },                                    ⟵  Using num_1
                "indexName" : "num_1",                    index
                "isMultiKey" : false,
                "direction" : "forward",
                "indexBounds" : {
                    "num" : [
                        "(19995.0, inf.0]"
                    ]
                }
            }
        },
        "rejectedPlans" : [ ]
    },
    "executionStats" : {
        "executionSuccess" : true,
  ⟶     "nReturned" : 4,
        "executionTimeMillis" : 0,                              ⟵─┐
        "totalKeysExamined" : 4,          Only four                │
        "totalDocsExamined" : 4,     ⟵    documents                │
        "executionStages" : {              scanned                 │
            "stage" : "FETCH",                                     │
  ⟶         "nReturned" : 4,                                       │
            "executionTimeMillisEstimate" : 0,          ⟵         │
            "works" : 5,                                           │
            "advanced" : 4,                                        │
            "needTime" : 0,                                        │
            "needFetch" : 0,                                       │
            "saveState" : 0,                                    Much
            "restoreState" : 0,                                faster!
            "isEOF" : 1,
            "invalidates" : 0,
            "docsExamined" : 4,
            "alreadyHasObj" : 0,
            "inputStage" : {
                "stage" : "IXSCAN",
                "nReturned" : 4,
                "executionTimeMillisEstimate" : 0,      ⟵         │
                "works" : 4,                                       │
                "advanced" : 4,                                   ─┘
                "needTime" : 0,
                "needFetch" : 0,
                "saveState" : 0,
                "restoreState" : 0,
                "isEOF" : 1,
                "invalidates" : 0,
                "keyPattern" : {
                    "num" : 1
                },                                    ⟵  Using num_1
                "indexName" : "num_1",                    index
```

Four documents returned

```
                    "isMultiKey" : false,
                    "direction" : "forward",
                    "indexBounds" : {
                        "num" : [
                            "(19995.0, inf.0]"
                        ]
                    },
                    "keysExamined" : 4,
                    "dupsTested" : 0,
                    "dupsDropped" : 0,
                    "seenInvalidated" : 0,
                    "matchTested" : 0
                }
            }
        },
        "serverInfo" : {
            "host" : "rMacBook.local",
            "port" : 27017,
            "version" : "3.0.6",
            "gitVersion" : "nogitversion"
        },
        "ok" : 1
    }
```

The `explain()` function for the aggregation framework is a bit different from the `explain()` used in the `find()` query function but it provides similar capabilities. As you might expect, for an aggregation pipeline you'll receive explain output for each operation in the pipeline, because each step in the pipeline is almost a call unto itself (see the following listing).

Listing 6.3 Example `explain()` output for aggregation framework

```
> countsByRating = db.reviews.aggregate([
...    {$match : {'product_id': product['_id']}},      ⟵┐ $match
...    {$group : { _id:'$rating',                        │ first
...                count:{$sum:1}}}
... ],{explain:true})                    ⟵┐ explain
{                                          │ option true
    "stages" : [
        {
            "$cursor" : {
                "query" : {
                    "product_id" : ObjectId("4c4b1476238d3b4dd5003981")
                },
                "fields" : {
                    "rating" : 1,
                    "_id" : 0
                },
                "plan" : {
                    "cursor" : "BtreeCursor ",      ⟵┐ Uses BTreeCursor, an
                    "isMultiKey" : false,             │ index-based cursor
                    "scanAndOrder" : false,
                    "indexBounds" : {
```

```
Range used is   ┌─▷        "product_id" : [
  for single    │              [
    product      │                   ObjectId("4c4b1476238d3b4dd5003981"),
                │                   ObjectId("4c4b1476238d3b4dd5003981")
                │              ]
                              ]
                          },
                          "allPlans" : [
                              ...
                          ]
                      }
                  }
              },
              {
                  "$group" : {
                      "_id" : "$rating",
                      "count" : {
                          "$sum" : {
                              "$const" : 1
                          }
                      }
                  }
              }
          ],
          "ok" : 1
}
```

Although the aggregation framework explain output shown in this listing isn't as extensive as the output that comes from `find().explain()` shown in listing 6.2, it still provides some critical information. For example, it shows whether an index is used and the range scanned within the index. This will give you an idea of how well the index was able to limit the query.

Aggregation `explain()` a work in progress?

The `explain()` function is new in MongoDB v2.6. Given the lack of details compared to the `find().explain()` output, it could be improved in the near future. As explained in the online MongoDB documentation at http://docs.mongodb.org/manual/reference/method/db.collection.aggregate/#example-aggregate-method-explain-option, "The intended readers of the explain output document are humans, and not machines, and the output format is subject to change between releases." Because the documentation states that the format may change between releases, don't be surprised if the output you see begins to look closer to the `find().explain()` output by the time you read this. But the `find().explain()` function has been further improved in MongoDB v3.0 and includes even more detailed output than the `find().explain()` function in MongoDB v2.6, and it supports three modes of operation: `"queryPlanner"`, `"executionStats"`, and `"allPlansExecution"`.

Now let's look at another option that solves a problem that previously limited the size of the data you could process.

As you already know, depending on the exact version of your MongoDB server, your output of the `explain()` function may vary.

6.5.3   *allowDiskUse option*

Eventually, if you begin working with large enough collections, you'll see an error similar to this:

```
assert: command failed: {
        "errmsg" : "exception: Exceeded memory limit for $group,
        but didn't allow external sort. Pass allowDiskUse:true to opt in.",
        "code" : 16945,
        "ok" : 0
} : aggregate failed
```

Even more frustrating, this error will probably happen after a long wait, during which your aggregation pipeline has been processing millions of documents, only to fail. What's happening in this case is that the pipeline has intermediate results that exceed the 100 MB of RAM limit allowed by MongoDB for pipeline stages. The fix is simple and is even specified in the error message: `Pass allowDiskUse:true` to opt in.

Let's see an example with your summary of sales by month, a pipeline that would need this option because your site will have huge sales volumes:

```
db.orders.aggregate([
    {$match: {purchase_data: {$gte: new Date(2010, 0, 1)}}},      ◁───┐ Use a $match
    {$group: {                                                         first to reduce
        _id: {year : {$year :'$purchase_data'},                       documents to
            month: {$month :'$purchase_data'}},                       process.
        count: {$sum:1},
        total: {$sum:'$sub_total'}}},
    {$sort: {_id:-1}}                   Allow MongoDB
], {allowDiskUse:true});         ◁───  to use the disk for
                                        intermediate storage.
```

Generally speaking, using the `allowDiskUse` option may slow down your pipeline, so we recommend that you use it only when needed. As mentioned earlier, you should also try to limit the size of your pipeline intermediate and final document counts and sizes by using `$match` to select which documents to process and `$project` to select which fields to process. But if you're running large pipelines that may at some future date encounter the problem, sometimes it's better to be safe and use it just in case.

Now for the last option available in the aggregation pipeline: `cursor`.

6.5.4   *Aggregation cursor option*

Before MongoDB v2.6, the result of your pipeline was a single document with a limit of 16 MB. Starting with v2.6, the default is to return a cursor if you're accessing MongoDB via the Mongo shell. But if you're running the pipeline from a program, to avoid "breaking" existing programs the default is unchanged and still returns a single document limited to 16 MB. In programs, you can access the new cursor capability by coding something like that shown here to return the result as a cursor:

```
countsByRating = db.reviews.aggregate([
  {$match : {'product_id': product['_id']}},
  {$group : { _id:'$rating',
            count:{$sum:1}}}                    Return a
], {cursor:{}})                                 cursor.
```

The cursor returned by the aggregation pipeline supports the following calls:

- `cursor.hasNext()`—Determine whether there's a next document in the results.
- `cursor.next()`—Return the next document in the results.
- `cursor.toArray()`—Return the entire result as an array.
- `cursor.forEach()`—Execute a function for each row in the results.
- `cursor.map()`—Execute a function for each row in the results and return an array of function return values.
- `cursor.itcount()`—Return a count of items (for testing only).
- `cursor.pretty()`—Display an array of formatted results.

Keep in mind that the purpose of the cursor is to allow you to stream large volumes of data. It can allow you to process a large result set while accessing only a few of the output documents at one time, thus reducing the memory needed to contain the results being processed at any one time. In addition, if all you need are a few of the documents, a cursor can allow you to limit how many documents will be returned from the server. With the methods `toArray()` and `pretty()`, you lose those benefits and all the results are read into memory immediately.

Similarly, `itcount()` will read all the documents and have them sent to the client, but it'll then throw away the results and return just a count. If all your application requires is a count, you can use the `$group` pipeline operator to count the output documents without having to send each one to your program—a much more efficient process.

Now let's wrap up by looking at alternatives to the pipeline for performing aggregations.

6.6   *Other aggregation capabilities*

Although the aggregation pipeline is now considered the preferred method for aggregating data in MongoDB, a few alternatives are available. Some are much simpler, such as the `.count()` function. Another, more complex alternative is the older MongoDB `map-reduce` function.

Let's start with the simpler alternatives first.

6.6.1 *.count( ) and .distinct( )*

You've already seen the `.count()` function earlier in section 6.2.1. Here's an excerpt from code in that section:

```
product = db.products.findOne({'slug': 'wheelbarrow-9092'})
reviews_count = db.reviews.count({'product_id': product['_id']})   ⟵⏤ Count reviews
                                                                       for a product
```

Now let's see an example of using the `distinct()` function. The following would return an array of the zip codes that we've shipped orders to:

```
db.orders.distinct('shipping_address.zip')
```

The size of the results of the `distinct()` function is limited to 16 MB, the current maximum size for a MongoDB document.

Next, let's take a look at one of the early attempts at providing aggregation: `map-reduce`.

6.6.2 *map-reduce*

`map-reduce` was MongoDB's first attempt at providing a flexible aggregation capability. With `map-reduce`, you have the ability to use JavaScript in defining your entire process. This provides a great deal of flexibility but generally performs much slower than the aggregation framework.[1] In addition, coding a map-reduce process is much more complex and less intuitive than the aggregation pipelines we've been building. Let's see an example of how a previous aggregation framework query would appear in `map-reduce`.

> **NOTE** For background on `map-reduce` as explained by two Google researchers, see the original paper on the MapReduce programming model at http://static.googleusercontent.com/media/research.google.com/en/us/archive/mapreduce-osdi04.pdf.

In section 6.2.2, we showed you an example aggregation pipeline that provided sales summary information:

```
db.orders.aggregate([
    {"$match": {"purchase_data":{"$gte" : new Date(2010, 0, 1)}}},
    {"$group": {
        "_id": {"year" : {"$year" :"$purchase_data"},
                "month" : {"$month" : "$purchase_data"}},
        "count": {"$sum":1},
        "total": {"$sum":"$sub_total"}}},
    {"$sort": {"_id":-1}}]);
```

---

[1] Although JavaScript performance has been improving in MongoDB, there are still some key reasons why map-reduce is still significantly slower than the aggregation framework. For a good synopsis of these issue see the wonderful write-up by William Zola in StackOverflow at http://stackoverflow.com/questions/12678631/map-reduce-performance-in-mongodb-2-2-2-4-and-2-6/12680165#12680165.

Let's create a similar result using map-reduce. The first step, as the name implies, is to write a map function. This function is applied to each document in the collection and, in the process, fulfills two purposes: it defines the keys that you're grouping on, and it packages all the data you'll need for your calculation. To see this process in action, look closely at the following function:

```
map = function() {
    var shipping_month = (this.purchase_data.getMonth()+1) +
        '-' + this.purchase_data.getFullYear();

    var tmpItems = 0;
    this.line_items.forEach(function(item) {
        tmpItems += item.quantity;
    });

    emit(shipping_month, {order_total: this.sub_total,
                          items_total: tmpItems});
};
```

First, know that the variable this always refers to a document being iterated over—orders, in this case. In the function's first line, you get an integer value specifying the month the order was created. You then call emit(), a special method that every map function must invoke. The first argument to emit() is the key to group by, and the second is usually a document containing values to be reduced. In this case, you're grouping by month, and you're going to reduce over each order's subtotal and item count. The corresponding reduce function should make this clearer:

```
reduce = function(key, values) {
    var result = { order_total: 0, items_total: 0 };
    values.forEach(function(value){
        result.order_total += value.order_total;
        result.items_total += value.items_total;
    });
    return ( result );
};
```

The reduce function will be passed a key and an array of one or more values. Your job in writing a reduce function is to make sure those values are aggregated together in the desired way and then returned as a single value. Because of map-reduce's iterative nature, reduce may be invoked more than once, and your code must take this into account. In addition, if only one value is emitted by the map function for a particular key, the reduce function won't be called at all. As a result, the structure returned by the reduce function must be identical to the structure emitted by the map function. Look closely at the example map and reduce functions and you'll see that this is the case.

ADDING A QUERY FILTER AND SAVING OUTPUT

The shell's map-reduce method requires a map and a reduce function as arguments. But this example adds two more. The first is a query filter that limits the documents involved in the aggregation to orders made since the beginning of 2010. The second argument is the name of the output collection:

```
filter = {purchase_data: {$gte: new Date(2010, 0, 1)}};
db.orders.mapReduce(map, reduce, {query: filter, out: 'totals'});
```

The process, as illustrated in figure 6.6, includes these steps:

1 `filter` will select only certain orders.

2 `map` then emits a key-value pair, usually one output for each input, but it can emit none or many as well.

3 `reduce` is passed a key with an array of values emitted by `map`, usually one array for each key, but it may be passed the same key multiple times with different arrays of values.

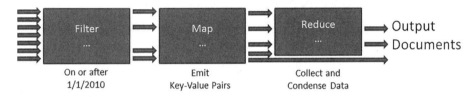

Figure 6.6 `map-reduce` **process**

One important point illustrated in figure 6.6 is that if the `map` function produces a single result for a given key, the `reduce` step is skipped. This is critical to understanding why you can't change the structure of the value output by the `map` output during the `reduce` step.

In the example, the results are stored in a collection called `totals`, and you can query this collection as you would any other. The following listing displays the results of querying one of these collections. The `_id` field holds your grouping key, the year, and the month, and the `value` field references the reduced totals.

Listing 6.4 Querying the `map-reduce` output collection

```
> db.totals.find()
{ "_id" : "11-2014", "value" : {"order_total" : 4897, "items_total" : 1 } }
{ "_id" : "4-2014", "value" : {"order_total" : 4897, "items_total" : 1 } }
{ "_id" : "8-2014", "value" : {"order_total" : 11093, "items_total" : 4 } }
```

The examples here should give you some sense of MongoDB's aggregation capabilities in practice. Compare this to the aggregation framework version of the equivalent process and you'll see why `map-reduce` is no longer the preferred method for this type of functionality.

But there may be some cases where you require the additional flexibility that JavaScript provides with `map-reduce`. We won't cover the topic further in this book, but you can find references and examples for `map-reduce` on the MongoDB website at http://docs.mongodb.org/manual/core/map-reduce/.

---

map-reduce—A good first try

At the first MongoDB World conference held in New York City in 2014, a group of MongoDB engineers presented results from benchmarks comparing different server configurations for processing a collection in the multi-terabyte range. An engineer presented a benchmark for the aggregation framework but none for `map-reduce`. When asked about this, the engineer replied that `map-reduce` was no longer the recommended option for aggregation and that it was "a good first try."

Although `map-reduce` provides the flexibility of JavaScript it's limited in being single threaded and interpreted. The Aggregation Framework, on the other hand, is executed as native C++ and multithreaded. Although `map-reduce` isn't going away, future enhancements will be limited to the Aggregation Framework.

6.7   Summary

This chapter has covered quite a bit of material. The `$group` operator provides the key functionality for the aggregation framework: the ability to aggregate data from multiple documents into a single document. Along with `$unwind` and `$project`, the aggregation framework provides you with the ability to generate summary data that's up to the minute or to process large amounts of data offline and even save the results as a new collection using the `$out` command.

Queries and aggregations make up a critical part of the MongoDB interface. So once you've read this chapter, put the query and aggregation mechanisms to the test. If you're ever unsure of how a particular combination of query operators will serve you, the MongoDB shell is always a ready test bed. So try practicing some of the key features of the aggregation framework, such as selecting documents via the `$match` operator, or restructuring documents using `$project`, and of course grouping and summarizing data using `$group`.

We'll use MongoDB queries pretty consistently from now on, and the next chapter is a good reminder of that. We'll tackle the usual document CRUD operations: create, read, update, and delete. Because queries play a key role in most updates, you can look forward to yet more exploration of the query language elaborated here. You'll also learn how updating documents, especially in a database that's designed for high volumes of updates, requires more capabilities than you may be familiar with if you've done similar work on a relational database.

Updates, atomic operations, and deletes

This chapter covers

- Updating documents
- Processing documents atomically
- Applying complex updates to a real-world example
- Using update operators
- Deleting documents

To update is to write to existing documents. Doing this effectively requires a thorough understanding of the kinds of document structures available and of the query expressions made possible by MongoDB. Having studied the e-commerce data model in the last two chapters, you should have a good sense of the ways in which schemas are designed and queried. We'll use all of this knowledge in our study of updates.

Specifically, we'll look more closely at why we model the category hierarchy in such a denormalized way, and how MongoDB's updates make that structure reasonable. We'll explore inventory management and solve a few tricky concurrency issues in the process. You'll get to know a host of new update operators, learn some tricks that take advantage of the atomicity of update operations, and experience the power of the findAndModify command. In this case *atomicity* refers to MongoDB's ability to search for a document and update it, with the guarantee that no other operation will interfere, a powerful property. After numerous examples, there will be a section devoted to the nuts and bolts of each update operator, which will expand on the examples to give you the full range of options for how you update. We'll also discuss how to delete data in MongoDB, and conclude with some notes on concurrency and optimization.

Most of the examples in this chapter are written for the JavaScript shell. The section where we discuss atomic document processing, though, requires a good bit more application-level logic, so for that section we'll switch over to Ruby.

By the end of the chapter, you'll have been exposed to the full range of MongoDB's CRUD operations, and you'll be well on your way to designing applications that best take advantage of MongoDB's interface and data model.

7.1   *A brief tour of document updates*

If you need to update a document in MongoDB, you have two ways of going about it. You can either replace the document altogether, or you can use update operators to modify specific fields within the document. As a way of setting the stage for the more detailed examples to come, we'll begin this chapter with a simple demonstration of these two techniques. We'll then provide reasons for preferring one over the other.

To start, recall the sample user document we developed in chapter 4. The document includes a user's first and last names, email address, and shipping addresses. Here's a simplified example:

```
{
  _id: ObjectId("4c4b1476238d3b4dd5000001"),
  username: "kbanker",
  email: "kylebanker@gmail.com",
  first_name: "Kyle",
  last_name: "Banker",
  hashed_password: "bd1cfa194c3a603e7186780824b04419",
  addresses: [
    {
      name: "work",
      street: "1 E. 23rd Street",
      city: "New York",
      state: "NY",
      zip: 10010
    }
  ]
}
```

You'll undoubtedly need to update an email address from time to time, so let's begin with that.

Please note that your ObjectId values might be a little different. Make sure that you're using valid ones and, if needed, manually add documents that will help you follow the commands of this chapter. Alternatively, you can use the following method to find a valid document, get its `ObjectId`, and use it elsewhere:

```
doc = db.users.findOne({username: "kbanker"})
user_id = doc._id
```

7.1.1 *Modify by replacement*

To replace the document altogether, you first query for the document, modify it on the client side, and then issue the update with the modified document. Here's how that looks in the JavaScript shell:

```
user_id = ObjectId("4c4b1476238d3b4dd5003981")
doc = db.users.findOne({_id: user_id})
doc['email'] = 'mongodb-user@mongodb.com'
print('updating ' + user_id)
db.users.update({_id: user_id}, doc)
```

With the user's `_id` at hand, you first query for the document. Next you modify the document locally, in this case changing the `email` attribute. Then you pass the modified document to the `update` method. The final line says, "Find the document in the users collection with the given `_id`, and replace that document with the one we've provided." The thing to remember is that the update operation replaces the entire document, which is why it must be fetched first. If multiple users update the same document, the last write will be the one that will be stored.

7.1.2 *Modify by operator*

That's how you modify by replacement; now let's look at modification by operator:

```
user_id = ObjectId("4c4b1476238d3b4dd5000001")
db.users.update({_id: user_id},
  {$set: {email: 'mongodb-user2@mongodb.com'}})
```

The example uses `$set`, one of several special update operators, to modify the email address in a single request to the server. In this case, the update request is much more targeted: find the given user document and set its `email` field to `mongodb-user2@mongodb.com`.

Syntax note: updates vs. queries

Users new to MongoDB sometimes have difficulty distinguishing between the update and query syntaxes. Targeted updates always begin with the update operator, and this operator is almost always a verb-like construct (set, push, and so on). Take the `$addToSet` operator, for example:

```
db.products.update({}, {$addToSet: {tags: 'Green'}})
```

> **(continued)**
>
> If you add a query selector to this update, note that the query operator is semantically adjectival (less than, equal to, and so on) and comes after the field name to query on (price, in this case):
>
> ```
> db.products.update({price: {$lte: 10}},
>     {$addToSet: {tags: 'cheap'}})
> ```
>
> This last query example only updates documents with a price ? 10 where it adds 'cheap' to their tags.
>
> Update operators use the *prefix* notation whereas query operators usually use the *infix* notation, meaning that $addToSet in the update operator comes first, and $lte in the query operator is within the hash in the price field.

7.1.3 *Both methods compared*

How about another example? This time you want to increment the number of reviews on a product. Here's how you'd do that as a document replacement:

```
product_id = ObjectId("4c4b1476238d3b4dd5003982")
doc = db.products.findOne({_id: product_id})
doc['total_reviews'] += 1        // add 1 to the value in total_reviews
db.products.update({_id: product_id}, doc)
```

And here's the targeted approach:

```
db.products.update({_id: product_id}, {$inc: {total_reviews: 1}})
```

The replacement approach, as before, fetches the user document from the server, modifies it, and then resends it. The update statement here is similar to the one you used to update the email address. By contrast, the targeted update uses a different update operator, $inc, to increment the value in total_reviews.

7.1.4 *Deciding: replacement vs. operators*

Now that you've seen a couple of updates in action, can you think of some reasons why you might use one method over the other? Which one do you find more intuitive? Which do you think is better for performance? What happens when multiple threads are updating simultaneously—are they isolated from one another?

Modification by replacement is the more generic approach. Imagine that your application presents an HTML form for modifying user information. With document replacement, data from the form post, once validated, can be passed right to MongoDB; the code to perform the update is the same regardless of which user attributes are modified. For instance, if you were going to build a MongoDB object mapper that needed to generalize updates, then updates by replacement would probably make for a sensible default.[1]

But targeted modifications generally yield better performance. For one thing, there's no need for the initial round-trip to the server to fetch the document to modify. And, just as important, the document specifying the update is generally small. If you're updating via replacement and your documents average 200 KB in size, that's 200 KB received and sent to the server per update! Recall chapter 5 when you used projections to fetch only part of a document. That isn't an option if you need to replace the document without losing information. Contrast that with the way updates are specified using $set and $push in the previous examples; the documents specifying these updates can be less than 100 bytes each, regardless of the size of the document being modified. For this reason, the use of targeted updates frequently means less time spent serializing and transmitting data.

In addition, targeted operations allow you to update documents atomically. For instance, if you need to increment a counter, updates via replacement are far from ideal. What if the document changes in between when you read and write it? The only way to make your updates atomic is to employ some sort of optimistic locking. With targeted updates, you can use $inc to modify a counter atomically. This means that even with a large number of concurrent updates, each $inc will be applied in isolation, all or nothing.[2]

> ### Optimistic locking
>
> *Optimistic locking*, or *optimistic concurrency control*, is a technique for ensuring a clean update to a record without having to lock it. The easiest way to understand this technique is to think of a wiki. It's possible to have more than one user editing a wiki page at the same time. But you never want a situation where a user is editing and updating an out-of-date version of the page. Thus, an optimistic locking protocol is used. When users try to save their changes, a timestamp is included in the attempted update. If that timestamp is older than the latest saved version of the page, the user's update can't go through. But if no one has saved any edits to the page, the update is allowed. This strategy allows multiple users to edit at the same time, which is much better than the alternative concurrency strategy of requiring each user to take out a lock to edit any one page.
>
> With pessimistic locking, a record is locked from the time it's first accessed in a transaction until the transaction is finished, making it inaccessible to other transactions during that time.

---

[1] This is the strategy employed by most MongoDB object mappers, and it's easy to understand why. If users are given the ability to model entities of arbitrary complexity, then issuing an update via replacement is much easier than calculating the ideal combination of special update operators to employ.

[2] The MongoDB documentation uses the term *atomic updates* to signify what we're calling *targeted updates*. This new terminology is an attempt to clarify the use of the word *atomic*. In fact, all updates issued to the core server occur atomically, isolated on a per-document basis. The update operators are called atomic because they make it possible to query and update a document in a single operation.

Now that you understand the kinds of available updates, you'll be able to appreciate the strategies we'll introduce in the next section. There, we'll return to the e-commerce data model to answer some of the more difficult questions about operating on that data in production.

7.2   *E-commerce updates*

It's easy to provide stock examples for updating this or that attribute in a MongoDB document. But with a production data model and a real application, complications will arise, and the update for any given attribute might not be a simple one-liner. In the following sections, we'll use the e-commerce data model you saw in the last two chapters to provide a representative sample of the kinds of updates you'd expect to make in a production e-commerce site. You may find certain updates intuitive and others not so much. But overall, you'll develop a better understanding of the schema developed in chapter 4 and an improved understanding of the features and limitations of MongoDB's update language.

7.2.1   *Products and categories*

Here you'll see a couple of examples of targeted updates in action, first looking at how you calculate average product ratings and then at the more complicated task of maintaining the category hierarchy.

AVERAGE PRODUCT RATINGS

Products are amenable to numerous update strategies. Assuming that administrators are provided with an interface for editing product information, the easiest update involves fetching the current product document, merging that data with the user's edits, and issuing a document replacement. At other times, you may only need to update a couple of values, where a targeted update is clearly the way to go. This is the case with average product ratings. Because users need to sort product listings based on average product rating, you store that rating in the product document itself and update the value whenever a review is added or removed.

Here's one way of issuing this update in JavaScript:

```
product_id = ObjectId("4c4b1476238d3b4dd5003981")
count = 0
total = 0
db.reviews.find({product_id: product_id}, {rating: 4}).forEach(
  function(review) {
    total += review.rating
    count++
  })
average = total / count
db.products.update({_id: product_id},
  {$set: {total_reviews: count, average_review: average}})
```

This code aggregates and produces the `rating` field from each product review and then produces an average. You also use the fact that you're iterating over each rating to count the total ratings for the product. This saves an extra database call to the `count` function. With the total number of reviews and their average rating, the code issues a targeted update, using `$set`.

If you don't want to hardcode an `ObjectId`, you can find a specific `ObjectId` as follows and use it afterwards:

```
product_id = db.products.findOne({sku: '9092'}, {'_id': 1})
```

Performance-conscious users may balk at the idea of re-aggregating all product reviews for each update. Much of this depends on the ratio of reads to writes; it's likely that more users will see product reviews than write their own, so it makes sense to re-aggregate on a write. The method provided here, though conservative, will likely be acceptable for most situations, but other strategies are possible. For instance, you could store an extra field on the product document that caches the review ratings total, making it possible to compute the average incrementally. After inserting a new review, you'd first query for the product to get the current total number of reviews and the ratings total. Then you'd calculate the average and issue an update using a selector like the following:

```
db.products.update({_id: product_id},
  {
    $set: {
      average_review: average,
      ratings_total: total
    },
    $inc: {
      total_reviews: 1
    }
  })
```

This example uses the `$inc` operator, which increments the field passed in by the given value—1, in this case.

Only by benchmarking against a system with representative data can you say whether this approach is worthwhile. But the example shows that MongoDB frequently provides more than one valid path. The requirements of the application will help you decide which is best.

THE CATEGORY HIERARCHY

With many databases, there's no easy way to represent a category hierarchy. This is true of MongoDB, although the document structure does help the situation somewhat. Documents encourage a strategy that optimizes for reads because each category can contain a list of its denormalized ancestors. The one tricky requirement is keeping all the ancestor lists up to date. Let's look at an example to see how this is done.

First you need a generic method for updating the ancestor list for any given category. Here's one possible solution:

```
var generate_ancestors = function(_id, parent_id) {
  ancestor_list = []
  var cursor = db.categories.find({_id: parent_id})
  while(cursor.size() > 0) {
    parent = cursor.next()
    ancestor_list.push(parent)
    parent_id = parent.parent_id
    cursor = db.categories.find({_id: parent_id})
  }
  db.categories.update({_id: _id}, {$set: {ancestors: ancestor_list}})
}
```

This method works by walking backward up the category hierarchy, making successive queries to each node's parent_id attribute until reaching the root node (where parent_id is null). All the while, it builds an in-order list of ancestors, storing that result in the ancestor_list array. Finally, it updates the category's ancestors attribute using $set.

Now that you have that basic building block, let's look at the process of inserting a new category. Imagine you have a simple category hierarchy that looks like the one in figure 7.1.

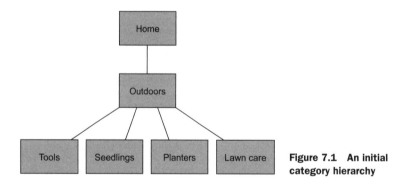

Figure 7.1   An initial category hierarchy

Suppose you want to add a new category called Gardening and place it under the Home category. You insert the new category document and then run your method to generate its ancestors:

```
parent_id = ObjectId("8b87fb1476238d3b4dd50003")
category = {
  parent_id: parent_id,
  slug: "gardening",
  name: "Gardening",
  description: "All gardening implements, tools, seeds, and soil."
}
db.categories.save(category)
generate_ancestors(category._id, parent_id)
```

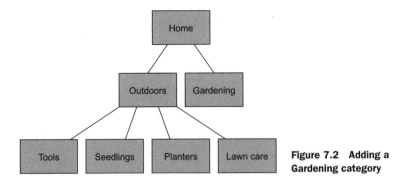

Figure 7.2　Adding a Gardening category

Note that save() puts the ID created for it into the original document. The ID is then used in the call to generate_ancestors(). Figure 7.2 displays the updated tree.

That's easy enough. But what if you now want to place the Outdoors category underneath Gardening? This is potentially complicated because it alters the ancestor lists of a number of categories. You can start by changing the parent_id of Outdoors to the _id of Gardening. This turns out to be not too difficult provided that you already have both an outdoors_id and a gardening_id available:

```
db.categories.update({_id: outdoors_id}, {$set: {parent_id: gardening_id}})
```

Because you've effectively moved the Outdoors category, all the descendants of Outdoors are going to have invalid ancestor lists. You can rectify this by querying for all categories with Outdoors in their ancestor lists and then regenerating those lists. MongoDB's power to query into arrays makes this trivial:

```
db.categories.find({'ancestors.id': outdoors_id}).forEach(
  function(category) {
    generate_ancestors(category._id, outdoors_id)
  })
```

That's how you handle an update to a category's parent_id attribute, and you can see the resulting category arrangement in figure 7.3.

But what if you update a category name? If you change the name of Outdoors to The Great Outdoors, you also have to change Outdoors wherever it appears in the ancestor lists of other categories. You may be justified in thinking, "See? This is where denormalization comes to bite you," but it should make you feel better to know that you can perform this update without recalculating any ancestor list. Here's how:

```
doc = db.categories.findOne({_id: outdoors_id})
doc.name = "The Great Outdoors"
db.categories.update({_id: outdoors_id}, doc)
db.categories.update(
  {'ancestors._id': outdoors_id},
  {$set: {'ancestors.$': doc}},
  {multi: true})
```

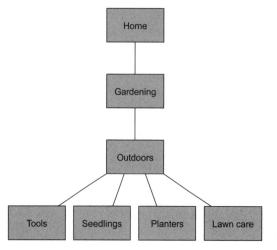

Figure 7.3 The category tree in its final state

You first grab the Outdoors document, alter the name attribute locally, and then update via replacement. Now you use the updated Outdoors document to replace its occurrences in the various ancestor lists. The multi parameter {multi: true} is easy to understand; it enables multi-updates causing the update to affect all documents matching the selector—without {multi: true} an update will only affect the first matching document. Here, you want to update each category that has the Outdoors category in its ancestor list.

The positional operator is more subtle. Consider that you have no way of knowing where in a given category's ancestor list the Outdoors category will appear. You need a way for the update operator to dynamically target the position of the Outdoors category in the array for any document. Enter the positional operator. This operator (here the $ in ancestors.$) substitutes the array index matched by the query selector with itself, and thus enables the update.

Here's another example of this technique. Say you want to change a field of a user address (the example document shown in section 7.1) that has been labeled as "work." You can accomplish this with a query like the following:

```
db.users.update({
    _id: ObjectId("4c4b1476238d3b4dd5000001"),
    'addresses.name': 'work'},
    {$set: {'addresses.$.street': '155 E 31st St.'}})
```

Because of the need to update individual subdocuments within arrays, you'll always want to keep the positional operator at hand. In general, these techniques for updating the category hierarchy will be applicable whenever you're dealing with arrays of subdocuments.

7.2.2 *Reviews*

Not all reviews are created equal, which is why this application allows users to vote on them. These votes are elementary; they indicate that the given review is helpful. You've modeled reviews so that they cache the total number of helpful votes and keep a list of each voter's ID. The relevant section of each review document looks like this:

```
{
  helpful_votes: 3,
  voter_ids: [
    ObjectId("4c4b1476238d3b4dd5000041"),
    ObjectId("7a4f0376238d3b4dd5000003"),
    ObjectId("92c21476238d3b4dd5000032")
  ]
}
```

You can record user votes using targeted updates. The strategy is to use the `$push` operator to add the voter's ID to the list and the `$inc` operator to increment the total number of votes, both in the same JavaScript console update operation:

```
db.reviews.update({_id: ObjectId("4c4b1476238d3b4dd5000041")}, {
    $push: {
      voter_ids: ObjectId("4c4b1476238d3b4dd5000001")
    },
    $inc: {
      helpful_votes: 1
    }
  })
```

This is almost correct. But you need to ensure that the update happens only if the voting user hasn't yet voted on this review, so you modify the query selector to match only when the `voter_ids` array doesn't contain the ID you're about to add. You can easily accomplish this using the `$ne` query operator:

```
query_selector = {
  _id: ObjectId("4c4b1476238d3b4dd5000041"),
  voter_ids: {
    $ne: ObjectId("4c4b1476238d3b4dd5000001")
  }
}
db.reviews.update(query_selector, {
    $push: {
      voter_ids: ObjectId("4c4b1476238d3b4dd5000001")
    },
    $inc : {
      helpful_votes: 1
    }
  })
```

This is an especially powerful demonstration of MongoDB's update mechanism and how it can be used with a document-oriented schema. Voting, in this case, is both atomic and efficient. The update is atomic because selection and modification occur in the same query. The atomicity ensures that, even in a high-concurrency environment, it will be impossible for any one user to vote more than once. The efficiency lies in the fact that the test for voter membership and the updates to the counter and the voter list all occur in the same request to the server.

Now, if you do end up using this technique to record votes, it's especially important that any other updates to the review document also be targeted—updating by replacement could result in an inconsistency. Imagine, for instance, that a user updates the content of their review and that this update occurs via replacement. When updating by replacement, you first query for the document you want to update. But between the time that you query for the review and replace it, it's possible that a different user might vote on the review. This is called a *race condition*. This sequence of events is illustrated in figure 7.4.

Review documents

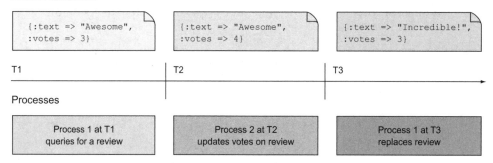

Figure 7.4 When a review is updated concurrently via targeted and replacement updates, data can be lost.

It should be clear that the document replacement at T3 will overwrite the votes update happening at T2. It's possible to avoid this by using the optimistic locking technique described earlier, but doing so requires additional application code to implement and it's probably easier to ensure that all updates in this case are targeted.

7.2.3 *Orders*

The atomicity and efficiency of updates that you saw in reviews can also be applied to orders. Specifically, you're going to see the MongoDB calls needed to implement an add_to_cart function using a targeted update. This is a three-step process. First, you construct the product document that you'll store in the order's line-item array. Then you issue a targeted update, indicating that this is to be an *upsert*—an update that will insert a new document if the document to be updated doesn't exist. (We'll describe upserts in detail in the next section.) The upsert will create a new order object if it doesn't yet exist, seamlessly handling both initial and subsequent additions to the shopping cart.[3]

Let's begin by constructing a sample document to add to the cart:

```
cart_item = {
  _id:  ObjectId("4c4b1476238d3b4dd5003981"),
  slug: "wheel-barrow-9092",
  sku:  "9092",
  name: "Extra Large Wheel Barrow",
  pricing: {
    retail: 5897,
    sale:   4897
  }
}
```

You'll most likely build this document by querying the `products` collection and then extracting whichever fields need to be preserved as a line item. The product's `_id`, `sku`, `slug`, `name`, and `price` fields should suffice. Next you'll ensure that there's an order for the customer with a status of `'CART'` using the parameter {upsert: true}. This operation will also increment the order `sub_total` using the `$inc` operator:

```
selector = {
  user_id: ObjectId("4c4b1476238d3b4dd5000001"),
  state: 'CART'
}
update = {
  $inc: {
    sub_total: cart_item['pricing']['sale']
  }
}
db.orders.update(selector, update, {upsert: true})
```

INITIAL UPSERT TO CREATE ORDER DOCUMENT

To make the code clearer, you're constructing the query selector and the update document separately. The update document increments the order subtotal by the sale price of the cart item. Of course, the first time a user executes the `add_to_cart` function, no shopping cart will exist. That's why you use an upsert here. The upsert will construct the document implied by the query selector including the update. Therefore, the initial upsert will produce an order document like this:

```
{
  user_id: ObjectId("4c4b1476238d3b4dd5000001"),
  state: 'CART',
  subtotal: 9794
}
```

---

[3] We're using the terms *shopping cart* and *order* interchangeably because they're both represented using the same document. They're formally differentiated only by the document's `state` field (a document with a state of CART is a shopping cart).

You then perform an update of the order document to add the line item if it's not already on the order:

```
selector = {user_id: ObjectId("4c4b1476238d3b4dd5000001"),
    state: 'CART',
    'line_items._id':
        {'$ne': cart_item._id}
    }

update = {'$push': {'line_items': cart_item}}
db.orders.update(selector, update)
```

ANOTHER UPDATE FOR QUANTITIES

Next you'll issue another targeted update to ensure that the item quantities are correct. You need this update to handle the case where the user clicks Add to Cart on an item that's already in the cart. In this case the previous update won't add a new item to the cart, but you'll still need to adjust the quantity:

```
selector = {
  user_id: ObjectId("4c4b1476238d3b4dd5000001"),
  state: 'CART',
  'line_items._id': ObjectId("4c4b1476238d3b4dd5003981")
}
update = {
  $inc: {
    'line_items.$.quantity': 1
  }
}
db.orders.update(selector, update)
```

We use the $inc operator to update the quantity on the individual line item. The update is facilitated by the positional operator, $, introduced previously. Thus, after the user clicks Add to Cart twice on the wheelbarrow product, the cart should look like this:

```
{
  user_id: ObjectId("4c4b1476238d3b4dd5000001"),
  state: 'CART',
  line_items: [
    {
      _id:  ObjectId("4c4b1476238d3b4dd5003981"),
      quantity:  2,
      slug: "wheel-barrow-9092",
      sku:  "9092",
      name: "Extra Large Wheel Barrow",
      pricing: {
        retail: 5897,
        sale:  4897
      }
    }
  ],
  subtotal: 9794
}
```

There are now two wheelbarrows in the cart, and the subtotal reflects that.

There are still more operations you'll need in order to fully implement a shopping cart. Most of these, such as removing an item from the cart or clearing a cart altogether, can be implemented with one or more targeted updates. If that's not obvious, the upcoming subsection describing each query operator should make it clear. As for the actual order processing, that can be handled by advancing the order document through a series of states and applying each state's processing logic. We'll demonstrate this in the next section, where we explain atomic document processing and the `findAndModify` command.

7.3 *Atomic document processing*

One tool you won't want to do without is MongoDB's `findAndModify` command.[4] This command allows you to atomically update a document and return it in the same round-trip. An atomic update is one where no other operation can interrupt or interleave itself with the update. What if another user tries to change the document after you find it but before you modify it? The find might no longer apply. An atomic update prevents this case; all other operations must wait for the atomic update to finish.

Every update in MongoDB is atomic, but the difference with `findAndModify` is that it also atomically returns the document to you. Why is this useful? If you fetch and then update a document (or update then fetch it), there can be changes made to the document by another MongoDB user in between those operations. Thus it's impossible to know the true state of the document you updated, before or after the update, even though the update is atomic, unless you use `findAndModify`. The other option is to use the optimistic locking mentioned in section 7.1, but that would require additional application logic to implement.

This atomic update capability is a big deal because of what it enables. For instance, you can use `findAndModify` to build job queues and state machines. You can then use these primitive constructs to implement basic transactional semantics, which greatly expand the range of applications you can build using MongoDB. With these transaction-like features, you can construct an entire e-commerce site on MongoDB—not just the product content, but the checkout mechanism and the inventory management as well.

To demonstrate, we'll look at two examples of the `findAndModify` command in action. First, we'll show how to handle basic state transitions on the shopping cart. Then we'll look at a slightly more involved example of managing a limited inventory.

---

[4] The way this command is identified can vary by environment. The shell helper is invoked camel case as `db.orders.findAndModify`, whereas Ruby uses underscores: `find_and_modify`. To confuse the issue even more, the core server knows the command as `findandmodify`. You'll use this final form if you ever need to issue the command manually.

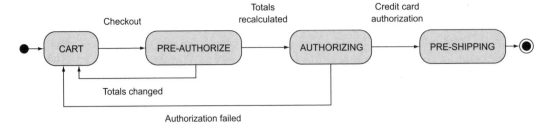

Figure 7.5   Order state transitions

7.3.1   *Order state transitions*

All state transitions have two parts: a query ensuring a valid initial state, and an update that effects the change of state. Let's skip forward a few steps in the order process and assume that the user is about to click the Pay Now button to authorize the purchase. If you're going to authorize the user's credit card synchronously on the application side, you need to ensure these four things:

1   You authorize for the amount that the user sees on the checkout screen.
2   The cart's contents never change while in the process of authorization.
3   Errors in the authorization process return the cart to its previous state.
4   If the credit card is successfully authorized, the payment information is posted to the order, and that order's state is transitioned to PRE-SHIPPING.

The state transitions that you'll use are shown in figure 7.5.

PREPARE THE ORDER FOR CHECKOUT

The first step is to get the order into the new PRE-AUTHORIZE state. You use find-AndModify to find the user's current order object and ensure that the object is in a CART state:

```
newDoc = db.orders.findAndModify({
    query: {
        user_id: ObjectId("4c4b1476238d3b4dd5000001"),
        state: 'CART'
    },
    update: {
        $set: {
            state: 'PRE-AUTHORIZE'
        }
    },
    'new': true
})
```

If successful, findAndModify will return the modified order object to newDoc.[5] Once the order is in the PRE-AUTHORIZE state, the user won't be able to edit the cart's

---

[5]   By default, the findAndModify command returns the document as it appears prior to the update. To return the modified document, you must specify 'new' : true as in this example.

contents. This is because all updates to the cart always ensure a state of CART. find-AndModify is useful here because you want to know the state of the document exactly when you changed its state to PRE-AUTHORIZE. What would happen to the total calculations if another thread was also attempting to move the user through the checkout process?

VERIFY THE ORDER AND AUTHORIZE

Now, in the preauthorization state, you take the returned order object and recalculate the various totals. Once you have those totals, you issue a new findAndModify that only transitions the document's state to AUTHORIZING if the new totals match the old totals. Here's what that findAndModify looks like:

```
oldDoc = db.orders.findAndModify({
    query: {
      user_id: ObjectId("4c4b1476238d3b4dd5000001"),
      total: 99000,
      state: "PRE-AUTHORIZE"
    },
    update: {
      '$set': {
        state: "AUTHORIZING"
      }
    }
  })
```

If this second findAndModify fails, then you must return the order's state to CART and report the updated totals to the user. But if it succeeds, you know that the total to be authorized is the same total that was presented to the user. This means you can move on to the actual authorization API call. Thus, the application now issues a credit card authorization request on the user's credit card. If the credit card fails to authorize, you record the failure and, as before, return the order to its CART state.

FINISHING THE ORDER

If the authorization is successful, you write the authorization information to the order and transition it to the next state. The following strategy does both in the same find-AndModify call. Here, the example uses a sample document representing the authorization receipt, which is attached to the original order:

```
auth_doc = {
  ts: new Date(),
  cc: 3432003948293040,
  id: 29238382910293844483949348,
  gateway: "Authorize.net"
}
db.orders.findAndModify({
    query: {
      user_id: ObjectId("4c4b1476238d3b4dd5000001"),
      state: "AUTHORIZING"
    },
```

```
      update: {
        $set: {
          state: "PRE-SHIPPING",
          authorization: auth_doc
        }
      }
    })
```

It's important to be aware of the MongoDB features that facilitate this transactional process. There's the ability to modify any one document atomically. There's the guarantee of consistent reads along a single connection. And finally, there's the document structure itself, which allows these operations to fit within the single-document atomicity that MongoDB provides. In this case, that structure allows you to fit line items, products, pricing, and user ownership into the same document, ensuring that you only ever need to operate on that one document to advance the sale.

This ought to strike you as impressive. But it may lead you to wonder, as it did us, whether any *multi-object* transaction-like behavior can be implemented with MongoDB. The answer is a cautious affirmative and can be demonstrated by looking into another e-commerce centerpiece: inventory management.

7.3.2   *Inventory management*

Not every e-commerce site needs strict inventory management. Most commodity items can be replenished in enough time to allow any order to go through regardless of the actual number of items on hand. In cases like these, managing inventory is easily handled by managing expectations; as soon as only a few items remain in stock, adjust the shipping estimates.

One-of-a-kind items present a different challenge. Imagine you're selling concert tickets with assigned seats or handmade works of art. These products can't be hedged; users will always need a guarantee that they can purchase the products they've selected. Here we'll present a possible solution to this problem using MongoDB. This will further illustrate the creative possibilities in the findAndModify command and the judicious use of the document model. It will also show how to implement transactional semantics across multiple documents. Although you'll only see a few of the key MongoDB calls used by this process, the full source code for the InventoryFetcher class is included with this book.

The way you model inventory can be best understood by thinking about a real store. If you're in a gardening store, you can see and feel the physical inventory; dozens of shovels, rakes, and clippers may line the aisles. If you take a shovel and place it in your cart, that's one less shovel available for the other customers. As a corollary, no two customers can have the same shovel in their shopping carts at the same time. You can use this simple principle to model inventory. For every physical piece of inventory in your warehouse, you store a corresponding document in an inventory collection. If there are 10 shovels in the warehouse, there are 10 shovel documents in the database. Each inventory item is linked to a product by sku, and each of these items can be in one of four states: AVAILABLE (0), IN_CART (1), PRE_ORDER (2), or PURCHASED (3).

Here's a method that inserts three shovels, three rakes, and three sets of clippers as available inventory. The examples in this section are in Ruby, since transactions require more logic, so it's useful to see a more concrete example of how an application would implement them:

```
3.times do
  $inventory.insert_one({:sku => 'shovel',   :state => AVAILABLE})
  $inventory.insert_one({:sku => 'rake',     :state => AVAILABLE})
  $inventory.insert_one({:sku => 'clippers', :state => AVAILABLE})
end
```

We'll handle inventory management with a special inventory fetching class. We'll first look at how this fetcher works and then we'll peel back the covers to reveal its implementation.

INVENTORY FETCHER

The inventory fetcher can add arbitrary sets of products to a shopping cart. Here you create a new order object and a new inventory fetcher. You then ask the fetcher to add three shovels and one set of clippers to a given order by passing an order ID and two documents specifying the products and quantities you want to the add_to_cart method. The fetcher hides the complexity of this operation, which is altering two collections at once:

```
$order_id = BSON::ObjectId('561297c5530a69dbc9000000')
$orders.insert_one({
    :_id => $order_id,
    :username => 'kbanker',
    :item_ids => []
  })

@fetcher = InventoryFetcher.new({
    :orders => $orders,
    :inventory => $inventory
  })

@fetcher.add_to_cart(@order_id,
    [
      {:sku => "shovel", :quantity => 3},
      {:sku => "clippers", :quantity => 1}
    ])

$orders.find({"_id" => $order_id}).each do |order|
    puts "\nHere's the order:"
    p order
end
```

The `add_to_cart` method will raise an exception if it fails to add every item to a cart. If it succeeds, the order should look like this:

```
{
  "_id" => BSON::ObjectId('4cdf3668238d3b6e3200000a'),
  "username" => "kbanker",
  "item_ids" => [
    BSON::ObjectId('4cdf3668238d3b6e32000001'),
    BSON::ObjectId('4cdf3668238d3b6e32000004'),
    BSON::ObjectId('4cdf3668238d3b6e32000007'),
    BSON::ObjectId('4cdf3668238d3b6e32000009')
      ]
    }
```

The `_id` of each physical inventory item will be stored in the order document. You can query for each of these items like this:

```
puts "\nHere's each item:"
order['item_ids'].each do |item_id|
  item = @inventory.find({"_id" => item_id}).each do |myitem|
    p myitem
  end
end
```

Looking at each of these items individually, you can see that each has a state of 1, corresponding to the `IN_CART` state. You should also notice that each item records the time of the last state change with a timestamp. You can later use this timestamp to expire items that have been in a cart for too long. For instance, you might give users 15 minutes to check out from the time they add products to their cart:

```
{
  "_id" => BSON::ObjectId('4cdf3668238d3b6e32000001'),
  "sku"=>"shovel",
  "state"=>1,
  "ts"=>"Sun Nov 14 01:07:52 UTC 2010"
}
{
  "_id"=>BSON::ObjectId('4cdf3668238d3b6e32000004'),
  "sku"=>"shovel",
  "state"=>1,
  "ts"=>"Sun Nov 14 01:07:52 UTC 2010"
}
{
  "_id"=>BSON::ObjectId('4cdf3668238d3b6e32000007'),
  "sku"=>"shovel",
  "state"=>1,
  "ts"=>"Sun Nov 14 01:07:52 UTC 2010"
}
```

INVENTORY MANAGEMENT

If this `InventoryFetcher`'s API makes any sense, you should have at least a few hunches about how you'd implement inventory management. Unsurprisingly, the `findAndModify` command resides at its core. The full source code for the InventoryFetcher is included with the source code of this book. We're not going to look at every line of code, but we'll highlight the three key methods that make it work.

First, when you pass a list of items to be added to your cart, the fetcher attempts to transition each item from the state of AVAILABLE to IN_CART. If at any point this operation fails (if any one item can't be added to the cart), the entire operation is rolled back. Have a look at the add_to_cart method that you invoked earlier:

```
def add_to_cart(order_id, *items)
  item_selectors = []
  items.each do |item|
    item[:quantity].times do
      item_selectors << {:sku => item[:sku]}
    end
  end
  transition_state(order_id, item_selectors,
      {:from => AVAILABLE, :to => IN_CART})
end
```

The *items syntax in the method arguments allows the user to pass in any number of objects, which are placed in an array called items. This method doesn't do much. It takes the specification for items to add to the cart and expands the quantities so that one item selector exists for each physical item that will be added to the cart. For instance, this document, which says that you want to add two shovels

```
{:sku => "shovel", :quantity => 2}
```

becomes this:

```
[{:sku => "shovel"}, {:sku => "shovel"}]
```

You need a separate query selector for each item you want to add to your cart. Thus, the method passes the array of item selectors to another method called transition _state. For example, the previous code specifies that the state should be transitioned from AVAILABLE to IN_CART:

```
def transition_state(order_id, selectors, opts={})
  items_transitioned = []
  begin # use a begin/end block so we can do error recovery

    for selector in selectors do
      query = selector.merge({:state => opts[:from]})
      physical_item = @inventory.find_and_modify({
          :query => query,
          :update => {
            '$set' => {
              :state => opts[:to],        # target state
              :ts => Time.now.utc         # get the current client time
            }
          }
      })
```

```
      if physical_item.nil?
        raise InventoryFetchFailure
      end

      items_transitioned << physical_item['_id']    # push item into array
      @orders.update_one({:_id => order_id}, {
          '$push' => {
            :item_ids => physical_item['_id']
          }
      })
    end # of for loop
  rescue Mongo::OperationFailure, InventoryFetchFailure
    rollback(order_id, items_transitioned, opts[:from], opts[:to])
    raise InventoryFetchFailure, "Failed to add #{selector[:sku]}"
  end

  return items_transitioned.size
end
```

To transition state, each selector gets an extra condition, {:state => AVAILABLE}, and the selector is then passed to findAndModify, which, if matched, sets a timestamp and the item's new state. The method then saves the list of items transitioned and updates the order with the ID of the item just added.

GRACEFUL FAILURE

If the findAndModify command fails and returns nil, then you raise an Inventory-FetchFailure exception. If the command fails because of networking errors, you rescue the inevitable Mongo::OperationFailure exception. In both cases, you rescue by rolling back all the items transitioned thus far and then raise an InventoryFetch-Failure, which includes the SKU of the item that couldn't be added. You can then rescue this exception on the application layer to fail gracefully for the user.

All that now remains is to examine the rollback code:

```
def rollback(order_id, item_ids, old_state, new_state)
  @orders.update_one({"_id" => order_id},
             {"$pullAll" => {:item_ids => item_ids}})

  item_ids.each do |id|
    @inventory. find_one_and_update({
        :query => {
          "_id" => id,
          :state => new_state
        }
      },
      {
        :update => {
          "$set" => {
            :state => old_state,
            :ts => Time.now.utc
          }
        }
      })
  end
end
```

You use the $pullAll operator to remove all of the IDs just added to the order's item_ids array. You then iterate over the list of item IDs and transition each one back to its old state. The $pullAll operator as well as many other array update operators are covered in further detail in section 7.4.2.

The transition_state method can be used as the basis for other methods that move items through their successive states. It wouldn't be difficult to integrate this into the order transition system that you built in the previous subsection, but that must be left as an exercise for the reader.

One scenario ignored in this implementation is the case when it's impossible to roll back all the inventory items to their original state. This could occur if the Ruby driver was unable to communicate with MongoDB, or if the process running the roll-back halted before completing. This would leave inventory items in an IN_CART state, but the orders collection wouldn't have the inventory. In such cases managing transactions becomes difficult. These could eventually be fixed, however, by the shopping cart timeout mentioned earlier that removes items that have been in the shopping cart longer than some specified period.

You may justifiably ask whether this system is robust enough for production. This question can't be answered easily without knowing more particulars, but what can be stated assuredly is that MongoDB provides enough features to permit a usable solution when you need transaction-like behavior. MongoDB was never intended to support transactions with multiple collections, but it allows the user to emulate such behavior with find_one_and_update and optimistic concurrency control. If you find yourself attempting to manage transactions often, it may be worth rethinking your schema or even using a different database. Not every application fits with MongoDB, but if you carefully plan your schema you can often obviate your need for such transactions.

7.4 Nuts and bolts: MongoDB updates and deletes

To understand updates in MongoDB, you need a holistic understanding of MongoDB's document model and query language, and the examples in the preceding sections are great for helping with that. But here, as promised in this chapter's introduction, we get down to brass tacks. This mostly involves brief summaries of each feature of the MongoDB update interface, but we also include several notes on performance. For brevity's sake, most of the upcoming examples will be in JavaScript.

7.4.1 Update types and options

As we've shown in our earlier examples, MongoDB supports both targeted updates and updates via replacement. The former are defined by the use of one or more update operators; the latter by a document that will be used to replace the document matched by the update's query selector.

Note that an update will fail if the update document is ambiguous. This is a common gotcha with MongoDB and an easy mistake to make given the syntax. Here, we've combined an update operator, $addToSet, with replacement-style semantics, {name: "Pitchfork"}:

```
db.products.update_one({}, {name: "Pitchfork", $addToSet: {tags: 'cheap'}})
```

If your intention is to change the document's name, you must use the $set operator:

```
db.products.update_one({},
  {$set: {name: "Pitchfork"}, $addToSet: {tags: 'cheap'}})
```

MULTIDOCUMENT UPDATES

An update will, by default, only update the first document matched by its query selector. To update all matching documents, you need to explicitly specify a multidocument update. In the shell, you can express this by adding the parameter multi: true. Here's how you'd add the cheap tags to all documents in the products collection:

```
db.products.update({}, {$addToSet: {tags: 'cheap'}}, {multi: true})
```

Updates are atomic at a document level, which means that a statement that has to update 10 documents might fail for some reason after updating the first 3 of them. The application has to deal with such failures according to its policy.

With the Ruby driver (and most other drivers), you can express multidocument updates in a similar manner:

```
@products.update_one({},
    {'$addToSet' => {'tags' => 'cheap'}},
    {:multi => true})
```

UPSERTS

It's common to need to insert an item if it doesn't exist but update it if it does. You can handle this normally tricky-to-implement pattern using upserts. If the query selector matches, the update takes place normally. But if no document matches the query selector, a new document will be inserted. The new document's attributes will be a logical merging of the query selector and the targeted update document.[6]

Here's a simple example of an upsert using the shell, setting the upsert: true parameter to allow an upsert:

```
db.products.update({slug: 'hammer'},
                   {$addToSet: {tags: 'cheap'}}, {upsert: true})
```

And here's an equivalent upsert in Ruby:

```
@products.update_one({'slug' => 'hammer'},
  {'$addToSet' => {'tags' => 'cheap'}}, {:upsert => true})
```

---

[6] Note that upserts don't work with replacement-style update documents.

As you'd expect, upserts can insert or update only one document at a time. You'll find upserts incredibly valuable when you need to update atomically and when there's uncertainly about a document's prior existence. For a practical example, see section 7.2.3, which describes adding products to a cart.

7.4.2 Update operators

MongoDB supports a host of update operators. Here we provide brief examples of each of them.

STANDARD UPDATE OPERATORS
This first set of operators is the most generic, and each works with almost any data type.

$INC
You use the $inc operator to increment or decrement a numeric value:

```
db.products.update({slug: "shovel"}, {$inc: {review_count: 1}})
db.users.update({username: "moe"}, {$inc: {password_retries: -1}})
```

You can also use $inc to add or subtract from numbers arbitrarily:

```
db.readings.update({_id: 324}, {$inc: {temp: 2.7435}})
```

$inc is as efficient as it is convenient. Because it rarely changes the size of a document, an $inc usually occurs in-place on disk, thus affecting only the value pair specified.[7] The previous statement is only true for the MMAPv1 storage engine. The WiredTiger storage engine works differently as it uses a write-ahead transaction log in combination with checkpoints to ensure data persistence.

As demonstrated in the code for adding products to a shopping cart, $inc works with upserts. For example, you can change the preceding update to an upsert like this:

```
db.readings.update({_id: 324}, {$inc: {temp: 2.7435}}, {upsert: true})
```

If no reading with an _id of 324 exists, a new document will be created with that _id and a temp with the value of the $inc, 2.7435.

$SET AND $UNSET
If you need to set the value of a particular key in a document, you'll want to use $set. You can set a key to a value having any valid BSON type. This means that all of the following updates are possible:

```
db.readings.update({_id: 324}, {$set: {temp: 97.6}})
db.readings.update({_id: 325}, {$set: {temp: {f: 212, c: 100}}})
db.readings.update({_id: 326}, {$set: {temps: [97.6, 98.4, 99.1]}})
```

If the key being set already exists, then its value will be overwritten; otherwise, a new key will be created.

---

[7] Exceptions to this rule arise when the numeric type changes. If the $inc results in a 32-bit integer being converted to a 64-bit integer, then the entire BSON document will have to be rewritten in-place.

$unset removes the provided key from a document. Here's how to remove the temp key from the reading document:

```
db.readings.update({_id: 324}, {$unset: {temp: 1}})
```

You can also use $unset on embedded documents and on arrays. In both cases, you specify the inner object using dot notation. If you have these two documents in your collection

```
{_id: 325, 'temp': {f: 212, c: 100}}
{_id: 326, temps: [97.6, 98.4, 99.1]}
```

then you can remove the Fahrenheit reading in the first document and the "zeroth" element in the second document like this:

```
db.readings.update({_id: 325}, {$unset: {'temp.f': 1}})
db.readings.update({_id: 326}, {$pop: {temps: -1}})
```

This dot notation for accessing subdocuments and array elements can also be used with $set.

> ### Using $unset with arrays
> Note that using $unset on individual array elements may not work exactly as you want it to. Instead of removing the element altogether, it merely sets that element's value to null. To completely remove an array element, see the $pull and $pop operators:
>
> ```
> db.readings.update({_id: 325}, {$unset: {'temp.f': 1}})
> db.readings.update({_id: 326}, {$unset: {'temps.0': 1}})
> ```

$RENAME
If you need to change the name of a key, use $rename:

```
db.readings.update({_id: 324}, {$rename: {'temp': 'temperature'}})
```

You can also rename a subdocument:

```
db.readings.update({_id: 325}, {$rename: {'temp.f': 'temp.fahrenheit'}})
```

$SETONINSERT
During an upsert, you sometimes need to be careful not to overwrite data that you care about. In this case it would be useful to specify that you only want to modify a field when the document is new, and you perform an insert, not when an update occurs. This is where the $setOnInsert operator comes in:

```
db.products.update({slug: 'hammer'}, {
    $inc: {
      quantity: 1
    },
```

```
  $setOnInsert: {
    state: 'AVAILABLE'
  }
}, {upsert: true})
```

You want to increment the quantity for a certain inventory item without interfering with `state`, which has a default value of `'AVAILABLE'`. If an insert is performed, then `qty` will be set to 1, and state will be set to its default value. If an update is performed, then only the increment to `qty` occurs. The `$setOnInsert` operator was added in MongoDB v2.4 to handle this case.

ARRAY UPDATE OPERATORS

The centrality of arrays in MongoDB's document model should be apparent. Naturally, MongoDB provides a handful of update operators that apply exclusively to arrays.

$PUSH, $PUSHALL, AND $EACH

If you need to append values to an array, `$push` is your friend. By default, it will add a single element to the end of an array. For example, adding a new tag to the shovel product is easy enough:

```
db.products.update({slug: 'shovel'}, {$push: {tags: 'tools'}})
```

If you need to add a few tags in the same update, you can use `$each` in conjunction with `$push`:

```
db.products.update({slug: 'shovel'},
  {$push: {tags: {$each: ['tools', 'dirt', 'garden']}}})
```

Note you can push values of any type onto an array, not just scalars. For an example, see the code in section 7.3.2 that pushed a product onto the shopping cart's line items array.

Prior to MongoDB version 2.4, you pushed multiple values onto an array by using the `$pushAll` operator. This approach is still possible in 2.4 and later versions, but it's considered deprecated and should be avoided if possible because `$pushAll` may be removed completely in the future. A `$pushAll` operation can be run like this:

```
db.products.update({slug: 'shovel'},
  {$pushAll: {'tags': ['tools', 'dirt', 'garden']}})
```

$SLICE

The `$slice` operator was added in MongoDB v2.4 to make it easier to manage arrays of values with frequent updates. It's useful when you want to push values onto an array but don't want the array to grow too big. It must be used in conjunction with the `$push` and `$each` operators, and it allows you to truncate the resulting array to a certain size, removing older versions first. The argument passed to `$slice` is an integer that must be less than or equal to zero. The value of this argument is -1 times the number of items that should remain in the array after the update.

These semantics can be confusing, so let's look at a concrete example. Suppose you want to update a document that looks like this:

```
{
  _id: 326,
  temps: [92, 93, 94]
}
```

You update this document with this command:

```
db.temps.update({_id: 326}, {
    $push: {
      temps: {
        $each: [95, 96],
        $slice: -4
      }
    }
  })
```

Beautiful syntax. Here you pass -4 to the $slice operator. After the update, your document looks like this:

```
{
  _id: 326,
  temps: [93, 94, 95, 96]
}
```

After pushing values onto the array, you remove values from the beginning until only four are left. If you'd passed -1 to the $slice operator, the resulting array would be [96]. If you'd passed 0, it would have been [], an empty array. Note also that starting with MongoDB 2.6 you can pass a positive number as well. If a positive number is passed to $slice, it'll remove values from the end of the array instead of the beginning. In the previous example, if you used $slice: 4 your result would've been temps: [92, 93, 94, 95].

$SORT

Like $slice, the $sort operator was added in MongoDB v2.4 to help with updating arrays. When you use $push and $slice, you sometimes want to order the documents before slicing them off from the start of the array. Consider this document:

```
{
  _id: 300,
  temps: [
    { day: 6, temp: 90 },
    { day: 5, temp: 95 }
  ]
}
```

You have an array of subdocuments. When you push a subdocument onto this array and slice it, you first want to make sure it's ordered by day, so you retain the higher day values. You can accomplish this with the following update:

```
db.temps.update({_id: 300}, {
    $push: {
      temps: {
        $each: [
          { day: 7, temp: 92 }
        ],
        $slice: -2,
        $sort: {
          day: 1
        }
      }
    }
  })
```

When this update runs, you first sort the temps array on day so that the lowest value is at the beginning. Then you slice the array down to two values. The result is the two subdocuments with the higher day values:

```
{
  _id: 300,
  temps: [
    { day: 6, temp: 90 },
    { day: 7, temp: 92 }
  ]
}
```

Used in this context, the $sort operator requires a $push, an $each, and a $slice. Though useful, this definitely handles a corner case, and you may not find yourself using the $sort update operator often.

$ADDTOSET AND $EACH

$addToSet also appends a value to an array, but it does so in a more discerning way: the value is added only if it doesn't already exist in the array. Thus, if your shovel has already been tagged as a tool, then the following update won't modify the document at all:

```
db.products.update({slug: 'shovel'}, {$addToSet: {'tags': 'tools'}})
```

If you need to add more than one value to an array uniquely in the same operation, you must use $addToSet with the $each operator. Here's how that looks:

```
db.products.update({slug: 'shovel'},
  {$addToSet: {tags: {$each: ['tools', 'dirt', 'steel']}}})
```

Only those values in $each that don't already exist in tags will be appended. Note that $each can only be used with the $addToSet and $push operators.

$POP

The most elementary way to remove an item from an array is with the $pop operator. If $push appends an item to an array, a subsequent $pop will remove that last item pushed. Though it's frequently used with $push, you can use $pop on its own. If your tags array contains the values ['tools', 'dirt', 'garden', 'steel'], then the following $pop will remove the steel tag:

```
db.products.update({slug: 'shovel'}, {$pop: {'tags': 1}})
```

Like $unset, $pop's syntax is {$pop: {'elementToRemove': 1}}. But unlike $unset, $pop takes a second possible value of -1 to remove the first element of the array. Here's how to remove the tools tag from the array:

```
db.products.update({slug: 'shovel'}, {$pop: {'tags': -1}})
```

One possible point of frustration is that you can't return the value that $pop removes from the array. Thus, despite its name, $pop doesn't work exactly like the stack operation you might have in mind.

$BIT

If you ever use bitwise operations in your application code, you may find yourself wishing that you could use the same operations in an update. Bitwise operations are used to perform logic on a value at the individual bit level. One common case (particularly in C programming) is to use bitwise operations to pass flags through a variable. In other words, if the fourth bit in an integer is 1, then some condition applies. There's often a clearer and more usable way to handle these operations, but this kind of storage does keep size to a minimum and matches how existing systems work. MongoDB includes the $bit operator to make bitwise OR and AND operations possible in updates.

Let's look at an example of storing bit-sensitive values in MongoDB and manipulating them in an update. Unix file permissions are often stored in this way. If you run ls -l in a Unix system, you'll see flags like drwxr-xr-x. The first flag, d, indicates the file is a directory. r denotes read permissions, w denotes write permissions, and x denotes execute permissions. There are three blocks of these flags, denoting these permissions for the user, the user's group, and everyone, respectively. Thus the example given says that the user has all permissions but others have only read and execute permissions.

A permission block is sometimes described with a single number, according to the spacing of these flags in the binary system. The x value is 1, the w value is 2, and the r value is 4. Thus you can use 7 to indicate a binary 111, or rwx. You can use 5 to indicate a binary 101, or r-x. And you can use 3 to indicate a binary 011, or -wx.

Let's store a variable in MongoDB that uses these characteristics. Start with the document:

```
{
  _id: 16,
  permissions: 4
}
```

The 4 in this case denotes binary 100, or r--. You can use a bitwise OR operation to add write permissions:

```
db.permissions.update({_id: 16}, {$bit: {permissions: {or: NumberInt(2)}}})
```

In the JavaScript shell you must use `NumberInt()` because it uses doubles for number by default. The resulting document contains a binary `100` ORed with a binary `010`, resulting in `110`, which is decimal `6`:

```
{
  _id: 16,
  permissions: 6
}
```

You can also use and instead of or, for a bit-wise AND operation. This is another corner-case operator, which you might not use often but that can be useful in certain situations.

$PULL AND $PULLALL

`$pull` is `$pop`'s more sophisticated cousin. With `$pull`, you specify exactly which array element to remove by value, not by position. Returning to the tags example, if you need to remove the tag `dirt`, you don't need to know where in the array it's located; you simply tell the `$pull` operator to remove it:

```
db.products.update({slug: 'shovel'}, {$pull: {tags: 'dirt'}})
```

`$pullAll` works similarly to `$pushAll`, allowing you to provide a list of values to remove. To remove both the tags `dirt` and `garden`, you can use `$pullAll` like this:

```
db.products.update({slug: 'shovel'},
  {$pullAll: {'tags': ['dirt', 'garden']}})
```

A powerful feature of `$pull` is the fact that you can pass in a query as an argument to choose which elements are pulled. Consider the document:

```
{_id: 326, temps: [97.6, 98.4, 100.5, 99.1, 101.2]}
```

Suppose you want to remove temperatures greater than 100. A query to do so might look like this:

```
db.readings.update({_id: 326}, {$pull: {temps: {$gt: 100}}})
```

This alters the document to the following:

```
{_id: 326, temps: [97.6, 98.4, 99.1]}
```

POSITIONAL UPDATES

It's common to model data in MongoDB using an array of subdocuments, but it wasn't so easy to manipulate those subdocuments until the positional operator came along. The positional operator allows you to update a subdocument in an array identified by using dot notation in your query selector. For example, suppose you have an order document that looks like this:

```
{
  _id: ObjectId("6a5b1476238d3b4dd5000048"),
  line_items: [
```

```
    {
      _id: ObjectId("4c4b1476238d3b4dd5003981"),
      sku: "9092",
      name: "Extra Large Wheelbarrow",
      quantity: 1,
      pricing: {
        retail: 5897,
        sale: 4897
      }
    },
    {
      _id: ObjectId("4c4b1476238d3b4dd5003982"),
      sku: "10027",
      name: "Rubberized Work Glove, Black",
      quantity: 2,
      pricing: {
        retail: 1499,
        sale: 1299
      }
    }
  ]
}
```

You want to be able to set the quantity of the second line item, with the SKU of 10027, to 5. The problem is that you don't know where in the line_items array this particular subdocument resides. You don't even know whether it exists. You can use a simple query selector and the positional operator to solve both these problems:

```
query = {
  _id: ObjectId("6a5b1476238d3b4dd5000048"),
  'line_items.sku': "10027"
}
update = {
  $set: {
    'line_items.$.quantity': 5
  }
}
db.orders.update(query, update)
```

The positional operator is the $ that you see in the line_items.$.quantity string. If the query selector matches, then the index of the document having a SKU of 10027 will replace the positional operator internally, thereby updating the correct document.

If your data model includes subdocuments, you'll find the positional operator useful for performing nuanced document updates.

7.4.3 The findAndModify command

With so many fleshed-out examples of using the findAndModify command earlier in this chapter, it only remains to enumerate its options when using it in the JavaScript shell. Here's an example of a simple findAndModify:

```
doc = db.orders.findAndModify({
    query: {
      user_id: ObjectId("4c4b1476238d3b4dd5000001"),
    },
    update: {
      $set: {
        state: "AUTHORIZING"
      }
    }
})
```

There are a number of options for altering this command's functionality. Of the following, the only options required are `query` and either `update` or `remove`:

- `query`—A document query selector. Defaults to `{}`.
- `update`—A document specifying an update. Defaults to `{}`.
- `remove`—A Boolean value that, when `true`, removes the object and then returns it. Defaults to `false`.
- `new`—A Boolean that, if `true`, returns the modified document as it appears after the update has been applied. Defaults to `false`, meaning the original document is returned.
- `sort`—A document specifying a sort direction. Because `findAndModify` will modify only one document at a time, the `sort` option can be used to help control which matching document is processed. For example, you might sort by `{created_at: -1}` to process the most recently created matching document.
- `fields`—If you only need to return a subset of fields, use this option to specify them. This is especially helpful with larger documents. The fields are specified as they'd be in any query. See the section on fields in chapter 5 for examples.
- `upsert`—A Boolean that, when `true`, treats `findAndModify` as an upsert. If the document sought doesn't exist, it will be created. Note that if you want to return the newly created document, you also need to specify `{new: true}`.

7.4.4 Deletes

You'll be relieved to learn that removing documents poses few challenges. You can remove an entire collection or you can pass a query selector to the `remove` method to delete only a subset of a collection. Deleting all reviews is simple:

```
db.reviews.remove({})
```

But it's much more common to delete only the reviews of a particular user:

```
db.reviews.remove({user_id: ObjectId('4c4b1476238d3b4dd5000001')})
```

All calls to `remove` take an optional query specifier for selecting exactly which documents to delete. As far as the API goes, that's all there is to say. But you'll have a few questions surrounding the concurrency and atomicity of these operations. We'll explain that in the next section.

7.4.5 *Concurrency, atomicity, and isolation*

It's important to understand how concurrency works in MongoDB. Prior to MongoDB v2.2, the locking strategy was rather coarse; a single global reader-writer lock reigned over the entire mongod instance. What this meant that at any moment in time, MongoDB permitted either one writer or multiple readers (but not both). In MongoDB v2.2 this was changed to a database-level lock, meaning these semantics apply at the database level rather than throughout the entire MongoDB instance; a database can have either one writer or multiple readers. In MongoDB v3.0, the WiredTiger storage engine works on the collection level and offers document-level locking. Other storage engines may offer other characteristics.

The locking characteristics sound a lot worse than they are in practice because quite a few concurrency optimizations exist around this lock. One is that the database keeps an internal map of which documents are in RAM. For requests to read or write documents not in RAM, the database yields to other operations until the document can be paged into memory.

A second optimization is the yielding of write locks. The issue is that if any one write takes a long time to complete, all other read and write operations will be blocked for the duration of the original write. All inserts, updates, and removes take a write lock. Inserts rarely take a long time to complete. But updates that affect, say, an entire collection, as well as deletes that affect a lot of documents, can run long. The current solution to this is to allow these long-running ops to yield periodically for other readers and writers. When an operation yields, it pauses itself, releases its lock, and resumes later.

Despite these optimizations, MongoDB's locking can affect performance in workloads where there are both heavy reads and heavy writes. A good but naive way to avoid trouble is to place heavily trafficked collections in separate databases, especially when you're using the MMAPv1 storage engine. But as mentioned earlier, the situation with MongoDB v3.0 is a lot better because WiredTiger works on the collection level instead of the database level.

When you're updating and removing documents, this yielding behavior can be a mixed blessing. It's easy to imagine situations where you'd want all documents updated or removed before any other operation takes place. For these cases, you can use a special option called $isolated to keep the operation from yielding. You add the $isolated operator to the query selector like this:

```
db.reviews.remove({user_id: ObjectId('4c4b1476238d3b4dd5000001'),
  $isolated: true})
```

The same can be applied to any multi-update. This forces the entire multi-update to complete in isolation:

```
db.reviews.update({$isolated: true}, {$set: {rating: 0}}, {multi: true})
```

This update sets each review's rating to 0. Because the operation happens in isolation, the operation will never yield, ensuring a consistent view of the system at all times.

Note that if an operation using $isolated fails halfway through, there's no implicit rollback. Half the documents will have been updated while the other half will still have their original value. Prior to MongoDB v2.2 the $isolated operator was called $atomic, a name that was deprecated presumably because these operations aren't classically atomic in this failure scenario. This, combined with the fact that the $isolated operator doesn't work in sharded collections, means that you should use it with care.

7.4.6 Update performance notes

The following information only applies to the MMAPv1 storage engine, which is currently the default storage engine. Chapter 10 talks about WiredTiger, which works differently and more efficiently than MMAPv1. If you're curious about WiredTiger, you're free to read chapter 10 right now!

Experience shows that having a basic mental model of how updates affect a document on disk helps users design systems with better performance. The first thing you should understand is the degree to which an update can be said to happen "in-place." Ideally, an update will affect the smallest portion of a BSON document on disk because this leads to the greatest efficiency. But this isn't always what happens.

There are essentially three kinds of updates to a document on disk. The first, and most efficient, takes place when only a single value is updated and the size of the overall BSON document doesn't change. This often happens with the $inc operator. Because $inc is only incrementing an integer, the size of that value on disk won't change. If the integer represents an int, it'll always take up four bytes on disk; long integers and doubles will require eight bytes. But altering the values of these numbers doesn't require any more space and, therefore, only that one value within the document must be rewritten on disk.

The second kind of update changes the size or structure of a document. A BSON document is literally represented as a byte array, and the first four bytes of the document always store the document's size. Thus, if you use the $push operator on a document, you're both increasing the overall document's size and changing its structure. This requires that the entire document be rewritten on disk. This isn't going to be horribly inefficient, but it's worth keeping in mind. But if you have extremely large documents—say, around 4 MB—and you're pushing values onto arrays in those documents, that's potentially a lot of work on the server side. This means that if you intend to do a lot of updates, it's best to keep your documents small.

The final kind of update is a consequence of rewriting a document. If a document is enlarged and can no longer fit in its allocated space on disk, not only does it need to be rewritten, but it must also be moved to a new space. This moving operation can be potentially expensive if it occurs often. MongoDB attempts to mitigate this by dynamically adjusting a padding factor on a per-collection basis. This means that if, within a given collection, lots of updates are taking place that require documents to be relocated, the internal padding factor will be increased. The padding factor is multiplied by the size of each inserted document to get the amount of extra space to create beyond the document itself. This may reduce the number of future document relocations. As of MongoDB 2.6, power of 2 is used to size the initial allocation of a new document, which is more efficient than the method described in this paragraph. Additionally, MongoDB 3.0 uses the power of 2 sizes allocation as the default record allocation strategy for MMAPv1.

To see a given collection's padding factor, run the collection stats command:

```
db.tweets.stats()
{
  "ns" : "twitter.tweets",
  "count" : 53641,
  "size" : 85794884,
  "avgObjSize" : 1599.4273783113663,
  "storageSize" : 100375552,
  "numExtents" : 12,
  "nindexes" : 3,
  "lastExtentSize" : 21368832,
  "paddingFactor" : 1.2,
  "flags" : 0,
  "totalIndexSize" : 7946240,
  "indexSizes" : {
    "_id_" : 2236416,
    "user.friends_count_1" : 1564672,
    "user.screen_name_1_user.created_at_-1" : 4145152
  },
  "ok" : 1
}
```

This collection of tweets has a padding factor of 1.2, which indicates that when a 100-byte document is inserted, MongoDB will allocate 120 bytes on disk. The default padding value is 1, which indicates that no extra space will be allocated.

Now, a brief word of warning. The considerations mentioned here apply especially to deployments where the data size exceeds RAM or where an extreme write load is expected. In these cases, rewriting or moving a document carries a particularly high cost. As you scale your MongoDB applications, think carefully about the best way to use update operations like $inc to avoid these costs.

7.5   *Reviewing update operators*

Table 7.1 lists the update operators we've discussed previously in this chapter.

Table 7.1 Operators

Operators	
$inc	Increment fields by given values.
$set	Set fields to the given values.
$unset	Unset the passed-in fields.
$rename	Rename fields to the given values.
$setOnInsert	In an upsert, set fields only when an insert occurs.
$bit	It performs a bitwise update of a field.
Array Operators	
$	Update the subdocument at the position discovered by the query selector.
$push	Add a value to an array.
$pushAll	Add an array of values to an array. Deprecated in favor of $each.
$addToSet	Add a value to an array but do nothing if it's a duplicate.
$pop	Remove first or last item from an array.
$pull	Remove values from an array that match a given query.
$pullAll	Remove multiple values from an array.
Array Operator Modifiers	
$each	Used with $push and $addToSet to apply these operators to multiple values.
$slice	Used with $push and $each to slice the updated array down to a certain size.
$sort	Used with $push, $each, and $slice to sort subdocuments in an array before slicing.
Isolation Operators	
$isolated	Don't allow other operations to interleave with an update of multiple documents.

7.6   *Summary*

We've covered a lot in this chapter. The variety of updates may at first feel like a lot to take in, but the power that these updates represent should be reassuring. The fact is that MongoDB's update language is as sophisticated as its query language. You can update a simple document as easily as you can a complex, nested structure. When needed, you can atomically update individual documents and, in combination with findAndModify, build transactional workflows.

If you've finished this chapter and feel like you can apply the examples here on your own, you're well on your way to becoming a MongoDB guru.

Part 3

MongoDB mastery

Having read the first two parts of the book, you should understand MongoDB quite well from a developer's perspective. Now it's time to switch roles. In this final part of the book, we'll look at MongoDB from the database administrator's perspective. This means we'll cover all the things you need to know about performance, deployments, fault tolerance, and scalability.

To get the best performance from MongoDB, you have to design efficient queries and then ensure that they're properly indexed. This is what you'll learn in chapter 8. You'll see why indexes are important, and you'll learn how they're chosen and then traversed by the query optimizer. You'll also learn how to use helpful tools like the query explainer and the profiler.

You'll find that many of the queries you're creating and optimizing have to do with searching for text. To make this easier and more powerful, MongoDB has some text search–specific features that we'll cover in chapter 9. These features will allow you to write queries that intelligently search for words and phrases similar to your search term, among other things.

Chapter 10 is about the WiredTiger storage engine. Chapter 11 is devoted to replication. You'll spend most of this chapter learning how replica sets work and how to deploy them intelligently for high availability and automatic failover. In addition, you'll learn how to use replication to scale application reads and to customize the durability of writes.

Horizontal scalability is the Holy Grail for modern database systems; MongoDB scales horizontally by partitioning data in a process known as sharding. Chapter 12 presents sharding theory and practice, showing you when to use it, how to design schemas around it, and how to deploy it.

The last chapter describes the niceties of deployment and administration. In chapter 13 we'll look at specific hardware and operating system recommendations. You'll then learn how to back up, monitor, and troubleshoot live MongoDB clusters.

Indexing and query optimization

This chapter covers

- Basic indexing concepts and theory
- Practical advice for managing indexes
- Using compound indexes for more complex queries
- Optimizing queries
- All the MongoDB indexing options

Indexes are enormously important. With the right indexes in place, MongoDB can use its hardware efficiently and serve your application's queries quickly. But the wrong indexes produce the opposite result: slow queries, slow writes, and poorly utilized hardware. It stands to reason that anyone wanting to use MongoDB effectively must understand indexing.

But for many developers, indexes are a topic shrouded in mystery. This need not be the case. Once you've finished this chapter, you should have a good mental model for thinking clearly about indexes. To introduce the concepts of indexing, we'll begin with a modest thought experiment. We'll then explore some core indexing concepts and provide an overview of the B-tree data structure underlying MongoDB indexes.

Then it's on to indexing in practice. We'll discuss unique, sparse, and multikey indexes, and provide a number of pointers on index administration. Next, we'll delve into query optimization, describing how to use `explain()` and work harmoniously with the query optimizer.

In versions 2.0, 2.4, 2.6, and 3.0, MongoDB gained more advanced indexing techniques. Most queries only require indexes that match a field's value or a range of values. But you may also want to run a query for words that are similar to a given word. This requires a text index, which is covered in chapter 9. Or perhaps you'd like to use a spatial index to find documents with latitude and longitude values near a given point. This chapter is intended to give you a good understanding of indexing fundamentals so that you'll be able to create indexes and use them effectively to optimize your queries.

8.1   Indexing theory

We'll proceed gradually, beginning with an extended analogy and ending with an exposition of some of MongoDB's key implementation details. Along the way, we'll define and provide examples of a number of important terms. If you're not familiar with compound-key indexes, virtual memory, and index data structures, you should find this section helpful.

8.1.1   A thought experiment

To understand indexing, you need a picture in your head. Imagine a cookbook. And not just any cookbook—a massive cookbook: 5,000 pages long with the most delicious recipes for every occasion, cuisine, and season, with all the good ingredients you might find at home. This is the cookbook to end them all. Let's call it *The Cookbook Omega*.

Although this might be the best of all possible cookbooks, there are two tiny problems with *The Cookbook Omega*. The first is that the recipes are in random order. On page 3,475 you have Australian Braised Duck, and on page 2 you'll find Zacatecan Tacos.

That would be manageable, were it not for the second problem: *The Cookbook Omega* has no index.

Here's the first question to ask yourself: with no index, how do you find the recipe for Rosemary Potatoes in *The Cookbook Omega*? Your only choice is to scan through every page of the book until you find the recipe. If the recipe is on page 3,973, that's how many pages you have to look through. In the worst case, where the recipe is on the last page, you have to look at every single page.

That would be madness. The solution is to build an index.

A SIMPLE INDEX

There are several ways you can imagine searching for a recipe, but the recipe's name is probably a good place to start. If you create an alphabetical listing of each recipe name followed by its page number, you'll have indexed the book by recipe name. A few entries might look like this:

- Tibetan Yak Soufflé: 45
- Toasted Sesame Dumplings: 4,011
- Turkey à la King: 943

As long as you know the name of the recipe (or even the first few letters of that name), you can use this index to quickly find any recipe in the book. If that's the only way you expect to search for recipes, your work is done.

But this is unrealistic because you can also imagine wanting to find recipes based on, say, the ingredients you have in your pantry. Or perhaps you want to search by cuisine. For those cases, you need more indexes.

Here's a second question: with only one index on the recipe name, how do you find all the cauliflower recipes? Again, lacking the proper indexes, you'd have to scan the entire book, all 5,000 pages. This is true for any search on ingredients or cuisine.

You need to build another index, this time on ingredients. In this index, you have an alphabetical listing of ingredients, each pointing to all the page numbers of recipes containing that ingredient. The most basic index on ingredients would look like this:

- Cashews: 3; 20; 42; 88; 103; 1,215…
- Cauliflower: 2; 47; 88; 89; 90; 275…
- Currants: 1,001; 1,050; 2,000; 2,133…

Is this the index you thought you were going to get? Is it even helpful?

A COMPOUND INDEX

This index is good if all you need is a list of recipes for a given ingredient. But if you want to include any other information about the recipe in your search, you still have some scanning to do—once you know the page numbers where cauliflower is referenced, you then need to go to each of those pages to get the name of the recipe and what type of cuisine it is. This is better than paging through the whole book, but you can do better.

For example, imagine that you randomly discovered a great cauliflower recipe in *The Cookbook Omega* several months ago but you've forgotten its name; you suspect that you'll recognize it when you see it. As of now, you have two indexes, one on recipe name and the other on ingredients. Can you think of a way to use these two indexes in combination to find your long-lost cauliflower recipe?

In fact, this is impossible. If you start with the index on recipe name, but don't remember the name of the recipe, then searching this index is little better than paging through the entire book. If you start with the index on ingredients, then you'll have a list of page numbers to check, but those page numbers can in no way be plugged into the index on recipe name. Therefore, you can only use one index in this case, and it happens that the one on ingredients is more helpful.

One index per query

Users commonly believe that a query on two fields can be resolved using two separate indexes on those fields. An algorithm exists for this: look up the page numbers in each index matching each term, and then scan the intersection of those pages for the individual recipes matching both terms. A number of pages won't match, but you'll still narrow down the total number of scanned items. Index intersection was first supported by version 2.6 of MongoDB. Note that whether the use of a compound index or the use of an index intersection is more efficient depends on the particular query and the system. Also, keep in mind that the database will use a single index per query if possible and that if you're going to be querying on more than one field frequently, ensure that a compound index for those fields exists.

What can you do? Happily, there's a solution to the long-lost cauliflower recipe, and its answer lies in the use of compound indexes.

The two indexes you've created so far are single-key indexes: they both order only one key from each recipe. You're going to build yet another index for *The Cookbook Omega*, but this time, instead of using one key per index, you'll use two. Indexes that use more than one key like this are called *compound indexes*.

This compound index uses both ingredients and recipe name, in that order. You'll notate the index like this: `ingredient-name`. Part of this index would look like what you see in figure 8.1.

The value of this index for a human is obvious. You can now search by ingredient and probably find the recipe you want, even if you remember only the initial part of the name. For a machine, it's still valuable for this use case and will keep the database from having to scan every recipe name listed for that ingredient. This compound index would be especially useful if, as with *The Cookbook Omega*, there were several hundred (or thousand) cauliflower recipes. Can you see why?

One thing to notice: with compound indexes, order matters. Imagine the reverse compound index on `name-ingredient`. Would this index be interchangeable with the compound index we just explored?

Cashews
 Cashew Marinade
  1,215
 Chicken with Cashews
  88
 Rosemary-Roasted Cashews
  103

Cauliflower
 Bacon Cauliflower Salad
  875
 Lemon-baked Cauliflower
  89
 Spicy Cauliflower Cheese Soup
  47

Currants
 Creamed Scones with Currants
  2,000
 Fettuccini with Glazed Duck
  2,133
 Saffron Rice with Currants
  1,050

Figure 8.1 **A compound index inside a cookbook**

Definitely not. With the new index, once you have the recipe name, your search is already limited to a single recipe; a single page in your cookbook. If this index were used on a search for the recipe Cashew Marinade and the ingredient Bananas, the index could confirm that no such recipe exists. But this use case is the opposite one: you know the ingredient, but not the recipe name.

The cookbook now has three indexes: one on `recipe` name, one on `ingredient`, and one on `ingredient-name`. This means that you can safely eliminate the single-key index on `ingredient`. Why? Because a search on a single ingredient can use the index on `ingredient-name`. That is, if you know the ingredient, you can traverse this compound index to get a list of all page numbers containing said ingredient. Look again at the sample entries for this index to see why this is so.

INDEXING RULES

The goal of this section was to present an extended metaphor to provide you with a better mental model of indexes. From this metaphor, you can derive a few simple concepts:

1   Indexes significantly reduce the amount of work required to fetch documents. Without the proper indexes, the only way to satisfy a query is to scan all documents linearly until the query conditions are met. This frequently means scanning entire collections.

2   Only one single-key index will be used to resolve a query.[1] For queries containing multiple keys (say, `ingredient` and `recipe name`), a compound index containing those keys will best resolve the query.

3   An index on `ingredient` can and should be eliminated if you have a second index on `ingredient-name`. More generally, if you have a compound index on `a-b`, then a second index on `a` alone will be redundant, but not one on `b`.

4   The order of keys in a compound index matters.

Bear in mind that this cookbook analogy can be taken only so far. It's a model for understanding indexes, but it doesn't fully correspond to the way MongoDB's indexes work. In the next section, we'll elaborate on the rules of thumb just presented, and we'll explore indexing in MongoDB in detail.

8.1.2   *Core indexing concepts*

The preceding thought experiment hinted at a number of core indexing concepts. Here and throughout the rest of the chapter, we'll unpack those ideas.

SINGLE-KEY INDEXES

With a single-key index, each entry in the index corresponds to a single value from each of the documents indexed. The default index on `_id` is a good example of a single-key index. Because this field is indexed, each document's `_id` also lives in an index for fast retrieval by that field.

---

[1] One exception is queries using the `$or` operator. But as a general rule, this isn't possible, or even desirable, in MongoDB.

COMPOUND-KEY INDEXES

Although when starting with MongoDB 2.6 you can use more than one index for a query, it's best if you use only a single index. But you often need to query on more than one attribute, and you want such a query to be as efficient as possible. For example, imagine that you've built two indexes on the products collection from this book's e-commerce example: one index on `manufacturer` and another on `price`. In this case, you've created two entirely distinct data structures that, when traversed, are ordered like the lists you see in figure 8.2.

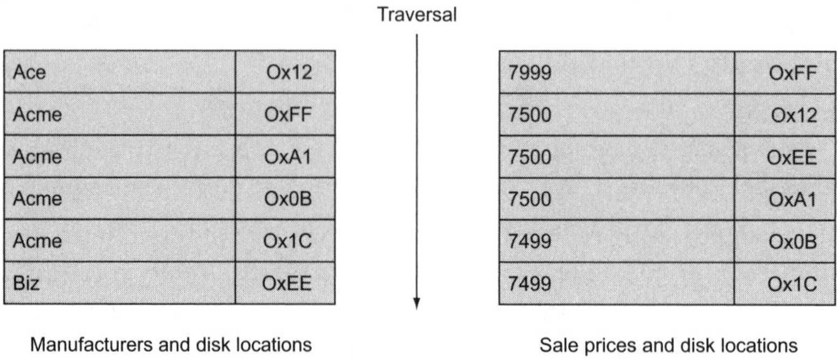

Traversal

Ace	Ox12
Acme	OxFF
Acme	OxA1
Acme	Ox0B
Acme	Ox1C
Biz	OxEE

7999	OxFF
7500	Ox12
7500	OxEE
7500	OxA1
7499	Ox0B
7499	Ox1C

Manufacturers and disk locations   Sale prices and disk locations

Figure 8.2   Single-key index traversal

Now, imagine your query looks like this:

```
db.products.find({
    'details.manufacturer': 'Acme',
    'pricing.sale': {
      $lt: 7500
    }
})
```

This query says to find all Acme products costing less than $75.00. If you issue this query with single-key indexes on `manufacturer` and `price`, only one of them will be used. The query optimizer will pick the more efficient of the two, but neither will give you an ideal result. To satisfy the query using these indexes, you'd have to traverse each structure separately and then grab the list of disk locations that match and calculate their intersection.

A compound index is a single index where each entry is composed of more than one key. If you were to build a *compound-key* index on manufacturer and price, the ordered representation would look like figure 8.3.

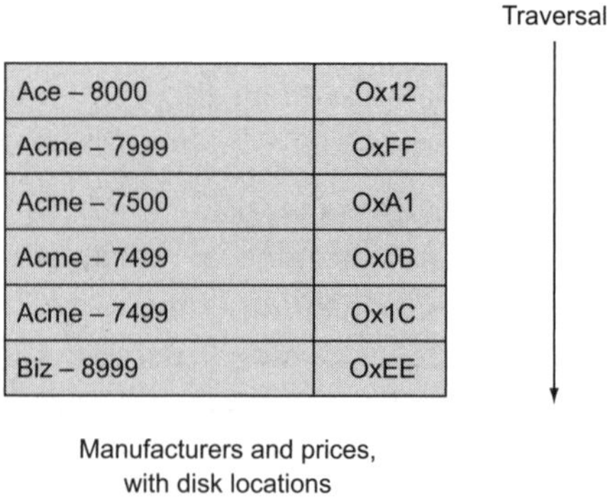

Traversal

Ace – 8000	Ox12
Acme – 7999	OxFF
Acme – 7500	OxA1
Acme – 7499	Ox0B
Acme – 7499	Ox1C
Biz – 8999	OxEE

Manufacturers and prices,
with disk locations

Figure 8.3   Compound-key index traversal

To fulfill your query, the query optimizer only needs to find the first entry in the index where `manufacturer` is `Acme` and `price` is `7500`. From there, the results can be retrieved with a simple scan of the successive index entries, stopping when the value of the manufacturer no longer equals Acme.

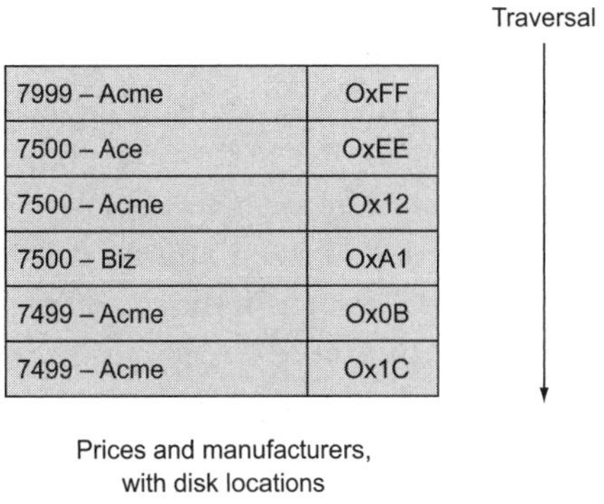

There are two things you should notice about the way this index and query work together. The first is that the order of the index's keys matters. If you'd declared a compound index where `price` was the first key and `manufacturer` the second, then your query would've been far less efficient. Can

	Traversal
7999 – Acme	0xFF
7500 – Ace	0xEE
7500 – Acme	0x12
7500 – Biz	0xA1
7499 – Acme	0x0B
7499 – Acme	0x1C

Prices and manufacturers, with disk locations

Figure 8.4 A compound-key index with the keys reversed

you see why? Take a look at the structure of the entries in such an index in figure 8.4.

Keys must be compared in the order in which they appear. Unfortunately, this index doesn't provide an easy way to jump to all the Acme products, so the only way to fulfill your query would be to look at every product whose price is less than $75.00 and then select only those products made by Acme. To put this in perspective, imagine that your collection had a million products, all priced under $100.00 and evenly distributed by price. Under these circumstances, fulfilling your query would require that you scan 750,000 index entries. By contrast, using the original compound index, where `manufacturer` precedes `price`, the number of entries scanned would be the same as the number of entries returned. This is because once you've arrived at the entry for (`Acme - 7500`), it's a simple, in-order scan to serve the query.

The order of keys in a compound index matters. If that seems clear, the second thing you should understand is why we've chosen the first ordering over the second. This may be obvious from the diagrams, but there's another way to look at the problem. Look again at the query: the two query terms specify different kinds of matches. On `manufacturer`, you want to match the term exactly. But on `price`, you want to match a range of values, beginning with 7500. As a general rule, a query where one term demands an exact match and another specifies a range requires a compound index where the range key comes second. We'll revisit this idea in the section on query optimization.

INDEX EFFICIENCY

Although indexes are essential for good query performance, each new index imposes a small maintenance cost. Whenever you add a document to a collection, each index on that collection must be modified to include the new document. If a particular collection has 10 indexes, that makes 10 separate structures to modify on each insert, in addition to writing the document itself. This holds for any write operation, whether you're removing a document, relocating a document because the allocated space isn't enough, or updating a given document's indexed keys.

For read-intensive applications, the cost of indexes is almost always justified. Just realize that indexes do impose a cost and that they therefore must be chosen with care. This means ensuring that all your indexes are used and that none are redundant. You can do this in part by profiling your application's queries; we'll describe this process later in the chapter.

But there's a second consideration. Even with all the right indexes in place, it's still possible that those indexes won't result in faster queries. This occurs when indexes and a working data set don't fit in RAM.

You may recall from chapter 1 that MongoDB tells the operating system to map all data files to memory using the mmap() system call when the MMAPv1 default storage engine is used. As you'll learn in chapter 10, the WiredTiger storage engine works differently. From this point on, the data files, which include all documents, collections, and their indexes, are swapped in and out of RAM by the operating system in 4 KB chunks called pages.[2] Whenever data from a given page is requested, the operating system must ensure that the page is available in RAM. If it's not, a kind of exception known as a *page fault* is raised, and this tells the memory manager to load the page from disk into RAM.

With sufficient RAM, all the data files in use will eventually be loaded into memory. Whenever that memory is altered, as in the case of a write, those changes will be flushed to disk asynchronously by the OS. The write, however, will be fast because it occurs directly in RAM; thus the number of disk accesses is reduced to a minimum. But if the working data set can't fit into RAM, page faults will start to creep up. This means that the operating system will be going to disk frequently, greatly slowing read and write operations. In the worst case, as data size becomes much larger than available RAM, a situation can occur where for any read or write, data must be paged to and from disk. This is known as *thrashing*, and it causes performance to take a severe dive.

Fortunately, this situation is relatively easy to avoid. At a minimum, you need to make sure that your indexes will fit in RAM. This is one reason why it's important to avoid creating any unneeded indexes. With extra indexes in place, more RAM will be required to maintain those indexes. Along the same lines, each index should have only the keys it needs. A triple-key compound index might be necessary at times, but be aware that it'll use more space than a simple single-key index. One example of where it might be valuable to create an index with more than one or two fields is if you can create a covering index for a frequent query. A *covering index* is one where the entire query can be satisfied from reading only the index, making queries very fast. Covering indexes are discussed more at the end of section 8.3.

---

[2] The 4 KB page size is standard but not universal.

Bear in mind that indexes are stored separately in RAM from the data they index and aren't clustered. In a clustered index, the order of the index corresponds directly to the order of the underlying data; if you index recipes by name in a clustered index, then all of the recipes starting with A will be stored together, followed by B, C, and so on. This isn't the case in MongoDB. Every name in the recipe index is essentially duplicated in the index, and the order of these names has no bearing on the order of the data. This is important when you scan through a collection sorted with an index because it means that every document fetched could be anywhere in the data set. There's no guaranteed locality with the previously fetched data.

Ideally, indexes and a working data set fit in RAM. But estimating how much RAM this requires for any given deployment isn't always easy. You can always discover total index size by looking at the results of the `stats` command. The working set is the subset of total data commonly queried and updated, which is different for every application. Suppose you have a million users for which you have data. If only half of them are active (thus half the user documents are queried), then your working set for the user collection is half the total data size. If these documents are evenly distributed throughout the entire data set, though, it's likely that untouched user documents are also being loaded into memory, which imposes a cost.

In chapter 10, we'll revisit the concept of the working set, and we'll look at specific ways to diagnose hardware-related performance issues. For now, be aware of the potential costs of adding new indexes, and keep an eye on the ratio of index and working set size to RAM. Doing so will help you to maintain good performance as your data grows.

8.1.3 B-trees

As mentioned, MongoDB represents most indexes internally as B-trees. B-trees are ubiquitous, having remained in popular use for database records and indexes since at least the late 1970s.[3] If you've used other database systems, you may already be familiar with the various aspects of using B-trees. This is good because it means you can effectively transfer most of your knowledge of indexing. If you don't know much about B-trees, that's okay, too; this section will present the concepts most relevant to your work with MongoDB.

B-trees have two overarching traits that make them ideal for database indexes. First, they facilitate a variety of queries, including exact matches, range conditions, sorting, prefix matching, and index-only queries. Second, they're able to remain balanced in spite of the addition and removal of keys.

We'll look at a simple representation of a B-tree and then discuss some principles that you'll want to keep in mind. Imagine that you have a collection of users and that

---

[3] The MMAPv1 storage engine uses B-trees for its indexes only; collections are stored as doubly linked lists. As you'll see in chapter 10, the WiredTiger storage engine works a little differently despite the fact that it also uses B-trees. But MMAPv1 remains the default MongoDB storage engine.

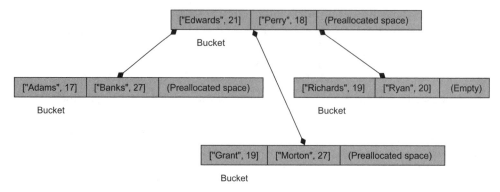

Figure 8.5   Sample B-tree structure

you've created a compound index on last name and age. An abstract representation of the resulting B-tree might look something like figure 8.5.

A *B-tree*, as you might guess, is a tree-like data structure. Each node in the tree can contain multiple keys. You can see in the example that the root node contains two keys, each of which is in the form of a BSON object representing an indexed value from the users collection. In reading the contents of the root node, you can see the keys for two documents, indicating last names Edwards and Perry, with ages of 21 and 18, respectively. Each of these keys includes two pointers: one to the data file it belongs to and another to the child node. Additionally, the node itself points to another node with values less than the node's smallest value.

In MongoDB's B-tree implementation, a new node is allocated 8,192 bytes, which means that in practice, each node may contain hundreds of keys. This depends on the average index key size; in this case, that average key size might be around 30 bytes. The maximum key size since MongoDB v2.0 is 1024 bytes. Add to this a per-key overhead of 18 bytes and a per-node overhead of 40 bytes, and this results in about 170 keys per node.[4] One thing to notice is that each node has some empty space (not to scale).

This is relevant because users frequently want to know why index sizes are what they are. You now know that each node is 8 KB, and you can estimate how many keys will fit into each node. To calculate this, keep in mind that B-tree nodes are usually intentionally kept around 60% full by default.

Given this information, you should now see why indexes aren't free, in terms of space or time required to update them. Use this information to help decide when to create indexes on your collections and when to avoid them.

---

[4] $(8192 - 40) / (30 + 18) = 169.8$

8.2 Indexing in practice

With most of the theory behind us, we'll now look at some refinements on our concept of indexing in MongoDB. We'll then proceed to some of the details of index administration.

8.2.1 Index types

MongoDB uses B-trees for indexes and allows you to apply several characteristics to these indexes. This section should give you an overview of your options when creating indexes.

UNIQUE INDEXES

Often you want to ensure that a field in your document, such as _id or username, is unique to that document. Unique indexes are a way to enforce this characteristic, and in fact are used by MongoDB to ensure that _id is a unique primary key.

To create a unique index, specify the unique option:

```
db.users.createIndex({username: 1}, {unique: true})
```

Unique indexes enforce uniqueness across all their entries. If you try to insert a document into this book's sample application's users collection with an already-indexed username value, the insert will fail with the following exception:

```
E11000 duplicate key error index:
  gardening.users.$username_1  dup key: { : "kbanker" }
```

If using a driver, this exception will be caught only if you perform the insert using your driver's safe mode, which is the default. You may have also encountered this error if you attempted to insert two documents with the same _id—every MongoDB collection has a unique index on this field because it's the primary key.

If you need a unique index on a collection, it's usually best to create the index before inserting any data. If you create the index in advance, you guarantee the uniqueness constraint from the start. When creating a unique index on a collection that already contains data, you run the risk of failure because it's possible that duplicate keys may already exist in the collection. When duplicate keys exist, the index creation fails.

If you do find yourself needing to create a unique index on an established collection, you have a couple of options. The first is to repeatedly attempt to create the unique index and use the failure messages to manually remove the documents with duplicate keys. But if the data isn't so important, you can also instruct the database to drop documents with duplicate keys automatically using the dropDups option. For example, if your users collection already contains data, and if you don't care that documents with duplicate keys are removed, you can issue the index creation command like this:

```
db.users.createIndex({username: 1}, {unique: true, dropDups: true})
```

> ### Be careful using dropDups
>
> Note that the choice of duplicate key documents to be preserved is arbitrary, so use this feature with extreme care. Typically you'll want to decide which duplicates to drop instead of having MongoDB choose for you.
>
> The `dropDups` option was removed starting with MongoDB 3.x and there's no direct replacement for the `dropDups` option. You can either create a new collection, create the unique index on this new collection, and copy all the documents from the old collection to the new one (while making sure that you're ignoring duplicated key errors during the process), or deal with duplicate key documents manually.

SPARSE INDEXES

Indexes are dense by default. This means that for every document in an indexed collection, a corresponding entry exists in the index, even if the document lacks the indexed key. For example, recall the products collection from your e-commerce data model, and imagine that you've built an index on the product attribute `category_ids`. Now suppose that a few products haven't been assigned to any categories. For each of these category-less products, there will still exist a null entry in the `category_ids` index. You can query for those null values like this:

```
db.products.find({category_ids: null})
```

Here, when searching for all products lacking a category, the query optimizer will still be able to use the index on `category_ids` to locate the corresponding products.

But in two cases a dense index is undesirable. The first is when you want a unique index on a field that doesn't appear in every document in the collection. For instance, you definitely want a unique index on every product's `sku` field. But suppose that, for some reason, products are entered into the system before a SKU is assigned. If you have a unique index on `sku` and attempt to insert more than one product without a SKU, the first insert will succeed, but all subsequent inserts will fail because there will already be an entry in the index where `sku` is `null`. This is a case where a dense index doesn't serve your purpose. Instead you want a unique and sparse index.

In a sparse index, only those documents having some value for the indexed key will appear. If you want to create a sparse index, all you have to do is specify `{sparse: true}`. For example, you can create a unique sparse index on `sku` like this:

```
db.products.createIndex({sku: 1}, {unique: true, sparse: true})
```

There's another case where a sparse index is desirable: when a large number of documents in a collection don't contain the indexed key. For example, suppose you allowed anonymous reviews on your e-commerce site. In this case, half the reviews might lack a `user_id` field, and if that field were indexed, half the entries in that index would be `null`. This would be inefficient for two reasons. First, it would increase the size of the index. Second, it'd require updates to the index when adding and removing documents with null `user_id` fields.

If you rarely (or never) expect queries on anonymous reviews, you might elect to build a sparse index on `user_id`. Again, setting the `sparse` option is simple:

```
db.reviews.createIndex({user_id: 1}, {sparse: true, unique: false})
```

Now only those reviews linked to a user via the `user_id` field will be indexed.

MULTIKEY INDEXES

In earlier chapters you saw several examples of indexing fields whose values are arrays.[5] This is made possible by what's known as a *multikey index*, which allows multiple entries in the index to reference the same document. This makes sense if we look at a simple example. Suppose you have a product document with a few tags like this:

```
{
  name: "Wheelbarrow",
  tags: ["tools", "gardening", "soil"]
}
```

If you create an index on `tags`, then each value in this document's `tags` array will appear in the index. This means that a query on any one of these array values can use the index to locate the document. This is the idea behind a multikey index: multiple index entries, or keys, end up referencing the same document.

Multikey indexes are always enabled in MongoDB, with a few exceptions, such as with hashed indexes. Whenever an indexed field contains an array, each array value will be given its own entry in the index.

The intelligent use of multikey indexes is essential to proper MongoDB schema design. This should be evident from the examples presented in chapters 4 through 6; several more examples are provided in the design patterns section of appendix B. But creating, updating, or deleting multikey indexes is more expensive than creating, updating, or deleting single-key indexes.

HASHED INDEXES

In the previous examples of B-tree indexes, we showed how MongoDB builds the index tree out of the values being indexed. Thus, in an index of recipes, the "Apple Pie" entry is near the "Artichoke Ravioli" entry. This may seem obvious and natural, but MongoDB also supports *hashed indexes* where the entries are first passed through a hash function.[6] This means the hashed values will determine the ordering, so these recipes will likely not be near each other in the index.

---

[5] Think of category IDs, for instance.

[6] Recall that a hash function takes some input and maps it to an output value of fixed length. For a given input, the hash output will always be consistent. A good hash function in this context will evenly distribute the output values so that they appear to be random.

Indexes of this kind can be created in MongoDB by passing `'hashed'` as the index sorting direction. For example:

```
db.recipes.createIndex({recipe_name: 'hashed'})
```

Because the indexed value is a hash of the original, these indexes carry some restrictions:

- Equality queries will work much the same, but range queries aren't supported.
- Multikey hashed indexes aren't allowed.
- Floating-point values are cast to an integer before being hashed; thus, 4.2 and 4.3 will have the same value in a hashed index.

Given these restrictions and peculiarities, you may wonder why anyone would use a hashed index. The answer lies in the fact that the entries in a hashed index are evenly distributed. In other words, when you have a non-uniform distribution of key data, then a hashed index will create uniformity if you can live with its restrictions. Recall that "Apple Pie" and "Artichoke Ravioli" are no longer next to each other in the hashed index; the data locality of the index has changed. This is useful in sharded collections where the shard index determines which shard each document will be assigned to. If your shard index is based on an increasing value, such as a MongoDB OIDs,[7] then new documents created will only be inserted to a single shard—unless the index is hashed.

Let's dig into that statement. Unless explicitly set, a MongoDB document will use an OID as its primary key. Here are a few sequentially generated OIDs:

```
5247ae72defd45a1daba9da9
5247ae73defd45a1daba9daa
5247ae73defd45a1daba9dab
```

Notice how similar the values are; the most significant bits are based on the time when they were generated. When new documents are inserted with these IDs, their index entries are likely to be near eachother. If the index using these IDs is being used to decide which shard (and thus machine) a document should reside on, these documents are also likely to be inserted on to the same machine. This can be detrimental if a collection is receiving heavy write load, because only a single machine is being used. Hashed indexes solve this issue by distributing these documents evenly in a namespace, and thus across shards and machines. To fully understand this example, wait until you read chapter 12.

If you're not familiar with sharding, it's described in much greater detail in chapter 11, and this example will make more sense once we describe sharding in detail.

---

[7] MongoDB object IDs (OIDs) are the default ids used for MongoDB documents. We discussed them in more detail in chapter 3, section 3.2.1.

For now, the important thing to remember is that hashed indexes change the locality of index entries, which can be useful in sharded collections.

GEOSPATIAL INDEXES

Another useful query capability is to find documents "close" to a given location, based on latitude and longitude values stored in each document. If you store a directory of restaurants in a MongoDB collection, for example, users are probably most eager to find restaurants located near their home. One answer to this is to run a query to find every restaurant within a 10-mile radius. Executing this query requires an index that can efficiently calculate geographic distances, including the curvature of the earth. Geospatial indexes can handle this and other types of queries.

8.2.2 Index administration

We've discussed simple index administration, such as creating indexes, in this and in previous chapters. When you use indexes in real-world applications, however, it's useful to understand this topic in greater depth. Here we'll see index creation and deletion in detail and address questions surrounding compaction and backups.

CREATING AND DELETING INDEXES

By now you've created quite a few indexes, so this should be easy. Simply call `create-Index()` either in the shell or with your language of choice. Please note that in MongoDB v3.0, `ensureIndex()`, which was previously used for creating indexes, has been replaced by the `createIndex()` command and shouldn't be used anymore. What you may not know is that this method works by creating a document defining the new index and putting it into the special `system.indexes` collection.

Though it's usually easier to use a helper method to create an index, you can also insert an index specification manually (this is what the helper methods do). You need to be sure you've specified the minimum set of keys: ns, key, and name. ns is the namespace, key is the field or combination of fields to index, and name is a name used to refer to the index. Any additional options, like sparse, can also be specified here. For example, let's create a sparse index on the users collection:

```
use green
spec = {ns: "green.users", key: {'addresses.zip': 1}, name: 'zip'}
db.system.indexes.insert(spec, true)
```

If no errors are returned on insert, the index now exists, and you can query the system.indexes collection to prove it:

```
db.system.indexes.find().pretty()
{
  "ns" : "green.users",
  "key" : {
    "addresses.zip" : 1
  },
  "name" : "zip",
  "v" : 1
}
```

The v field was added in MongoDB v2.0 to store the version of the index. This version field allows for future changes in the internal index format but should be of little concern to application developers.

To delete an index, you might think that all you need to do is remove the index document from system.indexes, but this operation is prohibited. Instead, you must delete indexes using the database command deleteIndexes. As with index creation, there are helpers for deleting indexes, but if you want to run the command itself, you can do that, too. The command takes as its argument a document containing the collection name and either the name of the index to drop or * to drop all indexes. To manually drop the index you created, issue the command like this:

```
use green
db.runCommand({deleteIndexes: "users", index: "zip"})
```

In most cases, you'll use the shell's helpers to create and drop indexes:

```
use green
db.users.createIndex({zip: 1})
```

You can then check the index specifications with the getIndexSpecs() method:

```
> db.users.getIndexes()
[
  {
    "v" : 1,
    "key" : {
      "_id" : 1
    },
    "ns" : "green.users",
    "name" : "_id_"
  },
  {
    "v" : 1,
    "key" : {
      "zip" : 1
    },
    "ns" : "green.users",
    "name" : "zip_1"
  }
]
```

Finally, you can drop the index using the dropIndex() method. Note that you must supply the index's name as specified in the spec:

```
use green
db.users.dropIndex("zip_1")
```

You can also supply your own name while creating an index using the name parameter.

Those are the basics of creating and deleting indexes. For what to expect when an index is created, read on.

BUILDING INDEXES

Most of the time, you'll want to declare your indexes before putting your application into production. This allows indexes to be built incrementally, as the data is inserted. But there are two cases where you might choose to build an index after the fact. The first case occurs when you need to import a lot of data before switching into production. For instance, you might be migrating an application to MongoDB and need to seed the database with user information from a data warehouse. You could create the indexes on your user data in advance, but doing so after you've imported the data will ensure an ideally balanced and compacted index from the start. It'll also minimize the net time to build the index.

The second (and more obvious) case for creating indexes on existing data sets is when you have to optimize for new queries. This occurs when you add or change functionality in your application, and it happens more than you might think. Suppose you allow users to log in using their username, so you index that field. Then you modify your application to also allow your users to log in using their email; now you probably need a second index on the email field. Watch out for cases like these because they require rethinking your indexing.

Regardless of why you're creating new indexes, the process isn't always pleasing. For large data sets, building an index can take hours, even days. But you can monitor the progress of an index build from the MongoDB logs. Let's take an example from a data set that we'll use in the next section. First, you declare an index to be built:

```
db.values.createIndex({open: 1, close: 1})
```

> ### Be careful declaring indexes
> Because it's so easy to declare indexes, it's also easy to inadvertently trigger an index build. If the data set is large enough, the build will take a long time. And in a production situation, this can be a nightmare because there's no easy way to kill an index build. If this ever happens, you may have to fail over to a backup or secondary. The most prudent advice is to treat an index build as a kind of database migration.

The index builds in two steps. In the first step, the values to be indexed are sorted. A sorted data set makes for a much more efficient insertion into the B-tree. If you look at the MongoDB server log, you'll see the progress printed for long index builds. Note that the progress of the sort is indicated by the ratio of the number of documents sorted to the total number of documents:

```
[conn1] building new index on { open: 1.0, close: 1.0 } for stocks.values
     1000000/4308303   23%
     2000000/4308303   46%
     3000000/4308303   69%
     4000000/4308303   92%
     Tue Jan  4 09:59:13 [conn1]    external sort used : 5 files  in 55 secs
```

For step two, the sorted values are inserted into the index. Progress is indicated in the same way, and when complete, the time it took to complete the index build is indicated as the insert time into system.indexes:

```
1200300/4308303   27%
    2227900/4308303   51%
    2837100/4308303   65%
    3278100/4308303   76%
    3783300/4308303   87%
    4075500/4308303   94%
Tue Jan  4 10:00:16 [conn1] done building bottom layer, going to commit
Tue Jan  4 10:00:16 [conn1] done for 4308303 records 118.942secs
Tue Jan  4 10:00:16 [conn1] insert stocks.system.indexes 118942ms
```

In addition to examining the MongoDB log, you can check the index build progress by running the shell's currentOp() method. This command's output varies from version to version, but it will probably look something like the next listing.[8]

Listing 8.1   Checking the index build process with the shell `currentOP()` **method**

```
> db.currentOp()
{
  "inprog" : [
    {
      "opid" : 83695,                              ◁────  Operation ID
      "active" : true,
      "secs_running" : 55,
      "op" : "insert",                                    Shows this is using
      "ns" : "stocks.system.indexes",        ◁────        indexes in the query
      "insert" : {                           ◁─
        "v" : 1,
        "key" : {                                   Stocks
          "desc" : 1                                database
        },
        "ns" : "stocks.values",
        "name" : "desc_1"
      },
      "client" : "127.0.0.1:56391",
      "desc" : "conn12",
      "threadId" : "0x10f20c000",
      "connectionId" : 12,                          Locks associated
      "locks" : {                            ◁────  with the operation
        "^" : "w",
        "^stocks" : "W"
      },
      "waitingForLock" : false,
      "msg" : "index: (1/3) external sort Index: (1/3)
              External Sort Progress: 3999999/4308303 92%",
```

---

[8] Note that if you've started the index build from the MongoDB shell, you'll have to open a new instance of the shell to run currentOp concurrently. For more about db.currentOp(), see chapter 10.

```
      "progress" : {
        "done" : 3999999,
        "total" : 4308303
      },
      "numYields" : 0,
      "lockStats" : {
        "timeLockedMicros" : {},
        "timeAcquiringMicros" : {
          "r" : NumberLong(0),
          "w" : NumberLong(723)
        }
      }
    }
  ]
}
```

The msg field describes the build's progress. Note also the locks element, which indicates that the index build takes a write lock on the stocks database. This means that no other client can read or write from the database at this time. If you're running in production, this is obviously a bad thing, and it's the reason why long index builds can be so vexing. Let's explore two possible solutions to this problem.

BACKGROUND INDEXING

If you're running in production and can't afford to halt access to the database, you can specify that an index be built in the background. Although the index build will still take a write lock, the job will yield to allow other readers and writers to access the database. If your application typically exerts a heavy load on MongoDB, a background index build will degrade performance, but this may be acceptable under certain circumstances. For example, if you know that the index can be built within a time window where application traffic is at a minimum, background indexing in this case might be a good choice.

To build an index in the background, specify {background: true} when you declare the index. The previous index can be built in the background like this:

```
db.values.createIndex({open: 1, close: 1}, {background: true})
```

OFFLINE INDEXING

Building an index in the background may still put an unacceptable amount of load on a production server. If this is the case, you may need to index the data offline. This will usually involve taking a replica node offline, building the index on that node by itself, and then allowing the node to catch up with the master replica. Once it's caught up, you can promote the node to primary and then take another secondary offline and build its version of the index. This tactic presumes that your replication oplog is large enough to prevent the offline node from becoming stale during the index build. Chapter 10 covers replication in detail and should help you plan for a migration such as this.

BACKUPS

Because indexes are hard to build, you may want to back them up. Unfortunately, not all backup methods include indexes. For instance, you might be tempted to use mongodump and mongorestore, but these utilities preserve collections and index declarations only. This means that when you run mongorestore, all the indexes declared for any collections you've backed up will be re-created. As always, if your data set is large, the time it takes to build these indexes may be unacceptable.

Consequently, if you want your backups to include indexes, you'll want to opt for backing up the MongoDB data files themselves. More details about this, as well as general instructions for backups, can be found in chapter 13.

DEFRAGMENTING

If your application heavily updates existing data or performs a lot of large deletions, you may end up with a highly fragmented index. B-trees will coalesce on their own somewhat, but this isn't always sufficient to offset a high delete volume. The primary symptom of a fragmented index is an index size much larger than you'd expect for the given data size. This fragmented state can result in indexes using more RAM than necessary. In these cases, you may want to consider rebuilding one or more indexes. You can do this by dropping and re-creating individual indexes or by running the reIndex command, which will rebuild all indexes for a given collection:

```
db.values.reIndex();
```

Be careful about reindexing: the command will take out a write lock for the duration of the rebuild, temporarily rendering your MongoDB instance unusable. Reindexing is best done offline, as described earlier for building indexes on a secondary. Note that the compact command, discussed in chapter 10, will also rebuild indexes for the collection on which it's run.

We've discussed how to create and manage your indexes, but despite this knowledge, you may still find yourself in a situation where your queries aren't fast enough. This can occur as you add data, traffic, or new queries. Let's learn how to identify these queries that could be faster and improve the situation.

8.3   *Query optimization*

Query optimization is the process of identifying slow queries, discovering why they're slow, and then taking steps to speed them up. In this section, we'll look at each step of the query optimization process in turn so that by the time you finish reading, you'll have a framework for addressing problematic queries on any MongoDB installation.

Before diving in, we must warn you that the techniques presented here can't be used to solve every query performance problem. The causes of slow queries vary too much. Poor application design, inappropriate data models, and insufficient physical hardware are all common culprits, and their remedies require a significant time investment. Here we'll look at ways to optimize queries by restructuring the queries themselves and by building the most useful indexes. We'll also describe other avenues for investigation when these techniques fail to deliver.

8.3.1 Identifying slow queries

If your MongoDB-based application feels sluggish, it's time to start profiling your queries. Any disciplined approach to application design should include a query audit, and MongoDB makes this easy. Though the requirements vary per application, it's safe to assume that for most apps, queries shouldn't take much longer than 100 ms. The MongoDB logger has this assumption ingrained because it prints a warning whenever any operation, including a query, takes longer than 100 ms. The logs, therefore, are the first place you should look for slow queries.

It's unlikely that any of the data sets we've worked with up until now have been large enough to generate queries lasting longer than 100 ms. For the following examples, we'll use a data set consisting of daily NASDAQ summaries. If you want to follow along, you'll need to have this data locally. To import it, first download the archive using http://mng.bz/ii49. Then unzip the file to a temporary folder. You'll see the following output:

```
$ unzip stocks.zip
Archive:  stocks.zip
   creating: dump/stocks/
   inflating: dump/stocks/system.indexes.bson
   inflating: dump/stocks/values.bson
```

Finally, after starting the mongod process if necessary, restore the dump like this:

```
$ mongorestore -d stocks dump/stocks
```

This process may take a few minutes. You may also receive some warning messages at the beginning and end of the process. Don't worry about those.

The stocks data set is large and easy to work with. For a certain subset of the NASDAQ stock exchange's symbols, there's a document for each day's high, low, close, and volume for a 25-year period beginning in 1983. Given the number and size of the documents in this collection, it's easy to generate one of the log warnings. Try querying for the first occurrence of Google's stock price:

```
use stocks
db.values.find({"stock_symbol": "GOOG"}).sort({date: -1}).limit(1)
```

You'll notice that this takes some time to run, and if you check the MongoDB log, you'll see the expected slow query warning. Here's a sample of the output to expect from MongoDB v2.6:

```
Mon Sep 30 21:48:58.066 [conn20] query stocks.values query: { query: {
    stock_symbol: "GOOG" }, orderby: { date: -1.0 } }
        ntoreturn:1 ntoskip:0 nscanned:4308303 scanAndOrder:1 keyUpdates:0
    numYields: 3 locks(micros) r:4399440
        nreturned:1 reslen:194 4011ms
```

A similar log message from MongoDB v3.0 using another collection has the follow-ing format:

```
2015-09-11T21:17:15.414+0300 I COMMAND   [conn99] command green.$cmd command:
insert { insert: "system.indexes", documents: [ { _id:
ObjectId('55f31aab9a50479be0a7dcd7'), ns: "green.users", key: {
addresses.zip: 1.0 }, name: "zip" } ], ordered: false } keyUpdates:0
writeConflicts:0 numYields:0 reslen:40 locks:{ Global: { acquireCount: { r:
1, w: 1 } }, MMAPV1Journal: { acquireCount: { w: 9 } }, Database: {
acquireCount: { W: 1 } }, Collection: { acquireCount: { W: 1 } }, Metadata: {
acquireCount: { W: 5 } } } } 102ms
```

There's a lot of information here, and we'll go over the meaning of all of it when we discuss explain(). For now, if you read the message carefully, you should be able to extract the most important parts: that it's a query on stocks.values; that the query selector consists of a match on stock_symbol and that a sort is being performed; and, maybe most significantly, that the query takes a whopping four seconds (4011 ms). The exact time may vary quite a bit depending on the speed of your computer.

Warnings like this must be addressed. They're so critical that it's worth your while to occasionally search for them in your MongoDB logs. This can be accomplished eas-ily with grep:

```
grep -E '[0-9]+ms' mongod.log
```

If 100 ms is too high a threshold, you can lower it with the --slowms server option when you start MongoDB. If you define slow as taking longer than 50 ms, then start mongod with --slowms 50.

Of course, using grep to search through logs isn't very systematic. You can use the MongoDB logs to check for slow queries, but the procedure is rather coarse and should be reserved as a kind of sanity check in a staging or production environment. To identify slow queries before they become a problem, you want a precision tool. MongoDB's built-in query profiler is exactly that.

USING THE PROFILER

For identifying slow queries, you can't beat the built-in profiler. Profiling is dis-abled by default, so let's get started by enabling it. From the MongoDB shell, enter the following:

```
use stocks
db.setProfilingLevel(2)
```

First you select the database you want to profile; profiling is always scoped to a particu-lar database. Then you set the profiling level to 2. This is the most verbose level; it directs the profiler to log every read and write. A couple of other options are available. To log only slow (100 ms) operations, set the profiling level to 1. To disable the query profiler altogether, set it to 0. And to log only operations taking longer than a certain threshold in milliseconds, pass the number of milliseconds as the second argument like this:

```
use stocks
db.setProfilingLevel(1, 50)
```

Once you've enabled the profiler, it's time to issue some queries. Let's run another query on the stocks database. Try finding the highest closing price in the data set:

```
db.values.find({}).sort({close: -1}).limit(1)
```

PROFILING RESULTS

The profiling results are stored in a special capped collection called `system.profile` which is located in the database where you executed the `setProfilingLevel` command. Recall that capped collections are fixed in size and that data is written to them in a circular way so that once the collection reaches its max size, new documents overwrite the oldest documents. The `system.profile` collection is allocated 128 KB, thus ensuring that the profile data never consumes much in the way of resources.

You can query `system.profile` as you would any capped collection. For instance, you can find all queries that took longer than 150 ms like this:

```
db.system.profile.find({millis: {$gt: 150}})
```

Because capped collections maintain natural insertion order, you can use the $natural operator to sort so that the most recent results are displayed first:

```
db.system.profile.find().sort({$natural: -1}).limit(5).pretty()
```

Returning to the query you just issued, you should see an entry in the result set that looks something like this:

```
{
  "op" : "query",
  "ns" : "stocks.values",            ⟵┐ Name of
  "query" : {                           │ collection
    "query" : { },
    "orderby" : {
      "close" : -1
    }
  },
  "ntoreturn" : 1,
  "ntoskip" : 0,
  "nscanned" : 4308303,              ⟵┐ Number of scanned
  "scanAndOrder" : true,                │ documents
  "keyUpdates" : 0,
  "numYield" : 3,
  "lockStats" : {
    "timeLockedMicros" : {
      "r" : NumberLong(12868747),
      "w" : NumberLong(0)
    },
```

```
  "timeAcquiringMicros" : {
    "r" : NumberLong(1838271),
    "w" : NumberLong(5)
  }
},
"nreturned" : 1,
"responseLength" : 194,
"millis" : 11030,
"ts" : ISODate("2013-09-30T06:44:40.988Z"),
"client" : "127.0.0.1",
"allUsers" : [ ],
"user" : ""
}
```

Number of returned documents

Response time in milliseconds

Another expensive query: this one took about 11 seconds! In addition to the time it took to complete, you get all same information about the query that you saw in the MongoDB log's slow query warning, which is enough to start the deeper investigation that we'll cover in the next section.

But before moving on, a few more words about profiling strategy are in order:

- A good way to use the profiler is to start it with a coarse setting and work downward. First ensure that no queries take longer than 100 ms, then move down to 75 ms, and so on.

- While the profiler is enabled, you'll want to put your application through its paces; this means testing all of your application's reads and writes.

- To be thorough, those reads and writes should be executed under real conditions, where the data sizes, query load, and hardware are representative of the application's production environment.

The query profiler is useful, but to get the most out of it, you need to be methodical. Better to be surprised with a few slow queries in development than in production, where the remedies are much more costly.

For reference, the following output presents a profiling entry from MongoDB v3.0.6:

```
> db.system.profile.find().limit(1).pretty()
{
    "op" : "query",
    "ns" : "products.system.profile",
    "query" : {

    },
    "ntoreturn" : 0,
    "ntoskip" : 0,
    "nscanned" : 0,
    "nscannedObjects" : 0,
    "keyUpdates" : 0,
    "writeConflicts" : 0,
    "numYield" : 0,
```

```
    "locks" : {
        "Global" : {
            "acquireCount" : {
                "r" : NumberLong(2)
            }
        },
        "MMAPV1Journal" : {
            "acquireCount" : {
                "r" : NumberLong(1)
            }
        },
        "Database" : {
            "acquireCount" : {
                "r" : NumberLong(1)
            }
        },
        "Collection" : {
            "acquireCount" : {
                "R" : NumberLong(1)
            }
        }
    },
    "nreturned" : 0,
    "responseLength" : 20,
    "millis" : 1,
    "execStats" : {
        "stage" : "COLLSCAN",
        "filter" : {
            "$and" : [ ]
        },
        "nReturned" : 0,
        "executionTimeMillisEstimate" : 0,
        "works" : 2,
        "advanced" : 0,
        "needTime" : 1,
        "needFetch" : 0,
        "saveState" : 0,
        "restoreState" : 0,
        "isEOF" : 1,
        "invalidates" : 0,
        "direction" : "forward",
        "docsExamined" : 0
    },
    "ts" : ISODate("2015-09-11T18:52:08.847Z"),
    "client" : "127.0.0.1",
    "allUsers" : [ ],
    "user" : ""
}
```

8.3.2 Examining slow queries

Finding slow queries is easy with MongoDB's profiler. Discovering why these queries are slow is trickier and may require some detective work. As mentioned, the causes of slow queries are manifold. If you're lucky, resolving a slow query may be as easy as adding an index. In more difficult cases, you might have to rearrange indexes, restructure the data model, or upgrade hardware. But you should always look at the simplest case first, and that's what we're going to do here.

In the simplest case, a lack of indexes, inappropriate indexes, or less-than-ideal queries will be the root of the problem. You can find out for sure by running an explain on the offending queries. Let's explore how to do that now.

USING AND UNDERSTANDING EXPLAIN( )

MongoDB's explain command provides detailed information about a given query's path. Let's dive right in and see what information can be gleaned from running an explain on the last query you ran in the previous section. To run explain from the shell, you only need to attach the explain() method call:

```
db.values.find({}).sort({close: -1}).limit(1).explain()
{
    "cursor" : "BasicCursor",
    "isMultiKey" : false,                        Number
    "n" : 1,                                     returned
    "nscannedObjects" : 4308303,
    "nscanned" : 4308303,                        Number
    "nscannedObjectsAllPlans" : 4308303,         scanned
    "nscannedAllPlans" : 4308303,
    "scanAndOrder" : true,
    "indexOnly" : false,
    "nYields" : 4,
    "nChunkSkips" : 0,
    "millis" : 10927,
    "indexBounds" : { },
    "server" : "localhost:27017"
}
```

The millis field indicates that this query takes about 11 seconds,[9] and there's an obvious reason for this. Look at the nscanned value: this shows that the query engine had to scan 4,308,303 documents to fulfill the query. Now, quickly run a count on the values collection:

```
db.values.count()
4308303
```

The number of documents scanned is the same as the total number of documents in the collection, so you've performed a complete collection scan. If your query were expected to return every document in the collection, this wouldn't be a bad thing. But you're returning one document, as indicated by the explain value n, so this is problematic. Furthermore, a full collection scan will only get more expensive if more documents are added. Generally speaking, you want the values of n and nscanned to be as

---

[9] If this doesn't seem like much, consider the case where a user is waiting on a web page to load because of a database query in the background. In that context, 11 seconds is an eternity.

close together as possible. When doing a collection scan, this is almost never the case. The cursor field tells you that you've been using a BasicCursor, which only confirms that you're scanning the collection itself and not an index. If you had used an index, the value would've been BTreeCursor.

A second datum here further explains the slowness of the query: the scanAndOrder field. This indicator appears when the query optimizer can't use an index to return a sorted result set. Therefore, in this case, not only does the query engine have to scan the collection, it also has to sort the result set manually.

The previous output from the explain() command is from an older MongoDB version. Here's a sample output from the explain() command using a MongoDB v3.0.6 server:

```
> db.inventory.find({}).sort({"quantity": -1}).limit(1).
    explain("executionStats")
{
    "queryPlanner" : {
        "plannerVersion" : 1,
        "namespace" : "tutorial.inventory",
        "indexFilterSet" : false,
        "parsedQuery" : {
            "$and" : [ ]
        },
        "winningPlan" : {
            "stage" : "SORT",
            "sortPattern" : {
                "quantity" : -1
            },
            "limitAmount" : 1,
            "inputStage" : {
                "stage" : "COLLSCAN",
                "filter" : {
                    "$and" : [ ]
                },
                "direction" : "forward"
            }
        },
        "rejectedPlans" : [ ]
    },
    "executionStats" : {
        "executionSuccess" : true,
        "nReturned" : 1,
        "executionTimeMillis" : 0,
        "totalKeysExamined" : 0,
        "totalDocsExamined" : 11,
        "executionStages" : {
            "stage" : "SORT",
            "nReturned" : 1,
            "executionTimeMillisEstimate" : 0,
            "works" : 16,
            "advanced" : 1,
            "needTime" : 13,
            "needFetch" : 0,
```

```
        "saveState" : 0,
        "restoreState" : 0,
        "isEOF" : 1,
        "invalidates" : 0,
        "sortPattern" : {
            "quantity" : -1
        },
        "memUsage" : 72,
        "memLimit" : 33554432,
        "limitAmount" : 1,
        "inputStage" : {
            "stage" : "COLLSCAN",
            "filter" : {
                "$and" : [ ]
            },
            "nReturned" : 11,
            "executionTimeMillisEstimate" : 0,
            "works" : 13,
            "advanced" : 11,
            "needTime" : 1,
            "needFetch" : 0,
            "saveState" : 0,
            "restoreState" : 0,
            "isEOF" : 1,
            "invalidates" : 0,
            "direction" : "forward",
            "docsExamined" : 11
        }
    }
},
"serverInfo" : {
    "host" : "rMacBook.local",
    "port" : 27017,
    "version" : "3.0.6",
    "gitVersion" : "nogitversion"
},
"ok" : 1
}
```

The explain() command displays more information when used with the execution-
Stats option.

ADD AN INDEX AND RETRY
The poor performance is unacceptable, but fortunately the fix is simple. All you need
to do is build an index on the close field. Go ahead and do that now:

```
db.values.createIndex({close: 1})
```

Note that building the index may take a few minutes. Once built, try the query again:

```
db.values.find({}).sort({close: -1}).limit(1).explain()
{
  "cursor" : "BtreeCursor close_1 reverse",
  "isMultiKey" : false,
```

```
    "n" : 1,
    "nscannedObjects" : 1,
    "nscanned" : 1,
    "nscannedObjectsAllPlans" : 1,
    "nscannedAllPlans" : 1,
    "scanAndOrder" : false,
    "indexOnly" : false,
    "nYields" : 0,
    "nChunkSkips" : 0,
    "millis" : 0,
    "indexBounds" : {
      "name" : [
        [
          {
            "$maxElement" : 1
          },
          {
            "$minElement" : 1
          }
        ]
      ]
    }
  },
  "server" : "localhost:27017"
}
```

What a difference! The query now takes less than a millisecond to process. You can see from the cursor field that you're using a BtreeCursor on the index named close_1 and that you're iterating over the index in reverse order. In the indexBounds field, you see the special values $maxElement and $minElement. These indicate that the query spans the entire index. In this case, the query optimizer walks the rightmost edge of the B-tree until it reaches the maximum key and then works its way backward. Because you've specified a limit of 1, the query is complete once the maxElement is found. And of course, the index keeps the entries in order, so there's no longer a need for the manual sort indicated by scanAndOrder.

Similarly, the MongoDB v3.0.6 output shows the improvement in the execution time and the number of documents that where examined:

```
> db.inventory.find({}).sort({"quantity": -
    1}).limit(1).explain("executionStats")
{
    "queryPlanner" : {
        "plannerVersion" : 1,
        "namespace" : "tutorial.inventory",
        "indexFilterSet" : false,
        "parsedQuery" : {
            "$and" : [ ]
        },
        "winningPlan" : {
            "stage" : "LIMIT",
            "limitAmount" : 0,
            "inputStage" : {
                "stage" : "FETCH",
```

```
                    "inputStage" : {
                        "stage" : "IXSCAN",
                        "keyPattern" : {
                            "quantity" : 1
                        },
                        "indexName" : "quantity_1",
                        "isMultiKey" : false,
                        "direction" : "backward",
                        "indexBounds" : {
                            "quantity" : [
                                "[MaxKey, MinKey]"
                            ]
                        }
                    }
                }
            }
        },
        "rejectedPlans" : [ ]
    },
    "executionStats" : {
        "executionSuccess" : true,
        "nReturned" : 1,
        "executionTimeMillis" : 0,
        "totalKeysExamined" : 1,
        "totalDocsExamined" : 1,
        "executionStages" : {
            "stage" : "LIMIT",
            "nReturned" : 1,
            "executionTimeMillisEstimate" : 0,
            "works" : 2,
            "advanced" : 1,
            "needTime" : 0,
            "needFetch" : 0,
            "saveState" : 0,
            "restoreState" : 0,
            "isEOF" : 1,
            "invalidates" : 0,
            "limitAmount" : 0,
            "inputStage" : {
                "stage" : "FETCH",
                "nReturned" : 1,
                "executionTimeMillisEstimate" : 0,
                "works" : 1,
                "advanced" : 1,
                "needTime" : 0,
                "needFetch" : 0,
                "saveState" : 0,
                "restoreState" : 0,
                "isEOF" : 0,
                "invalidates" : 0,
                "docsExamined" : 1,
                "alreadyHasObj" : 0,
                "inputStage" : {
                    "stage" : "IXSCAN",
                    "nReturned" : 1,
                    "executionTimeMillisEstimate" : 0,
```

```
                        "works" : 1,
                        "advanced" : 1,
                        "needTime" : 0,
                        "needFetch" : 0,
                        "saveState" : 0,
                        "restoreState" : 0,
                        "isEOF" : 0,
                        "invalidates" : 0,
                        "keyPattern" : {
                            "quantity" : 1
                        },
                        "indexName" : "quantity_1",
                        "isMultiKey" : false,
                        "direction" : "backward",
                        "indexBounds" : {
                            "quantity" : [
                                "[MaxKey, MinKey]"
                            ]
                        },
                        "keysExamined" : 1,
                        "dupsTested" : 0,
                        "dupsDropped" : 0,
                        "seenInvalidated" : 0,
                        "matchTested" : 0
                    }
                }
            }
        },
        "serverInfo" : {
            "host" : "rMacBook.local",
            "port" : 27017,
            "version" : "3.0.6",
            "gitVersion" : "nogitversion"
        },
        "ok" : 1
}
```

The reason for showing the output from both 2.x and 3.0 MongoDB versions is for you to have it as a reference.

USING AN INDEXED KEY

You'll see slightly different output if you use the indexed key in your query selector. Take a look at the explain plan for a query selecting closing values greater than 500:

```
> db.values.find({close: {$gt: 500}}).explain()
{
    "cursor" : "BtreeCursor close_1",
    "isMultiKey" : false,
    "n" : 309,
    "nscannedObjects" : 309,
    "nscanned" : 309,
    "nscannedObjectsAllPlans" : 309,
    "nscannedAllPlans" : 309,
    "scanAndOrder" : false,
```

```
"indexOnly" : false,
"nYields" : 0,
"nChunkSkips" : 0,
"millis" : 1,
"indexBounds" : {
  "close" : [
    [
      500,
      1.7976931348623157e+308
    ]
  ]
},
"server" : "localhost:27017"
}
```

You're still scanning the same number of documents that you're returning (n and nscanned are the same), which is ideal. But note the difference in the way the index boundaries are specified. Instead of the $maxElement and $minElement keys, the boundaries are actual values. The lower bound is 500 and the upper bound is effectively infinite. These values must share the same class of data type that you're querying on; you're querying on a number, which means the index bounds are numeric. If you were to query on a string range instead, the boundaries would be strings.[10]

As usual, output from a similar query using MongoDB v3.0 will be presented here:

```
> db.inventory.find({"quantity":{$gt:
    150}}).limit(1).explain("executionStats")
{
    "queryPlanner" : {
        "plannerVersion" : 1,
        "namespace" : "tutorial.inventory",
        "indexFilterSet" : false,
        "parsedQuery" : {
            "quantity" : {
                "$gt" : 150
            }
        },
        "winningPlan" : {
            "stage" : "LIMIT",
            "limitAmount" : 0,
            "inputStage" : {
                "stage" : "FETCH",
                "inputStage" : {
                    "stage" : "IXSCAN",
                    "keyPattern" : {
                        "quantity" : 1
                    },
                    "indexName" : "quantity_1",
                    "isMultiKey" : false,
                    "direction" : "forward",
```

---

[10] If this isn't making any sense, recall that a given index can contain keys of multiple data types. Thus, query results will always be limited by the data type used in the query.

```
            "indexBounds" : {
                "quantity" : [
                    "(150.0, inf.0]"
                ]
            }
        }
    }
}
},
"rejectedPlans" : [ ]
},
"executionStats" : {
    "executionSuccess" : true,
    "nReturned" : 1,
    "executionTimeMillis" : 0,
    "totalKeysExamined" : 1,
    "totalDocsExamined" : 1,
    "executionStages" : {
        "stage" : "LIMIT",
        "nReturned" : 1,
        "executionTimeMillisEstimate" : 0,
        "works" : 2,
        "advanced" : 1,
        "needTime" : 0,
        "needFetch" : 0,
        "saveState" : 0,
        "restoreState" : 0,
        "isEOF" : 1,
        "invalidates" : 0,
        "limitAmount" : 0,
        "inputStage" : {
            "stage" : "FETCH",
            "nReturned" : 1,
            "executionTimeMillisEstimate" : 0,
            "works" : 1,
            "advanced" : 1,
            "needTime" : 0,
            "needFetch" : 0,
            "saveState" : 0,
            "restoreState" : 0,
            "isEOF" : 0,
            "invalidates" : 0,
            "docsExamined" : 1,
            "alreadyHasObj" : 0,
            "inputStage" : {
                "stage" : "IXSCAN",
                "nReturned" : 1,
                "executionTimeMillisEstimate" : 0,
                "works" : 1,
                "advanced" : 1,
                "needTime" : 0,
                "needFetch" : 0,
                "saveState" : 0,
                "restoreState" : 0,
                "isEOF" : 0,
                "invalidates" : 0,
```

```
                              "keyPattern" : {
                                  "quantity" : 1
                              },
                              "indexName" : "quantity_1",
                              "isMultiKey" : false,
                              "direction" : "forward",
                              "indexBounds" : {
                                  "quantity" : [
                                      "(150.0, inf.0]"
                                  ]
                              },
                              "keysExamined" : 1,
                              "dupsTested" : 0,
                              "dupsDropped" : 0,
                              "seenInvalidated" : 0,
                              "matchTested" : 0
                          }
                      }
                  }
              },
          "serverInfo" : {
              "host" : "rMacBook.local",
              "port" : 27017,
              "version" : "3.0.6",
              "gitVersion" : "nogitversion"
          },
          "ok" : 1
      }
```

Before continuing, try running `explain()` on a few queries of your own using all MongoDB versions you have, and pay attention to the difference between n and nscanned, as well as the difference between `totalDocsExamined` and `nReturned`. Optimizing a query in MongoDB v2.x usually means making nscanned as small as possible, but every result must be scanned, so nscanned will never be lower than n, the number of results a query returns. In MongoDB v3.0 the nReturned value indicates the number of documents a query matches and returns. The value of `totalDocsExamined` indicates the number of documents that MongoDB scanned. Lastly, `totalKeysExamined` shows the number of index entries that MongoDB scanned.

MONGODB'S QUERY OPTIMIZER

The query optimizer is the piece of software that determines which index, if any, will most efficiently serve a given query. To select an ideal index for your queries, the query optimizer uses a fairly simple set of rules:

1. Avoid `scanAndOrder`. If the query includes a sort, attempt to sort using an index.
2. Satisfy all fields with useful indexing constraints—attempt to use indexes for the fields in the query selector.
3. If the query implies a range or includes a sort, choose an index where that last key used can help satisfy the range or sort.

If all of these conditions can be met for any one index, that index will be considered optimal and will be used. If more than one index qualifies as optimal, one of the optimal indexes will be chosen arbitrarily. There's a lesson here: if you can build optimal indexes for your queries, you make the query optimizer's job a lot easier. Strive for that if you can.

Let's look at a query that satisfies an index (and the query optimizer) perfectly. Go back to the stock symbol data set. Now imagine you want to issue the following query, which fetches all of Google's closing values greater than 200:

```
db.values.find({stock_symbol: "GOOG", close: {$gt: 200}})
```

If you use .explain() with this query, you'll see that n is 730 but nscanned is 5299. The previously created index on close helps, but the optimal index for this query includes both keys and places the close key last to allow for the range query:

```
db.values.createIndex({stock_symbol: 1, close: 1})
```

You'll see that if you run the query, both keys are used, and the index bounds are as expected:

```
db.values.find({stock_symbol: "GOOG", close: {$gt: 200}}).explain()
{
  "cursor" : "BtreeCursor stock_symbol_1_close_1",
  "isMultiKey" : false,
  "n" : 730,
  "nscannedObjects" : 730,
  "nscanned" : 730,
  "nscannedObjectsAllPlans" : 730,
  "nscannedAllPlans" : 730,
  "scanAndOrder" : false,
  "indexOnly" : false,
  "nYields" : 0,
  "nChunkSkips" : 0,
  "millis" : 2,
  "indexBounds" : {
    "stock_symbol" : [
      [
        "GOOG",
        "GOOG"
      ]
    ],
    "close" : [
      [
        200,
        1.7976931348623157e+308
      ]
    ]
  },
  "server" : "localhost:27017"
}
```

This is the optimal `explain` output for this query: the values of n and nscanned are the same. But now consider the case where no one index perfectly serves the query. For example, imagine that you don't have an index on {stock_symbol: 1, close: 1} but instead, you have a separate index on each of those fields. Using the shorthand `get-IndexKeys()` to list indexes, you'd see this:

```
db.values.getIndexKeys()
[
  {
    "_id" : 1
  },
  {
    "close" : 1
  },
  {
    "stock_symbol" : 1
  }
]
```

Because your query includes both the stock_symbol and close keys, there's no obvious index to use. This is where the query optimizer comes in, and the heuristic is more straightforward than you might imagine. It's based purely on the value of nscanned. In other words, the optimizer chooses the index that requires scanning the least number of index entries. When the query is first run, the optimizer creates a query plan for each index that might efficiently satisfy the query. The optimizer then runs each plan in parallel.[11] Usually, the plan that finishes with the lowest value for nscanned is declared the winner; but in rare occasions, the optimizer may select the full collection scan as the winning plan for a given query. The optimizer then halts any long-running plans and saves the winner for future use.

The following output is from MongoDB v3.0 using a much smaller collection:

```
> db.inventory.find({"quantity": 500,
    "type":"toys"}).limit(1).explain("executionStats")
{
    "queryPlanner" : {
        "plannerVersion" : 1,
        "namespace" : "tutorial.inventory",
        "indexFilterSet" : false,
        "parsedQuery" : {
            "$and" : [
                {
                    "quantity" : {
                        "$eq" : 500
                    }
                },
```

---

[11] Technically, the plans are interleaved.

```
                {
                    "type" : {
                        "$eq" : "toys"
                    }
                }
            ]
        },
        "winningPlan" : {
            "stage" : "LIMIT",
            "limitAmount" : 0,
            "inputStage" : {
                "stage" : "KEEP_MUTATIONS",
                "inputStage" : {
                    "stage" : "FETCH",
                    "filter" : {
                        "type" : {
                            "$eq" : "toys"
                        }
                    },
                    "inputStage" : {
                        "stage" : "IXSCAN",
                        "keyPattern" : {
                            "quantity" : 1
                        },
                        "indexName" : "quantity_1",
                        "isMultiKey" : false,
                        "direction" : "forward",
                        "indexBounds" : {
                            "quantity" : [
                                "[500.0, 500.0]"
                            ]
                        }
                    }
                }
            }
        },
        "rejectedPlans" : [ ]
    },
    "executionStats" : {
        "executionSuccess" : true,
        "nReturned" : 1,
        "executionTimeMillis" : 1,
        "totalKeysExamined" : 2,
        "totalDocsExamined" : 2,
        "executionStages" : {
            "stage" : "LIMIT",
            "nReturned" : 1,
            "executionTimeMillisEstimate" : 0,
            "works" : 3,
            "advanced" : 1,
            "needTime" : 1,
            "needFetch" : 0,
            "saveState" : 0,
            "restoreState" : 0,
            "isEOF" : 1,
```

```
"invalidates" : 0,
"limitAmount" : 0,
"inputStage" : {
    "stage" : "KEEP_MUTATIONS",
    "nReturned" : 1,
    "executionTimeMillisEstimate" : 0,
    "works" : 2,
    "advanced" : 1,
    "needTime" : 1,
    "needFetch" : 0,
    "saveState" : 0,
    "restoreState" : 0,
    "isEOF" : 0,
    "invalidates" : 0,
    "inputStage" : {
        "stage" : "FETCH",
        "filter" : {
            "type" : {
                "$eq" : "toys"
            }
        },
        "nReturned" : 1,
        "executionTimeMillisEstimate" : 0,
        "works" : 2,
        "advanced" : 1,
        "needTime" : 1,
        "needFetch" : 0,
        "saveState" : 0,
        "restoreState" : 0,
        "isEOF" : 1,
        "invalidates" : 0,
        "docsExamined" : 2,
        "alreadyHasObj" : 0,
        "inputStage" : {
            "stage" : "IXSCAN",
            "nReturned" : 2,
            "executionTimeMillisEstimate" : 0,
            "works" : 2,
            "advanced" : 2,
            "needTime" : 0,
            "needFetch" : 0,
            "saveState" : 0,
            "restoreState" : 0,
            "isEOF" : 1,
            "invalidates" : 0,
            "keyPattern" : {
                "quantity" : 1
            },
            "indexName" : "quantity_1",
            "isMultiKey" : false,
            "direction" : "forward",
            "indexBounds" : {
                "quantity" : [
                    "[500.0, 500.0]"
                ]
```

```
                },
                "keysExamined" : 2,
                "dupsTested" : 0,
                "dupsDropped" : 0,
                "seenInvalidated" : 0,
                "matchTested" : 0
              }
            }
          }
        }
      },
      "serverInfo" : {
        "host" : "rMacBook.local",
        "port" : 27017,
        "version" : "3.0.6",
        "gitVersion" : "nogitversion"
      },
      "ok" : 1
}
```

The aforementioned query examined two documents to return the desired document. Now it's time to create another index that combines two fields:

```
> db.inventory.createIndex( { quantity: 1, type: 1 } )
{
    "createdCollectionAutomatically" : false,
    "numIndexesBefore" : 2,
    "numIndexesAfter" : 3,
    "ok" : 1
}
```

Now you're going to rerun the previous query:

```
> db.inventory.find({"quantity": 500,
    "type":"toys"}).limit(1).explain("executionStats")
{
    "queryPlanner" : {
        "plannerVersion" : 1,
        "namespace" : "tutorial.inventory",
        "indexFilterSet" : false,
        "parsedQuery" : {
            "$and" : [
                {
                    "quantity" : {
                        "$eq" : 500
                    }
                },
                {
                    "type" : {
                        "$eq" : "toys"
                    }
                }
            ]
        },
```

```
"winningPlan" : {
    "stage" : "LIMIT",
    "limitAmount" : 0,
    "inputStage" : {
        "stage" : "FETCH",
        "inputStage" : {
            "stage" : "IXSCAN",
            "keyPattern" : {
                "quantity" : 1,
                "type" : 1
            },
            "indexName" : "quantity_1_type_1",
            "isMultiKey" : false,
            "direction" : "forward",
            "indexBounds" : {
                "quantity" : [
                    "[500.0, 500.0]"
                ],
                "type" : [
                    "[\"toys\", \"toys\"]"
                ]
            }
        }
    }
},
"rejectedPlans" : [
    {
        "stage" : "LIMIT",
        "limitAmount" : 1,
        "inputStage" : {
            "stage" : "KEEP_MUTATIONS",
            "inputStage" : {
                "stage" : "FETCH",
                "filter" : {
                    "type" : {
                        "$eq" : "toys"
                    }
                },
                "inputStage" : {
                    "stage" : "IXSCAN",
                    "keyPattern" : {
                        "quantity" : 1
                    },
                    "indexName" : "quantity_1",
                    "isMultiKey" : false,
                    "direction" : "forward",
                    "indexBounds" : {
                        "quantity" : [
                            "[500.0, 500.0]"
                        ]
                    }
                }
            }
        }
    }
```

```
            ]
        },
        "executionStats" : {
            "executionSuccess" : true,
            "nReturned" : 1,
            "executionTimeMillis" : 1,
            "totalKeysExamined" : 1,
            "totalDocsExamined" : 1,
            "executionStages" : {
                "stage" : "LIMIT",
                "nReturned" : 1,
                "executionTimeMillisEstimate" : 0,
                "works" : 2,
                "advanced" : 1,
                "needTime" : 0,
                "needFetch" : 0,
                "saveState" : 0,
                "restoreState" : 0,
                "isEOF" : 1,
                "invalidates" : 0,
                "limitAmount" : 0,
                "inputStage" : {
                    "stage" : "FETCH",
                    "nReturned" : 1,
                    "executionTimeMillisEstimate" : 0,
                    "works" : 1,
                    "advanced" : 1,
                    "needTime" : 0,
                    "needFetch" : 0,
                    "saveState" : 0,
                    "restoreState" : 0,
                    "isEOF" : 1,
                    "invalidates" : 0,
                    "docsExamined" : 1,
                    "alreadyHasObj" : 0,
                    "inputStage" : {
                        "stage" : "IXSCAN",
                        "nReturned" : 1,
                        "executionTimeMillisEstimate" : 0,
                        "works" : 1,
                        "advanced" : 1,
                        "needTime" : 0,
                        "needFetch" : 0,
                        "saveState" : 0,
                        "restoreState" : 0,
                        "isEOF" : 1,
                        "invalidates" : 0,
                        "keyPattern" : {
                            "quantity" : 1,
                            "type" : 1
                        },
                        "indexName" : "quantity_1_type_1",
                        "isMultiKey" : false,
                        "direction" : "forward",
                        "indexBounds" : {
```

```
                              "quantity" : [
                                  "[500.0, 500.0]" ,
                              ],
                              "type" : [
                                  "[\"toys\", \"toys\"]"
                              ]
                          },
                          "keysExamined" : 1,
                          "dupsTested" : 0,
                          "dupsDropped" : 0,
                          "seenInvalidated" : 0,
                          "matchTested" : 0
                      }
                  }
              }
          },
          "serverInfo" : {
              "host" : "rMacBook.local",
              "port" : 27017,
              "version" : "3.0.6",
              "gitVersion" : "nogitversion"
          },
          "ok" : 1
  }
```

This time only one document was examined to return one document. This means that the new index helped the process.

SHOWING THE QUERY PLANS AND HINT( )

You can see this process in action by issuing your query and running `explain()`. First, drop the compound index on `{stock_symbol: 1, close: 1}` and build separate indexes on each of these keys:

```
db.values.dropIndex("stock_symbol_1_close_1")
db.values.createIndex({stock_symbol: 1})
db.values.createIndex ({close: 1})
```

Then pass `true` to the `explain()` method, which will include the list of plans the query optimizer attempts. You can see the output in listing 8.2. When using MongoDB v3.0 the possible modes are `queryPlanner`, `executionStats`, and `allPlansExecution`. For backwards compatibility with earlier versions of `cursor.explain()`, MongoDB v3.0 interprets `true` as `allPlansExecution` and `false` as `queryPlanner`.

Listing 8.2   Viewing query plans with `explain(true)`

```
db.values.find({stock_symbol: "GOOG", close: {$gt: 200}}).explain(true)
{
  "cursor" : "BtreeCursor stock_symbol_1",
  "isMultiKey" : false,
  "n" : 730,
  "nscannedObjects" : 894,
```

```
"nscanned" : 894,                                ⟵─┐  Scanned
"nscannedObjectsAllPlans" : 1097,                  │  documents
"nscannedAllPlans" : 1097,
"scanAndOrder" : false,
"indexOnly" : false,
"nYields" : 0,
"nChunkSkips" : 0,                     ──┐  Query time
"millis" : 4,                        ⟵──┘
"indexBounds" : {                          ⟵──┐  Since this is querying
  "stock_symbol" : [[          ⟵──┐            │  on equality ...
      "GOOG",                     │
      "GOOG"                      │  ... the index bounds
    ]                             │  are identical
  ]
},
"allPlans" : [                             ⟵──┐  Array of attempted
  {                                           │  query plans
    "cursor" : "BtreeCursor close_1",
    "n" : 0,
    "nscannedObjects" : 102,
    "nscanned" : 102,
    "indexBounds" : {
      "close" : [
        [
          200,
          1.7976931348623157e+308
        ]
      ]
    }
  },
  {
    "cursor" : "BtreeCursor stock_symbol_1",
    "n" : 730,
    "nscannedObjects" : 894,
    "nscanned" : 894,
    "indexBounds" : {
      "stock_symbol" : [
        [
          "GOOG",
          "GOOG"
        ]
      ]
    }
  },
  {
    "cursor" : "BasicCursor",
    "n" : 0,
    "nscannedObjects" : 101,
    "nscanned" : 101,
    "indexBounds" : { }
  }
],
"server" : "localhost:27017"
}
```

You'll see right away that the query plan chooses the index on {stock_symbol: 1} to fulfill the query. Lower down, the allPlans key points to a list that includes two additional query plans: one for the index on {close: 1}, and the other a collection scan with a BasicCursor. MongoDB v3.0 calls this list rejectedPlans.

It's understandable why the optimizer rejects the collection scan, but it might be less clear why the index on {close: 1} doesn't satisfy. You can use hint() to find out. hint() forces the query optimizer to use a particular index:

```
query = {stock_symbol: "GOOG", close: {$gt: 200}}
db.values.find(query).hint({close: 1}).explain()
{
  "cursor" : "BtreeCursor close_1",
  "isMultiKey" : false,
  "n" : 730,
  "nscannedObjects" : 5299,
  "nscanned" : 5299,
  "nscannedObjectsAllPlans" : 5299,
  "nscannedAllPlans" : 5299,
  "scanAndOrder" : false,
  "indexOnly" : false,
  "nYields" : 0,
  "nChunkSkips" : 0,
  "millis" : 22,
  "indexBounds" : {
    "close" : [
      [
        200,
        1.7976931348623157e+308
      ]
    ]
  },
  "server" : "localhost:27017"
}
```

Look at the value for nscanned: 5,299. This is much greater than the 894 entries scanned previously, and the time it takes to complete the query bears this out.

Running the same query using MongoDB v3.0 and interpreting its output is left as an exercise for the reader.

QUERY PLAN CACHE

All that's left to understand is how the query optimizer caches and expires its choice of query plan. After all, you wouldn't want the optimizer running all those plans in parallel on each query.

When a successful plan is discovered, the query pattern, the value for nscanned, and the index spec are recorded. For the query we've been working with, the recorded structure looks something like this:

```
{
  pattern: {
    stock_symbol: 'equality',
    close: 'bound',
```

```
    index: {
      stock_symbol: 1
    },
    nscanned: 894
  }
}
```

The query pattern records the kind of match for each key. Here, you're requesting an exact match on `stock_symbol` (equality), and a range match on `close` (bound).[12] Whenever a new query matches this pattern, the index will be used.

But this shouldn't hold forever, and it doesn't. The optimizer automatically expires a plan after any of the following events:

- 100 writes are made to the collection.
- Indexes are added or removed from the collection.
- A query using a cached query plan does a lot more work than expected. Here, what qualifies as "a lot more work" is a value for `nscanned` exceeding the cached `nscanned` value by at least a factor of 10.

In the last of these cases, the optimizer will immediately begin interleaving other query plans in case a different index proves more efficient. As you spend time optimizing queries, you'll likely notice several patterns of queries and indexes that work well together. In the next section, we codify some of these patterns.

If you're running MongoDB v3.0 you can find more information about query plan cache methods at http://docs.mongodb.org/manual/reference/method/js-plan-cache/.

8.3.3 Query patterns

Here we present several common query patterns and the indexes to use with them. This section's goal is to help you plan out how to pair your application's queries with MongoDB's indexes.

SINGLE-KEY INDEXES

To review single-key indexes, recall the index you created for the stock values collection on closing numbers in section 8.3.2, `{close: 1}`. This index can be used in the following scenarios.

EXACT MATCHES

An exact match. The index is used whether 0, 1, or many results are returned. An exact match is used in this query, returning all entries with a closing value of 100:

```
db.values.find({close: 100})
```

SORTING

A sort on the indexed field. For example:

```
db.values.find({}).sort({close: 1})
```

---

[12] In case you're interested, three kinds of range matches are stored: upper, lower, and upper-and-lower. The query pattern also includes any sort specification.

In the case of a sort with no query selector, you'll probably want to tack on a limit unless you actually plan to iterate over the entire collection.

RANGE QUERIES

A range query with or without a sort on the same field. For example, all closing values greater than or equal to 100:

```
db.values.find({close: {$gte: 100}})
```

If you add a sort clause on the same key, the optimizer will still be able to use the same index:

```
db.values.find({close: {$gte: 100}}).sort({close: 1})
```

COMPOUND-KEY INDEXES

Compound-key indexes are a little more complicated, but their uses are analogous to those of single-key indexes. The main thing to remember is that a compound-key index can efficiently serve only a single range or sort per query. Let's imagine a triple-compound key index, again for stock values, on {close: 1, open: 1, date: 1}. Let's look at some possible scenarios.

EXACT MATCHES

An exact match on the first key, the first and second keys, or the first, second, and third keys, in that order:

```
db.values.find({close: 1})
db.values.find({close: 1, open: 1})
db.values.find({close: 1, open: 1, date: "1985-01-08"})
```

RANGE MATCHES

An exact match on any set of leftmost keys (including none), followed by either a range or a sort using the next key to the right. Thus, all the following queries are ideal for the triple-key index:

```
db.values.find({}).sort({close: 1})
db.values.find({close: {$gt: 1}})
db.values.find({close: 100}).sort({open: 1})
db.values.find({close: 100, open: {$gt: 1}})
db.values.find({close: 1, open: 1.01, date: {$gt: "2005-01-01"}})
db.values.find({close: 1, open: 1.01}).sort({date: 1})
```

COVERING INDEXES

If you've never heard of covering indexes, realize from the start that the term is something of a misnomer. A *covering index* isn't, as the name would suggest, a kind of index but rather a special use of an index. In particular, an index can be said to cover a query if all the data required by the query resides in the index itself. Covered index queries are also known as index-only queries because these queries are served without having to reference the indexed documents themselves. This can result in increased query performance.

Using a covering index in MongoDB is easy. Simply select a set of fields that reside in a single index and exclude the _id field (this field likely isn't part of the index you're using). Here's an example that uses the triple-compound index you created in the previous section:

```
db.values.find({close: 1}, {open: 1, close: 1, date: 1, _id: 0})
```

In earlier versions of MongoDB, cursor.explain() returned the indexOnly field to indicate whether the index covered a query and no actual collection data was used to serve the query. In MongoDB v3.0, when an index covers a query, the explain result has an IXSCAN stage that isn't a descendant of a FETCH stage, and in the execution-Stats, the value of totalDocsExamined is 0.

8.4   Summary

This chapter is hefty, as indexing is an admittedly rich subject. If some of the ideas are unclear, that's okay. You should at least come away with a few techniques for examining indexes and avoiding slow queries, and you should know enough to keep learning.

Query optimization is always application-specific, but our hope is that the ideas and techniques provided here will help you tune your queries for the better. Empirical approaches are always useful. Make a habit of profiling and explaining your queries. In the process, you'll continue learning about the hidden corners of the query optimizer, and you'll ensure efficient queries for your application.

As you write your own applications, here are some things to remember:

- Indexes are incredibly useful but carry a cost—they make writes slower.
- MongoDB generally uses only one index in a query, so queries on multiple fields require compound indexes to be efficient.
- Order matters when you declare compound indexes.
- You should plan for, and avoid, expensive queries. Use MongoDB's explain command, its expensive query logs, and its profiler to discover queries that should be optimized.
- MongoDB gives you several commands for building indexes, but these always include a cost and may interfere with your application. This means you should optimize your queries and create indexes early, before you have much traffic or data.
- Optimize queries by reducing the number of documents scanned. The explain command is immensely useful for discovering what a query is doing; use it as a guide for optimization.

With the complexity involved in indexing and query optimization, plain old experimentation may be your best teacher from here on out.

Text search

In chapters 5 and 6, which explored constructing queries and using aggregation, you learned how to perform database queries using a fairly sophisticated query language. For many applications, searches using these types of queries may be sufficient. But when you're dealing with large amounts of unstructured data, or trying to support users finding the product they want to buy from a huge catalog of possible products, this type of searching may not be enough. Website visitors who have become accustomed to using Google or Amazon for searches expect much more and have come to rely increasingly on more sophisticated search technology.

In this chapter you'll see how MongoDB can provide some of the capabilities that more sophisticated text search engines provide—much more than the queries you've seen so far. These additional capabilities include indexing for fast word searches, matching exact phrases, excluding documents with certain words or phrases, supporting multiple languages, and scoring search result documents based on how well they match a search string. Although MongoDB text search isn't intended to replace dedicated search engines, it may provide enough capabilities that you won't need one.

Let's look at the various types of search capabilities dedicated search engines provide. In section 9.1.3 you'll see the subset of those capabilities provided by MongoDB.

If you've got it, why not use it?

On a LinkedIn MongoDB group discussion, someone asked what the benefit was to using MongoDB text search versus a dedicated search engine such as Elasticsearch. Here's the reply from Kelly Stirman, director of Products at MongoDB:

"In general Elasticsearch has a much richer set of features than MongoDB. This makes sense—it is a dedicated search engine. Where MongoDB text search makes sense is for very basic search requirements. If you're already storing your data in MongoDB, text indexes add some overhead to your deployment, but in general it is far simpler than deploying MongoDB and Elasticsearch side by side."

NOTE You can read more about Elasticsearch in *Elasticsearch in Action* by Radu Gheorghe et al (Manning Publications, 2015). You can also read a book on another popular dedicated search engine also built on top of Apache Lucene: *Solr in Action,* by Trey Grainger and Timothy Potter (Manning Publications, 2014).

9.1 *Text searches—not just pattern matching*

You probably perform some type of search on a daily basis, if not many times every day. As a programmer, you may search the internet for help dealing with particularly vexing programming bugs. You may then go home at night and search Amazon or another website for products; you may have even used the custom search on Manning.com, supported by Google, to find this book.

If you go to Manning.com, you'll see a "Search manning.com" text search box in the upper-right corner of the site. Type a keyword, such as "java," into the text box and click the Search button; you'll see something like the display shown in figure 9.1.

Note that since the search is run against live data, your exact results may vary. Perhaps the book *Java 8 in Action,* newly published at the time this chapter was written, will be replaced with Java 9, 10, or even 11.

About 28,500 results (0.60 seconds)

Manning **Java** Books
www.manning.com/catalog/**java**/
Manning **Java** Books. **Java** Titles in Print. Out of Print titles listed here may still be available
in eBook format or in revised editions. A list of Cancelled MEAPs that ...

Manning: **Java** 8 in Action
www.manning.com/urma/

     Java 8 in Action Lambdas, streams, and functional-style programming. Raoul-
Gabriel Urma, Mario Fusco, and Alan Mycroft August 2014 | 424 pages | B&W

Manning: The Well-Grounded **Java** Developer
www.manning.com/evans/

     The Well-Grounded **Java** Developer Vital techniques of **Java** 7 and polyglot
programming. Benjamin J. Evans and Martijn Verburg Foreword by Dr. Heinz
Kabutz

Figure 9.1   Search results from search for term "java" at www.manning.com

The point of this search is to illustrate a couple of important features that text search
engines provide that you may take for granted:

- The search has performed a *case-insensitive search*, meaning that no matter how
  you capitalize the letters in your search term, even using "jAVA" instead of "Java"
  or "java," you'll see results for "Java" or any uppercase, lowercase combination
  spelling of the word.
- You won't see any results for "JavaScript," even though books on JavaScript contain the text string "Java." This is because the search engine recognizes that
  there's a difference between the words "Java" and "JavaScript."

As you may know, you could perform this type of search in MongoDB using a regular
expression, specifying whole word matches only and case-insensitive matches. But in
MongoDB, such pattern-matching searches can be slow when used on large collections
if they can't take advantage of indexes, something text search engines routinely do to
sift through large amounts of data. Even those complex MongoDB searches won't provide the capabilities of a true text search.

Let's illustrate that using another example.

9.1.1   *Text searches vs. pattern matching*

Now try a second search on Manning.com; this time use the search term "script." You
should see something similar to the results shown in figure 9.2.

Notice that in this case the results will include results for books that contain the
word "scripting" as well as the word "script," but not the word "JavaScript." This is due

About 5,010 results (0.32 seconds)

powered by Google™ Custom Search

Sample Chapter 8
www.manning.com/maher/ch08.pdf

File Format: PDF/Adobe Acrobat

Scripting techniques. 8.1 Exploiting **script**-oriented functions 248. 8.2 Pre-processing arguments 256. 8.3 Executing code conditionally with if/else 259.

Programming with Pig - Hadoop in Action
www.manning.com/lam/SampleCh10.pdf

File Format: PDF/Adobe Acrobat

Computing similar documents efficiently, using a simple Pig Latin **script**. □ ... 2 A compiler that compiles and runs your Pig Latin **script** in a choice of evaluation ...

Table of Contents
www.manning.com/maher/excerpt_contents.html

Using aliases for common types of Perl commands. Constructing programs. Constructing an output-only one-liner, Constructing an input/output **script**. Summary.

Figure 9.2   Results from searching for term "script" on www.manning.com

to the ability of search engines to perform what's known as *stemming*, where words in both the text being searched, as well as the search terms you entered, are converted to the "stem" or root word from which "scripting" is derived—"script" in this case. This is where search engines have to understand the language in which they're storing and searching in order to understand that "script" could refer to "scripts," "scripted," or "scripting," but not "JavaScript."

Although web page searches use many of the same text search capabilities, they also provide additional searching capabilities. Let's see what those search capabilities are as well as how they might help or hinder your user.

9.1.2   *Text searches vs. web page searches*

Web page search engines contain many of the same search capabilities as a dedicated text search engine and usually much more. Web page searches are focused on searching a network of web pages. This can be an advantage when you're trying to search the World Wide Web, but it may be overkill or even a disadvantage when you're trying to search a product catalog. This ability to search based on relationships between documents isn't something you'll find in dedicated text search engines, nor will you find it in MongoDB, even with the new text search capabilities.

One of the original search algorithms used by Google was referred to as "Page Rank," a play on words, because not only was it intended to rank web pages, but it was developed by the co-founder of Google, Larry Page. Page Rank rates the importance, or weight, of a page based on the importance of pages that link to it. Figure 9.3, based

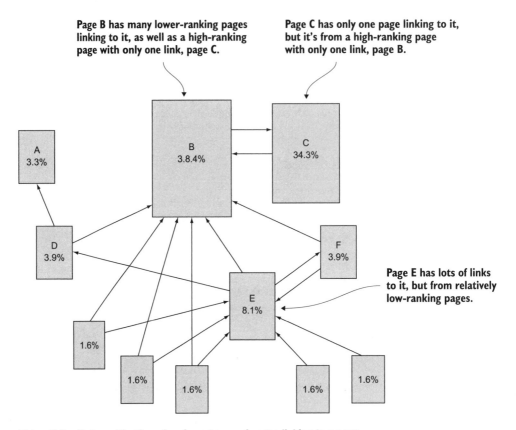

Page B has many lower-ranking pages linking to it, as well as a high-ranking page with only one link, page C.

Page C has only one page linking to it, but it's from a high-ranking page with only one link, page B.

A
3.3%

B
3.8.4%

C
34.3%

D
3.9%

F
3.9%

E
8.1%

Page E has lots of links to it, but from relatively low-ranking pages.

1.6%

1.6%

1.6%

1.6%

1.6%

Figure 9.3   Page ranking based on importance of pages linking to a page

on the Wikipedia entry for Page Rank, http://en.wikipedia.org/wiki/PageRank, illustrates this algorithm.

As you can see in figure 9.3, page C is almost as important as B because it has a very important page pointing to it: page B. The algorithm, which is still taught in university courses on data mining, also takes into account the number of outgoing links a page has. In this case, not only is B very important, but it also has only one outgoing link, making that one link even more critical. Note also that page E has lot of links to it, but they're all from relatively low-ranking pages, so page E doesn't have a high rating.

Google today uses many algorithms to weight pages, over 200 by some counts, making it a full-featured web search engine. But keep in mind that web page searching isn't the same as the type of search you might want to use when searching a catalog. Web page searches will access the web pages you generate from your database, but not the database itself. For example, look again at the page that searched for "java," shown in figure 9.4. You'll see that the first result isn't a product at all—it's the list of Manning books on Java.

Manning **Java** Books

www.manning.com/catalog/**java**/

Manning **Java** Books. **Java** Titles in Print. Out of Print titles listed here may still be available
in eBook format or in revised editions. A list of Cancelled MEAPs that ...

Figure 9.4   Searching results in more than just books.

Perhaps having a list of Java books as the first result might not be so bad, but because
the Google search doesn't have the concept of a book, if you search for "javascript,"
you don't have to scroll down very far before you'll see a web page for errata for a
book already in the list. This is illustrated in figure 9.5. This type of "noise" can be dis-
tracting if what you're looking for is a book on JavaScript. It can also require you to
scroll down further than you might otherwise have to.

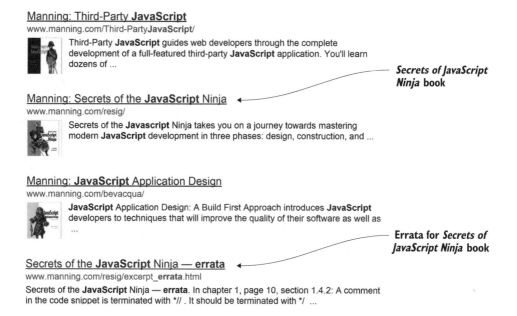

Manning: Third-Party **JavaScript**

www.manning.com/Third-Party**JavaScript**/

Third-Party **JavaScript** guides web developers through the complete
development of a full-featured third-party **JavaScript** application. You'll learn
dozens of ...

Secrets of JavaScript
Ninja **book**

Manning: Secrets of the **JavaScript** Ninja

www.manning.com/resig/

Secrets of the **Javascript** Ninja takes you on a journey towards mastering
modern **JavaScript** development in three phases: design, construction, and ...

Manning: **JavaScript** Application Design

www.manning.com/bevacqua/

JavaScript Application Design: A Build First Approach introduces **JavaScript**
developers to techniques that will improve the quality of their software as well as
...

Errata for *Secrets of*
JavaScript Ninja **book**

Secrets of the **JavaScript** Ninja — **errata**

www.manning.com/resig/excerpt_**errata**.html

Secrets of the **JavaScript** Ninja — **errata**. In chapter 1, page 10, section 1.4.2: A comment
in the code snippet is terminated with */// . It should be terminated with */ ...

Figure 9.5   A search showing how a book can appear more than once

Although web page search engines are great at searching a large network of pages and
ranking results based on how the pages are related, they aren't intended to solve the
problem of searching a database such as a product database. To solve this type of
problem, you can look to full-featured text search engines that can search a product
database, such as the one you'd expect to find on Amazon.

9.1.3   *MongoDB text search vs. dedicated text search engines*

Dedicated text search engines can go beyond indexing web pages to indexing extremely large databases. Text search engines can provide capabilities such as spelling correction, suggestions as to what you're looking for, and relevancy measures—things many web search engines can do as well. But dedicated search engines can provide further improvements such as facets, custom synonym libraries, custom stemming algorithms, and custom stop word dictionaries.

> **Facets? Synonym libraries? Custom stemming? Stop word dictionaries?**
>
> If you've never looked into dedicated search engines, you might wonder what all these terms mean. In brief: *facets* allow you to group together products by a particular characteristic, such as the "Laptop Computer" category shown on the left side of the page in figure 9.6. *Synonym libraries* allow you to specify different words that have the same meaning. For example, if you search for "intelligent" you might also want to see results for "bright" and "smart." As previously covered in section 9.1.1, *stemming* allows you to find different forms of a word, such as "scripting" and "script." *Stop words* are common words that are filtered out prior to searching, such as "the," "a," and "and."
>
> We won't cover these terms in great depth, but if you want to find out more about them you can read a book on dedicated search engines such as *Solr in Action* or *Elasticsearch in Action*.

Faceted search is something that you'll see almost any time you shop on a modern large e-commerce website, where results will be grouped by certain categories that allow the user to further explore. For example, if you go to the Amazon website and search using the term "apple" you'll see something like the page in figure 9.6.

On the left side of the web page, you'll see a list of different groupings you might find for Apple-related products and accessories. These are the results of a faceted search. Although we did provide similar capabilities in our e-commerce data model using categories and tags, facets make it easy and efficient to turn almost any field into a type of category. In addition, facets can go beyond groupings based on the different values in a field. For example, in figure 9.6 you see groupings based on weight ranges instead of exact weight. This approach allows you to narrow the search based on the weight range you want, something that's important if you're searching for a portable computer.

Facets allow the user to easily drill down into the results to help narrow their search results based on different criteria of interest to them. Facets in general are a tremendous aid to help you find what you're looking for, especially in a product database as large as Amazon, which sells more than 200 million products. This is where a faceted search becomes almost a necessity.

Show results for different "facets" based on department.

List of most common facets

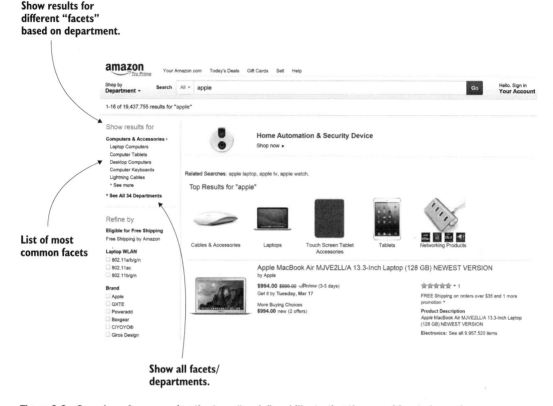

Show all facets/ departments.

Figure 9.6   Search on Amazon using the term "apple" and illustrating the use of faceted search

MONGODB'S TEXT SEARCH: COSTS VS. BENEFITS

Unfortunately, many of the capabilities available in a full-blown text search engine are beyond the capabilities of MongoDB. But there's good news: MongoDB can still provide you with about 80% of what you might want in a catalog search, with less complexity and effort than is needed to establish a full-blown text search engine with faceted search and suggestive terms. What does MongoDB give you?

- Automatic real-time indexing with stemming
- Optional assignable weights by field name
- Multilanguage support
- Stop word removal
- Exact phrase or word matches
- The ability to exclude results with a given phrase or word

NOTE   Unlike more full-featured text search engines, MongoDB doesn't allow you to edit the list of stop words. There's a request to add this: https://jira.mongodb.org/browse/SERVER-10062.

All these capabilities are available for the price of defining an index, which then gives you access to some decent word-search capabilities without having to copy your entire database to a dedicated search engine. This approach also avoids the additional administrative and management overhead that would go along with a dedicated search engine. Not a bad trade-off if MongoDB gives you enough of the capabilities you need.

Now let's see the details of how MongoDB provides this support. It's pretty simple:

- First, you define the indexes needed for text searching.
- Then, you'll use text search in both the basic queries as well as aggregation framework.

One more critical component you'll need is MongoDB 2.6 or later. MongoDB 2.4 introduced text search in an experimental stage, but it wasn't until MongoDB 2.6 that text search became available by default and text search–related functions became fully integrated with the find() and aggregate() functions.

What you'll need to know to use text searching in MongoDB

Although it will help to fully understand chapter 8 on indexing, the text search indexes are fairly easy to understand. If you want to use text search for basic queries or the aggregation framework, you'll have to be familiar with the related material in chapter 5, which covers how to perform basic queries, and chapter 6, which covers how to use the aggregation framework.

MONGODB TEXT SEARCH: A SIMPLE EXAMPLE

Before taking a detailed look at how MongoDB's text search works, let's explore an example using the e-commerce data. The first thing you'll need to do is define an index; you'll begin by specifying the fields that you want to index. We'll cover the details of using text indexes in section 9.3, but here's a simple example using the e-commerce products collection:

```
db.products.createIndex(                        Index name field
    {name: 'text',
     description: 'text',                        Index description
     tags: 'text'}                              field
);
                                                Index tags field
```

This index specifies that the text from three fields in the products collection will be searched: name, description, and tags. Now let's see a search example that looks for gardens in the products collection:

```
> db.products
    .find({$text: {$search: 'gardens'}},
          {_id:0, name:1,description:1,tags:1})   Search for text
    .pretty()                                     field gardens
```

```
{
    "name" : "Rubberized Work Glove, Black",
    "description" : "Black Rubberized Work Gloves...",
    "tags" : [
        "gardening"                     ◁─┐  gardening
    ]                                     │  matches search
}
{
    "name" : "Extra Large Wheel Barrow",
    "description" : "Heavy duty wheel barrow...",
    "tags" : [
        "tools",
        "gardening",                    ◁─┐  gardening
        "soil"                            │  matches search
    ]
}
```

Even this simple query illustrates a few key aspects of MongoDB text search and how it differs from normal text search. In this example, the search for *gardens* has resulted in a search for the stemmed word *garden*. That in turn has found two products with the tag gardening, which has been stemmed and indexed under garden.

In the next few sections, you'll learn much more about how MongoDB text search works. But first let's download a larger set of data to use for the remaining examples in this chapter.

9.2 *Manning book catalog data download*

Our e-commerce data has been fine for the examples shown so far in the book. For this chapter, though, we're going to introduce a larger set of data with much more text in order to better illustrate the use of MongoDB text search and its strengths as well as limitations. This data set will contain a snapshot of the Manning book catalog created at the time this chapter was written. If you want to follow along and run examples yourself, you can download the data to your local MongoDB database by following these steps:

- In the source code included with this book, find the chapter9 folder, and copy the file catalog.books.json from that folder to a convenient location on your computer.
- Run the command shown here. You may have to change the command to prefix the filename, catalog.books.json, with the name of the directory where you saved the file.

```
mongoimport --db catalog --collection books --type json --drop
➥   --file catalog.books.json
```

You should see something similar to the results shown in the following listing. Please note that the findOne() function returns a randomly selected document.

Listing 9.1   Loading sample data in the `books` collections

```
> use catalog                                          ◁         Switch to catalog
switched to db catalog                                           database
> db.books.findOne()                                   ◁
{                                                                Show a randomly selected
        "_id" : 1,                                              book from catalog
nerat        "title" : "Unlocking Android",
        "isbn" : "1933988673",
        "pageCount" : 416,
        "publishedDate" : ISODate("2009-04-01T07:00:00Z"),
        "thumbnailUrl" : "https://s3.amazonaws.com/AKIAJC5RLADLUMVRPFDQ
.book-thumb-images/ableson.jpg",
        "shortDescription" : "Unlocking Android: A Developer's Guide
provides concise, hands-on instruction for the Android operating system and
development tools. This book teaches important architectural concepts in a
straightforward writing style and builds on this with practical and useful
examples throughout.",
        "longDescription" : "Android is an open source mobile phone
platform based on the Linux operating system and developed by the Open
Handset Alliance, a consortium of over 30 hardware, software and telecom
...
* Notification methods    * OpenGL, animation & multimedia    * Sample
      "status" : "PUBLISH",
        "authors" : [
                "W. Frank Ableson",
                "Charlie Collins",
                "Robi Sen"
        ],
        "categories" : [
                "Open Source",
                "Mobile"
        ]
}
```

The listing also shows the structure of a document. For each document you'll have the following:

- `title`—A text field with the book title
- `isbn`—International Standard Book Number (ISBN)
- `pageCount`—The number of pages in the book
- `publishedDate`—The date on which the book was published (only present if the `status` field is `PUBLISH`)
- `thumbnailUrl`—The URL of the thumbnail for the book cover
- `shortDescription`—A short description of the book
- `longDescription`—A long description of the book
- `status`—The status of the book, either `PUBLISH` or `MEAP`
- `authors`—The array of author names
- `categories`—The array of book categories

Now that you have the list of books loaded, let's create a text index for it.

9.3   *Defining text search indexes*

Text indexes are similar to the indexes you saw in section 7.2.2, which covered creating and deleting indexes. One important difference between the regular indexes you saw there and text indexes is that you can have only a single text index for a given collection. The following is a sample text index definition for the books collection:

```
db.books.createIndex(
    {title: 'text',                         ◁─┐  Specify fields to
     shortDescription: 'text',                │  be text-indexed.
     longDescription: 'text',
     authors: 'text',
     categories: 'text'},

    {weights:                               ◁─┐  Optionally
        {title: 10,                           │  specify weights
         shortDescription: 1,                 │  for each field.
         longDescription:1,
         authors: 1,
         categories: 5}
    }
);
```

There are a few other important differences between the regular indexes covered in section 7.2.2 and text indexes:

- Instead of specifying a 1 or -1 after the field being indexed, you use text.
- You can specify as many fields as you want to become part of the text index and all the fields will be searched together as if they were a single field.
- You can have only one text search index per collection, but it can index as many fields as you like.

Don't worry yet about weights assigned to the fields. The weights allow you to specify how important a field is to scoring the search results. We'll discuss that further and show how they're used when we explore text search scoring in section 9.4.2.

9.3.1   *Text index size*

An index entry is created for each unique, post-stemmed word in the document. As you might imagine, text search indexes tend to be large. To reduce the number of index entries, some words (called *stop words*) are ignored. As we discussed earlier when we talked about faceted searches, stop words are words that aren't generally searched for. In English this include words such as "the," "an," "a," and "and." Trying to perform a search for a stop word would be pretty useless because it would return almost every document in your collection.

The next listing shows the results of a stats() command on our books collection. The stats() command shows you the size of the books collection, along with the size of indexes on the collection.

Listing 9.2   books collection statistics showing space use and index name

```
> db.books.stats()
{
        "ns" : "catalog.books",
        "count" : 431,
        "size" : 772368,              ◁─┐  Size of books
        "avgObjSize" : 1792,             │  collection
        "storageSize" : 2793472,
        "numExtents" : 5,
        "nindexes" : 2,
        "lastExtentSize" : 2097152,
        "paddingFactor" : 1,
        "systemFlags" : 0,
        "userFlags" : 1,
        "totalIndexSize" : 858480,
        "indexSizes" : {
                "_id_" : 24528,
"title_text_shortDescription_text_longDescription_text_authors_text
_categories_text" : 833952                           ◁─┐
        },                                               │  Name and size of
        "ok" : 1                                         │  text search index
}
```

Notice that the size of the books collection (size in listing 9.2) is 772,368. Looking at the indexSizes field in the listing, you'll see the name and size of the text search index. Note that the size of the text search index is 833,952—larger than the books collection itself! This might startle or concern you at first, but remember the index must contain an index entry for each unique stemmed word being indexed for the document, as well as a pointer to the document being indexed. Even though you remove stop words, you'll still have to duplicate most of the text being indexed as well as add a pointer to the original document for each word.

Another important point to take note of is the length of the index name:

```
"title_text_shortDescription_text_longDescription_text_authors_text
_categories_text."
```

MongoDB namespaces have a maximum length of 123 bytes. If you index a few more text fields, you can see how you might easily exceed the 123-byte limit. Let's see how you can assign an index a user-defined name to avoid this problem. We'll also show you a simpler way to specify that you want to index all text fields in a collection.

9.3.2   Assigning an index name and indexing all text fields in a collection

In MongoDB a *namespace* is the name of an object concatenated with the name of the database and collection, with a dot between the three names. Namespaces can have a maximum length of 123 bytes. In the previous example, you're already up to 84 characters for the namespace for the index.

There are a couple of ways to avoid this problem. First, as with all MongoDB indexes, you have the option of specifying the name of the index, as shown here:

```
db.books.createIndex(
    {title: 'text',
     shortDescription: 'text',
     longDescription: 'text',
     authors: 'text',
     categories: 'text'},          Specify weights for
                                    fields with weights
                                    other than 1.
    {weights:
        {title: 10,
         categories: 5},
     name : 'books_text_index'      User-defined
    }                               index name
);
```

This example also specifies weights for `title` and `categories`, but all other fields will default to a weight of 1. You'll find out more about how weights affect the sorting of your search results in section 9.4.3 when we cover sorting by text search score.

Please note that if an index already exists, you won't be able to create it again even if you're using a different name (the error message will be `"all indexes already exist"`). In that case, you'll first need to drop it using `dropIndex()` and then recreate it with the desired name.

WILDCARD FIELD NAME

Text search indexes also have a special wildcard field name: `$**`. This name specifies that you want to index any field that contains a string. For text indexes with the wildcard specification, the default index name is `$**_text`, thus enabling you to avoid the namespace 123-byte limit problem:

```
db.books.createIndex(
    {'$**': 'text'},               Index all fields
                                    with strings.
    {weights:
        {title: 10,
         categories: 5},
);
```

You can also include other fields in the text index to create a compound index, but there are some restrictions on how you can search a compound text index. You can read more about this and other details of the text index at http://docs.mongodb.org/manual/core/index-text/.

Now that you have a text index, let's see how to use it for searching.

9.4 Basic text search

Let's start with an example of a simple MongoDB text search:

```
db.books.find({$text: {$search: 'actions'}},{title:1})
```

This query looks much like the queries covered in chapter 5 using the `find()` command. The `$text` operator defines the query as a text search. The `$search` parameter then defines the string you want to use for the search. This query would return these results or something similar as results are returned in a random order:

```
{ "_id" : 256, "title" : "Machine Learning in Action" }
{ "_id" : 146, "title" : "Distributed Agile in Action" }
{ "_id" : 233, "title" : "PostGIS in Action" }
{ "_id" : 17, "title" : "MongoDB in Action" }
...
```

Even for this simple query there's quite a bit going on under the covers:

- The word *actions* was stemmed to *action*.
- MongoDB then used an index to quickly find all documents with the stemmed word *action*.

Although not noticeable on our relatively small collection, you can see how using an index to find the documents instead of scanning all the text fields for all the documents in the collection can be much faster even for modest-sized collections.

Next, try a more complex search, one using a phrase with more than one word:

```
db.books.find({$text: {$search: 'MongoDB in Action'}},{title:1})
```

So far the results will appear the same as for the previous example:

```
{ "_id" : 256, "title" : "Machine Learning in Action" }
{ "_id" : 146, "title" : "Distributed Agile in Action" }
{ "_id" : 233, "title" : "PostGIS in Action" }
{ "_id" : 17, "title" : "MongoDB in Action" }
...
```

For this query, the search string is split into words, stop words are removed, the remaining words are stemmed, and MongoDB then uses the text index to perform a case-insensitive compare. This is illustrated in figure 9.7.

In the figure, there's only one stop word, *in*, and the stemmed versions of each word are the same as the original word. MongoDB will next use the results to perform a case-insensitive search using the text index twice: once to search for *mongodb*, and then again to search for *action*. The results will be any documents that contain either of the two words, the equivalent of an or search.

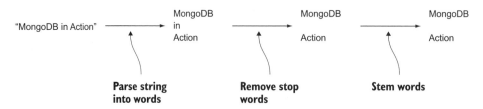

Figure 9.7   Text search string processing

Now that you've seen the basics of simple text searching, let's move on to more advanced searches.

9.4.1 *More complex searches*

In addition to searching for any of a number of words, the equivalent of an *or* search, MongoDB search allows you to do the following:

- Specify *and* word matches instead of *or* word matches.
- Perform exact phrase matches.
- Exclude documents with certain words.
- Exclude documents with certain phrases.

Let's start by seeing how to specify that a given word must be in the result document. You've already seen a search for *mongodb in action*, which returned not only books on MongoDB, but also any book with the word *action*. If you enclose a word in double quotes within the search string, it specifies that the word must always be in the result document. Here's an example:

```
db.books.
    find({$text: {$search: ' "mongodb" in action'}})    ◁┐
```
"mongodb" in double quotes means the word must be present.

This query returns only the books with titles that include the word *mongodb*:

```
{ "title" : "MongoDB in Action"}
{ "title" : "MongoDB in Action, Second Edition" }
```

EXACT MATCH ON PHRASES

Using double quotes also works for phrases, so if you specify the phrase *second edition*, only the second edition book is shown because multiple phrases make it an "and" search:

```
> db.books.
...     find({$text: {$search: ' "mongodb" "second edition" '}},    ◁┐
...     {_id:0, title:1})
{ "title" : "MongoDB in Action, Second Edition" }
```
Phrase "second edition" required as well as the word "mongodb"

Although the exact match logic will perform a case-insensitive compare, it won't remove stop words, nor will it stem the search terms. You can illustrate this by searching using the search string `'books'` with and without double quotes:

```
> db.books.
...     find({$text: {$search: ' books '}}).    ◁┐
...     count()
414
>
> db.books.
...     find({$text: {$search: ' "books" '}}).    ◁┐
...     count()
21
```
Stemmed version of word "books"—414

Exact word "books"—21

Here you can see that when you specified the word *books* without double quotes, MongoDB stemmed the word and could find 414 results. When you specify the exact match, using double quotes around the word *books*, MongoDB returned only the count of documents that contained the exact word *books*, 21 documents in all. The total number of results you will get may vary depending on the input data.

EXCLUDING DOCUMENTS WITH SPECIFIC WORDS OR PHRASES

To exclude all documents that contain a word, put a minus sign in front of the word. For example, if you wanted all books with the word *MongoDB* but not those with the word *second* you could use the following:

```
> db.books.
...      find({$text: {$search: ' mongodb -second '}},        ⟵ Exclude documents
...      {_id:0, title:1 })                                          with the word
{ "title" : "MongoDB in Action" }                                    "second."
```

Note that the three dots on the second and the third lines are automatically added by the mongo shell to show that the input is longer than one line—in this case it's three lines long.

Similarly, you can exclude documents with a particular phrase by enclosing the phrase in double quotes and preceding it with a minus sign:

```
> db.books.
...      find({$text: {$search: ' mongodb -"second edition" '}},  ⟵ Exclude
...      {_id:0, title:1})                                              documents
{ "title" : "MongoDB in Action" }                                      with the phrase
                                                                       "second edition."
```

MORE COMPLEX SEARCH SPECIFICATIONS

You can combine the text search with most other find() search criteria to further limit your search. For example, if you wanted to search for all Java books that still have a status of MEAP, you could use this:

```
> db.books.
...      find({$text: {$search: ' mongodb '}, status: 'MEAP' },  ⟵ status must
...      {_id:0, title:1, status:1})                                   be MEAP
{ "title" : "MongoDB in Action, Second Edition",
 "status" : "MEAP"}
```

Limits on combining text search criteria

There are a few limits as to what you can combine with a text search and how text indexes are limited. These limits are further defined at http://docs.mongodb.org/manual/core/index-text/ under restrictions. A few key limits include the following:

- Multikey compound indexes aren't allowed.
- Geospatial compound key indexes aren't allowed.
- hint() cannot be used if a query includes a $text query expression.
- Sort operations cannot obtain sort order from a text field index.

If you add more stop words, such as *the*, and change the search terms to use non-stemmed words, you'll see the same results. This doesn't prove that the stop words are in fact ignored or that the nonstemmed word is treated the same as the stemmed word.

To prove that, you'll have to look at the text search score to confirm that you're receiving the same score regardless of extra stop words or different words with the same stem. Let's see what the text search score is and how you can include it in your results.

9.4.2 Text search scores

The text search score provides a number that rates the relevancy of the document based on how many times the word appeared in the document. The scoring also uses any weights assigned to different fields when the index was created, as described in section 9.3.

To show the text search score, you use a projection field such as `score: { $meta: "textScore" }` in your `find()` command. Note that the name you assign the text score—`score` in this case—can be any name you want. The next listing shows an example of the same search shown earlier but with the text score displayed, followed by the search with a slightly different but equivalent search string. Please note that the output you're going to get may be different from the one presented here.

> **Listing 9.3 Displaying text search score**

Search for "Mongodb in Action."

Include text search score in results.

```
> db.books.
...     find({$text: {$search: 'mongodb in action'}},
...     {_id:0, title:1, score: { $meta: "textScore" }}).
...     limit(4);
{ "title" : "Machine Learning in Action", "score" : 16.83933933933934 }
{ "title" : "Distributed Agile in Action", "score" : 19.371088861076345 }
{ "title" : "PostGIS in Action", "score" : 17.67825896762905 }
{ "title" : "MongoDB in Action", "score" : 49.48653394500073 }
>
>
> db.books.
...     find({$text: {$search: 'the mongodb and actions in it'}},
...     {_id:0, title:1, score: { $meta: "textScore" }}).
...     limit(4);
{ "title" : "Machine Learning in Action", "score" : 16.83933933933934 }
{ "title" : "Distributed Agile in Action", "score" : 19.371088861076345 }
{ "title" : "PostGIS in Action", "score" : 17.67825896762905 }
{ "title" : "MongoDB in Action", "score" : 49.48653394500073 }
```

Text search scores for first search string

Second string text scores—identical to first set of scores

Second text string with extra stop words and plural word "actions"

In this listing, the search string "MongoDB in Action" is changed to "the mongodb and actions in it." This new search string uses the plural form of *action*, and also adds a number of stop words. As you can see, the text scores are identical in both cases, illustrating that the stop words are in fact ignored and that the remaining words are stemmed.

WEIGHT FIELD TO INFLUENCE WORD IMPORTANCE

In the index created in section 9.3.2, you'll notice the definition of a field called weights. Weights influence the importance of words found in a particular field, compared to the same word found in other fields. The default weight for a field is 1, but as you can see, we've assigned a weight of 5 to the categories field and a weight of 10 to the title field. This means that a word found in categories carries five times the weight of the same word found in the short or long description fields. Similarly, a word found in the title field will carry 10 times the weight of the same word found in one of the description fields and twice the weight of the same word found in categories. This will affect the score assigned to a document:

```
db.books.createIndex(
    {'$**': 'text'},

    {weights:                           Specify weights for
        {title: 10,                     fields with weights
          categories: 5}                other than 1.
    }
);
```

This search is fine if you want to find all the books with the words *mongodb* or *action*. But for most searches, you also want to view the most relevant results first. Let's see how to do that.

9.4.3 *Sorting results by text search score*

To sort the results by relevancy, sort by the same text search score shown in the previous example. In fact, to sort by the text search score, you must also include the $meta function in your find() projection specification. Here's an example:

```
db.books.
    find({$text: {$search: 'mongodb in action'}},      Projection for
        {title:1, score: { $meta: "textScore" }}).     text score
    sort({ score: { $meta: "textScore" } })
                                                        Sort by text score.
```

This example will result in a list sorted by the text score:

```
{ "_id" : 17, "title" : "MongoDB in Action", "score" : 49.48653394500073 }
{ "_id" : 186, "title" : "Hadoop in Action", "score" : 24.99910329985653 }
{ "_id" : 560, "title" : "HTML5 in Action", "score" : 23.02156177156177 }
```

As mentioned earlier, you can name the text search score anything you want. We've named it `score` in our examples, but you may choose something like `textSearchScore`. But keep in mind that the name specified in the `sort()` function must be the same as the name specified in the preceding `find()` function. In addition, you can't specify the order (ascending or descending) for the sort by text sort field. The sort is always from highest score to lowest score, which makes sense, because you normally want the most relevant results first. If for some reason you do need to sort with least relevant results first, you can use the aggregation framework text search (which is covered in the next section).

Now that you've seen how to use the text search with the `find()` command, let's see how you can also use it in the aggregation framework.

The projection field `$meta:"textScore"`

As you learned in chapter 5, section 5.1.2, you use a projection to limit the fields returned from the `find()` function. But if you specify any fields in the find projection, only those fields specified will be returned.

You can only sort by the text search score if you include the text search meta score results in your projection. Does this mean you must always specify all the fields you want returned if you sort by the text search score?

Luckily, no. If you specify only the meta text score in your find projection, all the other fields in your document will also be returned, along with the text search meta score.

9.5 Aggregation framework text search

As you learned in chapter 6, by using the aggregation framework, you can transform and combine data from multiple documents to generate new information not available in any single document. In this section you'll learn how to use the text search capabilities within the aggregation framework. As you'll see, the aggregation framework provides all the text search capabilities you saw for the `find()` command and a bit more.

In section 9.4.3, you saw a simple example in which you found books with the words *mongodb in action* and then sorted the results by the text score:

```
db.books.
    find({$text: {$search: 'mongodb in action'}},
        {title:1, score: { $meta: "textScore" }}).
    sort({ score: { $meta: "textScore" } })
```

Search for documents with the words mongodb or action.

Projection for text score

Sort by text score.

Using the aggregation framework, you can produce the same results using the following code:

```
db.books.aggregate(                                          Search for documents
   [                                                         with the words
      { $match: { $text: { $search: 'mongodb in action' } } },   mongodb or action.
      { $sort: { score: { $meta: 'textScore' } } },              Sort by
      { $project: { title: 1, score: { $meta: 'textScore' } } }  text score.
   ]
)                                            Projection for
                                             text score
```

As expected, this code will produce the same results you saw in the previous section:

```
{ "_id" : 17, "title" : "MongoDB in Action", "score" : 49.48653394500073 }
{ "_id" : 186, "title" : "Hadoop in Action", "score" : 24.99910329985653 }
{ "_id" : 560, "title" : "HTML5 in Action", "score" : 23.02156177156177 }
{ "_id" : 197, "title" : "Erlang and OTP in Action", "score" :
22.069632021922096 }
```

Notice that the two versions of the text search use many of the same constructs to specify the find/match criteria, the projection attributes, and the sort criteria. But as we promised, the aggregation framework can do even more. For example, you can take the previous example and by swapping the $sort and $project operators, simplify the $sort operator a bit:

```
db.books.aggregate(
   [
      { $match: { $text: { $search: 'mongodb in action' } } },   Sort by
      { $project: { title: 1, score: { $meta: 'textScore' } } },  descending
      { $sort: { score: -1 } }                                    score.
   ]
)
```

One big difference in the second aggregation example is that, unlike with the find() function, you can now reference the score attribute you defined in the preceding $project operation. Notice, though, that you're sorting the scores in *descending* order, and therefore you're using score: -1 instead of score: 1. But this does provide the option of showing lowest scoring books first if desired by using score: 1.

Using the $text search in the aggregation framework has some limitations:

- The $match operator using $text function search must be the first operation in the pipeline and must precede any other references to $meta:'textScore'.
- The $text function can appear only once in the pipeline.
- The $text function can't be used with $or or $not.

With the $match text search string, use the same format you would with the find()
command:

- If a word or phrase is enclosed in double quotes, the document must contain an
  exact match of the word or phrase.
- A word or phrase preceded by a minus sign (–) excludes documents with that
  word or phrase.

In the next section, you'll learn how to use the ability to access the text score to further customize the search.

9.5.1 *Where's MongoDB in Action, Second Edition?*

If you look closely at the results from our previous text searches using the string
"MongoDB in Action", you may have wondered why the results didn't include the second edition of *MongoDB in Action* as well as the first edition. To find out why, use the
same search string but enclose monogdb in double quotes so that you find only those
documents that have the word *mongodb* in them:

```
> db.books.aggregate(
...      [
...            { $match: { $text: { $search: ' "mongodb" in action ' } } },
...            { $project: {_id:0, title: 1, score: { $meta: 'textScore' } } }
...      ]
... )
{ "title" : "MongoDB in Action", "score" : 49.48653394500073 }
{ "title" : "MongoDB in Action, Second Edition", "score" : 12.5 }
```

When you see the low text score for the second edition of *MonogDB in Action*, it
becomes obvious why it hasn't shown up in the top scoring matches. But now the question is why the score is so low for the second edition. If you do a find only on the second edition, the answer becomes more obvious:

```
> db.books.findOne({"title" : "MongoDB in Action, Second Edition"})
{
        "_id" : 755,
        "title" : "MongoDB in Action, Second Edition",
        "isbn" : "1617291609",
        "pageCount" : 0,
        "thumbnailUrl" :
"https://s3.amazonaws.com/AKIAJC5RLADLUMVRPFDQ.book-thumb-
images/banker2.jpg",
        "status" : "MEAP",
        "authors" : [
                "Kyle Banker",
                "Peter Bakkum",
                "Tim Hawkins",
                "Shaun Verch",
                "Douglas Garrett"
        ],
        "categories" : [ ]
}
```

As you can see, because this data is from before the second edition was printed, the second edition didn't have the shortDescription or longDescription fields. This is true for many of the books that hadn't yet been published, and as a result those books will end up with a lower score.

You can use the flexibility of the aggregation framework to compensate for this somewhat. One way to do this is to multiply the text search score by a factor—say, 3— if a document doesn't have a longDescription field. The following listing shows an example of how you might do this.

Listing 9.4 Add text multiplier if `longDescription` isn't present

```
> db.books.aggregate(
      ...        [
      ...                { $match: { $text: { $search: 'mongodb in action' } } },
...
      ...        { $project: {                          Calculate multiplier: 3.0 if
      ...            title: 1,                          longDescription doesn't exist
      ...            score: { $meta: 'textScore' },
      ...            multiplier: { $cond: [ '$longDescription',1.0,3.0] } }    ⊲─┘
      ...        },
...
      ...        { $project: {                                   ┐ Calculate
      ...            _id:0, title: 1, score: 1, multiplier: 1,    │ adjusted
      ...            adjScore: {$multiply: ['$score','$multiplier']}}    ⊲─┤ score: score
      ...        },                                               │ * multiplier
...                                                               ┘
      ...        { $sort: {adjScore: -1}}    ⊲─┤ Sort by descending
      ...    ]                                └  adjusted score
... );
{ "title" : "MongoDB in Action", "score" : 49.48653394500073,
  "multiplier" : 1, "adjScore" : 49.48653394500073 }                ┐ Second
{ "title" : "MongoDB in Action, Second Edition", "score" : 12.5,    │ edition
  "multiplier" : 3, "adjScore" : 37.5 }                          ⊲─┤ now second
{ "title" : "Spring Batch in Action", "score" : 11.666666666666666, │ on list
  "multiplier" : 3, "adjScore" : 35 }                               ┘
{ "title" : "Hadoop in Action", "score" : 24.99910329985653,
  "multiplier" : 1, "adjScore" : 24.99910329985653 }
{ "title" : "HTML5 in Action", "score" : 23.02156177156177,
  "multiplier" : 1, "adjScore" : 23.02156177156177 }
```

As you can see in the first $project operator in the pipeline, you're calculating a multiplier by testing whether longDescription exists. A condition is considered false if it's null or doesn't exist, so you can use the $cond function to set a multiplier of 1.0 if longDescription exists and a multiplier of 3.0 if longDescription doesn't exist.

You then have a second $project operator in the aggregation pipeline that calculates an adjusted score by multiplying the text search score by the multiplier 1.0 or 3.0. Finally, you sort by the adjusted score in descending order.

As you can see, the MongoDB text search does have its limitations. Missing text fields can cause you to miss some results. The MongoDB text search also provides some ways to improve your search by requiring certain words or phrases to be in the search results, or by excluding documents that contain certain words. The aggregation framework offers additional flexibility and functionality and can be useful in extending the value of your text search.

Now that you've seen the basics and a few advanced features of MongoDB text search, you're ready to tackle another complex issue: searching languages other than English.

9.6 Text search languages

Remember that much of MongoDB's text search power comes from being able to stem words. Searching for the word *action* will return the same results as searching for the word *actions*, because they have the same stem. But stemming is language-specific. MongoDB won't recognize the plural or other unstemmed version of a non-English word unless you tell MongoDB what language you're using.

There are three points at which you can tell MongoDB what language you're using:

- *In the index*—You can specify the default language for a particular collection.
- *When you insert a document*—You can override this default to tell MongoDB that a particular document or field within the document is a language other than the index-specified default.
- *When you perform the text search in a* find() *or* aggregate() *function*—You can tell MongoDB what language your search is using.

> ### Stemming and stop words: Simple but limited
> Currently MongoDB uses "simple language-specific suffix stemming" (see http://docs.mongodb.org/manual/core/index-text/). Various stemming algorithms, including suffix stripping, are further described at http://en.wikipedia.org/wiki/Stemming. If you require processing of a language not supported by the suffix stemming approach, such as Chinese, or wish to use a different or customized stemmer, your best bet is to go to a more full-featured text search engine.
>
> Similarly, although MongoDB will use a different stop word dictionary based on the language, it doesn't allow you to customize the stop word dictionaries. Again, this is something that dedicated text search engines typically support.

Let's take a look at how you use each of these options.

9.6.1 Specifying language in the index

Returning to the example index you created in section 9.3.2, you can modify the index definition to define a default language. Before changing the language for the books collection, run the following text search command. You should find no results because you're searching for a stop word: *in*. Remember, stop words aren't indexed:

```
> db.books.find({$text: {$search: 'in '}}).count()
0
```

Now delete the previous index and create the same index, but with the language `french`:

```
db.books.dropIndex('books_text_index');        ◁┐  Drop existing text
                                                 │  index on books
db.books.createIndex(
    {'$**': 'text'},

    {weights:
        {title: 10,
         categories: 5},

     name : 'books_text_index',              ┐ Add new index with
                                             │ language french
     default_language: 'french'          ◁──┘
    }
);
```

Now if you rerun the previous `find()`, you'll now find some books, because in French, the word *in* isn't a stop word:

```
> db.books.find({$text: {$search: 'in '}}).count()
334
```

If you check the indexes on the books collection, you'll see the language is now French:

```
> db.books.getIndexes()
[
        {
                "v" : 1,
                "key" : {
                        "_id" : 1
                },
                "name" : "_id_",
                "ns" : "catalog.books"
        },
        {
                "v" : 1,
                "key" : {
                        "_fts" : "text",
                        "_ftsx" : 1
                },
                "name" : "books_text_index",
                "ns" : "catalog.books",
                "weights" : {
                        "$**" : 1,
                        "categories" : 5,
                        "title" : 10                   ┐ Default text index
                },                                     │ language is French
                "default_language" : "french",     ◁──┘
                "language_override" : "language",
                "textIndexVersion" : 2
        }
]
```

9.6.2 Specifying the language in the document

Before you insert an example document that specifies the document language, change
the index back to English by running the following commands:

```
db.books.dropIndex('books_text_index');

db.books.createIndex(
    {'$**': 'text'},

    {weights:
        {title: 10,
         categories: 5},

     name : 'books_text_index',

     default_language: 'english'     ◁──┐ Specify default
     }                                   │ language of English
);
```

Now insert a new document specifying the language as French:

```
db.books.insert({
    _id: 999,
    title: 'Le Petite Prince',
    pageCount: 85,
    publishedDate:  ISODate('1943-01-01T01:00:00Z'),
    shortDescription: "Le Petit Prince est une œuvre de langue française,
la plus connue d'Antoine de Saint-Exupéry. Publié en 1943 à New York
simultanément en anglais et en français. C'est un conte poétique et
philosophique sous l'apparence d'un conte pour enfants.",
    status: 'PUBLISH',
    authors: ['Antoine de Saint-Exupéry'],
    language: 'french'              ◁──┐ Specify language
})                                     │ as 'french'
```

MongoDB text search also allows you to change the name of the field used to specify
the document language when you define the index, if you want to use something other
than language. You can also specify different parts of the document to be in different
languages. You can read more about these features at http://docs.mongodb.org/
manual/tutorial/specify-language-for-text-index/.

Now that you've inserted a document in French, let's see how you can search for it
in French as well.

9.6.3 Specifying the language in a search

What language your text search string represents can make a big difference in the
results. Remember that the language affects how MongoDB interprets your string by
defining the stop words as well as stemming. Let's see how the specified language
affects both how the document was indexed and how MongoDB performs the search.
Our first example, shown in the next listing, shows the effect of stemming on our document indexes as well as on our search terms.

Listing 9.5   Example of how language affects stemming

```
> db.books.find({$text: {$search:                        Language French; only
    'simultanment',$language:'french'}},{title:1})       finds "Le Petit Prince"
{ "_id" : 999, "title" : "Le Petit Prince" }

> db.books.find({$text: {$search: 'simultanment'}},{title:1})
{ "_id" : 186, "title" : "Hadoop in Action" }             Same search in
{ "_id" : 293, "title" : "Making Sense of Java" }         English finds two
{ "_id" : 999, "title" : "Le Petite Prince" }             different books

> db.books.find({$text: {$search: 'prince'}},{title:1})
{ "_id" : 145, "title" : "Azure in Action" }            Search for prince in English
{ "_id" : 999, "title" : "Le Petit Prince" }            finds both French and
                                                        English language books
```

When you search for `simultanment` and specify the language as French, you find only the French book *Le Petit Prince*. Yet when you do the same search without specifying the language—meaning you use the default language English—you return two completely different books.

How can this be? With just this example, you might assume MongoDB is ignoring any documents that aren't in the specified language. But if you look at the third `find()`, where you search for the word *prince* you see that MongoDB can indeed find books in either French or English.

What's up with this? The answer lies in stemming. When you specify a search string, MongoDB will search for the stemmed words in your search string, not the actual words from the string. A similar process is used for creating the index for the documents where the index will contain the stemmed versions of words in the document, not the words themselves. As a result, the stemmed word MongoDB comes up with for *simultanment* will be different for French and English.

For French, it's easy to see how MongoDB found the one document because the book description contained the word *simultanment*. For the English documents, though, the reason is less clear. The next listing helps clarify the situation a bit and also illustrates some of the limitations of stemming.

Listing 9.6   Results of stemming `simultaneous`

```
> db.books.find({$text: {$search: 'simultaneous'}},{title:1})
{ "_id" : 186, "title" : "Hadoop in Action" }          English
{ "_id" : 293, "title" : "Making Sense of Java" }      search for
{ "_id" : 999, "title" : "Le Petite Prince" }          simultaneous

 > db.books.find({$text: {$search: 'simultaneous',
    $language:'french'}},{title:1})                    French search for
 >                                                     simultaneous; nothing found
```

In this listing you searched for the word *simultaneous* in both English and French. As you expected, when you searched in English, you found the two books previously found when you searched for *simultanment*.

But if you now search for *simultaneous* in French, you won't find the French book. Unfortunately, in this case what MongoDB calculates as the stem word in French isn't the same as the calculated stem word for *simultanment*.

This result can be confusing, and the process of calculating the stem for a word isn't an exact science. But in most cases you'll find what you'll expect.

Fortunately, the effect of language on stop words is much simpler. For stop words, MongoDB can use a dictionary to access a list of known stop words for a given language. As a result, the effect of language on the interpretation of stop words is much clearer. The next listing shows a simple example.

Listing 9.7 Example of how language affects stop words

```
> db.books.find({$text: {$search: 'de'}},{title:1})
{ "_id" : 36, "title" : "ASP.NET 4.0 in Practice" }          Search for "de" finds
{ "_id" : 629, "title" : "Play for Java" }                   only English books
{ "_id" : 199, "title" : "Doing IT Right" }
{ "_id" : 10, "title" : "OSGi in Depth" }
{ "_id" : 224, "title" : "Entity Framework 4 in Action" }
{ "_id" : 761, "title" : "jQuery in Action, Third Edition" }
> db.books.find({$text: {$search: 'de', $language: 'french'}}).count()
0                                                            Search for "de" in
                                                            French finds nothing
```

In this example, you search for the word *de* first in English and then in French. When the search is done in English, you find a number of books. In this case you're finding books with authors who have the word *de* in their name. You won't find the French book because in French *de* is a stop word and therefore isn't indexed.

If you perform this same search in French, you won't find any results because *de* is a stop word in French. As a result, the parsed search string won't contain any words to search for once the stop words are removed.

As you can see, language can have a big effect on the results of your text search as well as the text search indexes created for a document. That's why it's important to specify the language you'll be using in your index, document, and search string. If you're only worried about English, then your task is much simpler. But if not, read on to see which languages MongoDB supports. Hopefully you'll find the languages you need.

9.6.4 *Available languages*

MongoDB supports quite a few languages, and you can expect the list to grow over time. The following lists the languages supported by MongoDB as of release 2.6 (the same languages are also supported by MongoDB v3.0). The list also shows the two-letter abbreviation you can use instead of the full word:

- da—danish
- nl—dutch
- en—english

- fi—finnish
- fr—french
- de—german
- hu—hungarian
- it—italian
- no—norwegian
- pt—portuguese
- ro—romanian
- ru—russian
- es—spanish
- sv—swedish
- tr—turkish

In addition to this list, you can specify none. When you do, MongoDB skips any processing for stemming and stop words. For example, a document with the language of none will have an index created for each unique word in the document. Only the exact words will be indexed, without any stemming, and the index won't exclude any stop words. This approach can be useful if your documents contain words that MongoDB is having a difficult time processing. The downside is that you won't be able to take advantage of stemming finding "similar" words and your results will contain only exact word matches.

9.7   *Summary*

As you can see, MongoDB can provide a great deal of capabilities in using a basic query text search for your database. The aggregation framework provides even more complex search capabilities if needed. But MongoDB text search has its limits and isn't intended to completely replace dedicated text search engines such as Elasticsearch or Solr. If you can get by with MongoDB text search, though, you'll save yourself the effort and complexity of maintaining a duplicate copy of the data within a dedicated search engine.

Now that you know the full capabilities of MongoDB searches, updates, and indexing, let's move on to a topic that's new to MongoDB v3.0 and has to do with how MongoDB stores, updates, and reads data: the WiredTiger storage engine!

WiredTiger and
pluggable storage

10

> **This chapter covers**
> - WiredTiger
> - Pluggable storage engines
> - A comparison between MMAPv1 and WiredTiger

With version 3.0, MongoDB introduced the Pluggable Storage Engine API as one of its major changes. In this chapter, we'll talk about what exactly it is and why it has been added to MongoDB. We'll talk about WiredTiger, a pluggable storage engine that's bundled with MongoDB, and compare it with the default storage engine that MongoDB has used up until version 3.0. We'll compare the two engines in terms of speed, disk use, and latency. We'll also introduce several other pluggable storage engines that are expected to become interesting alternatives. For the more advanced readers, we'll uncover the technology behind pluggable storage engines.

10.1 Pluggable Storage Engine API

An application programming interface (API) is a relatively strict set of routines, protocols, and tools for building software applications. As an example, you should be aware by now that MongoDB offers an API that allows other software to interact with MongoDB without using the MongoDB shell: each of the MongoDB drivers that you've been using use the API provided by MongoDB to add driver functionality. They allow your application to communicate with the MongoDB database and to perform the basic CRUD operations on your documents in the database.

A storage engine is an interface between the database and the hardware. A storage engine doesn't change how you perform your queries in the shell or in the driver, and it doesn't interfere with MongoDB at the cluster level. But storage engines interfere with how data is written to, deleted from, and read from disk, as well as which data structure will be used for storing the data.

The Pluggable Storage Engine API allows third parties to develop storage engines for MongoDB. Before the Pluggable Storage Engine API, the only storage engine available to MongoDB was MMAPv1.

MongoDB still uses the MMAPv1 storage engine, and it's still the default storage engine in version 3.0 and later. The MMAPv1 storage engine is based on memory mapping, and has been a stable solution for MongoDB so far. One drawback to MMAPv1 that you'll notice soon if you have a lot of data to store is that it quickly consumes an enormous amount of disk space as your data set grows, to the extent that it preallocates 2 GB blocks every time it needs to grow in size. But preallocation is done by most database systems, and MongoDB is no exception. It does this in small, growing increments at first, but once it becomes larger than 2 GB, every next increment will preallocate another 2 GB, so as a system administrator you'll have to keep this in mind when managing disk space for your servers.

The database administrator has to choose from the different storage alternatives, which dictate how data is stored on disk. Since version 3.0, it's now possible to tell MongoDB to use a different module for storage, and that's what the Pluggable Storage Engine API does. It provides functions that MongoDB needs to use to store data. MongoDB 3.0 comes bundled with an alternative to MMAPv1, which is WiredTiger. We'll talk more about WiredTiger and how you can switch to using it in a later section in this chapter, but first let's consider why MongoDB has offered the ability to use different storage engines.

10.1.1 Why use different storages engines?

Let's consider two different applications:

- A news site, like Huffington Post
- A social media site, like Twitter or Facebook

On news sites you'll see news articles. The Huffington Post averages 1,200 editorial pieces per day, but they're read by tens of millions of people around the world.[1] Bring this into contrast with a social media site where people share their own stories, which are much shorter than news articles. Twitter tweets are at most 140 characters, and Facebook or Google+ status updates are short as well. These two different

---

[1] According to a 2013 article on DigiDay: http://digiday.com/publishers/whos-winning-at-volume-in-publishing/.

use cases have different requirements in terms of database storage and access, as table 10.1 shows.

News sites have much less data to delve into compared to social media sites, and for many visitors, the front page looks the same. Social media sites, on the other hand, have to go through millions and millions of tweets or status updates. Every visitor has their own feed, which should show only those tweets and updates that matter to the visitor. In addition to delivering millions of status updates for different visitors, the social media platforms also need to be able to store millions of new tweets every day.[2]

Table 10.1 Different requirements for different cases/users

	News site	Social media site
Number of documents	Hundreds of articles	Millions of updates
Average size	A few kilobytes	Tens of bytes
Dynamic content	None—same for every visitor	Content depends on visitor

For news sites, the application needs to collect the same articles over and over again for every user visiting the news site at the same time. Many database systems have a query cache that will quickly deliver the data that was requested by the same query a few minutes ago. Such news site applications can also make use of an external in-memory cache system such as Memcached or Redis to deliver the same data at high speeds. But these technologies will not help social media sites where the requested data is different every time, even per visitor. Such applications need a different kind of storage system that has much better performance when reading filtered data from a humongous set of records. Social media sites also need a storage system that has excellent write performance to be able to store millions of new records every day. News sites don't need this kind of performance because their number of write operations only runs in the mere thousands.

To cater to these different kinds of systems, MongoDB has implemented the concept of a pluggable storage engine so that the database administrators or system engineers can choose the storage engine that gives the best performance for their use case. In the next section we'll introduce a storage plugin that's bundled with MongoDB: WiredTiger.

10.2 *WiredTiger*

WiredTiger is a high-performance, scalable, open source data engine that focuses on multicore scalability and optimal RAM use. Multicore scaling is achieved by using

---

[2] According to Domo, in 2014, every minute of the day over 2.4 million pieces of content were shared on Facebook, and over 270,000 tweets were sent on Twitter. These numbers translate to over 3.5 billion shares per day, and 400 million tweets per day.

modern programming techniques such as hazard pointers[3] and lock-free algorithms,[4] resulting in more work done by each CPU core than alternative engines.

WiredTiger was developed by Michael Cahill and Keith Bostic, both architects at Sleepycat Software, which was founded by Bostic and his wife. At Sleepycat Software they designed and developed the Berkeley DB, the most widely used embedded data-management software in the world.

10.2.1 Switching to WiredTiger

Before you start using WiredTiger, make sure you're running a 64-bit system, with a 64-bit OS, because this is required. This should be the case in most modern computer equipment. Also, when setting up MongoDB to use WiredTiger, it's crucial that you start the MongoDB server with the WiredTiger configuration on a fresh dbPath directory. If you start the server with a dbPath that's in the MMAPv1 structure, it won't start. This is because the storage structure of MMAPv1 isn't compatible with that of Wired-Tiger, and there's no on-the-fly conversion available between storage structures. But there's a way to migrate your MMAPv1-based databases to WiredTiger, and vice versa, using `mongodump` and `mongorestore`. See chapter 13 to learn more about dumping and restoring your databases.

All you need to do to enable WiredTiger in your MongoDB installation is to set the storage configuration in your default YAML configuration file (see appendix A for more information about YAML) as follows:

```
storage:
    dbPath: "/data/db"
    journal:
        enabled: true
    engine: "wiredTiger"
    wiredTiger:
        engineConfig:
            cacheSizeGB: 8
            journalCompressor: none
        collectionConfig:
            blockCompressor: none
        indexConfig:
            prefixCompression: false
```

---

[3] In multithreading programming it's important to keep track of which memory blocks need to be accessible by the threads, and whether any thread is accessing it. Hazard pointers are a list of pointers to such memory blocks that are being accessed by a thread, and other threads are prohibited from modifying or deleting the pointers and the memory blocks they point to, as long as they're in the hazard pointers list.

[4] Resource locking is an important concept in multithreaded programming. Lock-free algorithms are programming patterns to avoid a program being stuck because several threads are waiting for each other to release their locks, and to guarantee that the program as a whole makes progress.

This is the basic, noncompressed configuration to enable WiredTiger for your MongoDB installation. Table 10.2 shows what the options do.

Table 10.2 Various options of the MongoDB configuration file

Option Name	Description
dbPath	The path where your database files are stored. Defaults to /data/db.
journal.enabled	Whether to enable journaling or not. It's recommended to enable this as it may save data that was lost during a power outage and hasn't been synchronized to disk. Defaults to true on 64-bit systems.
engine	Which storage engine to use. Defaults to mmapv1. To use WiredTiger, set this to wiredTiger.
wiredTiger	This is where WiredTiger-specific options are set.
engineConfig.cacheSize	This is how much RAM memory WiredTiger needs to reserve for the in-memory data, which would then serve as a cache to rapidly serve your data. Defaults to half the physical RAM on your system, at least 1 GB.
engineConfig.journalCompressor	Tells WiredTiger what kind of compressor to use for the journaling data. Defaults to snappy, but this is best set to none to achieve the best performance.
collectionConfig.blockCompressor	This tells WiredTiger what kind of compressor to use for the collection data. The three supported options are none, snappy, and zlib. You'll see in the benchmarks which is the best option for you. Defaults to snappy.
indexConfig.prefixCompression	This tells WiredTiger whether to use compression for its index data. Defaults to true.

10.2.2 *Migrating your database to WiredTiger*

Because you can't run MongoDB with the WiredTiger set up on a data directory that's in MMAPv1 format, you'll need to migrate your database to the WiredTiger installation. This is basically done by creating dumps and restoring from them (see chapter 13 for more information):

1 Create a MongoDB dump of your MMAPv1-based database:

```
$ mkdir ~/mongo-migration
$ cd ~/mongo-migration
$ mongodump
```

This will create a dump directory called mongo-migration in your home directory.

2   Stop the `mongod` instance, and make sure there's no `mongod` process running:

```
$ ps ax | grep mongo
```

3   Update the MongoDB configuration to use WiredTiger, as described in the previous section.

4   Move the MMAPv1-based database away. Assuming `dbPath` is set to /data/db:

```
$ sudo mv /data/db /data/db-mmapv1
```

5   Create a fresh directory and give the MongoDB user/group (assuming `mongodb`) permission to write to it:

```
$ mkdir /data/db
$ chown mongodb:mongodb /data/db
$ chmod 755 /data/db
```

6   Start your WiredTiger-enabled MongoDB instance.

7   Import your dump into the WiredTiger-enabled MongoDB instance:

```
$ cd ~/mongo-migration
$ mongorestore dump
```

Now you should have your database in your newly configured MongoDB environment. If you examine the WiredTiger-based /data/db and compare it with your old MMAPv1-based /data/db-mmapv1, you'll see considerable differences in how they're managed. For one, if you have large databases, you'll notice that the disk use of both directories differs greatly. You'll see that when we do the benchmark testing in the next section.

To convert your WiredTiger-based database back into MMAPv1, repeat the process, but now you'll make a dump of the data in your WiredTiger storage, stopping the MongoDB instance, changing the configuration to use MMAPv1, starting the MongoDB instance with this configuration, and restoring the data dump into the MMAPv1-enabled instance.

An alternative method is to run a second MongoDB instance with a WiredTiger configuration, and add this instance to your replica set, together with your existing MMAPv1 instance. Replica sets are covered in chapter 11.

10.3   *Comparison with MMAPv1*

How does WiredTiger's performance compare to a MongoDB instance with MMAPv1? In this chapter, you'll test three WiredTiger configurations against MMAPv1 using a couple of JavaScript and shell scripts. You'll test the following configurations:

- Default configuration using MMAPv1
- Normal WiredTiger, no compression

- WiredTiger with snappy compression
- WiredTiger with zlib compression

Zlib and snappy are compression algorithms. The former is an abstraction of the DEFLATE compression algorithm, which is an LZ77 variant that uses Huffman coding. Zlib is very common on many software platforms, and is the basis for the gzip file compression program. Snappy is developed by Google and is widely used in Google's projects such as BigTable. Snappy is more of an intermediate solution, which doesn't aim for maximum compression, but instead goes for high speeds, along with reasonable compression.

You're going to test the insert performance first to fill up the test databases. Then you'll use these test databases to measure the read performance. When going through the benchmark testing in the following sections, please keep in mind that it's difficult to draw the correct conclusions from these test results. The data sets in these tests are much smaller than real-world examples, and in real-world examples you'd have many more different search filters to collect the data that you need. There would also be a larger variety in the data structures in real-world examples, which will affect the compression algorithms in use. The tests in this chapter are only simple examples to give you a general idea. They'll also hopefully give you some insight into how you'd proceed testing the MongoDB instances with your own data and the filters that your application uses.

10.3.1 Configuration files

To be able to compare the disk use of the different storage configurations, you'll use different database paths in the storage configuration files. In a production system, however, you'd end up with the common database path for a MongoDB installation on your machine.

The configuration file for the MMAPv1 instance, called mmapv1.conf, is as follows, in YAML format:

```
storage:
    dbPath: "./data-mmapv1"
    directoryPerDB: true
    journal:
        enabled: true
systemLog:
    destination: file
    path: "./mongodb-server.log"
    logAppend: true
    timeStampFormat: iso8601-utc
net:
    bindIp: 127.0.0.1
    port: 27017
    unixDomainSocket:
        enabled : true
```

For the WiredTiger configurations, it's the same as the previous code, except for the storage part. For the no-compression version you'll use the following storage configuration for WiredTiger, naming it wiredtiger-uncompressed.conf:

```
storage:
    dbPath: "./data-wt-uncompressed"
    directoryPerDB: true
    journal:
        enabled: true
    engine: "wiredTiger"
    wiredTiger:
        engineConfig:
            cacheSizeGB: 8
            journalCompressor: none
        collectionConfig:
            blockCompressor: none
        indexConfig:
            prefixCompression: false
```

For the snappy instance, you'll use the following configuration for storage; what's different from the uncompressed WiredTiger instance is shown in bold. This file is called "wiredtiger-snappy.conf":

```
storage:
    dbPath: "./data-wt-zlib"
    directoryPerDB: true
    journal:
        enabled: true
    engine: "wiredTiger"
    wiredTiger:
        engineConfig:
            cacheSizeGB: 8
            journalCompressor: none
        collectionConfig:
            blockCompressor: snappy
        indexConfig:
            prefixCompression: true
```

Finally, for the zlib instance, you'll use the following storage configuration, naming it wiredtiger-zlib.conf:

```
storage:
    dbPath: "./data-wt-snappy"
    directoryPerDB: true
    journal:
        enabled: true
    engine: "wiredTiger"
    wiredTiger:
        engineConfig:
            cacheSizeGB: 8
            journalCompressor: none
        collectionConfig:
            blockCompressor: zlib
```

```
indexConfig:
    prefixCompression: true
```

If you have a legacy MongoDB installation in some directory, and these configuration files in a configs directory, you can use this MongoDB installation with these configurations by, for example running the following for the MMAPv1 configuration:

```
$ bin/mongod --config configs/mmapv1.conf &
```

This should run a MongoDB instance in the background with the given configuration.

10.3.2 *Insertion script and benchmark script*

You'll use the following JavaScript code to fill up the benchmark database with documents that have four fields of different types, an array field with eight document elements with four differently typed fields each, and eight subdocuments, also with four differently typed fields each. This is by no means a real-world situation, and compression algorithms will work differently with different data sets that are more heterogeneous than this test data:

```
for (var j = 0; j < 10000; j++) {
    var r1 = Math.random();

    // A nice date around year 2000
    var dateFld = new Date(1.5e12 * r1);
    var intFld = Math.floor(1e8 * r1);
    // A nicely randomized string of around 40 characters
    var stringFld = Math.floor(1e64 * r1).toString(36);
    var boolFld = intFld % 2;

    doc = {
        random_date: dateFld,
        random_int: intFld,
        random_string: stringFld,
        random_bool: boolFld
    }

    doc.arr = [];

    for (var i = 0; i < 16; i++) {
        var r2 = Math.random();

        // A nice date around year 2000
        var dateFld = new Date(1.5e12 * r2);
        var intFld = Math.floor(1e8 * r2);
        var stringFld = Math.floor(1e64 * r2).toString(36);
        var boolField = intFld % 2;

        if (i < 8) {
            doc.arr.push({
                date_field: dateFld,
                int_field: intFld,
                string_field: stringFld,
                bool_field: boolFld
            });
```

```
        } else {
           doc["sub" + i] = {
               date_field: dateFld,
               int_field: intFld,
               string_field: stringFld,
               bool_field: boolFld
           };
        }
    }

    db.benchmark.insert(doc);
}
```

This piece of JavaScript code, stored in insert.js, will insert 10,000 documents into the benchmark database. This script will be run by the following batch script that will go through all the four configurations, and does the same insert job for each configuration, 16 times:

```
#!/bin/bash

export MONGO_DIR=/storage/mongodb
export NUM_LOOPS=16

configs=(
    mmapv1.conf
    wiredtiger-uncompressed.conf
    wiredtiger-snappy.conf
    wiredtiger-zlib.conf
)

cd $MONGO_DIR
for config in "${configs[@]}"; do
    echo "===== RUNNING $config ====="
    echo "Cleaning up data directory"
    DATA_DIR=$(grep dbPath configs/$config | awk -F\" '{ print $2 }')
    rm -rf $MONGO_DIR/$DATA_DIR/*

    echo -ne "Starting up mongod... "
    T="$(date +%s)"
    ./bin/mongod --config configs/$config &

    # wait for mongo to start
    while [ 1 ]; do
        ./bin/mongostat -n 1 > /dev/null 2>&1
        if [ "$?" -eq 0 ]; then
            break
        fi
        sleep 2
    done
    T="$(($(date +%s)-T))"
    echo "took $T seconds"

    T="$(date +%s)"
    for l in $(seq 1 $NUM_LOOPS); do
        echo -ne "\rRunning import loop $l"
        ./bin/mongo benchmark --quiet insert.js >/dev/null 2>&1
```

```
    done
    T="$(($(date +%s)-T))"

    echo
    echo "Insert performance for $config: $T seconds"

    echo -ne "Shutting down server... "
    T="$(date +%s)"
    ./bin/mongo admin --quiet --eval "db.shutdownServer({force: true})" >/
     dev/null 2>&1

    while [ 1 ]; do
        pgrep -U $USER mongod > /dev/null 2>&1
        if [ "$?" -eq 1 ]; then
            break
        fi
        sleep 1
    done
    T="$(($(date +%s)-T))"
    echo "took $T seconds"

    SIZE=$(du -s --block-size=1 $MONGO_DIR/$DATA_DIR | cut -f1)
    SIZE_MB=$(echo "scale=2; $SIZE/(1024*1024)" | bc)
    echo "Disk usage for $config: ${SIZE_MB}MB"
done
```

This script assumes a legacy MongoDB installation in the bin directory inside the same directory as the script, and starts up a MongoDB instance according to the given configuration parameter. Therefore, you should make sure that you stop your MongoDB instance before running this script.

10.3.3 *Insertion benchmark results*

After running this batch script, you'll see output that looks like the following. The timings may be different on each machine, depending on the hardware and even on the operating system's kernel. This output was generated on a QuadCore i5-3570K running at 3.4 GHz, with 16 GB of RAM, and the storage medium being an ext4-formatted LVM partition, spread over two Hitachi Deskstar T7K250 250 GB disks connected to a SATA port, with a 7200 RPM rotational speed. The system runs on an Ubuntu 14.04 machine with a default Linux kernel 3.13.0 for the Intel 64-bit architecture:

```
===== RUNNING mmapv1.conf =====
Cleaning up data directory
Starting up mongod... took 102 seconds
Running import loop 16
Insert performance for mmapv1.conf: 105 seconds
Shutting down server... took 1 seconds
Disk usage for mmapv1.conf: 4128.04MB
===== RUNNING wiredtiger-uncompressed.conf =====
Cleaning up data directory
Starting up mongod... took 2 seconds
Running import loop 16
Insert performance for wiredtiger-uncompressed.conf: 92 seconds
Shutting down server... took 3 seconds
```

```
Disk usage for wiredtiger-uncompressed.conf: 560.56MB
===== RUNNING wiredtiger-snappy.conf =====
Cleaning up data directory
Starting up mongod... took 1 seconds
Running import loop 16
Insert performance for wiredtiger-snappy.conf: 93 seconds
Shutting down server... took 2 seconds
Disk usage for wiredtiger-snappy.conf: 380.27MB
===== RUNNING wiredtiger-zlib.conf =====
Cleaning up data directory
Starting up mongod... took 2 seconds
Running import loop 16
Insert performance for wiredtiger-zlib.conf: 104 seconds
Shutting down server... took 3 seconds
Disk usage for wiredtiger-zlib.conf: 326.67MB
```

It timed the server startup, the duration of the insert job, and the server shutdown processes, and measured the disk use of the storage directory after shutdown. You can see the results in table 10.3.

Table 10.3   Comparing MMAPv1 and WiredTiger operations

	MMAPv1	WT	WT snappy	WT zlib
Starting up	102 sec	2 sec	1 sec	2 sec
Insert job	105 sec	92 sec	93 sec	104 sec
Shut down	1 sec	3 sec	2 sec	3 sec
Disk use	4128.04 MB	560.56 MB	380.27 MB	326.67 MB

From this table it appears that WiredTiger has a tremendous gain in the time to start up the server and initialize the storage directory. But this is a one-time process, and therefore not a crucial measurement. Another test of the startup and shutdown times of the MongoDB instances with a preinitialized storage directory showed that the MMAPv1 startup took four seconds. You'll see this in a test in the next section, where you'll put the read performance to the test.

There's little gain to be had for the insert job when using WiredTiger, although the difference can be considerable when dealing with more data than this data set. Also keep in mind that this test doesn't test running the insert job using multiple Mongo client connections simultaneously.

The most striking feature of these test results is the disk use: WiredTiger without compression uses less than 15% of what MMAPv1 uses, and if you add compression, it's less than 10%! You'll also see that the snappy compression configuration finds a good middle ground between the insert speeds and the disk use. It's almost as fast as a bare WiredTiger instance with no compression, but still gains 180 MB on this data set. The zlib configuration has better compression, but in exchange for this, it takes 10 seconds more to do the insert job.

10.3.4 *Read performance scripts*

Up until now you've benchmarked the write performance of the different storage configurations, but for some applications you might be more interested in the read performance. Here's the simple JavaScript that will fetch all records in the benchmark collection and sequentially go through each of them. Note that this doesn't benchmark searches and filtering, which would need a predefined set of values to search for:

```
c = db.benchmark.find();
while(c.hasNext()) c.next();
```

This simple JavaScript is put in a read.js file and run by the following read.sh shell script, which is similar to the insert script:

```
#!/bin/bash

export MONGO_DIR=/storage/mongodb
export NUM_LOOPS=16

configs=(
    mmapv1.conf
    wiredtiger-uncompressed.conf
    wiredtiger-snappy.conf
    wiredtiger-zlib.conf
)

sudo echo "Acquired root permissions"

cd $MONGO_DIR
for config in "${configs[@]}"; do
    echo "===== RUNNING $config ====="
    echo "Clearing memory caches"
    sync
    echo 3 | sudo tee /proc/sys/vm/drop_caches

    echo -ne "Starting up mongod... "
    T="$(date +%s)"
    ./bin/mongod --config configs/$config &

    # wait for mongo to start
    while [ 1 ]; do
        ./bin/mongostat -n 1 > /dev/null 2>&1
        if [ "$?" -eq 0 ]; then
            break
        fi
        sleep 2
    done
    T="$(($(date +%s)-T))"
    echo "took $T seconds"

    rm -f timings-${config}.txt
    T="$(date +%s)"
    for l in $(seq 1 $NUM_LOOPS); do
        echo -ne "\rRunning read loop $l"
        /usr/bin/time -f "%e" -o timings-${config}.txt -a --quiet ./bin/mongo
  benchmark --quiet read.js >/dev/null 2>&1
```

```
    done
    T="$(($(date +%s)-T))"

    echo
    echo "Read performance for $config: $T seconds"

    echo -ne "Shutting down server... "
    T="$(date +%s)"
    ./bin/mongo admin --quiet --eval "db.shutdownServer({force: true})" >/
    dev/null 2>&1

    while [ 1 ]; do
        pgrep -U $USER mongod > /dev/null 2>&1
        if [ "$?" -eq 1 ]; then
            break
        fi
        sleep 1
    done
    T="$(($(date +%s)-T))"
    echo "took $T seconds"
done
```

This script also times the startup and shutdown processes of the MongoDB server instance again, so you can see that it starts up faster with a storage directory that's already initialized. Because the script needs to clear the memory caches to get an accurate timing of cold fetches—that is, fetches that aren't from the cache, but from the storage system itself—you'll need to enter your password to give it sudo access so it can flush the memory cache.

10.3.5 *Read performance results*

When running the script, you'll see an output similar to the following:

```
===== RUNNING mmapv1.conf =====
Clearing memory caches
3
Starting up mongod... took 3 seconds
Running read loop 16
Read performance for mmapv1.conf: 33 seconds
Shutting down server... took 1 seconds
===== RUNNING wiredtiger-uncompressed.conf =====
Clearing memory caches
3
Starting up mongod... took 2 seconds
Running read loop 16
Read performance for wiredtiger-uncompressed.conf: 23 seconds
Shutting down server... took 2 seconds
===== RUNNING wiredtiger-snappy.conf =====
Clearing memory caches
3
Starting up mongod... took 3 seconds
Running read loop 16
Read performance for wiredtiger-snappy.conf: 21 seconds
Shutting down server... took 1 seconds
```

```
===== RUNNING wiredtiger-zlib.conf =====
Clearing memory caches
3
Starting up mongod... took 2 seconds
Running read loop 16
Read performance for wiredtiger-zlib.conf: 21 seconds
Shutting down server... took 1 seconds
```

The 3's on their own lines are from the echo to clear the memory caches, so you can ignore those. You can now clearly see that the startup and shutdown times are similar for all MongoDB configurations, as shown in table 10.4.

Table 10.4 Comparing shutdown and startup times of various configurations

	MMAPv1	WT	WT snappy	WT zlib
Starting up	3 sec	2 sec	3 sec	2 sec
Read job	33 sec	23 sec	21 sec	21 sec
Shut down	1 sec	2 sec	1 sec	1 sec

The read job took at least 10 seconds longer on the MMAPv1 configuration than on the WiredTiger configurations. If you check the timings files, you'll see why. The timings have been graphed in figure 10.1.

It's clear that the first iteration took the longest because each subsequent iteration will take the results directly from the memory cache. For the cold fetch, MMAPv1 is clearly the slowest. The compressed configurations of WiredTiger have the best performance during the cold fetch. But for cached results, MMAPv1 is slightly faster than

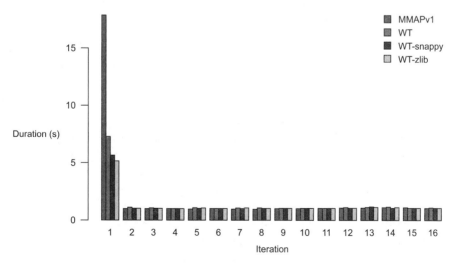

Figure 10.1 The read performance of MMAPv1 and WiredTiger

the WiredTiger alternatives. The graph doesn't show this clearly, but the timings files do, and their contents are shown in the table 10.5.

Table 10.5   Timing fetching operations using various storage engines (all times are in seconds)

	MMAPv1	WT	WT-snappy	WT-zlib
1	17.88	7.37	5.67	5.17
2	1.01	1.1	1.05	1.05
3	1	1.05	1.02	1.08
4	1.03	1.03	1.05	1.08
5	0.99	1.07	1.04	1.08
6	1.03	1.03	1.05	1.08
7	0.96	1.06	0.99	1.07
8	0.99	1.08	1.01	1.06
9	0.97	1.03	1.02	1.03
10	0.96	1.03	1.03	1.03
11	0.99	1.03	1.06	1.06
12	1.01	1.07	1.06	1.07
13	0.98	1.04	1.08	1.06
14	1.01	1.08	1.03	1.07
15	1.08	1.05	1.05	1.05
16	1.02	1.06	1.04	1.06

10.3.6 Benchmark conclusion

How much better is WiredTiger is than MMAPv1 in different aspects? You've seen the server startup and shutdown times, the insertion of thousands of averagely sized documents, and the fetching and iterating through these documents, repeatedly. You've also looked at the disk use of the storage directories.

You haven't tested how the MongoDB instances perform when there are several clients connecting and making requests at the same time. You also haven't tested the random search and filtering performances. These two are what happens most in a real-world example, and require a more complicated benchmark testing setup than what is used in this chapter. We hope that the benchmark examples give you some insight into how you want to benchmark the other aspects of the MongoDB installations.

From the results in this chapter, you can conclude that there's a tremendous gain to be had in terms of disk use. For small-scale applications where resource use is a concern, this will be the deciding factor, and you should go with a compressed version of WiredTiger. The zlib version will give the best performance-versus-cost ratio. For critical applications where extra storage cost is worthwhile, the WiredTiger configuration without compression, or, if needed, using the snappy compression algorithm, will give slightly better speeds over the zlib configuration.

Even when disk storage isn't an issue for enterprise users, the speed of cold fetches will often be an important factor. This is especially true for social network sites where every visitor will have specific filters, so that cache misses will often occur.

Again, remember that the benchmarks in this chapter aren't totally representative of real-world situations, and therefore no hard conclusions should be drawn from the results of these benchmarks. But we hope that these benchmarks will give you a basic idea of what you can do with the data in your application, and that you'll be able to tune the benchmark scripts to best match the workload in your application. This way you'll be able to draw better conclusions as to what storage engine is better for your application's specific use case.

There are also several other environmental factors that depend on the hardware and software (OS kernel) configuration of your system. They haven't been taken into account in this chapter, but they may affect the performance of these benchmarks. When comparing storage engines, one should remember to fix all the environmental factors, even though some storage systems may perform better with a certain operating system setting, which may have a negative effect on other storage systems. Therefore, you should be cautious when drawing conclusions from such benchmarks.

10.4 Other examples of pluggable storage engines

We talked about WiredTiger in the previous sections and how it performs against MMAPv1 in terms of disk use and read/write speeds. In this section we'll introduce you to several other storage engines that are available.

An example is RocksDB, developed by Facebook, and based on Google's LevelDB with significant inspiration from Apache's Hbase. RocksDB is a key-value store that was developed to exploit the full potential of high read/write rates offered by Flash or RAM subsystems to offer low-latency database access by using an LSM tree engine.[5] This makes RocksDB a good storage plugin for applications that need high write performance, such as social media applications. MongoDB can be built with RocksDB support so that you can also enjoy the performance of RocksDB. For more information on how to do this, check out the announcement on the RocksDB blog.[6]

Tokutek's TokuFT (formerly known as TokuKV) is another key-value store that uses fractal tree indexing[7] instead of the default B-tree data structure used in WiredTiger.

---

[5] Log Structure Merge trees are data structures that outperform B-trees in the most useful record updating scenarios. The WiredTiger team compared B-trees vs. LSM trees: https://github.com/wiredtiger/wiredtiger/wiki/Btree-vs-LSM. For more information on LSM trees, see https://en.wikipedia.org/wiki/Log-structured_merge-tree.

[6] See http://rocksdb.org/blog/1967/integrating-rocksdb-with-mongodb-2/ for more information.

[7] Fractal tree indexing is a Tokutek innovation that keeps write performance consistent while your data set grows larger. See http://www.tokutek.com/resources/technology/.

Before MongoDB version 3.0, Tokutek offered a fork of MongoDB called TokuMX, which uses their TokuFT technology as the storage engine. Because MongoDB supports pluggable storage engines, Tokutek is offering a storage engine–only solution based on the MongoDB Pluggable Storage API, called TokuMXse,[8] where se stands for storage engine. While the TokuMX fork incorporates many features, such as clustering indexes and fast read-free updates by updating the MongoDB codebase, the TokuMXse version can't have them because of how the Pluggable Storage Engine API is currently designed. In this sense, TokuMXse will empower your standard MongoDB installation with reliably high-performance storage and compression.

Tokutek has been acquired by Percona, so all the TokuFT-related development will be done by Percona. Percona has announced an experimental build of MongoDB using TokuMXse.[9]

A last example that's familiar to MySQL users is InnoDB. This engine is used by MySQL as an alternative to the sequential MyISAM storage engine. InnoDB makes use of a transaction log that's replayed when a crash has occurred to get the latest operations from before the crash synchronized to disk, similar to how journaling works in WiredTiger and MMAPv1. MyISAM has to go through the whole database after a crash to repair any indexes or tables that haven't been flushed to disk, and as the database grows in size, this has an impact on the availability of the database. InnoDB doesn't have that problem and therefore offers better availability on bigger databases. The InnoDB technology isn't partial to MySQL. There's a fork from InnoDB called XtraDB, which is used by MariaDB, and it's possible that there will be an InnoDB module for MongoDB in the future.

10.5 Advanced topics

In this section we'll talk about the more advanced topics to get a better understanding of how storage engines work and why there are so many different ones with different technologies out there. The material covered in this section is absolutely not necessary to get a MongoDB instance running with one of the storage engines, but provides nice background information for those who are curious to know more.

10.5.1 How does a pluggable storage engine work?

The MongoDB source code comes with special classes to deal with storage modules. At the time of writing, the MongoDB source code was exposing the following classes:

- `StorageEngine`—A virtual class that forms the basis of the storage engines
- `MMAPV1Engine`—The MMAPv1 storage engine plugin class
- `KVStorageEngine`—The key-value-based storage engine class

---

[8] Announced in January 2015 by Tokutek: http://www.tokutek.com/2015/01/announcing-tokumxse-v1-0-0-rc-0/.

[9] Percona announcement in May 2015: https://www.percona.com/blog/2015/05/08/mongodb-percona-tokumxse-experimental-build-rc5-available/.

- KVEngine—The key-value engine that's used by the KVStorageEngine class
- MMAPV1DatabaseCatalogEntry—The catalog entry class for MMAPv1-based databases
- RecordStore—The base class for record store objects
- RecordStoreV1Base—The base class for MMAPv1 record store objects; the MMAPV1DatabaseCatalogEntry uses these
- WiredTigerKVEngine—The WiredTiger engine
- WiredTigerFactory—The factory class that creates a KVStorageEngine that uses the WiredTigerKVEngine class for its key-value engine
- WiredTigerRecordStore—The record store class that's used by the WiredTigerKVEngine class

You can see these classes in figure 10.2.

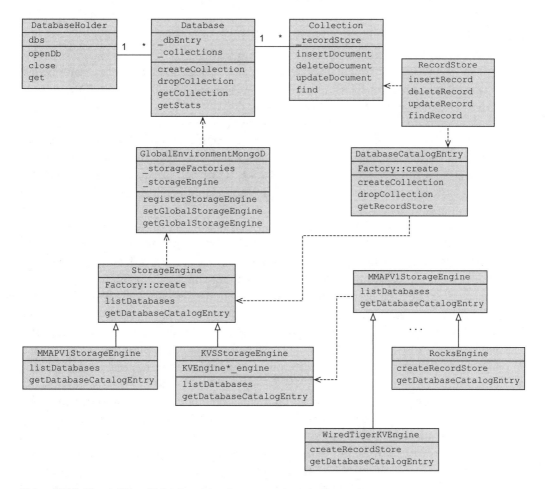

Figure 10.2 MongoDB multiple storage engines support mechanisms

There are three levels:

- *The storage engine at the top*—This works as the interface for MongoDB to the storage plugin.
- *The storage management*—This is the catalog entry class in the MMAPv1 case, and the key-value store (KVEngine) in the key-value-based storage engine case.
- *The record store*—This manages the actual MongoDB data, such as collections and entries. At this level, it communicates with the actual storage engine for the CRUD operations.

Together, these levels form the translator, if you will, between how MongoDB sees their data structures and how the storage engines store them. What MongoDB cares about is its own data structure—BSON—and its own scripting language based on JavaScript, which is used by the MongoDB drivers to communicate with MongoDB. How the data is stored or collected is left to the storage engine.

10.5.2 *Data structure*

In the MongoDB Pluggable Storage Engine API there are base classes for key-value storage systems. A key-value storage system is a storage system that guarantees fast access to the records by looking up the keys in the collection. You can tell the storage system to index certain keys for faster lookup.

A common data structure for storing such key-value data is a B-tree, which is also used in the WiredTiger storage plugin. B-trees were invented by Rudolf Bayer and Ed McCreight while working at Boeing Research Labs. There are speculations that the B in B-tree stands for Bayer, named after Rudolf Bayer, but others say that it stands for Boeing, where it was developed. In any case, the origin of the name is a mystery, but what's more interesting is how it works.

The power of the B-tree lies in the fact that disk-based storage is done in blocks. Each piece of data that's stored on disk is put in a block on the filesystem. In a real-world situation, these blocks are usually 4 KB in size, which is the default for many filesystems such as ExtFS and NTFS. A larger block size will allow for much larger files to be stored on the disk, but then we're talking about files larger than 4 TB.

A B-tree storage system uses these blocks as its nodes to store the indexes to the data elements. Each node can hold at most 4096 bytes of index information, and this index information is basically sorted. In the following examples, assume that each node can hold at most three indexes, but keep in mind that in a real-world example that number is much larger.

A B-tree starts with a root node, and within this node, you can store data records using their keys. These data records may have pointers to the actual value assigned to the key, or may have that value inside the data record. The more interesting part is how these records are found, because that's what needs to be done fast. Each node has several data records, indexed by an index key, and between each record, there's a diamond that's a placeholder for a pointer to another node containing other data records. The diamond placeholder to the left of the 12 goes to a whole tree of data records with index values less than 12. Similarly, the whole tree that's pointed to by the diamond between 12 and 65 contains records with index values all between 12 and 65. This way, when doing a search, an algorithm will quickly know which node to traverse into.

For this to work well, it's important that the index keys in each node of a B-tree structure be sorted. To optimize the disk seek times, it's preferable to store as much data as you can within a node that's optimally the same size as a disk block; in most real-world examples this size is 4096 bytes.

Imagine an empty database with an empty root node. You start adding records with certain keys in an arbitrary order, and once the node becomes full, you create new nodes for the next data records to be added. Let's say you have the following keys to be added in this order:

{ 2, 63, 42, 48, 1, 62, 4, 24, 8, 23, 58, 99, 38, 41, 81, 30, 17, 47, 66 }

Remember that you use a maximum node size of three elements. You'll have a root node with the keys shown in figure 10.3, which are the first three elements from the example sequence, in sorted order.

Figure 10.3   Root node with three elements

When you add the fourth element from the sequence, which is 48, it will create a new node between 42 and 63, and put 48 there, because 48 is between 42 and 63. The next element, 1, will be in the node before 2, because 1 is less than 2. Then the next element, 62, will join 48 in its node, because 62 lies between 42 and 63. The following three keys—4, 24, and 8—will go into the node that's pointed to between 2 and 42, because these numbers are all between 2 and 42. Within this new node, the keys will be sorted, as is always the case within nodes. After these first steps, the node tree graph will look like figure 10.4. Note how the numbers are sorted within each node.

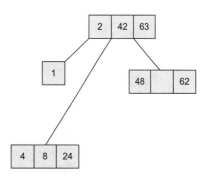

Figure 10.4   Early version of B-tree

You continue along the sequence. The next key, 23, is between 2 and 42 and will go into the node containing 4, 8, and 24, but because that node is already full, it will go into a new node between 8 and 24, because 23 is between 8 and 24. Then the next one, 58, will join 48 and 62. Key 99 will be in a new node pointed to after 63, because

99 is more than 63. Key 38, being between 2 and 42, will visit the node containing 4, 8, and 24, but because that node is full, it will go into a new node after 24, because 38 is more than 24. Key 41 joins key 38 in that new node at the second level. Key 81 joins 99, and 30 joins 38 and 41. Key 17 joins key 23 in the second-level node. Key 47 lies between 42 and 63, and so it goes to the node that holds 48, 58, and 62. Because that node is already full, it goes a level deeper, into a node before 48. Finally, key 66 will join 81 and 99, because 66 is more than 63. The final structure will look like figure 10.5, with the keys in each node in a sorted order.

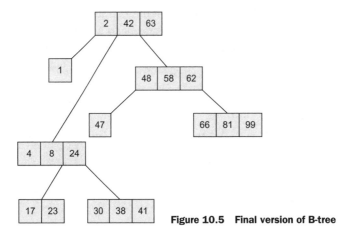

Figure 10.5   Final version of B-tree

Because the nodes contain the data in a sorted order, you will find out where you have to be very quickly. It will also be very fast at adding new records into the tree, as it will traverse through the tree at the same speed as finding a record, until it finds a free slot in a node, or until it needs to create a new node from a full node.

10.5.3 *Locking*

In the early days of MongoDB, locking was done for every connection, on a server level, using mutexes (mutual exclusions), a mechanism that ensures that multiple clients or threads can access the same resource—in this case, the database server—but not simultaneously. This is the worst method of locking, especially if you want to be a Big Data database engine, accessed by thousands of clients at the same time.

This changed with version 2.2, which is when database-level locking was implemented. The mutexes were applied on databases instead of on the whole MongoDB server instance, which was an improvement. But MongoDB threads would try to acquire subsequent write locks in a queue and deal with them in a serial fashion, letting the threads continue whenever the currently locking thread released its lock. While in a small-sized database, this can be rather fast, without any significant performance impact; in larger databases with thousands of write requests per second, this will become problematic and degrade the application's performance.

This changed with MongoDB version 3.0, which introduced collection-level locking for the MMAPv1 storage engine. This moved the locking mechanism a level lower, to collections. This means that multiple requests will be served simultaneously, without blocking each other, as long as they're writing into different collections.

With WiredTiger in version 3.0, MongoDB also supports document-level locking. This is an even more granular level of locking—multiple requests can now access the same collection simultaneously without blocking each other, as long as they aren't writing into the same document.

10.6 Summary

MongoDB version 3.0 introduced the concept of a pluggable storage engine architecture, and in this chapter you've seen what this entails and what it means for the system administrator or the application developer working with MongoDB. A real-world comparison has been given between a news site and a social network platform, both having different requirements for their database systems.

We compared the default engine that MongoDB used in previous versions, MMAPv1, with the newly bundled WiredTiger engine. WiredTiger performs well in both read and write operations, and offers document-level locking, whereas MMAPv1 doesn't go further than collection-level locking. WiredTiger isn't as greedy as MMAPv1 in terms of disk use, and it makes MongoDB a viable database system, even for small-scale applications. While MMAPv1 may be faster in certain situations, the performance versus cost ratio that WiredTiger offers far outweighs the performance versus cost ratio for MMAPv1.

While this comparison is based on a simple benchmark kit to give you a general idea of what benchmarking scripts do, it should give you insight into how to do your own benchmarks specific to your application's use case. The benchmarks are simple without taking into account several environmental factors, such as the hardware and software (OS kernel) configuration of your system. Tweaking these may affect the results of your benchmarks, so be cautious when comparing the results of the different storage engines.

You also learned about a few other storage engine platforms such as RocksDB and TokuFT, both of which are still in the experimental phase, but offer interesting features, because RocksDB is based on LSM trees and TokuFT is based on fractal trees. It will be interesting to see how they perform against WiredTiger in different situations.

You also read about some advanced concepts that come into play when designing a storage engine. Maximizing read and write performance, minimizing disk I/O, and offering optimal concurrency by using smart locking mechanisms on higher levels all play a crucial role in developing a storage engine.

Enough with the theory; the topic of the next chapter is used in true production databases—replication.

Replication

11

This chapter covers

- Understanding basic replication concepts
- Connecting a driver to a replica set
- Administering replica sets and handling failover
- Increasing the durability of writes with write concerns
- Optimizing your reads with the read preference
- Managing complex replica sets using tagging

Replication is central to most database management systems because of one inevitable fact: failures happen. If you want your live production data to be available even after a failure, you need to be sure that your production databases are available on more than one machine. Replication provides data protection, high availability, and disaster recovery.

We'll begin this chapter by introducing replication and discussing its main use cases. Then we'll cover MongoDB's replication through a detailed study of replica sets. Finally, we'll describe how to connect to replicated MongoDB clusters using the drivers, how to use write concerns, and how to load-balance reads across replicas.

11.1 Replication overview

Replication is the distribution and maintenance of data across multiple MongoDB servers (nodes). MongoDB can copy your data to one or more nodes and constantly keep them in sync when changes occur. This type of replication is provided through a mechanism called *replica sets*, in which a group of nodes are configured to automatically synchronize their data and fail over when a node disappears. MongoDB also supports an older method of replication called *master-slave*, which is now considered deprecated, but master-slave replication is still supported and can be used in MongoDB v3.0. For both methods, a single primary node receives all writes, and then all secondary nodes read and apply those writes to themselves asynchronously.

Master-slave replication and replica sets use the same replication mechanism, but replica sets additionally ensure automated failover: if the primary node goes offline for any reason, one of the secondary nodes will automatically be promoted to primary, if possible. Replica sets provide other enhancements too, such as easier recovery and more sophisticated deployment topologies. For these reasons you'd rarely want to use simple master-slave replication.[1] Replica sets are thus the recommended replication strategy for production deployments; we'll devote the bulk of this chapter to explanations and examples of replica sets, with only a brief overview of master-slave replication.

It's also important to understand the pitfalls of replication, most importantly the possibility of a rollback. In a replica set, data isn't considered truly committed until it's been written to a majority of member nodes, which means more than 50% of the servers; therefore, if your replica set has only two servers, this means that no server can be down. If the primary node in a replica set fails before it replicates its data, other members will continue accepting writes, and any unreplicated data must be rolled back, meaning it can no longer be read. We'll describe this scenario in detail next.

11.1.1 Why replication matters

All databases are vulnerable to failures of the environments in which they run. Replication provides a kind of insurance against these failures. What sort of failure are we talking about? Here are some of the more common scenarios:

- The network connection between the application and the database is lost.
- Planned downtime prevents the server from coming back online as expected. Most hosting providers must schedule occasional downtime, and the results of this downtime aren't always easy to predict. A simple reboot will keep a database server offline for at least a few minutes. Then there's the question of what happens when the reboot is complete. For example, newly installed software or

---

[1] The only time you should opt for MongoDB's master-slave replication is when you'd require more than 51 slave nodes, because a replica set can have no more than 50 members, which should never happen under normal circumstances.

hardware can prevent MongoDB or even the operating system from starting up properly.

- There's a loss of power. Although most modern datacenters feature redundant power supplies, nothing prevents user error within the datacenter itself or an extended brownout or blackout from shutting down your database server.

- A hard drive fails on the database server. Hard drives have a mean time to failure of a few years and fail more often than you might think.[2] Even if it's acceptable to have occasional downtime for your MongoDB, it's probably not acceptable to lose your data if a hard drive fails. It's a good idea to have at least one copy of your data, which replication provides.

In addition to protecting against external failures, replication has been particularly important for MongoDB's durability. When running without journaling enabled, MongoDB's data files aren't guaranteed to be free of corruption in the event of an unclean shutdown—with journaling enabled data files can't get corrupted. Without journaling, replication should always be run to guarantee a clean copy of the data files if a single node shuts down hard.

Of course, replication is desirable even when running with journaling. After all, you still want high availability and fast failover. In this case, journaling expedites recovery because it allows you to bring failed nodes back online simply by replaying the journal. This is much faster than resyncing from an existing replica to recover from failure.

It's important to note that although they're redundant, replicas aren't a replacement for backups. A backup represents a snapshot of the database at a particular time in the past, whereas a replica is always up to date. There are cases where a data set is large enough to render backups impractical, but as a general rule, backups are prudent and recommended even when running with replication. In other words, backups are there in case of a logical failure such as an accidental data loss or data corruption.

We highly recommend running a production MongoDB instance with both replication and journaling, unless you're prepared to lose data; to do otherwise should be considered poor deployment practice. When (not if) your application experiences a failure, work invested in thinking through and setting up replication will pay dividends.

11.1.2 *Replication use cases and limitations*

You may be surprised at how versatile a replicated database can be. In particular, replication facilitates redundancy, failover, maintenance, and load balancing. Let's take a brief look at each of these use cases.

Replication is designed primarily for redundancy. It ensures that replicated nodes stay in sync with the primary node. These replicas can live in the same datacenter as

---

[2] You can read a detailed analysis of consumer hard drive failure rates in Google's article "Failure Trends in a Large Disk Drive Population" (http://research.google.com/archive/disk_failures.pdf).

the primary, or they can be distributed geographically as an additional failsafe. Because replication is asynchronous, any sort of network latency or partition between nodes will have no effect on the performance of the primary. As another form of redundancy, replicated nodes can also be delayed by a constant number of seconds, minutes, or even hours behind the primary. This provides insurance against the case where a user inadvertently drops a collection or an application somehow corrupts the database. Normally, these operations will be replicated immediately; a delayed replica gives administrators time to react and possibly save their data.

Another use case for replication is failover. You want your systems to be highly available, but this is possible only with redundant nodes and the ability to switch over to those nodes in an emergency. Conveniently, MongoDB's replica sets almost always make this switch automatically.

In addition to providing redundancy and failover, replication simplifies maintenance, usually by allowing you to run expensive operations on a node other than the primary. For example, it's common practice to run backups on a secondary node to keep unnecessary load off the primary and to avoid downtime. Building large indexes is another example. Because index builds are expensive, you may opt to build on a secondary node first, swap the secondary with the existing primary, and then build again on the new secondary.

Finally, replication allows you to balance reads across replicas. For applications whose workloads are overwhelmingly read-heavy, this is the easiest, or if you prefer, the most naïve, way to scale MongoDB. But for all its promise, a replica set doesn't help much if any of the following apply:

- The allotted hardware can't process the given workload. As an example, we mentioned working sets in the previous chapter. If your working data set is much larger than the available RAM, then sending random reads to the secondaries likely won't improve your performance as much as you might hope. In this scenario, performance becomes constrained by the number of I/O operations per second (IOPS) your disk can handle—generally around 80–100 for non-SSD hard drives. Reading from a replica increases your total IOPS, but going from 100 to 200 IOPS may not solve your performance problems, especially if writes are occurring at the same time and consuming a portion of that number. In this case, sharding may be a better option.

- The ratio of writes to reads exceeds 50%. This is an admittedly arbitrary ratio, but it's a reasonable place to start. The issue here is that every write to the primary must eventually be written to all the secondaries as well. Therefore, directing reads to secondaries that are already processing a lot of writes can sometimes slow the replication process and may not result in increased read throughput.

- The application requires consistent reads. Secondary nodes replicate asynchronously and therefore aren't guaranteed to reflect the latest writes to the primary node. In pathological cases, secondaries can run hours behind. As we'll explain later, you can guarantee your writes go to secondaries before returning to the driver, but this approach carries a latency cost.

Replica sets are excellent for scaling reads that don't require immediate consistency, but they won't help in every situation. If you need to scale and any of the preceding conditions apply, then you'll need a different strategy, involving sharding, augmented hardware, or some combination of the two.

11.2   Replica sets

Replica sets are the recommended MongoDB replication strategy. We'll start by configuring a sample replica set. We'll then describe how replication works because this knowledge is incredibly important for diagnosing production issues. We'll end by discussing advanced configuration details, failover and recovery, and best deployment practices.

11.2.1   Setup

The minimum recommended replica set configuration consists of three nodes, because in a replica set with only two nodes you can't have a majority in case the primary server goes down. A three-member replica set can have either three members that hold data or two members that hold data and an arbiter. The primary is the only member in the set that can accept write operations. Replica set members go through a process in which they "elect" a new master by voting. If a primary becomes unavailable, elections allow the set to recover normal operations without manual intervention. Unfortunately, if a majority of the replica set is inaccessible or unavailable, the replica set cannot accept writes and all remaining members become read-only. You may consider adding an arbiter to a replica set if it has an equal number of nodes in two places where network partitions between the places are possible. In such cases, the arbiter will break the tie between the two facilities and allow the set to elect a new primary.

In the minimal configuration, two of these three nodes serve as first-class, persistent mongod instances. Either can act as the replica set primary, and both have a full copy of the data. The third node in the set is an arbiter, which doesn't replicate data but merely acts as a kind of observer. Arbiters are lightweight mongod servers that participate in the election of a primary but don't replicate any of the data. You can see an illustration of the replica set you're about to set up in figure 11.1. The arbiter is located at the secondary data center on the right.

Now let's create a simple three-node replica set to demonstrate how to do it. Normally you would create a replica set with each member on a separate machine. To keep this tutorial simple, we're going to start all three on a single machine. Each MongoDB instance we start is identified by its hostname and its port; running the set locally means that when we connect, we'll use the local hostname for all three and start each on a separate port.

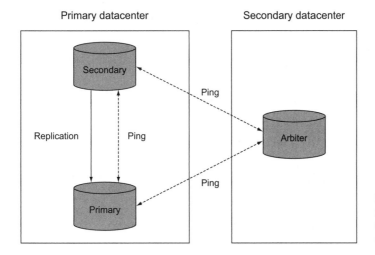

Primary datacenter   Secondary datacenter

**Figure 11.1 A basic
replica set consisting of
a primary, a secondary,
and an arbiter**

Begin by creating a data directory for each replica set member:

```
mkdir ~/node1
mkdir ~/node2
mkdir ~/arbiter
```

Next, start each member as a separate mongod. Because you'll run each process on the same machine, it's easiest to start each mongod in a separate terminal window:

```
mongod --replSet myapp --dbpath ~/node1 --port 40000
mongod --replSet myapp --dbpath ~/node2 --port 40001
mongod --replSet myapp --dbpath ~/arbiter --port 40002
```

Note how we tell each mongod that it will be a member of the myapp replica set and that we start each mongod on a separate port. If you examine the mongod log output, the first thing you'll notice are error messages saying that the configuration can't be found. This is completely normal:

```
[rsStart] replSet info you may need to run replSetInitiate
    -- rs.initiate() in the shell -- if that is not already done
[rsStart] replSet can't get local.system.replset config from self
    or any seed (EMPTYCONFIG)
```

On MongoDB v3.0 the log message will be similar to the following:

```
2015-09-15T16:27:21.088+0300 I REPL      [initandlisten] Did not find local
replica set configuration document at startup;  NoMatchingDocument Did not
find replica set configuration document in local.system.replset
```

To proceed, you need to configure the replica set. Do so by first connecting to one of the non-arbiter mongods just started. These instances aren't running on MongoDB's default port, so connect to one by running

```
mongo --port 40000
```

These examples were produced running these mongod processes locally, so you'll see the name of the example machine, iron, pop up frequently; substitute your own hostname.

Connect, and then run the rs.initiate() command:[3]

```
> rs.initiate()
{
    "info2" : "no configuration explicitly specified -- making one",
    "me" : "iron.local:40000",
    "info" : "Config now saved locally.  Should come online in about a
    minute.",
    "ok" : 1
}
```

On MongoDB v3.0 the output will be similar to the following:

```
{
    "info2" : "no configuration explicitly specified -- making one",
    "me" : "iron.local:40000",
    "ok" : 1
}
```

Within a minute or so, you'll have a one-member replica set. You can now add the other two members using rs.add():

```
> rs.add("iron.local:40001")
{ "ok" : 1 }
> rs.add("iron.local:40002", {arbiterOnly: true})
{ "ok" : 1 }
```

On MongoDB v3.0 you can also add an arbiter with the following command:

```
> rs.addArb("iron.local:40002")
{ "ok" : 1 }
```

Note that for the second node, you specify the arbiterOnly option to create an arbiter. Within a minute, all members should be online. To get a brief summary of the replica set status, run the db.isMaster() command:

```
> db.isMaster()
{
  "setName" : "myapp",
  "ismaster" : true,
  "secondary" : false,
  "hosts" : [
    "iron.local:40001",
    "iron.local:40000"
  ],
```

---

[3] Some users have reported trouble with this step because they have the line bind_ip = 127.0.0.1 in their mongod.conf file at /etc/mongod.conf or /usr/local/etc/mongod.conf. If initiating the replica set prints an error, look for and remove that configuration.

```
  "arbiters" : [
    "iron.local:40002"
  ],
  "primary" : "iron.local:40000",
  "me" : "iron.local:40000",
  "maxBsonObjectSize" : 16777216,
  "maxMessageSizeBytes" : 48000000,
  "localTime" : ISODate("2013-11-06T05:53:25.538Z"),
  "ok" : 1
}
```

The same command produces the following output on a MongoDB v3.0 machine:

```
myapp:PRIMARY> db.isMaster()
{
    "setName" : "myapp",
    "setVersion" : 5,
    "ismaster" : true,
    "secondary" : false,
    "hosts" : [
        "iron.local:40000",
        "iron.local:40001"
    ],
    "arbiters" : [
        "iron.local:40002"
    ],
    "primary" : "iron.local:40000",
    "me" : "iron.local:40000",
    "electionId" : ObjectId("55f81dd44a50a01e0e3b4ede"),
    "maxBsonObjectSize" : 16777216,
    "maxMessageSizeBytes" : 48000000,
    "maxWriteBatchSize" : 1000,
    "localTime" : ISODate("2015-09-15T13:37:13.798Z"),
    "maxWireVersion" : 3,
    "minWireVersion" : 0,
    "ok" : 1
}
```

A more detailed view of the system is provided by the rs.status() method. You'll see state information for each node. Here's the complete status listing:

```
> rs.status()
{
  "set" : "myapp",
  "date" : ISODate("2013-11-07T17:01:29Z"),
  "myState" : 1,
  "members" : [
    {
      "_id" : 0,
      "name" : "iron.local:40000",
      "health" : 1,
      "state" : 1,
      "stateStr" : "PRIMARY",
      "uptime" : 1099,
```

```
        "optime" : Timestamp(1383842561, 1),
        "optimeDate" : ISODate("2013-11-07T16:42:41Z"),
        "self" : true
    },
    {
        "_id" : 1,
        "name" : "iron.local:40001",
        "health" : 1,
        "state" : 2,
        "stateStr" : "SECONDARY",
        "uptime" : 1091,
        "optime" : Timestamp(1383842561, 1),
        "optimeDate" : ISODate("2013-11-07T16:42:41Z"),
        "lastHeartbeat" : ISODate("2013-11-07T17:01:29Z"),
        "lastHeartbeatRecv" : ISODate("2013-11-07T17:01:29Z"),
        "pingMs" : 0,
        "lastHeartbeatMessage" : "syncing to: iron.local:40000",
        "syncingTo" : "iron.local:40000"
    },
    {
        "_id" : 2,
        "name" : "iron.local:40002",
        "health" : 1,
        "state" : 7,
        "stateStr" : "ARBITER",
        "uptime" : 1089,
        "lastHeartbeat" : ISODate("2013-11-07T17:01:29Z"),
        "lastHeartbeatRecv" : ISODate("2013-11-07T17:01:29Z"),
        "pingMs" : 0
    }
    ],
        "ok" : 1
}
```

The rs.status() command produces a slightly different output on a MongoDB v3.0
server:

```
{
    "set" : "myapp",
    "date" : ISODate("2015-09-15T13:41:58.772Z"),
    "myState" : 1,
    "members" : [
        {
            "_id" : 0,
            "name" : "iron.local:40000",
            "health" : 1,
            "state" : 1,
            "stateStr" : "PRIMARY",
            "uptime" : 878,
            "optime" : Timestamp(1442324156, 1),
            "optimeDate" : ISODate("2015-09-15T13:35:56Z"),
            "electionTime" : Timestamp(1442323924, 2),
            "electionDate" : ISODate("2015-09-15T13:32:04Z"),
            "configVersion" : 5,
```

```
                      "self" : true
            },
            {
                "_id" : 1,
                "name" : "iron.local:40001",
                "health" : 1,
                "state" : 2,
                "stateStr" : "SECONDARY",
                "uptime" : 473,
                "optime" : Timestamp(1442324156, 1),
                "optimeDate" : ISODate("2015-09-15T13:35:56Z"),
                "lastHeartbeat" : ISODate("2015-09-15T13:41:56.819Z"),
                "lastHeartbeatRecv" : ISODate("2015-09-15T13:41:57.396Z"),
                "pingMs" : 0,
                "syncingTo" : "iron.local:40000",
                "configVersion" : 5
            },
            {
                "_id" : 2,
                "name" : "iron.local:40002",
                "health" : 1,
                "state" : 7,
                "stateStr" : "ARBITER",
                "uptime" : 360,
                "lastHeartbeat" : ISODate("2015-09-15T13:41:57.676Z"),
                "lastHeartbeatRecv" : ISODate("2015-09-15T13:41:57.676Z"),
                "pingMs" : 10,
                "configVersion" : 5
            }
        ],
        "ok" : 1
}
```

Unless your MongoDB database contains a lot of data, the replica set should come online within 30 seconds. During this time, the stateStr field of each node should transition from RECOVERING to PRIMARY, SECONDARY, or ARBITER.

Now even if the replica set status claims that replication is working, you may want to see some empirical evidence of this. Go ahead and connect to the primary node with the shell and insert a document:

```
$ mongo --port 40000
myapp:PRIMARY> use bookstore
switched to db bookstore
myapp:PRIMARY> db.books.insert({title: "Oliver Twist"})
myapp:PRIMARY> show dbs
bookstore 0.203125GB
local 0.203125GB
```

Notice how the MongoDB shell prints out the replica set membership status of the instance it's connected to.

Initial replication of your data should occur almost immediately. In another terminal window, open a new shell instance, but this, time point it to the secondary node. Query for the document just inserted; it should have arrived:

```
$ mongo --port 40001
myapp:SECONDARY> show dbs
bookstore 0.203125GB
local 0.203125GB
myapp:SECONDARY> use bookstore
switched to db bookstore
myapp:SECONDARY> rs.slaveOk()
myapp:SECONDARY> db.books.find()
{ "_id" : ObjectId("4d42ebf28e3c0c32c06bdf20"), "title" : "Oliver Twist" }
```

If replication is working as displayed here, you've successfully configured your replica set. By default, MongoDB attempts to protect you from accidentally querying a secondary because this data will be less current than the primary, where writes occur. You must explicitly allow reads from the secondary in the shell by running rs.slaveOk().

It should be satisfying to see replication in action, but perhaps more interesting is automated failover. Let's test that now and kill a node. You could kill the secondary, but that merely stops replication, with the remaining nodes maintaining their current status. If you want to see a change of system state, you need to kill the primary. If the primary is running in the foreground of your shell, you can kill it by pressing Ctrl-C; if it's running in the background, then get its process ID from the mongod.lock file in ~/node1 and run kill -3 <process id>. You can also connect to the primary using the shell and run commands to shut down the server:

```
$ mongo --port 40000

PRIMARY> use admin
PRIMARY> db.shutdownServer()
```

Once you've killed the primary, note that the secondary detects the lapse in the primary's heartbeat. The secondary then elects itself primary. This election is possible because a majority of the original nodes (the arbiter and the original secondary) are still able to ping each other. Here's an excerpt from the secondary node's log:

```
Thu Nov  7 09:23:23.091 [rsHealthPoll] replset info iron.local:40000
    heartbeat failed, retrying
Thu Nov  7 09:23:23.091 [rsHealthPoll] replSet info iron.local:40000
    is down (or slow to respond):
Thu Nov  7 09:23:23.091 [rsHealthPoll] replSet member iron.local:40000
    is now in state DOWN
Thu Nov  7 09:23:23.092 [rsMgr] replSet info electSelf 1
Thu Nov  7 09:23:23.202 [rsMgr] replSet PRIMARY
```

If you connect to the new primary node and check the replica set status, you'll see that the old primary is unreachable:

```
$ mongo --port 40001

> rs.status()
...
  {
    "_id" : 0,
    "name" : "iron.local:40000",
    "health" : 0,
    "state" : 8,
    "stateStr" : "(not reachable/healthy)",
    "uptime" : 0,
    "optime" : Timestamp(1383844267, 1),
    "optimeDate" : ISODate("2013-11-07T17:11:07Z"),
    "lastHeartbeat" : ISODate("2013-11-07T17:30:00Z"),
    "lastHeartbeatRecv" : ISODate("2013-11-07T17:23:21Z"),
    "pingMs" : 0
  },
...
```

Post-failover, the replica set consists of only two nodes. Because the arbiter has no data, your application will continue to function as long as it communicates with the primary node only.[4] Even so, replication isn't happening, and there's now no possibility of failover. The old primary must be restored. Assuming that the old primary was shut down cleanly, you can bring it back online, and it'll automatically rejoin the replica set as a secondary. Go ahead and try that now by restarting the old primary node.

That's a quick overview of replica sets. Some of the details are, unsurprisingly, messier. In the next two sections, you'll see how replica sets work and look at deployment, advanced configuration, and how to handle tricky scenarios that may arise in production.

11.2.2 How replication works

Replica sets rely on two basic mechanisms: an oplog and a heartbeat. The oplog enables the replication of data, and the heartbeat monitors health and triggers failover. You'll now see how both of these mechanisms work in turn. You should begin to understand and predict replica set behavior, particularly in failure scenarios.

ALL ABOUT THE OPLOG

At the heart of MongoDB's replication stands the oplog. The oplog is a capped collection that lives in a database called `local` on every replicating node and records all changes to the data. Every time a client writes to the primary, an entry with enough information to reproduce the write is automatically added to the primary's oplog. Once the write is replicated to a given secondary, that secondary's oplog also stores a

---

[4] Applications sometimes query secondary nodes for read scaling. If that's happening, this kind of failure will cause read failures,sSo it's important to design your application with failover in mind. More on this at the end of the chapter.

record of the write. Each oplog entry is identified with a BSON timestamp, and all secondaries use the timestamp to keep track of the latest entry they've applied.[5]

To better see how this works, let's look more closely at a real oplog and at the operations recorded in it. First connect with the shell to the primary node started in the previous section and switch to the `local` database:

```
myapp:PRIMARY> use local
switched to db local
```

The `local` database stores all the replica set metadata and the oplog. Naturally, this database isn't replicated itself. Thus it lives up to its name; data in the `local` database is supposed to be unique to the local node and therefore shouldn't be replicated.

If you examine the `local` database, you'll see a collection called `oplog.rs`, which is where every replica set stores its oplog. You'll also see a few system collections. Here's the complete output:

```
myapp:PRIMARY> show collections
me
oplog.rs
replset.minvalid
slaves
startup_log
system.indexes
system.replset
```

`replset.minvalid` contains information for the initial sync of a given replica set member, and `system.replset` stores the replica set config document. Not all of your mongod servers will have the `replset.minvalid` collection. `me` and `slaves` are used to implement write concerns, described at the end of this chapter, and `system.indexes` is the standard index spec container.

First we'll focus on the oplog. Let's query for the oplog entry corresponding to the book document you added in the previous section. To do so, enter the following query. The resulting document will have four fields, and we'll discuss each in turn:

```
> db.oplog.rs.findOne({op: "i"})
{
  "ts" : Timestamp(1383844267, 1),
  "h" : NumberLong("-305734463742602323"),
  "v" : 2,
  "op" : "i",
  "ns" : "bookstore.books",
  "o" : {
    "_id" : ObjectId("527bc9aac2595f18349e4154"),
    "title" : "Oliver Twist"
  }
}
```

---

[5] The BSON timestamp is a unique identifier consisting of the number of seconds since the epoch and an incrementing counter. For more details, see http://en.wikipedia.org/wiki/Unix_time.

The first field, ts, stores the entry's BSON timestamp. The timestamp includes two numbers; the first representing the seconds since epoch and the second representing a counter value—1 in this case. To query with a timestamp, you need to explicitly construct a timestamp object. All the drivers have their own BSON timestamp constructors, and so does JavaScript. Here's how to use it:

```
db.oplog.rs.findOne({ts: Timestamp(1383844267, 1)})
```

Returning to the oplog entry, the op field specifies the opcode. This tells the secondary node which operation the oplog entry represents. Here you see an i, indicating an insert. After op comes ns to signify the relevant namespace (database and collection) and then the lowercase letter o, which for insert operations contains a copy of the inserted document.

As you examine oplog entries, you may notice that operations affecting multiple documents are analyzed into their component parts. For multi-updates and mass deletes, a separate entry is created in the oplog for each document affected. For example, suppose you add a few more Dickens books to the collection:

```
myapp:PRIMARY> use bookstore
myapp:PRIMARY> db.books.insert({title: "A Tale of Two Cities"})
myapp:PRIMARY> db.books.insert({title: "Great Expectations"})
```

Now with four books in the collection, let's issue a multi-update to set the author's name:

```
myapp:PRIMARY> db.books.update({}, {$set: {author: "Dickens {multi:true})
```

How does this appear in the oplog?

```
myapp:PRIMARY> use local
myapp:PRIMARY> db.oplog.rs.find({op: "u"})
{
  "ts" : Timestamp(1384128758, 1),
  "h" : NumberLong("5431582342821118204"),
  "v" : 2,
  "op" : "u",
  "ns" : "bookstore.books",
  "o2" : {
    "_id" : ObjectId("527bc9aac2595f18349e4154")
  },
  "o" : {
    "$set" : {
      "author" : "Dickens"
    }
  }
}
{
  "ts" : Timestamp(1384128758, 2),
  "h" : NumberLong("3897436474689294423"),
  "v" : 2,
  "op" : "u",
  "ns" : "bookstore.books",
```

```
      "o2" : {
        "_id" : ObjectId("528020a9f3f61863aba207e7")
      },
      "o" : {
        "$set" : {
          "author" : "Dickens"
        }
      }
    }
    {
      "ts" : Timestamp(1384128758, 3),
      "h" : NumberLong("2241781384783113"),
      "v" : 2,
      "op" : "u",
      "ns" : "bookstore.books",
      "o2" : {
        "_id" : ObjectId("528020a9f3f61863aba207e8")
      },
      "o" : {
        "$set" : {
          "author" : "Dickens"
        }
      }
    }
```

As you can see, each updated document gets its own oplog entry. This normalization is done as part of the more general strategy of ensuring that secondaries always end up with the same data as the primary. To guarantee this, every applied operation must be *idempotent*—it can't matter how many times a given oplog entry is applied. The result must always be the same. But the secondaries must apply the oplog entries in the same order as they were generated for the oplog. Other multidocument operations, like deletes, will exhibit the same behavior. You can try different operations and see how they ultimately appear in the oplog.

To get some basic information about the oplog's current status, you can run the shell's db.getReplicationInfo() method:

```
myapp:PRIMARY> db.getReplicationInfo()
{
  "logSizeMB" : 192,
  "usedMB" : 0.01,
  "timeDiff" : 286197,
  "timeDiffHours" : 79.5,
  "tFirst" : "Thu Nov 07 2013 08:42:41 GMT-0800 (PST)",
  "tLast" : "Sun Nov 10 2013 16:12:38 GMT-0800 (PST)",
  "now" : "Sun Nov 10 2013 16:19:49 GMT-0800 (PST)"
}
```

Here you see the timestamps of the first and last entries in this oplog. You can find these oplog entries manually by using the $natural sort modifier. For example, the following query fetches the latest entry:

```
db.oplog.rs.find().sort({$natural: -1}) .limit(1)
```

The only important thing left to understand about replication is how the secondaries keep track of their place in the oplog. The answer lies in the fact that secondaries also keep an oplog. This is a significant improvement upon master-slave replication, so it's worth taking a moment to explore the rationale.

Imagine you issue a write to the primary node of a replica set. What happens next? First, the write is recorded and then added to the primary's oplog. Meanwhile, all secondaries have their own oplogs that replicate the primary's oplog. When a given secondary node is ready to update itself, it does three things. First, it looks at the timestamp of the latest entry in its own oplog. Next, it queries the primary's oplog for all entries greater than that timestamp. Finally, it writes the data and adds each of those entries to its own oplog.[6] This means that in case of failover, any secondary promoted to primary will have an oplog that the other secondaries can replicate from. This feature essentially enables replica set recovery.

Secondary nodes use long polling to immediately apply new entries from the primary's oplog. Long polling means the secondary makes a long-lived request to the primary. When the primary receives a modification, it responds to the waiting request immediately. Thus, secondaries will usually be almost completely up to date. When they do fall behind because of network partitions or maintenance on secondaries, the latest timestamp in each secondary's oplog can be used to monitor any replication lag.

Master-slave replication

Master-slave replication is the original replication paradigm in MongoDB. This flavor of replication is easy to configure and has the advantage of supporting any number of slave nodes. But master-slave replication is no longer recommended for production deployments. There are a couple reasons for this. First, failover is completely manual. If the master node fails, then an administrator must shut down a slave and restart it as a master node. Then the application must be reconfigured to point to the new master. Second, recovery is difficult. Because the oplog exists only on the master node, a failure requires that a new oplog be created on the new master. This means that any other existing nodes will need to resync from the new master in the event of a failure.

In short, there are few compelling reasons to use master-slave replication. Replica sets are the way forward, and they're the flavor of replication you should use. If for some reason you must use master-slave replication, consult the MongoDB manual for more information.

---

[6] When journaling is enabled, documents are written to the core data files and to the oplog simultaneously in an atomic transaction.

HALTED REPLICATION

Replication will halt permanently if a secondary can't find the point it's synced to in the primary's oplog. When that happens, you'll see an exception in the secondary's log that looks like this:

```
repl: replication data too stale, halting
Fri Jan 28 14:19:27 [replsecondary] caught SyncException
```

Recall that the oplog is a capped collection. This means that the collection can only hold so much data. If a secondary is offline for an extended period of time, the oplog may not be large enough to store every change made in that period. Once a given secondary fails to find the point at which it's synced in the primary's oplog, there's no longer any way of ensuring that the secondary is a perfect replica of the primary. Because the only remedy for halted replication is a complete resync of the primary's data, you'll want to strive to avoid this state. To do that, you'll need to monitor secondary delay, and you'll need to have a large enough oplog for your write volume. You'll learn more about monitoring in chapter 12. Choosing the right oplog size is what we'll cover next.

SIZING THE REPLICATION OPLOG

The oplog is a capped collection; as such, MongoDB v2.6 doesn't allow you to resize it once it's been created. This makes it important to choose an initial oplog size carefully. But in MongoDB v3.0 you can change the size of the oplog. The procedure requires you to stop the mongod instance and start it as a standalone instance, modify the oplog size, and restart the member.

The default oplog sizes vary somewhat. On 32-bit systems, the oplog will default to 50 MB, whereas on 64-bit systems, the oplog will be the larger of 1 GB or 5% of free disk space, unless you're running on Mac OS X, in which case the oplog will be 192 MB. This smaller size is due to the assumption that OS X machines are development machines. For many deployments, 5% of free disk space will be more than enough. One way to think about an oplog of this size is to recognize that once it overwrites itself 20 times, the disk will likely be full (this is true for insert-only workloads).

That said, the default size won't be ideal for all applications. If you know that your application will have a high write volume, you should do some empirical testing before deploying. Set up replication and then write to the primary at the rate you'll have in production. You'll want to hammer the server in this way for at least an hour. Once done, connect to any replica set member and get the current replication information:

```
db.getReplicationInfo()
```

Once you know how much oplog you're generating per hour, you can then decide how much oplog space to allocate. The goal is to eliminate instances where your secondaries get too far behind the primary to catch up using the oplog. You should probably shoot for being able to withstand at least eight hours of secondary downtime. You want to avoid having to completely resync any node, and increasing the oplog size will buy you time in the event of network failures and the like.

If you want to change the default oplog size, you must do so the first time you start each member node using mongod's `--oplogSize` option. The value is in megabytes. Thus you can start mongod with a 1 GB oplog like this:[7]

```
mongod --replSet myapp --oplogSize 1024
```

HEARTBEAT AND FAILOVER

The replica set heartbeat facilitates election and failover. By default, each replica set member pings all the other members every two seconds. In this way, the system can ascertain its own health. When you run `rs.status()`, you see the timestamp of each node's last heartbeat along with its state of health (`1` means healthy and `0` means unresponsive).

As long as every node remains healthy and responsive, the replica set will hum along its merry way. But if any node becomes unresponsive, action may be taken. Every replica set wants to ensure that exactly one primary node exists at all times. But this is possible only when a majority of nodes is visible. For example, look back at the replica set you built in the previous section. If you kill the secondary, then a majority of nodes still exists, so the replica set doesn't change state but simply waits for the secondary to come back online. If you kill the primary, then a majority still exists but there's no primary. Therefore, the secondary is automatically promoted to primary. If more than one secondary exists, the most current secondary will be the one elected.

But other possible scenarios exist. Imagine that both the secondary and the arbiter are killed. Now the primary remains but there's no majority—only one of the three original nodes remains healthy. In this case, you'll see a message like this in the primary's log:

```
[rsMgr] can't see a majority of the set, relinquishing primary
[rsMgr] replSet relinquishing primary state
[rsMgr] replSet SECONDARY
[rsMgr] replSet closing client sockets after relinquishing primary
```

With no majority, the primary demotes itself to a secondary. This may seem puzzling, but think about what might happen if this node were allowed to remain primary. If the heartbeats fail due to some kind of network partition, the other nodes will still be online. If the arbiter and secondary are still up and able to see each other, then according to the rule of the majority, the remaining secondary will become a primary. If the original primary doesn't step down, you're suddenly in an untenable situation: a replica set with two primary nodes. If the application continues to run, it might write to and read from two different primaries, a sure recipe for inconsistency and truly bizarre application behavior. Therefore, when the primary can't see a majority, it must step down.

---

[7] For a tutorial on how to resize the oplog, see http://docs.mongodb.org/manual/tutorial/change-oplog-size/.

COMMIT AND ROLLBACK

One final important point to understand about replica sets is the concept of a commit. In essence, you can write to a primary node all day long, but those writes won't be considered committed until they've been replicated to a majority of nodes. What do we mean by committed? The idea can best be explained by example.

Please note that operations on a single document are always atomic with MongoDB databases, but operations that involve multiple documents aren't atomic as a whole.

Imagine again the replica set you built in the previous section. Suppose you issue a series of writes to the primary that don't get replicated to the secondary for some reason (connectivity issues, secondary is down for backup, secondary is lagging, and so on). Now suppose that the secondary is suddenly promoted to primary. You write to the new primary, and eventually the old primary comes back online and tries to replicate from the new primary. The problem here is that the old primary has a series of writes that don't exist in the new primary's oplog. This situation triggers a rollback.

In a rollback, all writes that were never replicated to a majority are undone. This means that they're removed from both the secondary's oplog and the collection where they reside. If a secondary has registered a delete, the node will look for the deleted document in another replica and restore it to itself. The same is true for dropped collections and updated documents.

The reverted writes are stored in the rollback subdirectory of the relevant node's data path. For each collection with rolled-back writes, a separate BSON file will be created the filename of which includes the time of the rollback. In the event that you need to restore the reverted documents, you can examine these BSON files using the bsondump utility and manually restore them, possibly using mongorestore.

If you ever have to restore rolled-back data, you'll realize that this is a situation you want to avoid, and fortunately you can, to some extent. If your application can tolerate the extra write latency, you can use write concerns, described later, to ensure that your data is replicated to a majority of nodes on each write (or perhaps after every several writes). Being smart about write concerns and about monitoring of replication lag in general will help you mitigate the problem of rollback, or even avoid it altogether.

In this section you learned perhaps a few more replication internals than expected, but the knowledge should come in handy. Understanding how replication works goes a long way in helping you to diagnose any issues you may have in production.

11.2.3 *Administration*

For all the automation they provide, replica sets have some potentially complicated configuration options. In what follows, we'll describe these options in detail. In the interest of keeping things simple, we'll also suggest which options can be safely ignored.

CONFIGURATION DETAILS

Here we'll present the `mongod` startup options pertaining to replica sets, and we'll describe the structure of the replica set configuration document.

Replication options

Earlier, you learned how to initiate a replica set using the shell's `rs.initiate()` and `rs.add()` methods. These methods are convenient, but they hide certain replica set configuration options. Let's look at how to use a configuration document to initiate and update a replica set's configuration.

A configuration document specifies the configuration of the replica set. To create one, first add a value for `_id` that matches the name you passed to the `--replSet` parameter:

```
> config = {_id: "myapp", members: []}
{ "_id" : "myapp", "members" : [ ] }
```

The individual `members` can be defined as part of the configuration document as follows:

```
config.members.push({_id: 0, host: 'iron.local:40000'})
config.members.push({_id: 1, host: 'iron.local:40001'})
config.members.push({_id: 2, host: 'iron.local:40002', arbiterOnly: true})
```

As noted earlier, `iron` is the name of our test machine; substitute your own hostname as necessary. Your configuration document should now look like this:

```
> config
{
  "_id" : "myapp",
  "members" : [
    {
      "_id" : 0,
      "host" : "iron.local:40000"
    },
    {
      "_id" : 1,
      "host" : "iron.local:40001"
    },
    {
      "_id" : 2,
      "host" : "iron.local:40002",
      "arbiterOnly" : true
    }
  ]
}
```

You can then pass the document as the first argument to `rs.initiate()` to initiate the replica set.

Technically, the document consists of an `_id` containing the name of the replica set, an array specifying between 3 and 50 `members`, and an optional subdocument for specifying certain global settings. This sample replica set uses the minimum required configuration parameters, plus the optional `arbiterOnly` setting. Please keep in mind that although a replica set can have up to 50 members, it can only have up to 7 voting members.

The document requires an `_id` that matches the replica set's name. The initiation command will verify that each member node has been started with the `--replSet` option with that name. Each replica set `member` requires an `_id` consisting of increasing integers starting from 0. Also, `members` require a `host` field with a hostname and optional port.

Here you initiate the replica set using the `rs.initiate()` method. This is a simple wrapper for the `replSetInitiate` command. Thus you could have started the replica set like this:

```
db.runCommand({replSetInitiate: config});
```

`config` is a variable holding your configuration document. Once initiated, each set member stores a copy of this configuration document in the `local` database's `system.replset` collection. If you query the collection, you'll see that the document now has a version number. Whenever you modify the replica set's configuration, you must also increment this version number. The easiest way to access the current configuration document is to run `rs.conf()`.

To modify a replica set's configuration, there's a separate command, `replSetReconfig`, which takes a new configuration document. Alternatively, you can use `rs.reconfig()` which also uses `replSetReconfig`. The new document can specify the addition or removal of set members along with alterations to both member-specific and global configuration options. The process of modifying a configuration document, incrementing the version number, and passing it as part of the `replSetReconfig` can be laborious, so a number of shell helpers exist to ease the way. To see a list of them all, enter `rs.help()` at the shell.

Bear in mind that whenever a replica set reconfiguration results in the election of a new primary node, all client connections will be closed. This is done to ensure that clients will no longer attempt to send writes to a secondary node unless they're aware of the reconfiguration.

If you're interested in configuring a replica set from one of the drivers, you can see how by examining the implementation of `rs.add()`. Enter `rs.add` (the method without the parentheses) at the shell prompt to see how the method works.

Configuration document options

Until now, we've limited ourselves to the simplest replica set configuration document. But these documents support several options for both replica set members and for the replica set as a whole. We'll begin with the member options. You've seen `_id`, `host`, and `arbiterOnly`. Here are these plus the rest, in all their gritty detail:

- `_id` *(required)*—A unique incrementing integer representing the member's ID. These `_id` values begin at 0 and must be incremented by one for each member added.

- host (required)—A string storing the hostname of this member along with an optional port number. If the port is provided, it should be separated from the hostname by a colon (for example, iron:30000). If no port number is specified, the default port, 27017, will be used. We've seen it before, but here's a simple document with a replica set _id and host:

```
{
  "_id" : 0,
  "host" : "iron:40000"
}
```

- arbiterOnly—A Boolean value, true or false, indicating whether this member is an arbiter. Arbiters store configuration data only. They're lightweight members that participate in primary election but not in the replication itself. Here's an example of using the arbiterOnly setting:

```
{
  "_id" : 0,
  "host" : "iron:40000",
  "arbiterOnly": true
}
```

- priority—A decimal number from 0 to 1000 that helps to determine the relative eligibility that this node will be elected primary. For both replica set initiation and failover, the set will attempt to elect as primary the node with the highest priority, as long as it's up to date. This might be useful if you have a replica set where some nodes are more powerful than the others; it makes sense to prefer the biggest machine as the primary.

  There are also cases where you might want a node never to be primary (say, a disaster recovery node residing in a secondary data center). In those cases, set the priority to 0. Nodes with a priority of 0 will be marked as passive in the results to the isMaster() command and will never be elected primary. Here's an example of setting the member's priority:

```
{
  "_id" : 0,
  "host" : "iron:40000",
  "priority" : 500
}
```

- votes—All replica set members get one vote by default. The votes setting allows you to give more than one vote to an individual member.

  This option should be used with extreme care, if at all. For one thing, it's difficult to reason about replica set failover behavior when not all members have the same number of votes. Moreover, the vast majority of production deployments will be perfectly well served with one vote per member. If you do choose to alter the number of votes for a given member, be sure to think through and simulate the various failure scenarios carefully. This member has an increased number of votes:

```
{
  "_id" : 0,
  "host" : "iron:40000",
  "votes" : 2
}
```

- hidden—A Boolean value that, when `true`, will keep this member from showing up in the responses generated by the `isMaster` command. Because the MongoDB drivers rely on `isMaster` for knowledge of the replica set topology, hiding a member keeps the drivers from automatically accessing it. This setting can be used in conjunction with `buildIndexes` and must be used with `slaveDelay`. This member is configured to be hidden:

```
{
  "_id" : 0,
  "host" : "iron:40000",
  "hidden" : true
}
```

- buildIndexes—A Boolean value, defaulting to `true`, that determines whether this member will build indexes. You'll want to set this value to `false` only on members that will never become primary (those with a priority of 0).

  This option was designed for nodes used solely as backups. If backing up indexes is important, you shouldn't use this option. Here's a member configured not to build indexes:

```
{
  "_id" : 0,
  "host" : "iron:40000",
  "buildIndexes" : false
}
```

- slaveDelay—The number of seconds that a given secondary should lag behind the primary. This option can be used only with nodes that will never become primary. To specify a `slaveDelay` greater than 0, be sure to also set a priority of 0.

  You can use a delayed slave as insurance against certain kinds of user errors. For example, if you have a secondary delayed by 30 minutes and an administrator accidentally drops a database, you have 30 minutes to react to this event before it's propagated. This member has been configured with a `slaveDelay` of one hour:

```
{
  "_id" : 0,
  "host" : "iron:40000",
  "slaveDelay" : 3600
}
```

- `tags`—A document containing a set of key-value pairs, usually used to identify this member's location in a particular datacenter or server rack. Tags are used for specifying granular write concern and read settings, and they're discussed in section 11.3.4. In the tag document, the values entered must be strings. Here's a member with two tags:

```
{
  "_id" : 0,
  "host" : "iron:40000",
  "tags" : {
    "datacenter" : "NY",
    "rack" : "B"
  }
}
```

That sums up the options for individual replica set members. There are also two global replica set configuration parameters scoped under a `settings` key. In the replica set configuration document, they appear like this:

```
{
  _id: "myapp",
  members: [ ... ],
  settings: {
    getLastErrorDefaults: {
      w: 1
    },
    getLastErrorModes: {
      multiDC: {
        dc: 2
      }
    }
  }
}
```

- `getLastErrorDefaults`—A document specifying the default arguments to be used when the client calls `getLastError` with no arguments. This option should be treated with care because it's also possible to set global defaults for `getLast-Error` within the drivers, and you can imagine a situation where application developers call `getLastError` not realizing that an administrator has specified a default on the server.

  For more details on `getLastError`, see its documentation at http://docs .mongodb.org/manual/reference/command/getLastError. Briefly, to specify that all writes are replicated to at least two members with a timeout of 500 ms, you'd specify this value in the config like this:

```
settings: {
  getLastErrorDefaults: {
    w: 2,
    wtimeout: 500
  }
}
```

- getLastErrorModes—A document defining extra modes for the getLastError command. This feature is dependent on replica set tagging and is described in detail in section 11.3.4.

REPLICA SET STATUS

You can see the status of a replica set and its members by running the replSetGetStatus command. To invoke this command from the shell, run the rs.status() helper method. The resulting document indicates the members and their respective states, uptime, and oplog times. It's important to understand replica set member state. You can see a complete list of possible values in table 11.1.

You can consider a replica set stable and online when all its nodes are in any of states 1, 2, or 7 and when at least one node is running as the primary. You can use the rs.status() or replSetGetStatus command from an external script to monitor overall state, replication lag, and uptime, and this is recommended for production deployments.[8]

Table 11.1   Replica set states

State	State string	Notes
0	STARTUP	Indicates that the replica set is negotiating with other nodes by pinging all set members and sharing config data.
1	PRIMARY	This is the primary node. A replica set will always have at most one primary node.
2	SECONDARY	This is a secondary, read-only node. This node may become a primary in the event of a failover if and only if its priority is greater than 0 and it's not marked as hidden.
3	RECOVERING	This node is unavailable for reading and writing. You usually see this state after a failover or upon adding a new node. While recovering, a data file sync is often in progress; you can verify this by examining the recovering node's logs.
4	FATAL	A network connection is still established, but the node isn't responding to pings. This usually indicates a fatal error on the machine hosting the node marked FATAL.
5	STARTUP2	An initial data file sync is in progress.
6	UNKNOWN	A network connection has yet to be made.
7	ARBITER	This node is an arbiter.
8	DOWN	The node was accessible and stable at some point but isn't currently responding to heartbeat pings.
9	ROLLBACK	A rollback is in progress.
10	REMOVED	The node was once a member of the replica set but has since been removed.

---

[8] Note that in addition to running the status command, you can get a useful visual through the web console. Chapter 13 discusses the web console and shows an example of its use with replica sets.

FAILOVER AND RECOVERY

In the sample replica set you saw a couple examples of failover. Here we summarize the rules of failover and provide some suggestions on handling recovery.

A replica set will come online when all members specified in the configuration can communicate with one another. Each node is given one vote by default, and those votes are used to form a majority and elect a primary. This means that a replica set can be started with as few as two nodes (and votes). But the initial number of votes also decides what constitutes a majority in the event of a failure.

Let's assume that you've configured a replica set of three complete replicas (no arbiters) and thus have the recommended minimum for automated failover. If the primary fails, and the remaining secondaries can see each other, then a new primary can be elected. As for deciding which one, the secondary with the most up-to-date oplog with the higher priority will be elected primary.

Failure modes and recovery

Recovery is the process of restoring the replica set to its original state following a failure. There are two overarching failure categories to be handled. The first is called *clean failure*, where a given node's data files can still be assumed to be intact. One example of this is a network partition. If a node loses its connections to the rest of the set, you need only wait for connectivity to be restored, and the partitioned node will resume as a set member. A similar situation occurs when a given node's mongod process is terminated for any reason but can be brought back online cleanly.[9] Again, once the process is restarted, it can rejoin the set.

The second type is called *categorical failure*, where a node's data files either no longer exist or must be presumed corrupted. Unclean shutdowns of the mongod process without journaling enabled and hard drive crashes are both examples of this kind of failure. The only ways to recover a categorically failed node are to completely replace the data files via a resync or to restore from a recent backup. Let's look at both strategies in turn.

To completely resync, start a mongod with an empty data directory on the failed node. As long as the host and port haven't changed, the new mongod will rejoin the replica set and then resync all the existing data. If either the host or port has changed, then after bringing the mongod back online you'll also have to reconfigure the replica set. As an example, suppose the node at iron:40001 is rendered unrecoverable and you bring up a new node at foobar:40000. You can reconfigure the replica set by grabbing the configuration document, modifying the host for the second node, and then passing that to the rs.reconfig() method:

```
> config = rs.conf()
{
  "_id" : "myapp",
  "version" : 1,
  "members" : [
```

---

[9] For instance, if MongoDB is shut down cleanly, then you know that the data files are okay. Alternatively, if running with journaling, the MongoDB instance should be recoverable regardless of how it's killed.

```
    {
      "_id" : 0,
      "host" : "iron:40000"
    },
    {
      "_id" : 1,
      "host" : "iron:40001"
    },
    {
      "_id" : 2,
      "host" : "iron:40002",
      "arbiterOnly" : true
    }
  ]
}
> config.members[1].host = "foobar:40000"
foobar:40000
> rs.reconfig(config)
```

Now the replica set will identify the new node, and the new node should start to sync from an existing member.

In addition to restoring via a complete resync, you have the option of restoring from a recent backup. You'll typically perform backups from one of the secondary nodes by making snapshots of the data files and then storing them offline.[10] Recovery via backup is possible only if the oplog within the backup isn't stale relative to the oplogs of the current replica set members. This means that the latest operation in the backup's oplog must still exist in the live oplogs. You can use the information provided by db.getReplicationInfo() to see right away if this is the case. When you do, don't forget to take into account the time it will take to restore the backup. If the backup's latest oplog entry is likely to go stale in the time it takes to copy the backup to a new machine, you're better off performing a complete resync.

But restoring from backup can be faster, in part because the indexes don't have to be rebuilt from scratch. To restore from a backup, copy the backed-up data files to a mongod data path. The resync should begin automatically, and you can check the logs or run rs.status() to verify this.

DEPLOYMENT STRATEGIES

You now know that a replica set can consist of up to 50 nodes in MongoDB v3.0, and you've been presented with a dizzying array of configuration options and considerations regarding failover and recovery. There are a lot of ways you might configure a replica set, but in this section we'll present a couple that will work for the majority of cases.

The most minimal replica set configuration providing automated failover is the one you built earlier consisting of two replicas and one arbiter. In production, the arbiter can run on an application server while each replica gets its own machine. This configuration is economical and sufficient for many production apps.

---

[10] Backups are discussed in detail in chapter 13.

But for applications where uptime is critical, you'll want a replica set consisting of three complete replicas. What does the extra replica buy you? Think of the scenario where a single node fails completely. You still have two first-class nodes available while you restore the third. As long as a third node is online and recovering (which may take hours), the replica set can still fail over automatically to an up-to-date node.

Some applications will require the redundancy afforded by two datacenters, and the three-member replica set can also work in this case. The trick is to use one of the datacenters for disaster recovery only. Figure 11.2 shows an example of this. Here, the primary datacenter houses a replica set primary and secondary, and a backup datacenter keeps the remaining secondary as a passive node (with priority 0).

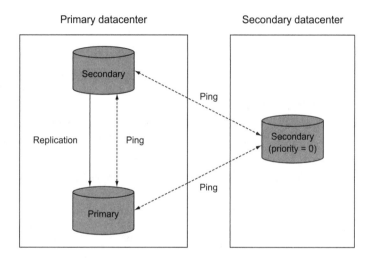

Figure 11.2   A three-node replica set with members in two datacenters

In this configuration, the replica set primary will always be one of the two nodes living in datacenter A. You can lose any one node or any one datacenter and still keep the application online. Failover will usually be automatic, except in the cases where both of A's nodes are lost. Because it's rare to lose two nodes at once, this would likely represent the complete failure or partitioning of datacenter A. To recover quickly, you could shut down the member in datacenter B and restart it without the --replSet flag. Alternatively, you could start two new nodes in datacenter B and then force a replica set reconfiguration. You're not supposed to reconfigure a replica set when the majority of the set is unreachable, but you can do so in emergencies using the force option. For example, if you've defined a new configuration document, config, you can force reconfiguration like this:

```
> rs.reconfig(config, {force: true})
```

As with any production system, testing is key. Make sure that you test for all the typical failover and recovery scenarios in a staging environment comparable to what you'll be running in production. Knowing from experience how your replica set will behave in these failures cases will secure some peace of mind and give you the wherewithal to calmly deal with emergencies as they occur.

11.3 *Drivers and replication*

If you're building an application using MongoDB's replication, you need to know about several application-specific topics. The first is related to connections and failover. Next comes the write concern, which allows you to decide to what degree a given write should be replicated before the application continues. The next topic, read scaling, allows an application to distribute reads across replicas. Finally, we'll discuss tagging, a way to configure more complex replica set reads and writes.

11.3.1 *Connections and failover*

The MongoDB drivers present a relatively uniform interface for connecting to replica sets.

SINGLE-NODE CONNECTIONS

You'll always have the option of connecting to a single node in a replica set. There's no difference between connecting to a node designated as a replica set primary and connecting to one of the vanilla stand-alone nodes we've used for the examples throughout the book. In both cases, the driver will initiate a TCP socket connection and then run the `isMaster` command. For a stand-alone node, this command returns a document like the following:

```
{
  "ismaster" : true,
  "maxBsonObjectSize" : 16777216,
  "maxMessageSizeBytes" : 48000000,
  "localTime" : ISODate("2013-11-12T05:22:54.317Z"),
  "ok" : 1
}
```

What's most important to the driver is that the `isMaster` field be set to `true`, which indicates that the given node is a stand-alone, a master running master-slave replication, or a replica set primary.[11] In all of these cases, the node can be written to, and the user of the driver can perform any CRUD operation.

But when connecting directly to a replica set secondary, you must indicate that you know you're connecting to such a node (for most drivers, at least). In the Ruby driver, you accomplish this with the `:read` parameter. To connect directly to the first secondary you created earlier in the chapter, the Ruby code would look like this:

```
@con = Mongo::Client.new(['iron: 40001'], {:read => {:mode => :secondary}})
```

---

[11] The `isMaster` command also returns a value for the maximum BSON object size for this version of the server. The drivers then validate that all BSON objects are within this limit prior to inserting them.

Without the :read argument, the driver will raise an exception indicating that it couldn't connect to a primary node (assuming that the mongod running at port 40001 is the secondary). This check is in place to keep you from inadvertently reading from a secondary node. Though such attempts to read will always be rejected by the server, you won't see any exceptions unless you're running the operations with safe mode enabled.

The assumption is that you'll usually want to connect to a primary node master; the :read parameter is enforced as a sanity check.

REPLICA SET CONNECTIONS

You can connect to any replica set member individually, but you'll normally want to connect to the replica set as a whole. This allows the driver to figure out which node is primary and, in the case of failover, reconnect to whichever node becomes the new primary.

Most of the officially supported drivers provide ways of connecting to a replica set. In Ruby, you connect by creating a new instance of Mongo::Client, passing in a list of seed nodes as well as the name of the replica set:

```
Mongo::Client.new(['iron:40000', 'iron:40001'], :replica_set => 'myapp')
```

Internally, the driver will attempt to connect to each seed node and then call the isMaster command. Issuing this command to a replica set returns a number of important set details:

```
> db.isMaster()
{
  "setName" : "myapp",
  "ismaster" : false,
  "secondary" : true,
  "hosts" : [
    "iron:40001",
    "iron:40000"
  ],
  "arbiters" : [
    "iron:40002"
  ],
  "me" : "iron:40000",
  "maxBsonObjectSize" : 16777216,
  "maxMessageSizeBytes" : 48000000,
  "localTime" : ISODate("2013-11-12T05:14:42.009Z"),
  "ok" : 1
}
```

Once a seed node responds with this information, the driver has everything it needs. Now it can connect to the primary member, again verify that this member is still primary, and then allow the user to read and write through this node. The response object also allows the driver to cache the addresses of the remaining secondary and arbiter nodes. If an operation on the primary fails, then on subsequent requests the driver can attempt to connect to one of the remaining nodes until it can reconnect to a primary.

When connecting to a MongoDB replica set in this way, drivers will automatically discover additional nodes. This means that when you're connecting to a replica set, you don't need to explicitly list every member of the set. The response from the isMaster command alerts the driver of the presence of the other members. If none of the replica set members listed in the connection arguments are active, the connection will fail, so it's wise to list as many as you can. But don't sweat it if a few nodes are missing from the connection list; they'll be found. If you have multiple data centers, it's considered good practice to include members from all data centers.

It's important to keep in mind that although replica set failover is automatic, the drivers don't attempt to hide the fact that a failover has occurred. The course of events goes something like this: First, the primary fails or a new election takes place. Subsequent requests will reveal that the socket connection has been broken, and the driver will then raise a connection exception and close any open sockets to the database. It's now up to the application developer to decide what happens next, and this decision will depend on both the operation being performed and the specific needs of the application.

Keeping in mind that the driver will automatically attempt to reconnect on any subsequent request, let's imagine a couple of scenarios. First, suppose that you only issue reads to the database. In this case, there's little harm in retrying a failed read because there's no possibility of changing database state. But now imagine that you also regularly write to the database. You can write to the database with or without checking for errors. As discussed in section 11.3.2, with a write concern of 1 or more, the driver will check for problems, including a failure of the write to reach the replica set, by calling the getLastError command. This is the default in most drivers since around MongoDB v2.0, but if you explicitly set the write concern to 0, the driver writes to the TCP socket without checking for errors. If you're using a relatively recent version of the drivers or the shell, you don't have to explicitly call getLastError(); writes send detailed ACK in any case.

If your application writes with a write concern of 0 and a failover occurs, you're left in an uncertain state. How many of the recent writes made it to the server? How many were lost in the socket buffer? The indeterminate nature of writing to a TCP socket makes answering these questions practically impossible. How big of a problem this is depends on the application. For logging, non-safe-mode writes are probably acceptable, because losing writes hardly changes the overall logging picture. But for users creating data in the application, non-safe-mode writes can be a disaster.

The important thing to remember is that the write concern is set to 1 by default, meaning the writes are guaranteed to have reached one member of a replica set, and there are risks in setting it to 0. Receiving a response doesn't eliminate the possibility of a rollback, as we discussed in section 11.2.2. MongoDB gives you some more advanced capabilities for managing this by controlling how writes work with the write concern.

11.3.2 *Write concern*

It should be clear now that the default write concern of 1 is reasonable for some applications because it's important to know that writes have arrived error-free at the primary server. But greater levels of assurance are required if you want to eliminate the possibility of a rollback, and the write concern addresses this by allowing developers to specify the extent to which a write should be replicated before getting an acknowledgment and allowing the application to continue. Technically, you control write concerns via two parameters on the getLastError command: w and wtimeout. The first value, w, indicates the total number of servers that the latest write should be replicated to; the second is a timeout that causes the command to return an error if the write can't be replicated in the specified number of milliseconds.

For example, if you want to make sure that a given write is replicated to at least one server, you can indicate a w value of 2. If you want the operation to time out if this level of replication isn't achieved in 500 ms, you include a wtimeout of 500. Note that if you don't specify a value for wtimeout, and the replication for some reason never occurs, the operation will block indefinitely.

When using a driver, you usually pass the write concern value in with the write, but it depends on the specific driver's API. In Ruby, you can specify a write concern on a single operation like this:

```
@collection.insert_one(doc, {:w => 2, :wtimeout => 200})
```

Many drivers support setting default write concern values for a given connection or database. It can be overwritten for a single operation, as shown earlier, but will become the default for the life of the connection:

```
Mongo::Client.new(['hostname:27017'], :write => {:w => 2})
```

Even fancier options exist. For instance, if you've enabled journaling, you can also force that the journal be synced to disk before acknowledging a write by adding the j option:

```
@collection.insert_one(doc, :write => {:w => 2, :j => true})
```

To find out how to set the write concern in your particular case, check your driver's documentation.

Write concerns work with both replica sets and master-slave replication. If you examine the local databases, you'll see a couple of collections, me on secondary nodes and slaves on the primary node. These are used to implement write concerns. Whenever a secondary polls a primary, the primary makes a note of the latest oplog entry applied to each secondary in its slaves collection. Thus, the primary knows what each secondary has replicated at all times and can therefore reliably answer the getLastError command's write requests.

Keep in mind that using write concerns with values of w greater than 1 will introduce extra latency. Configurable write concerns essentially allow you to make the trade-off between speed and durability. If you're running with journaling, then a write concern with w equal to 1 should be fine for most applications. On the other hand, for logging or analytics, you might elect to disable journaling and write concerns altogether and rely solely on replication for durability, allowing that you may lose some writes in the event of a failure. Consider these trade-offs carefully and test the different scenarios when designing your application.

11.3.3   *Read scaling*

Replicated databases are great for read scaling. If a single server can't handle the application's read load, you have the option to route queries to more than one replica. Most of the drivers have built-in support for sending queries to secondary nodes through a read preference configuration. With the Ruby driver, this is provided as an option on the Mongo::Client constructor:

```
Mongo::Client.new(
    ['iron:40000', 'iron:40001'],
    {:read => {:mode => :secondary}})
```

Note in the connection code that we configure which nodes the new client will read from. When the :read argument is set to {:mode => :secondary}, the connection object will choose a random, nearby secondary to read from. This configuration is called the read preference, and it can be used to direct your driver to read from certain nodes. Most MongoDB drivers have these available read preferences:

- *primary*—This is the default setting and indicates that reads will always be from the replica set primary and thus will always be consistent. If the replica set is experiencing problems and there's no secondary available, an error will be thrown.
- *primaryPreferred*—Drivers with this setting will read from the primary unless for some reason it's unavailable or there's no primary, in which case reads will go to a secondary. This means that reads aren't guaranteed to be consistent.
- *secondary*—This setting indicates the driver should always read from the secondary. This is useful in cases where you want to be sure that your reads will have no impact on the writes that occur on the primary. If no secondaries are available, the read will throw an exception.
- *secondaryPreferred*—This is a more relaxed version of the previous setting. Reads will go to secondaries, unless no secondaries are available, in which case reads will go to the primary.
- *nearest*—A driver configured with this setting will attempt to read from the nearest member of the replica set, as measured by network latency. This could be either a primary or a secondary. Thus, reads will go to the member that the driver believes it can communicate with the quickest.

Remember, the primary read preference is the only one where reads are guaranteed to be consistent. Writing is always done first on the primary. Because there may be a lag in updating the secondary, it's possible that a document that has just been written won't be found on a read immediately following the write, unless you're reading the primary.

It turns out that even if you're not using the nearest setting, if a MongoDB driver has a read preference that allows it to query secondaries, it will still attempt to communicate with a nearby node. It does this according to its member selection strategy. The driver first ranks all the nodes by their network latency. Then it excludes all the nodes for which network latency is at least 15 ms larger than the lowest latency. Finally, it picks one of the remaining nodes at random. Fifteen milliseconds is the default for this value, but some drivers will allow configuration of the acceptable latency window. For the Ruby driver, this configuration might look like this:

```
Mongo::Client.new(
    ['iron:40000', 'iron:40001'],
    :read => {:mode => :secondary},:local_threshold => '0.0015')
```

The :local_threshold option specifies the maximum latency in seconds as a float.

Note that the nearest read preference uses this strategy to pick a node to read from as well, but it includes the primary in the selection process. Overall, the advantage of this approach is that a driver will be likely to have lower latency on a query than with totally random selection but is still able to distribute reads to multiple nodes if they have similarly low latency.

Many MongoDB users scale with replication in production, but there are three cases where this sort of scaling won't be sufficient. The first relates to the number of servers needed. As of MongoDB v2.0, replica sets support a maximum of 12 members, 7 of which can vote. As of MongoDB v3.0, replica sets support a maximum of 50 members, 7 of which can vote. If you need even more replicas for scaling, you can use master-slave replication. But if you don't want to sacrifice automated failover and you need to scale beyond the replica set maximum, you'll need to migrate to a sharded cluster.

The second case involves applications with a high write load. As mentioned at the beginning of this chapter, secondaries must keep up with this write load. Sending reads to write-laden secondaries may inhibit replication.

A third situation that replica scaling can't handle is consistent reads. Because replication is asynchronous, replicas aren't always going to reflect the latest writes to the primary. Therefore, if your application reads arbitrarily from secondaries, the picture presented to end users isn't always guaranteed to be fully consistent. For some applications, this isn't an issue, but for others you need consistent reads; in our shopping cart example from chapter 4, there would be serious problems if we weren't reading the most current data. In fact, atomic operations that read and write must be run on the primary. In these cases, you have two options. The first is to separate the parts of the application that need consistent reads from the parts that don't. The former can always be read from the primary, and the latter can be distributed to secondaries. When this strategy is either too complicated or doesn't scale, sharding is the way to go.[12]

11.3.4 Tagging

If you're using either write concerns or read scaling, you may find yourself wanting more granular control over exactly which secondaries receive writes or reads. For example, suppose you've deployed a five-node replica set across two data geographically separate centers, *NY* and *FR*. The primary datacenter, NY, contains three nodes, and the secondary datacenter, FR, contains the remaining two. Let's say that you want to use a write concern to block until a certain write has been replicated to at least one node in datacenter FR. With what you know about write concerns right now, you'll see that there's no good way to do this. You can't use a w value of a majority of nodes (3) because the most likely scenario is that the three nodes in NY will acknowledge first. You could use a value of 4, but this won't hold up well if, say, you lose one node from each datacenter.

Replica set tagging solves this problem by allowing you to define special write concern modes that target replica set members with certain tags. To see how this works, you first need to learn how to tag a replica set member. In the config document, each member can have a key called `tags` pointing to an object containing key-value pairs. Here's an example:

```
{
  "_id" : "myapp",
  "version" : 1,
  "members" : [
    {
      "_id" : 0,
      "host" : "ny1.myapp.com:30000",
      "tags": { "dc": "NY", "rackNY": "A" }
    },
    {
      "_id" : 1,
      "host" : "ny2.myapp.com:30000",
      "tags": { "dc": "NY", "rackNY": "A" }
    },
    {
      "_id" : 2,
      "host" : "ny3.myapp.com:30000",
      "tags": { "dc": "NY", "rackNY": "B" }
    },
    {
      "_id" : 3,
      "host" : "fr1.myapp.com:30000",
      "tags": { "dc": "FR", "rackFR": "A" }
    },
```

---

[12] Note that to get consistent reads from a sharded cluster, you must always read from the primary nodes of each shard, and you must issue safe writes.

```
    {
      "_id" : 4,
      "host" : "fr2.myapp.com:30000",
      "tags": { "dc": "FR", "rackFR": "B" }
    }
  ],
  settings: {
    getLastErrorModes: {
      multiDC: { dc: 2 } },
      multiRack: { rackNY: 2 } },
    }
  }
}
```

This is a tagged configuration document for the hypothetical replica set spanning two datacenters. Note that each member's tag document has two key-value pairs: the first identifies the datacenter and the second names the local server rack for the given node. Keep in mind that the names used here are completely arbitrary and only meaningful in the context of this application; you can put anything in a tag document (though the value must be a string). What's most important is how you use it.

That's where `getLastErrorModes` comes into play. This allows you to define modes for the `getLastError` command that implement specific write concern requirements. In the example, we've defined two of these. The first, `multiDC`, is defined as `{ "dc": 2 }`, which indicates that a write should be replicated to nodes tagged with at least two different values for `dc`. If you examine the tags, you'll see this will necessarily ensure that the write has been propagated to both datacenters. The second mode specifies that at least two server racks in NY should've received the write. Again the tags should make this clear.

In general, a `getLastErrorModes` entry consists of a document with one or more keys (in this case, `dc` and `rackNY`) the values of which are integers. These integers indicate the number of different tagged values for the key that must be satisfied for the `getLastError` command to complete successfully. Once you define these modes, you can use them as values for `w` in your application. For example, using the first mode in Ruby looks like this:

```
@collection.with(:write => {:w => "multiDC"}).insert_one(doc)
```

In addition to making write concerns more sophisticated, tagging also works with most of the read preferences discussed in section 11.3.3. With reads, tagging works by restricting reads to those with a specific tag. For example, if using a read preference of secondary, the driver will ignore all the nodes that don't have the given tag value. Because the primary read preference can only ever read from one node, it's not compatible with tags, but all the other read preferences are. Here's an example of this using the Ruby driver:

```
@collection.find({user: "pbakkum"},
{
  :read => :secondary,
  :tag_sets => {
```

```
    :dc => "NY"
  }
})
```

This configuration reads from a secondary node that has the dc:NY tag.

Tagging is an element of MongoDB that you may never use, but it can be incredibly useful in certain situations. Keep it in mind if you're managing complex replica set configurations.

11.4   Summary

It should be clear from all that we've discussed that replication is essential for most deployments. MongoDB's replication is supposed to be easy, and setting it up usually is. But when it comes to backing up and failing over, there are bound to be hidden complexities. For these complex cases, let experience, and some help from this chapter, breed familiarity.

To finish up, here are some key things to remember as you move on and manage your own replica sets:

- We recommend that every production deployment of MongoDB where data protection is critical should use a replica set. Failing that, frequent backups are especially essential.
- A replica set should include at least three members, though one of these can be an arbiter.
- Data isn't considered committed until it has been written to a majority of replica set members. In a failure scenario, if a majority of members remain they'll continue to accept writes. Writes that haven't reached a majority of members in this situation will be placed in the rollback data directory and must be handled manually.
- If a replica set secondary is down for a period of time, and the changes made to the database don't fit into MongoDB's oplog, this node will be unable to catch up and must be resynced from scratch. To avoid this, try to minimize the downtime of your secondaries.
- The driver's write concern controls how many nodes must be written to before returning. Increase this value to increase durability. For real durability, we recommend you set it to a majority of members to avoid rollback scenarios, though this approach carries a latency cost.
- MongoDB give you fine-grained controls over how reads and writes behave in more complex replica sets using read preferences and tagging. Use these options to optimize the performance of your replica set, especially if you have set members in multiple datacenters.

As always, think through your deployments and test thoroughly. Replica sets can be an especially valuable tool when used effectively.

Scaling your system with sharding

With the increasing scale of modern applications, it's become more and more expensive, and in some cases impossible, to get a single machine powerful enough to handle the load. One solution to the problem is to pool the capacity of a large number of less powerful machines. *Sharding* in MongoDB is designed to do just that: partition your database into smaller pieces so that no single machine has to store all the data or handle the entire load. On top of that, sharding in MongoDB is transparent to the application, which means the interface for querying a sharded cluster is exactly the same as the interface for querying a replica set or a single mongod server instance.

We'll begin the chapter with an overview of sharding. We'll go into detail about what problems it tries to solve and how to know when you need it. Next, we'll talk about the components that make up a sharded cluster. Then, we'll cover the two different ways to shard, and scratch the surface of MongoDB's range-based partitioning.

These three sections will give you a basic working knowledge of sharding, but you won't fully understand how these ideas all come together until you set up your own sharded cluster. That's what you'll do in the fourth section, where you'll build a sample cluster to host data from a massive Google Docs–like application.

We'll then discuss some sharding mechanics, describing how queries and indexing work across shards. We'll look at the ever-important choice of shard key, and we'll end the chapter with some specific advice on running sharding in production.

> ### Google Docs instead of e-commerce
>
> We're using a Google Docs–like application here, rather than the e-commerce application we've used in the rest of the book, because the schema is simpler and allows us to focus on the sharding itself.
>
> In an e-commerce application, you may have multiple collections. Some of these collections may be large, such as a collection storing all user comments, whereas some may be smaller, such as a collection storing all user profiles. In a more complex application such as this, you'd only shard the collections that would benefit from the added capacity of sharding while leaving the smaller collections unsharded for simplicity. Because sharded and unsharded collections can exist in the same system, all of this will work together, completely transparently to the application. In fact, if later you find that one of the collections that didn't need to be sharded is becoming larger, you can enable sharding at any time.
>
> The same principles that we'll see when looking at our Google Docs–like application apply to any sharded collection. We'll stick with this example to keep things simple and focus on what's new in this chapter.

12.1 Sharding overview

Before you build your first sharded cluster, it's useful to have a general understanding of the concepts behind sharding. In this section, we'll cover what problems sharding solves, discuss some of the challenges inherent in sharding, and then talk about how to know when sharding is the correct solution in practice.

12.1.1 What is sharding?

Sharding is the process of partitioning a large dataset into smaller, more manageable pieces. Until this point in the book, you've used MongoDB as a single server, where each mongod instance contains a complete copy of your application's data. Even when using replication (as we did in chapter 11), each replica clones every other replica's data entirely. For the majority of applications, storing the complete data set on each server is perfectly acceptable. But as the size of the data grows, and as an application demands greater read-and-write throughput, commodity servers may not be sufficient. In particular, these servers may not be able to address enough RAM, or they might not have enough CPU cores, to process the workload efficiently. In addition, as the size of the data grows, it may become impractical to store and manage backups for such a large data set on one disk or RAID array. If you're to continue to use commodity or virtualized hardware to host the database, the solution to these problems is to distribute the database across more than one server. The method for doing this in MongoDB is called sharding. Sharding in MongoDB can help your application scale, but remember that it's a large hammer. It's a complex system that adds administrative and performance overhead, so make absolutely sure it's what your application needs. In the next section we'll cover how you can tell when sharding is your best option.

Sharding: Learn by doing

Sharding is complicated. To get the most out of this chapter, you should run the examples.

You'll have no trouble running the sample cluster entirely on one machine; once you've successfully set up your cluster, start experimenting with it. There's nothing like having a live, sharded deployment on hand for understanding MongoDB as a distributed system.

12.1.2 *When should you shard?*

The question of when to shard is straightforward in theory but requires a solid understanding of how your system is being used. In general, there are two main reasons to shard: storage distribution and load distribution. Keep in mind that sharding doesn't solve all performance issues, and it adds additional complexity and overhead, so it's important to understand why you're sharding. In many cases, sharding may not be the optimal solution.

STORAGE DISTRIBUTION

Understanding the storage requirements of your system is usually not difficult. MongoDB stores all its data in ordinary files in the directory specified by the `--dbpath` option, which you can read more about in appendix A, so you should be able to use whatever utilities are present on your host operating system to monitor the storage usage of MongoDB. In addition, running `db.stats()` and `db.collection.stats()` in the `mongo` shell will output statistics about the storage usage of the current database and the collection within it named `collection`, respectively.

If you carefully monitor your storage capacity as your application grows, you'll be able to clearly see when the storage that your application requires exceeds the capacity of any one node. In that case, if adding more capacity isn't possible, sharding may be your best option.

LOAD DISTRIBUTION

Understanding the *load*—the CPU, RAM, and I/O bandwidth used by requests from clients—that your system must support is a bit more nuanced. In chapter 8 we talked about the importance of keeping indexes and the working data set in RAM, and this is the most common reason to shard. If an application's data set continues to grow unbounded, a moment will come when that data no longer fits in RAM. If you're running on Amazon's EC2, you'll hit that threshold when you've exceeded the available RAM on the largest available instance. Alternatively, you may run your own hardware with much more RAM, in which case you'll probably be able to delay sharding for some time. But no machine has infinite capacity for RAM; therefore, sharding eventually becomes necessary.

To be sure, the relationship between the load your servers can handle and the amount of RAM they have available isn't always straightforward. For instance, using solid-state drives (an increasingly affordable prospect) or arranging your disks in a striped RAID configuration will increase the number of IOPS (input/output operations per second) that your disks can handle, which may allow you to push the data-to-RAM ratio without negatively affecting performance. It may also be the case that your working set is a fraction of your total data size and that, therefore, you can operate with relatively little RAM. On the flip side, if you have an especially demanding write load, you may want to shard well before data reaches the size of RAM, simply because you need to distribute the load across machines to get the desired write throughput.

> **Leave some elbow room**
> Although it may be tempting to wait to shard until all your disks are 100% full and all your machines are overloaded, that's a bad idea. Sharding itself puts some load on your system because the process of automatic balancing has to move data off overloaded shards. If your system is already so overloaded that this can't happen, your empty shards will remain empty, your overloaded shards will remain overloaded, and your system will grind to a halt. Chapter 13 gives some practical advice for how to keep track of the important metrics, so you can scale up smoothly as your application grows.

Whatever the case, the decision to shard an existing system will always be based on regular analyses of network usage, disk usage, CPU usage, and the ever-important ratio of working set size, or the amount of data actively being used, to available RAM.

Now that you understand the background and theory behind sharding and know when you need it, let's look at the components that make up a sharded cluster in MongoDB.

12.2 Understanding components of a sharded cluster

Several components need to work together to make sharding possible. When they're all functioning together, this is known as a *sharded cluster*. To understand how MongoDB's sharding works, you need to know about all the components that make up a sharded cluster and the role of each component in the context of the cluster as a whole.

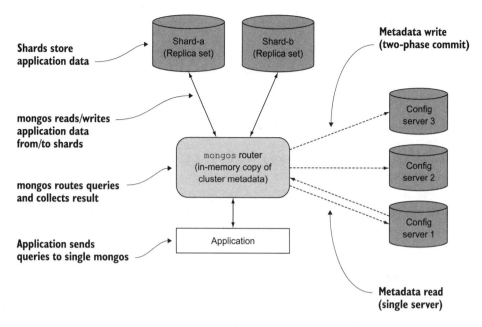

Figure 12.1　Components in a MongoDB shard cluster

A sharded cluster consists of shards, mongos routers, and config servers, as shown in figure 12.1.

Let's examine each component in figure 12.1:

- *Shards* (upper left) store the application data. In a sharded cluster, only the mongos routers or system administrators should be connecting directly to the shards. Like an unsharded deployment, each shard can be a single node for development and testing, but should be a replica set in production.
- mongos *routers* (center) cache the cluster metadata and use it to route operations to the correct shard or shards.
- *Config servers* (upper right) persistently store metadata about the cluster, including which shard has what subset of the data.

Now, let's discuss in more detail the role each of these components plays in the cluster as a whole.

12.2.1　*Shards: storage of application data*

A shard, shown at the upper left of figure 12.1, is either a single mongod server or a replica set that stores a partition of the application data. In fact, the shards are the only places where the application data gets saved in a sharded cluster. For testing, a shard can be a single mongod server but should be deployed as a replica set in production because then it will have its own replication mechanism and can fail over automatically. You can connect to an individual shard as you would to a single node or a replica set, but if you try to run operations on that shard directly, you'll see only a portion of the cluster's total data.

12.2.2 *Mongos router: router of operations*

Because each shard contains only part of the cluster's data, you need something to route operations to the appropriate shards. That's where mongos comes in. The mongos process, shown in the center of figure 12.1, is a router that directs all reads, writes, and commands to the appropriate shard. In this way, mongos provides clients with a single point of contact with the cluster, which is what enables a sharded cluster to present the same interface as an unsharded one.

mongos processes are lightweight and nonpersistent.[1] Because of this, they're often deployed on the same machines as the application servers, ensuring that only one network hop is required for requests to any given shard. In other words, the application connects locally to a mongos, and the mongos manages connections to the individual shards.

12.2.3 *Config servers: storage of metadata*

mongos processes are nonpersistent, which means something must durably store the metadata needed to properly manage the cluster. That's the job of the config servers, shown in the top right of figure 12.1. This metadata includes the global cluster configuration; the locations of each database, collection, and the particular ranges of data therein; and a change log preserving a history of the migrations of data across shards.

The metadata held by the config servers is central to the proper functioning and upkeep of the cluster. For instance, every time a mongos process is started, the mongos fetches a copy of the metadata from the config servers. Without this data, no coherent view of the shard cluster is possible. The importance of this data, then, informs the design and deployment strategy for the config servers.

If you examine figure 12.1, you'll see there are three config servers, but they're not deployed as a replica set. They demand something stronger than asynchronous replication; when the mongos process writes to them, it does so using a two-phase commit. This guarantees consistency across config servers. You must run exactly three config servers in any production deployment of sharding, and these servers must reside on separate machines for redundancy.[2]

Now you know what a shard cluster consists of, but you're probably still wondering about the sharding machinery itself. How is data actually distributed? We'll explain that in the next section, first introducing the two ways to shard in MongoDB, and then covering the core sharding operations.

---

[1] The mongos server caches a local copy of the config server metadata in memory. This metadata has a version identifier that changes when the metadata changes, so when a mongos with old metadata tries to contact a shard with a newer metadata version, it receives a notification that it must refresh its local copy.

[2] You can also run a single config server, but only as a way of more easily testing sharding. Running with only one config server in production is like taking a transatlantic flight in a single-engine jet: it might get you there, but lose an engine and you're hosed.

12.3 Distributing data in a sharded cluster

Before discussing the different ways to shard, let's discuss how data is grouped and organized in MongoDB. This topic is relevant to a discussion of sharding because it illustrates the different boundaries on which we can partition our data.

To illustrate this, we'll use the Google Docs–like application we'll build later in the chapter. Figure 12.2 shows how the data for such an application would be structured in MongoDB.

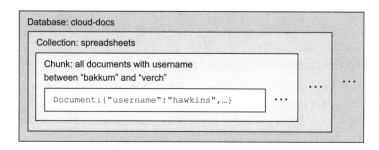

Figure 12.2 Levels of granularity available in a sharded MongoDB deployment

Looking at the figure from the innermost box moving outward, you can see there are four different levels of granularity in MongoDB: document, chunk, collection, and database.

These four levels of granularity represent the units of data in MongoDB:

- *Document*—The smallest unit of data in MongoDB. A document represents a single object in the system and can't be divided further. You can compare this to a row in a relational database. Note that we consider a document and all its fields to be a single atomic unit. In the innermost box in figure 12.2, you can see a document with a `username` field with a value of `"hawkins"`.
- *Chunk*—A group of documents clustered by values on a field. A chunk is a concept that exists only in sharded setups. This is a logical grouping of documents based on their values for a field or set of fields, known as a *shard key*. We'll cover the shard key when we go into more detail about chunks later in this section, and then again in section 12.6. The chunk shown in figure 12.2 contains all the documents that have the field `username` with values between `"bakkum"` and `"verch"`.
- *Collection*—A named grouping of documents within a database. To allow users to separate a database into logical groupings that make sense for the application, MongoDB provides the concept of a collection. This is nothing more than a named grouping of documents, and it must be explicitly specified by the application to run any queries. In figure 12.2, the collection name is `spreadsheets`. This collection name essentially identifies a subgroup within the `cloud-docs` database, which we'll discuss next.
- *Database*—Contains collections of documents. This is the top-level named grouping in the system. Because a database contains collections of documents, a

collection must also be specified to perform any operations on the documents themselves. In figure 12.2, the database name is cloud-docs. To run any queries, the collection must also be specified—spreadsheets in our example. The combination of database name and collection name together is unique throughout the system, and is commonly referred to as the *namespace*. It is usually represented by concatenating the collection name and database together, separated by a period character. For the example shown in figure 12.2, that would look like cloud-docs.spreadsheets.

Databases and collections were covered in section 4.3, and are present in unsharded deployments as well, so the only unfamiliar grouping here should be the chunk.

12.3.1 *Ways data can be distributed in a sharded cluster*

Now you know the different ways in which data is logically grouped in MongoDB. The next questions are, how does this interact with sharding? On which of these groupings can we partition our data? The quick answer to these questions is that data can be distributed in a sharded cluster on two of these four groupings:

- On the level of an entire database, where each database along with all its collections is put on its own shard.
- On the level of partitions or *chunks* of a collection, where the documents within a collection itself are divided up and spread out over multiple shards, based on values of a field or set of fields called the *shard key* in the documents.

You may wonder why MongoDB does partitioning based on chunks rather than on individual documents. It seems like that would be the most logical grouping because a document is the smallest possible unit. But when you consider the fact that not only do we have to partition the data, but we also have to be able to find it again, you'll see that if we partition on a document level—for example, by allowing each spreadsheet in our Google Docs–like application to be independently moved around—we need to store metadata on the config servers, keeping track of every single document independently. If you imagine a system with small documents, half of your data may end up being metadata on the config servers just keeping track of where your actual data is stored.

> **Granularity jump from database to partition of collection**
>
> You may also wonder why there's a jump in granularity from an entire database to a partition of a collection. Why isn't there an intermediate step where we can distribute on the level of whole collections, without partitioning the collections themselves?
>
> The real answer to this question is that it's completely theoretically possible. It just hasn't been implemented yet. Fortunately, because of the relationship between databases and collections, there's an easy workaround. If you're in a situation where you

have different collections—say, `files.spreadsheets` and `files.powerpoints`—
that you want to be put on separate servers, you can store them in separate databases. For example, you could store spreadsheets in `files_spreadsheets.spread-`
`sheets` and PowerPoint files in `files_powerpoints.powerpoints`. Because `files`
`_spreadsheets` and `files_powerpoints` are two separate databases, they'll be
distributed, and so will the collections.

In the next two sections, we'll cover each of the supported distribution methods. First
we'll discuss distributing entire databases, and then we'll move on to the more common and useful method of distributing chunks within a collection.

12.3.2 Distributing databases to shards

As you create new databases in a sharded cluster, each database is assigned to a different shard. If you do nothing else, a database and all its collections will live forever
on the shard where they were created. The databases themselves don't even need to
be sharded.

Because the name of a database is specified by the application, you can think of this
as a kind of manual partitioning. MongoDB has nothing to do with how well-partitioned
your data is. To see why this is manual, consider using this method to shard the `spread-`
`sheets` collection in our documents example. To shard this two ways using database
distribution, you'd have to make two databases—say `files1` and `files2`—and evenly
divide the data between the `files1.spreadsheets` and the `files2.spreadsheets` collections. It's completely up to you to decide which spreadsheet goes in which collection and come up with a scheme to query the appropriate database to find them later.
This is a difficult problem, which is why we don't recommend this approach for this
type of application.

When is the database distribution method really useful? One example of a real
application for database distribution is MongoDB as a service. In one implementation
of this model, customers can pay for access to a single MongoDB database. On the
backend, each database is created in a sharded cluster. This means that if each client
uses roughly the same amount of data, the distribution of the data will be optimal due
to the distribution of the databases throughout the cluster.

12.3.3 Sharding within collections

Now, we'll review the more powerful form of MongoDB sharding: sharding an individual collection. This is what the phrase automatic sharding refers to, because this is the
form of sharding in which MongoDB itself makes all the partitioning decisions, without any direct intervention from the application.

To allow for partitioning of an individual collection, MongoDB defines the idea of
a *chunk*, which as you saw earlier is a logical grouping of documents, based on the values

of a predetermined field or set of fields called a *shard key*. It's the user's responsibility to choose the shard key, and we'll cover how to do this in section 12.8.

For example, consider the following document from a spreadsheet management application:

```
{
  _id: ObjectId("4d6e9b89b600c2c196442c21")
  filename: "spreadsheet-1",
  updated_at: ISODate("2011-03-02T19:22:54.845Z"),
  username: "banks",
  data: "raw document data"
}
```

If all the documents in our collection have this format, we can, for example, choose a shard key of the _id field and the username field. MongoDB will then use that information in each document to determine what *chunk* the document belongs to.

How does MongoDB make this determination? At its core, MongoDB's sharding is *range-based;* this means that each "chunk" represents a range of shard keys. When MongoDB looks at a document to determine what chunk it belongs to, it first extracts the values for the shard key and then finds the chunk whose shard key range contains the given shard key values.

To see a concrete example of what this looks like, imagine that we chose a shard key of username for this spreadsheets collection, and we have two shards, "A" and "B." Our chunk distribution may look something like table 12.1.

Table 12.1   Chunks and shards

Start	End	Shard
-∞	Abbot	B
Abbot	Dayton	A
Dayton	Harris	B
Harris	Norris	A
Norris	∞	B

Looking at the table, it becomes a bit clearer what purpose chunks serve in a sharded cluster. If we gave you a document with a username field of "Babbage", you'd immediately know that it should be on shard A, just by looking at the table above. In fact, if we gave you any document that had a username field, which in this case is our shard key, you'd be able to use table 12.1 to determine which chunk the document belonged to, and from there determine which shard it should be sent to. We'll look into this process in much more detail in sections 12.5 and 12.6.

12.4   *Building a sample shard cluster*

The best way to get a handle on sharding is to see how it works in action. Fortunately, it's possible to set up a sharded cluster on a single machine, and that's exactly what we'll do now.[3]

The full process of setting up a sharded cluster involves three phases:

1   *Starting the* mongod *and* mongos *servers*—The first step is to spawn all the individual mongod and mongos processes that make up the cluster. In the cluster we're setting up in this chapter, we'll spawn nine mongod servers and one mongos server.

2   *Configuring the cluster*—The next step is to update the configuration so that the replica sets are initialized and the shards are added to the cluster. After this, the nodes will all be able to communicate with each other.

3   *Sharding collections*—The last step is to shard a collection so that it can be spread across multiple shards. The reason this exists as a separate step is because MongoDB can have both sharded and unsharded collections in the same cluster, so you must explicitly tell it which ones you want to shard. In this chapter, we'll shard our only collection, which is the spreadsheets collection of the cloud-docs database.

We'll cover each of these steps in detail in the next three sections. We'll then simulate the behavior of the sample cloud-based spreadsheet application described in the previous sections. Throughout the chapter we'll examine the global shard configuration, and in the last section, we'll use this to see how data is partitioned based on the shard key.

12.4.1   *Starting the mongod and mongos servers*

The first step in setting up a sharded cluster is to start all the required mongod and mongos processes. The shard cluster you'll build will consist of two shards and three config servers. You'll also start a single mongos to communicate with the cluster. Figure 12.3 shows a map of all the processes that you'll launch, with their port numbers in parentheses.

You'll run a bunch of commands to bring the cluster online, so if you find yourself unable to see the forest because of the trees, refer back to this figure.

---

[3]   The idea is that you can run every mongod and mongos process on a single machine for testing. In section 12.7 we'll look at production sharding configurations and the minimum number of machines required for a viable deployment.

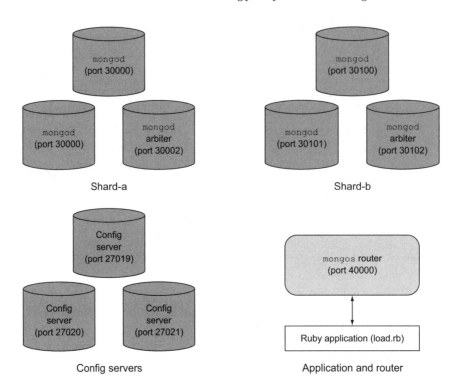

Figure 12.3   **A map of processes comprising the sample shard cluster**

STARTING THE SHARDING COMPONENTS

Let's start by creating the data directories for the two replica sets that will serve as our shards:

```
$ mkdir /data/rs-a-1
$ mkdir /data/rs-a-2
$ mkdir /data/rs-a-3
$ mkdir /data/rs-b-1
$ mkdir /data/rs-b-2
$ mkdir /data/rs-b-3
```

Next, start each mongod. Because you're running so many processes, you'll use the --fork option to run them in the background.[4] The commands for starting the first replica set are as follows:

```
$ mongod --shardsvr --replSet shard-a --dbpath /data/rs-a-1 \
  --port 30000 --logpath /data/rs-a-1.log --fork
$ mongod --shardsvr --replSet shard-a --dbpath /data/rs-a-2 \
  --port 30001 --logpath /data/rs-a-2.log --fork
```

---

[4] If you're running Windows, note that fork won't work for you. Because you'll have to open a new terminal window for each process, you're best off omitting the logpath option as well.

```
$ mongod --shardsvr --replSet shard-a  --dbpath /data/rs-a-3 \
  --port 30002 --logpath /data/rs-a-3.log --fork
```

Here are the commands for the second replica set:

```
$ mongod --shardsvr --replSet shard-b --dbpath /data/rs-b-1 \
  --port 30100 --logpath /data/rs-b-1.log --fork
$ mongod --shardsvr --replSet shard-b --dbpath /data/rs-b-2 \
  --port 30101 --logpath /data/rs-b-2.log --fork
$ mongod --shardsvr --replSet shard-b --dbpath /data/rs-b-3 \
  --port 30102 --logpath /data/rs-b-3.log --fork
```

> **Make careful note of all the options that differ between nodes.**

We won't cover all the command-line options used here. To see what each of these flags means in more detail, it's best to refer to the MongoDB documentation at http://docs.mongodb.org/manual/reference/program/mongod/ for the mongod program. As usual, you now need to initiate these replica sets. Connect to each one individually, run rs.initiate(), and then add the remaining nodes. The first should look like this:

```
$ mongo localhost:30000
> rs.initiate()
```

You'll have to wait a minute or so before the initial node becomes primary. During the process, the prompt will change from shard-a:SECONDARY> to shard-a:PRIMARY. Using the rs.status() command will also reveal more information about what's going on behind the scenes. Once it does, you can add the remaining nodes:

```
> rs.add("localhost:30001")
> rs.addArb("localhost:30002")
```

> **addArb means to add this node to replica set as an arbiter.**

Using localhost as the machine name might cause problems in the long run because it only works if you're going to run all processes on a single machine. If you know your hostname, use it to get out of trouble. On a Mac, your hostname should look something like MacBook-Pro.local. If you don't know your hostname, make sure that you use localhost everywhere!

Configuring a replica set that you'll use as a shard is exactly the same as configuring a replica set that you'll use on its own, so refer back to chapter 10 if any of this replica set setup looks unfamiliar to you.

Initiating the second replica set is similar. Again, wait a minute after running rs.initiate():

```
$ mongo localhost:30100
> rs.initiate()
> rs.add("localhost:30100")
> rs.addArb("localhost:30101")
```

Finally, verify that both replica sets are online by running the rs.status() command from the shell on each one. If everything checks out, you're ready to start the config servers.[5] Now you create each config server's data directory and then start a mongod for each one using the configsvr option:

```
$ mkdir /data/config-1
$ mongod --configsvr --dbpath /data/config-1 --port 27019 \
  --logpath /data/config-1.log --fork --nojournal
$ mkdir /data/config-2
$ mongod --configsvr --dbpath /data/config-2 --port 27020 \
  --logpath /data/config-2.log --fork --nojournal
$ mkdir /data/config-3
$ mongod --configsvr --dbpath /data/config-3 --port 27021 \
  --logpath /data/config-3.log --fork --nojournal
```

Ensure that each config server is up and running by connecting with the shell, or by tailing the log file (tail -f <log_file_path>) and verifying that each process is listening on the configured port. Looking at the logs for any one config server, you should see something like this:

```
Wed Mar  2 15:43:28 [initandlisten] waiting for connections on port 27020
Wed Mar  2 15:43:28 [websvr] web admin interface listening on port 28020
```

If each config server is running, you can go ahead and start the mongos. The mongos must be started with the configdb option, which takes a comma-separated list of config database addresses:[6]

```
$ mongos --configdb localhost:27019,localhost:27020,localhost:27021 \
  --logpath /data/mongos.log --fork --port 40000
```

Once again, we won't cover all the command line options we're using here. If you want more details on what each option does, refer to the docs for the mongos program at http://docs.mongodb.org/manual/reference/program/mongos/.

12.4.2 *Configuring the cluster*

Now that you've started all the mongod and mongos processes that we'll need for this cluster (see figure 12.2), it's time to configure the cluster. Start by connecting to the mongos. To simplify the task, you'll use the sharding helper methods. These are methods run on the global sh object. To see a list of all available helper methods, run sh.help().

You'll enter a series of configuration commands beginning with the addShard command. The helper for this command is sh.addShard(). This method takes a string consisting of the name of a replica set, followed by the addresses of two or more seed

---

[5] Again, if running on Windows, omit the --fork and --logpath options, and start each mongod in a new window.

[6] Be careful not to put spaces between the config server addresses when specifying them.

nodes for connecting. Here you specify the two replica sets you created along with the addresses of the two non-arbiter members of each set:

```
$ mongo localhost:40000
> sh.addShard("shard-a/localhost:30000,localhost:30001")
  { "shardAdded" : "shard-a", "ok" : 1 }
> sh.addShard("shard-b/localhost:30100,localhost:30101")
  { "shardAdded" : "shard-b", "ok" : 1 }
```

If successful, the command response will include the name of the shard just added. You can examine the config database's `shards` collection to see the effect of your work. Instead of using the `use` command, you'll use the `getSiblingDB()` method to switch databases:

```
> db.getSiblingDB("config").shards.find()
{ "_id" : "shard-a", "host" : "shard-a/localhost:30000,localhost:30001" }
{ "_id" : "shard-b", "host" : "shard-b/localhost:30100,localhost:30101" }
```

As a shortcut, the `listshards` command returns the same information:

```
> use admin
> db.runCommand({listshards: 1})
```

While we're on the topic of reporting on sharding configuration, the shell's `sh.status()` method nicely summarizes the cluster. Go ahead and try running it now.

12.4.3 *Sharding collections*

The next configuration step is to enable sharding on a database. This doesn't do anything on its own, but it's a prerequisite for sharding any collection within a database. Your application's database will be called `cloud-docs`, so you enable sharding like this:

```
> sh.enableSharding("cloud-docs")
```

As before, you can check the config data to see the change you just made. The config database holds a collection called `databases` that contains a list of databases. Each document specifies the database's primary shard location and whether it's partitioned (whether sharding is enabled):

```
> db.getSiblingDB("config").databases.find()
{ "_id" : "admin", "partitioned" : false, "primary" : "config" }
{ "_id" : "cloud-docs", "partitioned" : true, "primary" : "shard-a" }
```

Now all you need to do is shard the `spreadsheets` collection. When you shard a collection, you define a shard key. Here you'll use the compound shard key {username: 1, _id: 1} because it's good for distributing data and makes it easy to view and comprehend chunk ranges:

```
> sh.shardCollection("cloud-docs.spreadsheets", {username: 1, _id: 1})
```

Again, you can verify the configuration by checking the config database for sharded collections:

```
> db.getSiblingDB("config").collections.findOne()
{
  "_id" : "cloud-docs.spreadsheets",
  "lastmod" : ISODate("1970-01-16T00:50:07.268Z"),
  "dropped" : false,
  "key" : {
    "username" : 1,
    "_id" : 1
  },
  "unique" : false
}
```

> **Full namespace of the collection we just sharded**

> **Shard key of the collection we just sharded**

Don't worry too much about understanding all the fields in this document. This is internal metadata that MongoDB uses to track collections, and it isn't meant to be accessed directly by users.

SHARDING AN EMPTY COLLECTION

This sharded collection definition may remind you of something: it looks a bit like an index definition, especially with its unique key. When you shard an empty collection, MongoDB creates an index corresponding to the shard key on each shard.[7] Verify this for yourself by connecting directly to a shard and running the getIndexes() method. Here you connect to your first shard, and the output contains the shard key index, as expected:

```
$ mongo localhost:30000
> use cloud-docs
> db.spreadsheets.getIndexes()
[
  {
    "name" : "_id_",
    "ns" : "cloud-docs.spreadsheets",
    "key" : {
      "_id" : 1
    },
    "v" : 0
  },
  {
    "ns" : "cloud-docs.spreadsheets",
    "key" : {
      "username" : 1,
      "_id" : 1
    },
    "name" : "username_1__id_1",
    "v" : 0
  }
]
```

> **_id index, which is automatically created for all collections**

> **Compound index on username and _id created, because we sharded this collection on that key**

---

[7] If you're sharding an existing collection, you'll have to create an index corresponding to the shard key before you run the shardcollection command.

Once you've sharded the collection, sharding is ready to go. You can now write to the cluster and data will distribute. You'll see how that works in the next section.

12.4.4 *Writing to a sharded cluster*

We'll insert some documents into the sharded cluster so you can observe the formation and movement of chunks, which is the essence of MongoDB's sharding. The sample documents, each representing a single spreadsheet, will look like this:

```
{
  _id: ObjectId("4d6f29c0e4ef0123afdacaeb"),
  filename: "sheet-1",
  updated_at: new Date(),
  username: "banks",
  data: "RAW DATA"
}
```

Note that the data field will contain a 5 KB string to simulate user data.

This book's source code for this chapter includes a Ruby script you can use to write documents to the cluster. The script takes a number of iterations as its argument, and for each iteration, it inserts one 5 KB document for each of 200 users. The script's source is here:

```
require 'rubygems'
require 'mongo'
require 'names'
@con  = Mongo::MongoClient.new("localhost", 40000)
@col  = @con['cloud-docs']['spreadsheets']
@data = "abcde" * 1000
def write_user_docs(iterations=0, name_count=200)
  iterations.times do |iteration|
    name_count.times do |name_number|
      doc = { :filename => "sheet-#{iteration}",
              :updated_at => Time.now.utc,
              :username => Names::LIST[name_number],
              :data => @data
            }
      @col.insert(doc)
    end
  end
end
if ARGV.empty? || !(ARGV[0] =~ /^\d+$/)
  puts "Usage: load.rb [iterations] [name_count]"
else
  iterations = ARGV[0].to_i
  if ARGV[1] && ARGV[1] =~ /^\d+$/
    name_count = ARGV[1].to_i
  else
    name_count = 200
  end
  write_user_docs(iterations, name_count)
end
```

Connection to MongoDB using the Ruby driver

Function to actually insert data into MongoDB

If you have the script on hand, you can run it from the command line with no arguments to insert the initial iteration of 200 values:

```
$ ruby load.rb 1
```

Now connect to mongos via the shell. If you query the spreadsheets collection, you'll
see that it contains exactly 200 documents and that they total around 1 MB. You can
also query a document, but be sure to exclude the sample data field (you don't want
to print 5 KB of text to the screen):

```
$ mongo localhost:40000
> use cloud-docs
> db.spreadsheets.count()
200
> db.spreadsheets.stats().size
1019496
> db.spreadsheets.findOne({}, {data: 0})
{
  "_id" : ObjectId("4d6d6b191d41c8547d0024c2"),
  "username" : "Cerny",
  "updated_at" : ISODate("2011-03-01T21:54:33.813Z"),
  "filename" : "sheet-0"
}
```

CHECK ON THE SHARDS

Now you can check out what's happened sharding-wise. Switch to the config database
and check the number of chunks:

```
> use config
> db.chunks.count()
1
```

There's only one chunk so far. Let's see how it looks:

```
> db.chunks.findOne()
{
  "_id" : "cloud-docs.spreadsheets-username_MinKey_id_MinKey",
  "lastmod" : {
    "t" : 1000,
    "i" : 0
  },
  "ns" : "cloud-docs.spreadsheets",
  "min" : {                              ◁——— min field
    "username" : { $minKey : 1 },
    "_id" : { $minKey : 1 }
  },
  "max" : {                              ◁——— max field
    "username" : { $maxKey : 1 },
    "_id" : { $maxKey : 1 }
  },
  "shard" : "shard-a"
}
```

Can you figure out what range this chunk represents? If there's only one chunk, it spans the entire sharded collection. That's borne out by the min and max fields, which show that the chunk's range is bounded by $minKey and $maxKey.

---

minKey and maxKey

$minKey and $maxKey are used in comparison operations as the boundaries of BSON types. BSON is MongoDB's native data format. $minKey always compares lower than all BSON types, and $maxKey compares greater than all BSON types. Because the value for any given field can contain any BSON type, MongoDB uses these two types to mark the chunk endpoints at the extremities of the sharded collection.

You can see a more interesting chunk range by adding more data to the spreadsheets collection. You'll use the Ruby script again, but this time you'll run 100 iterations, which will insert an extra 20,000 documents totaling 100 MB:

```
$ ruby load.rb 100
```

Verify that the insert worked:

```
> db.spreadsheets.count()
20200
> db.spreadsheets.stats().size
103171828
```

Sample insert speed

Note that it may take several minutes to insert this data into the shard cluster. There are two main reasons for the slowness:

1 You're performing a round-trip for each insert, whereas you might be able to perform bulk inserts in a production situation.

2 Most significantly, you're running all of the shard's nodes on a single machine. This places a huge burden on the disk because four of your nodes are being written to simultaneously (two replica set primaries and two replicating secondaries).

Suffice it to say that in a proper production installation, this insert would run much more quickly.

Having inserted this much data, you'll definitely have more than one chunk. You can check the chunk state quickly by counting the number of documents in the chunks collection:

```
> use config
> db.chunks.count()
10
```

You can see more detailed information by running `sh.status()`. This method prints all of the chunks along with their ranges. For brevity, we'll only show the first two chunks:

```
> sh.status()
sharding version: { "_id" : 1, "version" : 3 }
 shards:
 { "_id": "shard-a", "host": "shard-a/localhost:30000,localhost:30001" }
 { "_id": "shard-b", "host": "shard-b/localhost:30100,localhost:30101" }
 databases:
 { "_id": "admin",  "partitioned": false, "primary": "config" }
 { "_id": "test",   "partitioned": false, "primary": "shard-a" }
 { "_id": "cloud-docs", "partitioned": true,  "primary": "shard-b" }
    shard-a 5
    shard-b 5
 { "username": { $minKey : 1 }, "_id" : { $minKey : 1 } } -->>   {
    "username": "Abdul",
    "_id": ObjectId("4e89ffe7238d3be9f0000012") }
 on: shard-a { "t" : 2000, "i" : 0 }
   { "username" : "Abdul",
    "_id" : ObjectId("4e89ffe7238d3be9f0000012") } -->> {
    "username" : "Buettner",
    "_id" : ObjectId("4e8a00a0238d3be9f0002e98") }
 on : shard-a { "t" : 3000, "i" : 0 }
```

First chunk starting from the minimum key

Second chunk starting from where the first chunk ended

SEEING DATA ON MULTIPLE SHARDS

The picture has definitely changed. As you can see in figure 12.4, you now have 10 chunks. Naturally, each chunk represents a contiguous range of data.

You can see in figure 12.4 that shard-a has a chunk that ranges from one of Abdul's documents to one of Buettner's documents, just as you saw in our output. This means that all the documents with a shard key that lies between these two values will either be inserted into, or found on, shard-a.[8] You can also see in the figure that shard-b has

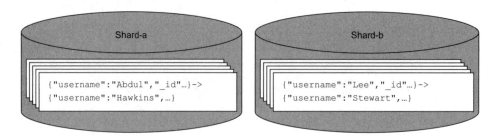

Figure 12.4 The chunk distribution of the `spreadsheets` collection

---

[8] If you're following along and running all these examples for yourself, note that your chunk distributions may differ somewhat.

some chunks too, in particular the chunk ranging from one of Lee's documents to one of Stewart's documents, which means any document with a shard key between those two values belongs on shard-b. You could visually scan the `sh.status()` output to see all the chunks, but there's a more direct way: running a query on the chunks collection that filters on the name of the shard and counting how many documents would be returned:

```
> db.chunks.count({"shard": "shard-a"})
5
> db.chunks.count({"shard": "shard-b"})
5
```

As long as the cluster's data size is small, the splitting algorithm dictates that splits happen often. That's what you see now. This is an optimization that gives you a good distribution of data and chunks early on. From now on, as long as writes remain evenly distributed across the existing chunk ranges, few migrations will occur.

Splits and migrations

Behind the scenes, MongoDB relies on two mechanisms to keep the cluster balanced: splits and migrations.

Splitting is the process of dividing a chunk into two smaller chunks. This happens when a chunk exceeds the maximum chunk size, currently 64 MB by default. Splitting is necessary because chunks that are too large are unwieldy and hard to distribute evenly throughout the cluster.

Migrating is the process of moving chunks between shards. When some shards have significantly more chunks than others, this triggers something called a *migration round*. During a migration round, chunks are migrated from shards with many chunks to shards with fewer chunks until the cluster is more evenly balanced. As you can imagine, of the two operations, migrating is significantly more expensive than splitting.

In practice, these operations shouldn't affect you, but it's useful to be aware that they're happening in case you run into a performance issue. If your inserts are well-distributed, the data set on all your shards should increase at roughly the same rate, meaning that the number of chunks will also grow at roughly the same rate and expensive migrations will be relatively infrequent.

Now the split threshold will increase. You can see how the splitting slows down, and how chunks start to grow toward their max size, by doing a more massive insert. Try adding another 800 MB to the cluster. Once again, we'll use the Ruby script, remembering that it inserts about 1 MB on each iteration:

```
$ ruby load.rb 800
```

This will take a lot of time to run, so you may want to step away and grab a snack after starting this load process. By the time it's done, you'll have increased the total data size by a factor of 8. But if you check the chunking status, you'll see that there are only around twice as many chunks:

```
> use config
> db.chunks.count()
21
```

Given that there are more chunks, the average chunk ranges will be smaller, but each chunk will include more data. For example, the first chunk in the collection spans from Abbott to Bender but it's already nearly 60 MB in size. Because the max chunk size is currently 64 MB by default, you'd soon see this chunk split if you were to continue inserting data.

Another thing to note is that the distribution still looks pretty even, as it did before:

```
> db.chunks.count({"shard": "shard-a"})
11
> db.chunks.count({"shard": "shard-b"})
10
```

Although the number of chunks has increased during the last 800 MB insert round, you can probably assume that no migrations occurred; a likely scenario is that each of the original chunks split in two, with a single extra split somewhere in the mix. You can verify this by querying the config database's changelog collection:

```
> db.changelog.count({what: "split"})
20
> db.changelog.find({what: "moveChunk.commit"}).count()
6
```

This is in line with these assumptions. A total of 20 splits have occurred, yielding 20 chunks, but only 6 migrations have taken place. For an extra-deep look at what's going on here, you can scan the change log entries. For instance, here's the entry recording the first chunk move:

```
> db.changelog.findOne({what: "moveChunk.commit"})
{
  "_id" : "localhost-2011-09-01T20:40:59-2",
  "server" : "localhost",
  "clientAddr" : "127.0.0.1:55749",
  "time" : ISODate("2011-03-01T20:40:59.035Z"),
  "what" : "moveChunk.commit",
  "ns" : "cloud-docs.spreadsheets",
```

```
    "details" : {
      "min" : {
        "username" : { $minKey : 1 },
        "_id" : { $minKey : 1 }
      },
      "max" : {
        "username" : "Abbott",
        "_id" : ObjectId("4d6d57f61d41c851ee000092")
      },
      "from" : "shard-a",
      "to" : "shard-b"
    }
}
```

Details about
the chunk that
was moved

Shard that the
chunk was
moved from

Shard that the
chunk was
moved to

Here you see the movement of chunks from shard-a to shard-b. In general, the documents you find in the change log are quite readable. As you learn more about sharding and begin prototyping your own shard clusters, the config change log makes an excellent live reference on split and migrate behavior. Refer to it often.

12.5 Querying and indexing a shard cluster

From the application's perspective, there's no difference between querying a sharded cluster and querying a single mongod. In both cases, the query interface and the process of iterating over the result set are the same. But behind the scenes, things are different, and it's worthwhile to understand exactly what's going on.

12.5.1 Query routing

Imagine you're querying a sharded cluster. How many shards does mongos need to contact to return a proper query response? If you give it some thought, you'll see that it depends on whether the shard key is present in the query selector that we pass to find and similar operations. Remember that the config servers (and thus mongos) maintain a mapping of shard key ranges to shards. These mappings are none other than the chunks we examined earlier in the chapter. If a query includes the shard key, then mongos can quickly consult the chunk data to determine exactly which shard contains the query's result set. This is called a *targeted query*.

But if the shard key isn't part of the query, the query planner will have to visit all shards to fulfill the query completely. This is known as a *global* or *scatter/gather query*. The diagram in figure 12.5 illustrates both query types.

Figure 12.5 shows a cluster with two shards, two mongos routers, and two application servers. The shard key for this cluster is {username: 1, _id: 1}. We'll discuss how to choose a good shard key in section 12.6.

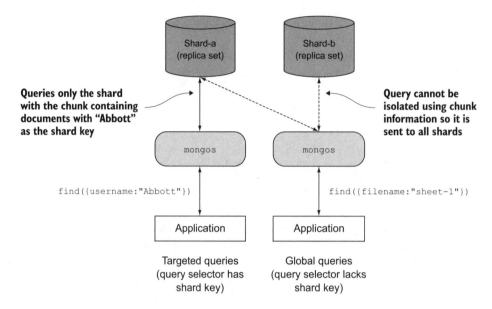

Figure 12.5   Targeted and global queries against a shard cluster

To the left of the figure, you can see a targeted query that includes the username field in its query selector. In this case, the mongos router can use the value of the username field to route the query directly to the correct shard.

To the right of the figure, you can see a global or scatter/gather query that doesn't include any part of the shard key in its query selector. In this case, the mongos router must broadcast the query to both shards.

The effect of query targeting on performance cannot be overstated. If all your queries are global, that means each shard must respond to every single query against your cluster. In contrast, if all your queries are targeted, each shard only needs to handle on average the total number of requests divided by the total number of shards. The implications for scalability are clear.

But targeting isn't the only thing that affects performance in a sharded cluster. As you'll see in the next section, everything you've learned about the performance of an unsharded deployment still applies to a sharded cluster, but to each shard individually.

12.5.2 *Indexing in a sharded cluster*

No matter how well-targeted your queries are, they must eventually run on at least one shard. This means that if your shards are slow to respond to queries, your cluster will be slow as well.

As in an unsharded deployment, indexing is an important part of optimizing performance. There are only a few key points to keep in mind about indexing that are specific to a sharded cluster:

- Each shard maintains its own indexes. When you declare an index on a sharded collection, each shard builds a separate index for its portion of the collection. For example, when you issue the `db.spreadsheets.createIndex()` command while connected to a `mongos` router, each shard processes the index creation command individually.
- It follows that the sharded collections on each shard should have the same indexes. If this ever isn't the case, you'll see inconsistent query performance.
- Sharded collections permit unique indexes on the `_id` field and on the shard key only. Unique indexes are prohibited elsewhere because enforcing them would require inter-shard communication, which is against the fundamental design of sharding in MongoDB.

Once you understand how queries are routed and how indexing works, you should be in a good position to write smart queries and indexes for your sharded cluster. Most of the advice on indexing and query optimization from chapter 8 will apply.

In the next section, we'll cover the powerful `explain()` tool, which you can use to see exactly what path is taken by a query against your cluster.

12.5.3 *The explain() tool in a sharded cluster*

The `explain()` tool is your primary way to troubleshoot and optimize queries. It can show you exactly how your query would be executed, including whether it can be targeted and whether it can use an index. The following listing shows an example of what this output might look like.

Listing 12.1   Index and query to return latest documents updated by a user

```
mongos> db.spreadsheets.createIndex({username:1, updated_at:-1})
{
    "raw" : {
        "shard-a/localhost:30000,localhost:30001" : {
            "createdCollectionAutomatically" : false,
            "numIndexesBefore" : 3,
            "numIndexesAfter" : 4,
            "ok" : 1
        },
        "shard-b/localhost:30100,localhost:30101" : {
            "createdCollectionAutomatically" : false,
            "numIndexesBefore" : 3,
            "numIndexesAfter" : 4,
            "ok" : 1
        }
    },
    "ok" : 1
}
```

```
mongos> db.spreadsheets.find({username: "Wallace"}).sort({updated_at:-
    1}).explain()
{
    "clusteredType" : "ParallelSort",
    "shards" : {
        "shard-b/localhost:30100,localhost:30101" : [
            {
                "cursor" : "BtreeCursor username_1_updated_at_-1",        ◁——┐
                "isMultiKey" : false,
                "n" : 100,                                              **Index on**
                "nscannedObjects" : 100,                          **updated_at and**
                "nscanned" : 100,                                **username used to**
                "nscannedObjectsAllPlans" : 200,                 **fetch documents** ➋
                "nscannedAllPlans" : 200,
                "scanAndOrder" : false,
                "indexOnly" : false,
                "nYields" : 1,
                "nChunkSkips" : 0,
                "millis" : 3,
                "indexBounds" : {
                    "username" : [
                        [
                            "Wallace",
                            "Wallace"
                        ]
                    ],
                    "updated_at" : [
                        [
                            {
                                "$maxElement" : 1
                            },
                            {
                                "$minElement" : 1
                            }
                        ]
                    ]
                },
                "server" : "localhost:30100",
                "filterSet" : false
            }
        ]
    },
    "cursor" : "BtreeCursor username_1_updated_at_-1",
    "n" : 100,
    "nChunkSkips" : 0,
    "nYields" : 1,
    "nscanned" : 100,
    "nscannedAllPlans" : 200,
    "nscannedObjects" : 100,
    "nscannedObjectsAllPlans" : 200,
    "millisShardTotal" : 3,                        ➊ **Number of shards**
    "millisShardAvg" : 3,                            **this query was**
    "numQueries" : 1,                                **sent to**
    "numShards" : 1,                              ◁——┘
    "indexBounds" : {
```

```
            "username" : [
                [
                    "Wallace",
                    "Wallace"
                ]
            ],
            "updated_at" : [
                [
                    {
                        "$maxElement" : 1
                    },
                    {
                        "$minElement" : 1
                    }
                ]
            ]
        },
        "millis" : 4
}
```

You can see from this explain() plan that this query was only sent to one shard ❶, and that when it ran on that shard it used the index we created to satisfy the sort more efficiently ❷. Note that this explain() plan output is from v2.6 and earlier, and it has changed in 3.0 and later versions. Chapter 8 contains output from the explain() command when used on a MongoDB v3.0 server. Consult the documentation at https://docs.mongodb.org/manual/reference/method/cursor.explain/ for your specific version if you see any fields you don't understand.

12.5.4 *Aggregation in a sharded cluster*

It's worth noting that the aggregation framework also benefits from sharding. The analysis of an aggregation is a bit more complicated than a single query, and may change between versions as new optimizations are introduced. Fortunately, the aggregation framework also has an explain() option that you can use to see details about how your query would perform. As a basic rule of thumb, the number of shards that an aggregation operation needs to contact is dependent on the data that the operation needs as input to complete. For example, if you're counting every document in your entire database, you'll need to query all shards, but if you're only counting a small range of documents, you may not need to query every shard. Consult the current documentation at https://docs.mongodb.org/manual/reference/method/db .collection.aggregate/ for more details.

12.6 *Choosing a shard key*

In section 12.3 you saw how the shard key is used to split a collection into logical ranges called chunks, and in section 12.5.1 you saw how the mongos can use this information to figure out where a set of documents might be located.

In this section, we'll discuss in depth the vitally important process of choosing a shard key. A poorly chosen shard key will prevent your application from taking advantage of many of the benefits provided by sharding. In the pathological case, both insert and query performance will be significantly impaired. Adding to the gravity of the decision is that once you've chosen a shard key, you're stuck with it. Shard keys are immutable.[9]

The best way to understand the pitfalls of a bad shard key is to walk through the process of finding a good one step by step and analyze in depth each shard key you consider along the way. That's exactly what we'll do now, using the spreadsheet application as an example.

After we find an optimal shard key for our spreadsheet application, at the end of the chapter we'll consider how our shard key choice would have been different if we'd instead been designing a system to support an email application. This will highlight how much the optimal shard key depends on the specifics of each application.

As we walk through the process of choosing a shard key for our spreadsheet application, you'll see three main pitfalls:

- *Hotspots*—Some shard keys result in situations where all reads or writes are going to a single chunk, on a single shard. This can cause one shard to be completely overwhelmed, while the others are sitting idle.
- *Unsplittable chunks*—A shard key that's too coarse-grained can result in a situation where there are many documents with the same shard key. Because sharding is based on ranges of shard keys, this means that the documents can't be split into separate chunks, which can limit MongoDB's ability to evenly distribute data.
- *Poor targeting*—Even if writes are distributed perfectly in the cluster, if our shard key doesn't have some relationship to our queries, we'll have poor query performance. You saw this in section 12.5.1 when we discussed global and targeted queries.

Now we'll begin the process of finding the best shard key for our spreadsheet application and see firsthand how each of these situations can come up in practice.

12.6.1 *Imbalanced writes (hotspots)*

The first shard key you may consider is { "_id" : 1 }, which will shard on the _id field. The _id field may initially seem like a great candidate: it must be present in every document, it has an index by default, you may have it in many of your queries, and it's automatically generated by MongoDB using the BSON Object ID type, which is essentially a GUID (globally unique identifier).

But there's one glaring problem with using an Object ID as a shard key: its values are strictly ascending. This means that every new document will have a shard key larger than any other document in the collection. Why is this a problem? If the system is already completely balanced, that means every new document will go to the same

---

[9]   Note that there's no good way to alter the shard key once you've created it. Your best bet is to create a new sharded collection with the proper key, export the data from the old sharded collection, and then restore the data to the new one.

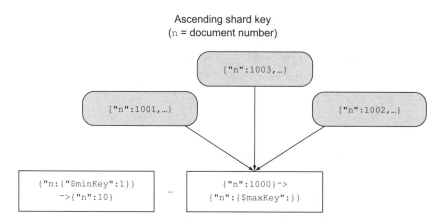

Ascending shard key
(n = document number)

Figure 12.6 The ascending shard key causing all writes to go to one chunk.

chunk, which is the chunk that ranges up to $maxKey. This issue is best understood with an example, as shown in figure 12.6.

For simplicity, rather than using a BSON Object ID to illustrate the problem with ascending shard keys, this example uses the document number, which is stored in the field n. As you can see, we've already inserted documents 1 to 1000, and we're about to insert documents 1001, 1002, and 1003. Because MongoDB hadn't seen anything above 1000 before that point, it had no reason to split the chunk ranging from 1000 to $maxKey. This means that the three new documents all belong in that chunk, and so will all new documents.

To see how this might affect a real application, consider using the ascending BSON Object id field as the shard key for the spreadsheet application. Practically, what this means is that every new spreadsheet that gets created will belong in the same chunk, which means that every new document will need to be written to the single shard responsible for storing that chunk. This is where the performance issue becomes clear. Even if you have a hundred shards, all your writes will be sent to a single one while the rest sit idle. On top of that, MongoDB will do its best to migrate data off the overloaded shard, which will slam it even more.

This effectively nullifies one of sharding's greatest benefits: the automatic distribution of the insert load across machines.[10] All that said, if you still want to use the _id field as your shard key, you have two options:

- First, you can override the _id field with your own identifier that isn't ascending. If you choose this approach, however, take care to remember that _id must be unique even in a sharded cluster.
- Alternatively, you can make your shard key on _id a *hashed shard key*. This instructs MongoDB to use the output of a hash function on the shard key, rather

---

[10] Note that an ascending shard key shouldn't affect updates as long as documents are updated randomly.

than using the shard key directly. Because the hash function is designed to have an output that appears randomly distributed, this will ensure that your inserts are evenly distributed throughout the cluster. But this also means that range queries will have to span multiple shards, because even documents with shard keys that are similar may hash to completely different values.

> **Uniqueness gotchas**
>
> MongoDB can only ensure that the shard key is unique. It can't enforce uniqueness on any other key because one shard can't check another shard to see if there are duplicates. Surprisingly, this also includes the _id field, which is required to be unique. By default, MongoDB generates the _id field using a BSON Object ID. Great care was taken in the design of this data type to ensure that, statistically speaking, it would be unique across the cluster. Because of this, beware of overriding the _id field yourself. If you don't properly enforce uniqueness on the client side, you could lose data when two documents with the same _id field are migrated to the same shard.

12.6.2 *Unsplittable chunks (coarse granularity)*

Now you know that { "_id" : 1 } won't work as a shard key, but what about { "username" : 1 }? This looks like a good candidate because when we're querying or updating a spreadsheet, we generally already know what user the spreadsheet belongs to, so we can include the username field in our query and get good targeting. Additionally, sharding on the username field will also lead to relatively well-balanced inserts because the distribution of inserts across users should be relatively even.

There's just one problem with this field: it's so coarse that we may end up in a situation where one chunk grows without bound. To see this, imagine that the user "Verch" decides to store 10 GB of spreadsheet data. This would bring the size of the chunk containing the documents with a username of "Verch" well above our 64 MB maximum.

Normally, when a chunk gets too large, MongoDB can split the chunk into smaller pieces and rebalance them across the cluster. However, in this case, there's no place the chunk can be split, because it already contains only a single shard key value. This causes a number of technical problems, but the end result is that your cluster will become imbalanced, and MongoDB won't be able to rebalance effectively.

12.6.3 *Poor targeting (shard key not present in queries)*

After seeing all these problems, you may want to throw up your hands and say "Fine, I'll just pick a completely random shard key. It's unique and it's not ascending." Although that does solve the problem of writes, it isn't a good shard key if you ever intend to read from your cluster. As you saw in section 12.5.1, queries can only be routed to the correct shard if they include the shard key. If your shard key is completely random, then at the time you're querying for a document, chances are you'll have no idea what the shard key is. You probably will know the username you're looking for, or the ID of the document, which is why those fields were so appealing in the first place. This means that the router will have to result to a global broadcast, which can hurt performance.

That said, if you're writing an application where all you need to do is dump a large amount of data and you don't need selective queries—for example, in an application where you're collecting sensor data to analyze later in large batches (where you're processing such a large portion of the data that you'll need to query all the shards anyway)—a random unique shard key may not be a bad idea. In fact, if you can guarantee uniqueness (by making it a GUID using some library that provides this guarantee) and ensure that it's not ascending, you can even override the _id field.

12.6.4 *Ideal shard keys*

So far you've seen three things that you need to consider when choosing a shard key. One is how reads are targeted, the second is how well writes are distributed, and the last is how effectively MongoDB can split and migrate chunks in your collection. Each key satisfied some of these properties but failed in others. How can you pick a shard key that works for all three? The answer, as you might expect, is using a compound shard key that provides all these benefits. In this case, that shard key is { username : 1, _id : 1 }. This has good targeting because the username field will often be present in our reads, has good write balancing because username has values that are evenly distributed throughout the alphabet, and is fine-grained enough for MongoDB to split chunks because it includes the _id field, which is unique. See figure 12.7 for an example.

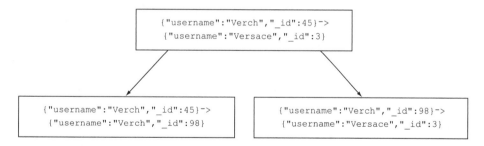

Figure 12.7   Splitting a chunk that was previously unsplittable when sharding only on username

Here we can see a split on a chunk that we couldn't split when we sharded only on the username field. Now, because we include the _id field, we can split all the documents from "Verch" into two separate chunks, which we couldn't have done if our shard key was { "username" : 1 }.

Indexing matters

This chapter is all about choosing an effective shard key, but it's important to keep in mind that indexing is still just as important as it was for a single node. As we discussed in section 12.5.2, even if your shard key is perfect and each query is routed to a single shard, if the performance on each shard is poor, your overall performance will still be poor. For this reason, MongoDB requires an index to be created on the shard key before a collection is sharded. There's no technical reason for this, other than the fact that it'd be a common mistake to leave this out if it wasn't done automatically. As you design your sharded system, be sure to keep in mind everything you learned about indexing on a single node. It's just as important in a sharded cluster, and likely more so because you're operating at a larger scale.

One important factor to consider is *index locality*. This refers to how close together subsequent inserts are in the index. In this case, random inserts will perform poorly because the entire index must be loaded into memory, whereas sequential inserts will perform well because only the end of the index will need to be in memory at any given time. This is in direct contrast to the requirement that shard keys aren't ascending and illustrates the fact that proper indexing and optimal shard key choice must be each given dedicated attention when designing a sharded system.

Fortunately, the shard key `{ "username" : 1, "_id" : 1 }` that we chose earlier satisfies all the requirements. It's well-distributed on `username`, so it's balanced from the cluster perspective, but it's ascending on `_id`, so it's also ascending for each username, thus providing good index locality.

12.6.5 *Inherent design trade-offs (email application)*

Sometimes in sharding there are inherent design trade-offs that must be dealt with. Our spreadsheet example was a clean example of sharding because both the writes (document creation) and reads (document viewing) are correlated by `username`, so the shard key we chose in the previous section provides good performance on both. But what if we have an application where we need to query based on a field that isn't correlated with our write patterns? For example, what if we're building an email application where we need to send emails and read inboxes? This may not seem like a problem at first, until you realize that writes are correlated to the sender whereas reads are correlated to the recipient. Because anyone can in theory send an email to anyone else, it's difficult to predict the relationship between these two fields. In this section, we'll consider two approaches. First, we'll take the more straightforward approach and shard based on sender, and then we'll see how sharding on recipient can change our usage patterns. These two approaches are shown in figure 12.8.

SHARDING ON SENDER

Our first tactic may be to shard on sender. This seems to be a sensible choice—each email has exactly one sender. In this case, our write patterns are good: each write will go to one and only one shard. What happens when we need to read a user's inbox? If we're sharding based on sender and then piecing together all the emails a user has

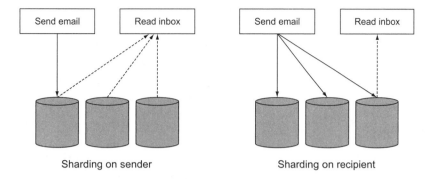

Figure 12.8 Overview of two ways an email application might be sharded

received, we need to do a full global broadcast query, as shown in figure 12.8, because we have no idea who any given user has received emails from.

SHARDING ON RECIPIENT

Our next tactic may be to shard on recipient. This is a bit more complicated because every email must be written to multiple locations to ensure every recipient gets a copy, as shown in figure 12.8. This unfortunately means that our writes will take longer and put more load on the cluster. But this approach has one nice side effect; the query to read a user's inbox is well-targeted, so reads will return quickly and scale well.

What's the right approach? That's a difficult question to answer precisely, but for this application, the second approach is likely better. This is for two reasons. One is that users may read their inbox more often than they send emails, and the other is that it's easier for users to conceptualize that taking an action such as sending an email requires real work but may not realize that reading their inbox does, too. How often have you heard "I can't even load my inbox!" as if that's somehow the easiest thing for their email application to do? In the end, this is all speculation and, like any real-world application, requires careful measurement and testing to determine what the usage patterns are.

What this example illustrates is the fact that your shard key depends on the specifics of your application. There's no magic bullet shard key that covers all use cases, so remember to think about what your read and write patterns are expected to be.

So far we've discussed in great detail the theory behind sharding, as well as how to configure the parameters in a way that will optimize the performance of your system. In the next section, we'll get to the details of what else you might want to think about when setting up a sharded cluster in the real world.

12.7 *Sharding in production*

Earlier in this chapter, we created a fully functional sharded cluster, all on one machine. Although this is great for testing, it'd be a terrible way to deploy sharding in production.

Fortunately, that's exactly what we'll cover in this next section. We'll look at the three general categories of production concerns and the order in which they arise. The first, provisioning, is how to best allocate machines and resources for use by MongoDB processes. The next, deployment, consists of things that you need to think about before you start running this cluster in production for the first time, and the last, maintenance, is how to keep your new cluster running and healthy.

12.7.1 Provisioning

The first thing to consider when thinking about how to deploy your system is provisioning, or how to allocate resources and machines to MongoDB.

DEPLOYMENT TOPOLOGIES

To launch the sample MongoDB shard cluster, you had to start a total of nine processes (three mongods for each replica set, plus three config servers). That's a potentially frightening number. First-time users might assume that running a two-shard cluster in production would require nine separate machines. Fortunately, fewer are needed. You can see why by looking at the expected resource requirements for each component of the cluster.

Consider first the replica sets. Each replicating member contains a complete copy of the data for its shard and may run as a primary or secondary node. These processes will always require enough disk space to store their copy of the data, and enough RAM to serve that data efficiently. Thus, replicating mongods are the most resource-intensive processes in a shard cluster and must be given their own machines.

What about replica set arbiters? These processes are like any other member of the replica set, except they don't store any data besides replica set config data, which is minimal. Hence, arbiters incur little overhead and certainly don't need their own servers.

Next are the config servers. These also store a relatively small amount of data. For instance, the data on the config servers managing the sample replica set totaled only about 30 KB. If you assume that this data will grow linearly with shard cluster data size, then a 1 TB shard cluster might swell the config servers' data size to a mere 30 MB.[11] This means that config servers don't necessarily need their own machines, either. But given the critical role played by the config servers, some users prefer to place them on a few modestly provisioned machines (or virtual instances).

From what you already know about replica sets and shard clusters, you can construct a list of minimum deployment requirements:

- Each member of a replica set, whether it's a complete replica or an arbiter, needs to live on a distinct machine.
- Every replicating replica set member needs its own machine.

---

[11] That's a highly conservative estimate. The real value will likely be far smaller.

- Replica set arbiters are lightweight enough to share a machine with another process. Refer back to chapter 10 for more on arbiters.
- Config servers can optionally share a machine. The only hard requirement is that all config servers in the config cluster reside on distinct machines.

Satisfying these rules might feel like tackling a logic problem. Fortunately, we'll apply them now by looking at two reasonable deployment topologies for the sample two-shard cluster. The first requires only four machines. The process layout is illustrated in figure 12.9.

This configuration satisfies all the deployment rules just mentioned. Predominant on each machine are the replicating nodes of each shard. The remaining processes are arranged so that all three config servers and all members of each replica set live on different machines. To speak of fault tolerance, this topology will tolerate the failure of any one machine. No matter which machine fails, the cluster will continue to process reads and writes. If the failing machine happens to host one of the config

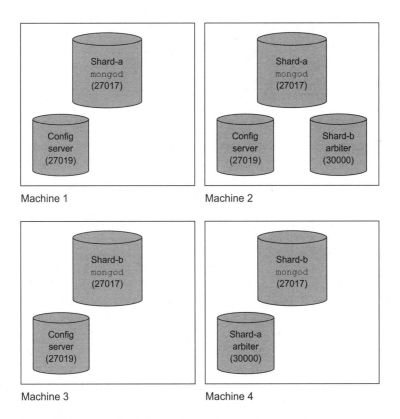

Figure 12.9 A two-shard cluster deployed across four machines

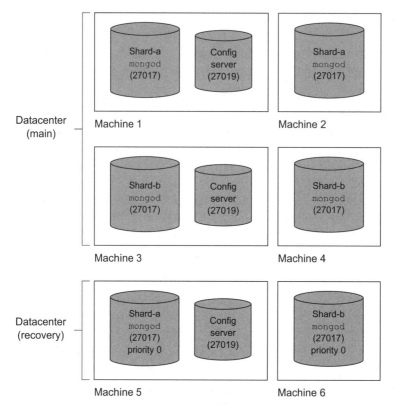

Figure 12.10 A two-shard cluster deployed across six machines and two datacenters

servers, all chunk splits and migrations will be suspended.[12] Fortunately, suspending sharding operations doesn't prevent the cluster from servicing operations; splitting and migrating can wait until the lost machine is recovered.

That's the minimum recommend setup for a two-shard cluster. But applications demanding the highest availability and the fastest paths to recovery will need something more robust. As discussed in the previous chapter, a replica set consisting of two replicas and one arbiter is vulnerable while recovering. Having three nodes reduces the fragility of the set during recovery and also allows you to keep a node in a secondary datacenter for disaster recovery. Figure 12.10 shows a robust two-shard cluster topology. Each shard consists of a three-node replica set, where each node contains a complete copy of the data. For disaster recovery, one config server and one node from each shard are located in a secondary datacenter; to ensure that those nodes never become primary, they're given a priority of 0.

---

[12] All three config servers need to be online for any sharding operations to take place.

With this configuration, each shard is replicated twice, not just once. Additionally, the secondary datacenter has all the data necessary for a user to completely reconstruct the shard cluster in the event of the failure of the first datacenter.

The decision about which sharding topology is best for your application should always be based on serious considerations about how much downtime you can tolerate, as measured by your recovery time objective (RTO). Think about the potential failure scenarios and simulate them. Consider the consequences for your application (and business) if a datacenter should fail.

12.7.2 Deployment

Now that you've settled on the topology of your cluster, it's time to discuss the actual deployment and configuration.

Fortunately, configuration of a production cluster follows exactly the same steps that we took to configure our example cluster in section 12.4. Here, we'll focus on the additional variables that must be considered in a production deployment.

ADDING NEW SHARDS

Users frequently want to know how many shards to deploy and how large each shard should be. Naturally, each additional shard introduces extra complexity, and each shard also requires replicas. Thus it's better to have a small number of large shards than a large number of small ones. But the question remains, how large can each shard be in practice?

The answer, of course, depends on the circumstances. In fact, the same concepts we discussed in section 12.1.2 for how to know when to shard in the first place apply here as well. Knowing when a single replica set—or, in this case, a shard—is at capacity is a matter of understanding the requirements of your application. Once you reach a point where your application requirements exceed the capacity of the shards you have or plan to have in your cluster, that's when you need a new shard. As always, make sure you add enough shards before your cluster grinds to a halt, or MongoDB may not be able to rebalance your data quickly enough.

SHARDING AN EXISTING COLLECTION

You can shard existing collections, but don't be surprised if it takes some time to distribute the data across shards. Only one balancing round can happen at a time, and the migrations will move only around 100–200 MB of data per minute. Thus, sharding a 50 GB collection will take around eight hours, and this will likely involve some moderate disk activity. In addition, when you initially shard a large collection like this, you may have to split manually to expedite the sharding process because splitting is triggered by inserts.

Given this, it should be clear that sharding a collection at the last minute isn't a good response to a performance problem. If you plan on sharding a collection at some point in the future, you should do so well in advance of any anticipated performance degradation.

PRESPLITTING CHUNKS FOR INITIAL LOAD

If you have a large data set that you need to load into a sharded collection, and you know something about the distribution of the data, then you can save a lot of time by presplitting and then premigrating chunks. For example, suppose you wanted to import the spreadsheet data into a fresh MongoDB shard cluster. You can ensure that the data distributes evenly upon import by first splitting and then migrating chunks across shards. You can use the split and moveChunk commands to accomplish this. These are aliased by the sh.splitAt() (or sh.splitFind()) and sh.moveChunks() helpers, respectively.

Here's an example of a manual chunk split. You issue the split command, specify the collection you want, and then indicate a split point:

```
> sh.splitAt( "cloud-docs.spreadsheets",
  { "username" : "Chen", "_id" : ObjectId("4d6d59db1d41c8536f001453") })
```

When run, this command will locate the chunk that logically contains the document where username is Chen and _id is ObjectId("4d6d59db1d41c8536f001453").[13] It then splits the chunk at that point, which results in two chunks. You can continue splitting like this until you have a set of chunks that nicely distribute the data. You'll want to make sure that you've created enough chunks to keep the average chunk size well within the 64 MB split threshold. If you expect to load 1 GB of data, you should plan to create around 20 chunks.

The second step is to ensure that all shards have roughly the same number of chunks. Because all chunks will initially reside on the same shard, you'll need to move them. Each chunk can be moved using the moveChunk command. The helper method simplifies this:

```
> sh.moveChunk("cloud-docs.spreadsheets", {username: "Chen"}, "shardB")
```

This says that you want to move the chunk that logically would contain the document {username: "Chen"} to shard B.

12.7.3 *Maintenance*

We'll round out this chapter with a few words about sharding maintenance and administration. Note that much of this can be done using MongoDB's official monitoring and automation tools, which we'll discuss in chapter 13, but here we explore the fundamentals of what's happening in the cluster, because that's still important to know. The MongoDB automation uses a lot of these commands under the hood to implement its functionality.

---

[13] Note that such a document need not exist. That should be clear from the fact that you're splitting chunks on an empty collection.

MONITORING

A shard cluster is a complex piece of machinery, and you should monitor it closely. The serverStatus and currentOp() commands can be run on any mongos, and their output will reflect aggregate statistics across shards. We'll discuss these commands in more detail in the next chapter.

In addition to aggregating server statistics, you'll want to keep an eye on the distribution of chunks and on individual chunk sizes. As you saw in the sample cluster, all of this information is stored in the config database. If you ever detect unbalanced chunks or unchecked chunk growth, you can use the split and movechunk commands to address these issues. Alternatively, you can consult the logs to see whether the balancing operation has halted for some reason.

MANUAL PARTITIONING

There are a couple of cases where you may want to manually split and migrate chunks on a live shard cluster. For example, as of MongoDB v2.6, the balancer doesn't directly take into account the load on any one shard. Obviously, the more a shard is written to, the larger its chunks become, and the more likely they are to eventually migrate. Nevertheless, it's not hard to imagine situations where you'd be able to alleviate load on a shard by migrating chunks. This is another situation where the movechunk command can be helpful.

ADDING A SHARD

If you've determined that you the need more capacity, you can add a new shard to an existing cluster using the same method you used earlier:

```
sh.addShard("shard-c/rs1.example.net:27017,rs2.example.net:27017")
```

When adding capacity in this way, be realistic about how long it will take to migrate data to the new shard. As stated earlier, you can expect data to migrate at a rate of 100–200 MB per minute. This means that if you need to add capacity to a sharded cluster, you should do so long before performance starts to degrade. To determine when you need to add a new shard, consider the rate at which your data set is growing. Obviously, you'll want to keep indexes and working set in RAM. A good rule of thumb is to plan to add a new shard at least several weeks before the indexes and working set on your existing shards reach 90% of RAM.

If you're not willing to play it safe, as described here, then you open yourself up to a world of pain. Once your indexes and working set don't fit in RAM, your application can come to a halt, especially if the application demands high write and read throughput. The problem is that the database will have to page to and from the disk, which will slow reads and writes, backlogging operations that can't be served into a read/ write queue. At that point, adding capacity is difficult because migrating chunks between shards adds read load to existing shards. Obviously, when a database is overloaded, the last thing you want to do is add load.

All of this is to emphasize that you should monitor your cluster and add capacity well before you need to.

REMOVING A SHARD

You may, in rare cases, want to remove a shard. You can do so using the removeshard command:

```
> use admin
> db.runCommand({removeshard: "shard-1/localhost:30100,localhost:30101"})
{
  "msg" : "draining started successfully",
  "state" : "started",
  "shard" : "shard-1-test-rs",
  "ok" : 1 }
```

The command response indicates that chunks are now being drained from the shard to be relocated to other shards. You can check the status of the draining process by running the command again:

```
> db.runCommand({removeshard: "shard-1/localhost:30100,localhost:30101"})
{
  "msg" : "draining ongoing",
  "state" : "ongoing",
  "remaining" : {
    "chunks" : 376,
    "dbs" : 3
  },
  "ok" : 1 }
```

Once the shard is drained, you also need to make sure that no database's primary shard is the shard you're going to remove. You can check database shard membership by querying the config.databases collection:

```
> use config
> db.databases.find()
{ "_id" : "admin", "partitioned" : false, "primary" : "config" }
{ "_id" : "cloud-docs", "partitioned" : true, "primary" : "shardA" }
{ "_id" : "test", "partitioned" : false, "primary" : "shardB" }
```

Here the cloud-docs database is owned by shardB but the test database is owned by shardA. Because you're removing shardB, you need to change the test database's primary node. You can accomplish that with the moveprimary command:

```
> db.runCommand({moveprimary: "test", to: "shard-0-test-rs" });
```

Run this command for each database whose primary is the shard to be removed. Then run the removeshard command again to verify that the shard is completely drained:

```
> db.runCommand({removeshard: "shard-1/localhost:30100,localhost:30101"})
{ "msg": "remove shard completed successfully",
  "stage": "completed",
  "host": "localhost:30100",
  "ok" : 1
}
```

Once you see that the removal is completed, it's safe to take the removed shard offline.

UNSHARDING A COLLECTION

Although you can remove a shard, there's no official way to unshard a collection. If you do need to unshard a collection, your best option is to dump the collection and then restore the data to a new collection with a different name.[14] You can then drop the sharded collection you dumped. For example, suppose that foo is a sharded collection. You must dump foo by connecting to mongos with mongodump:

```
$ mongodump -h localhost --port 40000 -d cloud-docs -c foo
connected to: localhost:40000
DATABASE: cloud-docs    to    dump/cloud-docs
  cloud-docs.foo to dump/cloud-docs/foo.bson
      100 objects
```

This will dump the collection to a file called foo.bson. You can then restore that file using mongorestore:

```
$ mongorestore -h localhost --port 40000 -d cloud-docs -c bar
Tue Mar 22 12:06:12 dump/cloud-docs/foo.bson
Tue Mar 22 12:06:12    going into namespace [cloud-docs.bar]
Tue Mar 22 12:06:12    100 objects found
```

Once you've moved the data into an unsharded collection, you're then free to drop the old sharded collection, foo. But when dropping collections, you should be extra careful because bad things can happen: first of all, make sure that you're dropping the correct collection!

BACKING UP A SHARDED CLUSTER

As you'll see in chapter 13, there are a few different options for backing up MongoDB. For the most part, these strategies also apply to backing up each shard in a sharded cluster. But there are two additional steps that must be taken when backing up a sharded cluster, regardless of which method you're using to back up the shards:

- *Disable chunk migrations*—The first thing to keep in mind when backing up a sharded cluster is that chunk migrations may be occurring. This means that unless you backup everything at exactly the same instant in time, which is essentially impossible, you may end up missing some data. We'll cover exactly how to disable chunk migrations in this section.
- *Config server metadata*—When backing up a sharded cluster, the config server metadata must also be backed up. To do this, perform a backup of a single config server node, because all config servers should have the same data. Like the backup of the shards, this should also be done after chunk migrations are disabled to avoid missing data.

Fortunately, there's a built-in mechanism to disable automatic chunk migrations. All migration of data between shards is handled by something called the *balancer* process.

---

[14] The utilities you use to dump and restore, mongodump and mongorestore, are covered in the next chapter.

Once you stop this process, you're guaranteed that no automatic migrations are happening. You can still trigger migrations manually or create new databases, however, which would disrupt a proper backup, so be sure you have no other processes running that do administrative operations.

STOPPING AND STARTING THE BALANCER

To disable the balancer, use the `sh.stopBalancer()` shell helper:

```
> use config
> sh.stopBalancer()
```

Note that this may take a long time to complete. This is because this helper only marks the balancer as disabled, and doesn't abort existing balancing rounds. This means it has to wait for in-progress balancing rounds to complete. Once it returns successfully, you can be sure that no chunk migrations are in progress. To start the balancer again, you can use the `sh.startBalancer()` helper:

```
> use config
> sh.startBalancer()
```

You should consult the MongoDB docs for additional balancer configuration, which includes a setting to enable the balancer only in a specified time window.

FAILOVER AND RECOVERY

Although we've covered general replica set failures, it's also important to note a sharded cluster's potential points of failure along with best practices for recovery.

FAILURE OF A SHARD MEMBER

Each shard consists of a replica set. If any member of one of these replica sets fails, a secondary member will be elected primary, and the `mongos` process will automatically connect to it. Chapter 11 describes the specific steps to take in restoring a failed replica set member. The method you choose depends on how the member has failed, but regardless, the instructions are the same whether or not the replica set is part of a sharded cluster.

FAILURE OF A CONFIG SERVER

A sharded cluster requires three config servers for normal operation, but up to two of these can fail. Whenever you have fewer than three config servers, your remaining config servers will become read-only, and all splitting and balancing operations will be suspended. Note that this won't negatively affect the cluster as a whole. Reads and writes to the cluster will still work, and the balancer will start from where it left off once all three config servers are restored.

To restore a config server, copy the data files from an existing config server to the failed config server's machine. Then restart the server.[15]

---

[15] As always, before you copy any data files, make sure you either lock the `mongod` (as described in chapter 11) or shut it down cleanly. Never copy data files while the server is live.

FAILURE OF A MONGOS

The failure of a mongos process is nothing to worry about. If you're hosting mongos on an application server and mongos fails, it's likely that your application server has failed, too. Recovery in this case simply means restoring the server.

Regardless of how mongos fails, the process has no state of its own. This means that recovering a mongos is a matter of restarting the mongos process and pointing it at the config servers.

12.8 Summary

Sharding is an effective strategy for maintaining high read-and write-performance on large data sets. MongoDB's sharding works well in numerous production deployments and can work for you, too. Instead of having to worry about implementing your own half-baked, custom sharding solution, you can take advantage of all the effort that's been put into MongoDB's sharding mechanism. If you follow the advice in this chapter, paying particular attention to the recommended deployment topologies, the strategies for choosing a shard key, and the importance of keeping data in RAM, then sharding will serve you well.

Deployment and administration

This chapter covers

- Provisioning and hardware requirements
- Monitoring and diagnostics
- Backups and administrative tasks
- Security
- Performance troubleshooting
- Deployment checklist

This book would be incomplete without a few notes on deployment and administration. After all, it's one thing to use MongoDB but quite another to keep it running smoothly in production. The goal of this final chapter is to prepare you to make good decisions when deploying and administering MongoDB. You can think of this chapter as providing the wisdom required to keep you from experiencing the unpleasantness of a production database meltdown.

We'll start this chapter with MongoDB's hardware requirements, as well as some options for deploying this hardware. Then, we'll move into a few sections that discuss how to keep your system running, resilient, and secure. Finally, we'll end with a deployment checklist you can look back on to make sure you've covered all your bases.

13.1 Hardware and provisioning

The first question you need to ask before you deploy MongoDB is, "What I should deploy it on?" If you ran an entire production cluster on a single laptop as we did earlier in this book, you'd be in big trouble. In this section, we'll discuss how to choose the right topology for your requirements, how different hardware affects MongoDB, and what options are available for provisioning this hardware.

13.1.1 Cluster topology

This section gives you some basic recommendations on cluster topologies, but for a more complete analysis of different deployment topologies in replicated and sharded setups, you can consult chapters 11 and 12.

Figure 13.1 shows the minimum setup for the three different cluster types, as well as when you'd want to upgrade to a different type of cluster.

In total, there are three different types of clusters in MongoDB:

- *Single node*—As you can see at the top of figure 13.1, MongoDB can be run as a single server to support testing and staging environments. But for production deployments, a single server isn't recommended, even if journaling is enabled. Having only one machine complicates backup and recovery, and when there's a server failure, there's nothing to fail over to. That said, if you don't need reliability and have a small enough data set, this is always an option.

- *Replica set*—As shown in the middle of figure 13.1, the minimum recommended deployment topology for a replica set is three nodes, at least two of which should be data-storing nodes rather than arbiters. A replica set is necessary for automatic failover, easier backups, and not having a single point of failure. Refer to chapter 10 for more details on replica sets.

- *Sharded cluster*—As you can see at the bottom of figure 13.1, the minimum recommended deployment for a sharded cluster has two shards because deploying a sharded cluster with only one shard would add additional overhead without any of the benefits of sharding. Each shard should also be a replica set and there should be three config servers to ensure that there's no single point of failure. Note that there are also two mongos processes. Loss of all mongos processes doesn't lead to any data loss, but it does lead to downtime, so we have two here as part of the minimum production topology to ensure high availability. A sharded cluster is necessary when you want to scale up the capacity of your cluster by pooling together the capacity of a number of less powerful commodity servers. Refer to chapter 12 for more details on sharded clusters.

Now that you have a high-level understanding of the types of clusters that are available, let's go into more specific details about the deployment of each individual server.

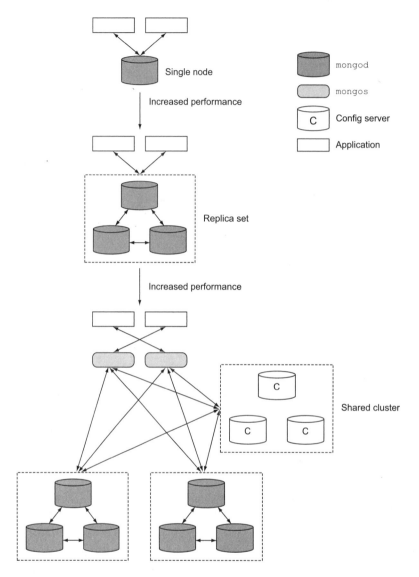

Figure 13.1   The minimum single node, replica set, and sharded cluster setups, as well as their purpose

13.1.2 *Deployment environment*

Here we'll present considerations for choosing good deployment environments for MongoDB. We'll discuss specific hardware requirements, such as CPU, RAM, and disks, and provide recommendations for optimizing the operating system environment. Figure 13.2 is a simplified visualization of the hardware and operating system components that MongoDB needs to interact with that we'll cover in this section. In the

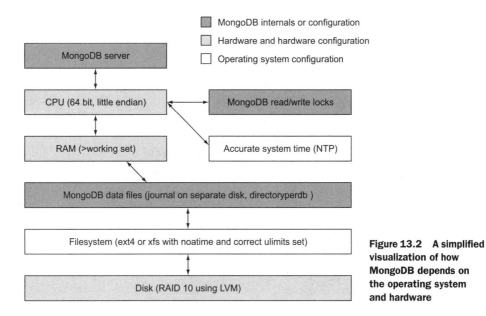

Figure 13.2 A simplified visualization of how MongoDB depends on the operating system and hardware

subsequent sections we'll discuss cluster topology and provide some advice for deploying in the cloud.

ARCHITECTURE

Two notes on hardware architecture are in order. First, because MongoDB maps all data files to a virtual address space, all production deployments should be run on 64-bit machines. A 32-bit architecture limits MongoDB to about 2 GB of storage. With journaling enabled, the limit is reduced at around 1.5 GB. This is dangerous in production because if these limits are ever surpassed, MongoDB will behave unpredictably.[1] Feel free to run on 32-bit machines for unit testing and staging, but in production and for load testing, stick to 64-bit architectures.

Next, the components that ship with the MongoDB servers must be run on little-endian machines.[2] This usually isn't difficult to comply with since the x86 architecture, which you're likely using if you're not sure, is little endian, but users running SPARC, PowerPC, PA-RISC, and other big-endian architectures will have to hold off.[3] The client drivers, though, are maintained as separate projects, and they're usually built to support both little- and big-endian byte orderings. This means that even

---

[1] In this case "unpredictably" means that the behavior is completely undefined. This essentially means that MongoDB "might" simply crash, or it might make demons fly out of your nose. We just don't know. The main point here is that you should avoid this scenario because even the maintainers of MongoDB can't help you.

[2] The "endianness" of a machine is a hardware detail referring to the order in which bytes are stored in memory. See https://en.wikipedia.org/wiki/Endianness for more information.

[3] If you're interested in big-endian support for the core server, see https://jira.mongodb.org/browse/SERVER-1625.

though the server must run on little endian machines, clients of MongoDB can usually run on either architecture.

CPU

MongoDB isn't particularly CPU-intensive; database operations are rarely CPU-bound, so this isn't the first place to look when diagnosing a performance issue. Your first priority when optimizing for MongoDB is to ensure operations aren't I/O-bound (we'll discuss I/O-bound issues more in the next two sections on RAM and disks).

But once your indexes and working set fit entirely in RAM, you may see some CPU-boundedness. If you have a single MongoDB instance serving tens (or hundreds) of thousands of queries per second, you can realize performance increases by providing more CPU cores.

If you do happen to see CPU saturation, check your logs for slow query warnings. There may be some types of queries that are inherently more CPU-intensive, or you may have an index issue that the logs will help you diagnose. But if that's not the case and you're still seeing CPU saturation, it's likely due to lock contention, which we'll briefly touch on here.

RAM

As with any database, MongoDB performs best with sufficient RAM. Be sure to select hardware with enough RAM to contain your frequently used indexes, plus your working data set. Then as your data grows, keep a close eye on the ratio of RAM-to–working set size. If you allow working set size to grow beyond RAM, you may start to see significant performance degradation. Paging from disk in and of itself isn't a problem—it's a necessary step in loading data into memory. But if you're unhappy with performance, excessive paging may be your problem. (Chapter 8 discusses the relationship between working set, index size, and RAM in great detail.) By the end of this chapter, you should have enough tools in your arsenal to diagnose RAM deficiencies.

There are a few use cases where you can safely let data size grow well beyond available RAM, but they're the exception, not the rule. One example is using MongoDB as an archive, where reads and writes seldom happen and you don't need fast responses. Because RAM is essentially a cache for pages on disk, it only provides a performance boost if a page will be used more than once in a short period of time. In the case of an archive application, this may not be the case, and the page will need to be loaded into memory from disk the first (and possibly only) time it's used anyway. On top of that, having as much RAM as data for this type of application might be prohibitively expensive. For all data sets, the key is testing. Test a representative prototype of your application to ensure that you get the necessary baseline performance.

DISKS

When choosing disks, you need to consider cost, IOPS (input/output operations per second), seek time, and storage capacity. The differences between running on a single consumer-grade hard drive, running in the cloud in a virtual disk (say, EBS), and running against a high-performance SAN can't be overemphasized. Some applications will perform acceptably against a single network-attached EBS volume, but demanding applications will require something more.

Disk performance is important for a few reasons:

- *High write workloads*—As you're writing to MongoDB, the server must flush the data back to disk. With a write-intensive app and a slow disk, the flushing may be slow enough to negatively affect overall system performance.
- *A fast disk allows a quicker server warm-up*—Any time you need to restart a server, you also have to load your data set into RAM. This happens lazily; each successive read or write to MongoDB will load a new virtual memory page into RAM until the physical memory is full. A fast disk will make this process much faster, which will increase MongoDB's performance following a cold restart.
- *A fast disk alters the required ratio of working set size to RAM for your application*— Using, say, a solid-state drive, you may be able to run with much less RAM (or much greater capacity) than you would otherwise.

Regardless of the type of disk used, serious deployments will generally use, not a single disk, but a redundant array of disks (RAID) instead. Users typically manage a RAID cluster using Linux's logical volume manager, LVM, with a RAID level of 10. RAID 10 provides redundancy while maintaining acceptable performance, and it's commonly used in MongoDB deployments.[4] Note that this is more expensive than a single disk, which illustrates the tradeoff between cost and performance. Even more advanced deployments will use a high-performance self-managed SAN, where the disks are all virtual and the idea of RAID may not even apply.

If your data is spread across multiple databases within the same MongoDB server, then you can also ensure capacity by using the server's `--directoryperdb` flag. This will create a separate directory in the data file path for each database. Using this, you can conceivably mount a separate volume (RAID'ed or not) for each database. This may allow you to take advantage of some performance increases, because you'll be able to read from separate sets of spindles (or solid-state drives).

LOCKS

MongoDB's locking model is a topic unto itself. We won't discuss all the nuances of concurrency and performance in MongoDB here, but we'll cover the basic concurrency models MongoDB supports. In practice, ensuring that you don't have lock contention will require careful monitoring or benchmarking because every workload is different and may have completely different points of contention.

In the early days, MongoDB took a global lock on the entire server. This was soon updated to a global lock on each database and support was added to release the lock before disk operations.

As of v3.0 MongoDB now supports two separate storage engines with different concurrency models. It has collection-level locking in its own native mmap-based storage

---

[4] For an overview of RAID levels, see http://en.wikipedia.org/wiki/Standard_RAID_levels.

engine, and document-level locking in the newly supported WiredTiger storage engine, which can be used instead of the native storage engine. Consult JIRA, MongoDB's bug-tracking system, as well as the latest release notes for the status of these improvements.[5]

FILESYSTEMS

You'll get the best performance from MongoDB if you run it on the right filesystem. Two in particular, ext4 and xfs, feature fast, contiguous disk allocation. Using these filesystems will speed up MongoDB's frequent preallocations.[6]

Once you mount your fast filesystem, you can achieve another performance gain by disabling updates to files' last access time: atime. Normally, the operating system will update a file's atime every time the file is read or written. In a database environment, this amounts to a lot of unnecessary work. Disabling atime on Linux is relatively easy:

1   First, make a backup of the filesystem config file:

```
sudo cp /etc/fstab /etc/fstab.bak
```

2   Open the original file in your favorite editor:

```
sudo vim /etc/fstab
```

3   For each mounted volume you'll find inside /etc/fstab, you'll see a list of set-tings aligned by column. Under the options column, add the noatime directive:

```
# file-system        mount  type    options  dump  pass
UUID=8309beda-bf62-43 /ssd   ext4    noatime  0     2
```

4   Save your work. The new settings should take effect immediately.[7]

You can see the list of all mounted filesystems with the help of the findmnt command, which exists on Linux machines:

```
$ findmnt -s
TARGET SOURCE     FSTYPE OPTIONS
/proc  proc       proc   defaults
/      /dev/xvda  ext3   noatime,errors=remount-ro
none   /dev/xvdb  swap   sw
```

The -s option makes findmnt get its data from the /etc/fstab file. Running findmnt without any command-line parameters shows more details yet more busy output.

FILE DESCRIPTORS

Some Linux systems cap the number of allowable open file descriptors at 1024. This is occasionally too low for MongoDB and may result in warning messages or even errors

---

[5]   Release notes can be found at https://jira.mongodb.org/browse/server and https://docs.mongodb.org/manual/release-notes/ for more information.

[6]   For more detailed filesystem recommendations, see https://docs.mongodb.org/manual/administration/production-notes/#kernel-and-file-systems.

[7]   Note that these are basic recommendations and by no means comprehensive. See https://en.wikipedia.org/wiki/Fstab for an overview of mount options.

when opening connections (which you'll see clearly in the logs). Naturally, MongoDB requires a file descriptor for each open file and network connection.

Assuming you store your data files in a folder with the word "*data*" in it, you can see the number of data file descriptors using `lsof` and a few well-placed pipes:

```
lsof | grep mongo | grep data | wc -l
```

Counting the number of network connection descriptors is just as easy:

```
lsof | grep mongo | grep TCP | wc -l
```

When it comes to file descriptors, the best strategy is to start with a high limit so that you never run out in production. You can check the current limit temporarily with the `ulimit` command:

```
ulimit -Hn
```

To raise the limit permanently, open your limits.conf file with your editor of choice:

```
sudo vim /etc/security/limits.conf
```

Then set the soft and hard limits. These are specified on a per-user basis. This example assumes that the `mongodb` user will run the `mongod` process:

```
mongodb soft nofile 2048
mongodb hard nofile 10240
```

The new settings will take effect when that user logs in again.[8]

CLOCKS

It turns out that replication is susceptible to "clock skew," which can occur if the clocks on the machines hosting the various nodes of a replica set get out of sync. Replication depends heavily on time comparisons, so if different machines in the same replica set disagree on the current time, that can cause serious problems. This isn't ideal, but fortunately there's a solution. You need to ensure that each of your servers uses NTP (Network Time Protocol)[9] or some other synchronization protocol to keep their clocks synchronized:

- On Unix variants, this means running the `ntpd` daemon.
- On Windows, the Windows Time Services fulfills this role.

JOURNALING

MongoDB v1.8 introduced journaling, and since v2.0 MongoDB enables journaling by default. When journaling is enabled, MongoDB will commit all writes to a journal

---

[8] This may not apply if the user is purely a daemon. In that case restarting the `mongodb` service using something like `sudo service mongodb restart` should do the trick.

[9] Make sure to verify that NTP is working correctly using diagnostic commands such as `ntpstat`.

before writing to the core data files. This allows the MongoDB server to come back online quickly and cleanly in the event of an unclean shutdown.

In the event of an unclean shutdown of a nonjournaled mongod process, restoring the data files to a consistent state requires running a repair. The repair process rewrites the data files, discarding anything it can't understand (corrupted data). Because downtime and data loss are generally frowned upon, repairing in this way is usually part of a last-ditch recovery effort. Resyncing from an existing replica is almost always easier and more reliable. Being able to recover in this way is one of the reasons why it's so important to run with replication.

Journaling obviates the need for database repairs because MongoDB can use the journal to restore the data files to a consistent state. In MongoDB v2.0 as well as v3.0, journaling is enabled by default, but you can disable it with the --nojournal flag:

```
$ mongod --nojournal
```

When enabled, the journal files will be kept in a directory called journal, located just below the main data path.

If you run your MongoDB server with journaling enabled, keep a of couple points in mind:

- First, journaling adds some additional overhead to writes.
- One way to mitigate this is to allocate a separate disk for the journal, and then either create a symlink[10] between the journal directory and the auxiliary volume or simply mount this disk where the journal directory should be. The auxiliary volume needn't be large; a 120 GB disk is more than sufficient, and a solid-state drive (SSD) of this size is affordable. Mounting a separate SSD for the journal files will ensure that journaling runs with the smallest possible performance penalty.
- Second, journaling by itself doesn't guarantee that no write will be lost. It guarantees only that MongoDB will always come back online in a consistent state. Journaling works by syncing a write buffer to disk every 100 ms, so an unclean shutdown can result in the loss of up to the last 100 ms of writes. If this isn't acceptable for any part of your application, you can change the write concern of operations through any client driver. You'd run this as a safe mode option (just like w and wtimeout). For example, in the Ruby driver, you might use the j option like this in order to have safe mode enabled all the time for one of the servers:

```
client = Mongo::Client.new( ['127.0.0.1:27017'], :write => {:j =>
true}, :database => 'garden')
```

---

[10] A symlink, or symbolic link, is essentially an object that looks like a file but is actually a reference to another location. Using this here means that MongoDB can still find the journal directory in the same place despite the fact that it's on a completely different disk. See https://en.wikipedia.org/wiki/Symbolic_link for more details.

Be aware that running this after every write is unwise because it forces every write to wait for the next journal sync.[11] Even then, these writes are subject to rollbacks in a replicated setup because journal acknowledged writes only wait until the primary writes to its journal and doesn't wait for replication to secondaries. Therefore, a more commonly used way to ensure your writes are durable is to use the "majority" write concern option. This ensures that the write reaches a majority of the replica set, which is usually sufficient and resilient to failures. See chapter 10 for more details on replication and write concern options.[12]

13.1.3 Provisioning

You can certainly deploy on your own hardware, and that approach does have its advantages, but this section will focus mostly on cloud deployments and automation. In-house deployments require a lot of specialized administration and setup that's outside the scope of this book.

THE CLOUD

More and more users are running MongoDB in hosted, virtualized environments, collectively known as the cloud. Among these, Amazon's EC2 has become a deployment environment of choice because of its ease of use, wide geographic availability, and competitive pricing. EC2, and other environments like it, can be adequate for deploying MongoDB. At a high level, there are three main components to consider when thinking about deploying on any cloud provider:

- The hosts themselves, which will actually run MongoDB
- The persistent storage system, which will store MongoDB's data files
- The network that MongoDB will use to communicate internally and with clients

First, EC2 hosts are convenient, because they're easy to provision and can be allocated as you need them, so the cost will scale with your needs. But one disadvantage of an EC2 host is that it's essentially a black box. You may experience service blips or instance slowdowns and have no way of diagnosing or remedying them. Sometimes you might get a "bad box," which means your virtual instance got allocated on a machine with slow hardware or several other active users.[13]

Second, EC2 allows you to mount virtual block devices known as EBS volumes as your persistent storage. EBS volumes provide a great deal of flexibility, allowing you to add storage and move volumes across machines as needed. EBS also lets you take snapshots, which you can use for backups.

---

[11] Recent versions of MongoDB allow changing the journal commit interval to reduce the latency on journal-acknowledged writes, using the `commitIntervalMs` option.

[12] For more details on the behavior of specific write concern levels, see https://docs.mongodb.org/manual/core/write-concern.

[13] Note that EC2 has many different instance types and purchasing options that may suffer more or less from these problems. Check with EC2 or your cloud provider to find out exactly how they provision your machine.

The problem with the cheapest EBS volumes is that they may not provide a high level of throughput compared to what's possible with physical disks. Be sure to check with your hosting provider to learn what their current offerings are. As of this writing, EBS volumes can be SSD-backed, and Amazon also provides an option to use disks local to the node. On top of that, another way to increase performance is to run whatever disks you're using with a RAID 10 for increased read throughput.

Finally, EC2's network is sufficient for most users, but like the storage and the hosts themselves, you give up a great deal of control by using EC2's network rather than one you set up yourself. You're sharing the same network with many others, so high traffic from other applications have the potential to affect your network performance. Like disks and instance types, this is "pay to play" when dealing with a hosting provider, so you may be able to pay more to mitigate these problems.

In summary, deploying on EC2 has many advantages, but it clearly has some notable drawbacks. For these reasons, rather than dealing with some of EC2's limitations and unpredictability, many users prefer to run MongoDB on their own physical hardware. Then again, EC2 and the cloud in general are convenient and perfectly acceptable for a wide variety of users. In the end, the best way to approach deploying in any environment is careful testing. Benchmarking the cloud platform that you want to deploy on will ultimately help you make the decision more than anything else.

MMS AUTOMATION

Another provisioning option that is relatively new is the MongoDB Management System (MMS) Automation. MMS Automation can provision instances from EC2 and setup of your entire cluster with the press of a button.[14] The MMS team at MongoDB is constantly adding new features to simplify MongoDB operations, so if you're interested in using this, refer to the current documentation at https://docs.mms.mongodb.com to find out what's available.

13.2 *Monitoring and diagnostics*

Once you've deployed MongoDB in production, you'll want to keep an eye on it. If performance is slowly degrading, or if failures are occurring frequently, you'll want to be apprised of these. That's where monitoring comes in.

Let's start with the simplest kind of monitoring: logging. Then we'll explore the built-in commands that provide the most information about the running MongoDB server; these commands underlie the `mongostat` utility and the web console, both of which we'll describe in brief.

Then we'll look at the MMS Monitoring provided by the MongoDB company. We'll make a couple of recommendations on external monitoring tools and end the section by presenting two diagnostic utilities: `bsondump` and `mongosniff`.

---

[14] MMS Automation can also deploy MongoDB onto preprovisioned hardware if you're not using EC2.

13.2.1 Logging

Logging is the first level of monitoring; as such, you should plan on keeping logs for all your deployments. This usually isn't a problem because MongoDB requires that you specify the `--logpath` option when running it in the background. But there are a few extra settings to be aware of. To enable verbose logging, start the `mongod` process with the `-vvvvv` option (the more vs, the more verbose the output). This is handy if, for instance, you need to debug some code and want to log every query. But do be aware that verbose logging will make your logs quite large and may affect server performance. If your logs become too unwieldy, remember that you can always store your logs on a different partition.

Next you can start `mongod` with the `--logappend` option. This will append to an existing log rather than moving it and appending a timestamp to the filename, which is the default behavior.

Finally, if you have a long-running MongoDB process, you may want to write a script that periodically rotates the log files. MongoDB provides the `logrotate` command for this purpose. Here's how to run it from the shell:

```
> use admin
> db.runCommand({logrotate: 1})
```

Sending the SIGUSR1[15] signal to the process also runs the `logrotate` command. Here's how to send that signal to process number 12345:

```
$ kill -SIGUSR1 12345
```

You can find the process ID of the process you want to send the signal to using the `ps` command, like this:

```
$ ps -ef | grep mongo
```

Note that the `kill` command isn't always as dire as it sounds. It only sends a signal to a running process, but was named in the days when most or all signals ended the process.[16] But running `kill` with the `-9` command-line option will end a process in a brutal way and should be avoided as much as possible on production systems.

13.2.2 *MongoDB diagnostic commands*

MongoDB has a number of database commands used to report internal state. These underlie all MongoDB monitoring applications. Here's a quick reference for a few of the commands that you might find useful:

- Global server statistics: `db.serverStatus()`
- Stats for currently running operation: `db.currentOp()`

---

[15] Unix-like systems support sending "signals" to running processes, which can trigger certain actions if the process that receives the signal is written to handle it. MongoDB is configured to handle receiving the SIGUSR1 signal and rotates the logs when it receives it.

[16] There's no Windows equivalent for this, so you'll have to rely on the `logrotate` command in that case.

- Include stats for idle system operations: `db.currentOp(true)`
- Per database counters and activity stats: `db.runCommand({top:1})`
- Memory and disk usage statistics: `db.stats()`

The output for all of these commands improves with each MongoDB release, so documenting it in a semi-permanent medium like this book isn't always helpful. Consult the documentation for your version of MongoDB to find out what each field in the output means.

13.2.3 *MongoDB diagnostic tools*

In addition to the diagnostic commands listed previously, MongoDB ships with a few handy diagnostic tools. Most of these are built on the previous commands and could be easily implemented using a driver or the mongo shell.

Here's a quick introduction to what we'll cover in this section:

- `mongostat`—Global system statistics
- `mongotop`—Global operation statistics
- `mongosniff` (advanced)—Dump MongoDB network traffic
- `bsondump`—Display BSON files as JSON

MONGOSTAT

The `db.currentOp()` method shows only the operations queued or in progress at a particular moment in time. Similarly, the `serverStatus` command provides a point-in-time snapshot of various system fields and counters. But sometimes you need a view of the system's real-time activity, and that's where `mongostat` comes in. Modeled after `iostat` and other similar tools, `mongostat` polls the server at a fixed interval and displays an array of statistics, from the number of inserts per second to the amount of resident memory, to the frequency of B-tree page misses.

You can invoke the `mongostat` command on localhost, and the polling will occur once a second:

```
$ mongostat
```

It's also highly configurable, and you can start it with `--help` to see all the options. For example, you can use the `--host` option to connect to a host and port besides the default of `localhost:27017`. One of the more notable features is cluster discovery; when you start `mongostat` with the `--discover` option, you can use the `--host` option to point it to a single node, and it'll discover the remaining nodes in a replica set or sharded cluster. It then displays the entire cluster's statistics in aggregate.

MONGOTOP

Similar to the way `mongostat` is the external tool for the `db.currentOp()` and `serverStatus` commands, `mongotop` is the external tool for the `top` command. You can run this in exactly the same way as `mongostat`, assuming you have a server running on the local machine and listening on the default port:

```
$ mongotop
```

As with `mongostat`, you can run this command with `-help` to see a number of useful configuration options.

MONGOSNIFF

The next command we'll cover is `mongosniff`, which sniffs packets from a client to the MongoDB server and prints them intelligibly. If you happen to be writing a driver or debugging an errant connection, then this is your tool. You can start it up like this to listen on the local network interface at the default port:

```
sudo mongosniff --source NET I0
```

Then when you connect with any client—say, the MongoDB shell—you'll get an easy-to-read stream of network chatter:

```
127.0.0.1:58022  -->> 127.0.0.1:27017 test.$cmd 61 bytes id:89ac9c1d
2309790749 query: { isMaster: 1.0 }  ntoreturn: -1
127.0.0.1:27017  <<-- 127.0.0.1:58022   87 bytes
reply n:1 cursorId: 0 { ismaster: true, ok: 1.0 }
```

Here you can see a client running the `isMaster` command, which is represented as a query for { `isMaster: 1.0` } against the special `test.$cmd` collection. You can also see that the response document contains `ismaster: true`, indicating that the node that this command was sent to was in fact the primary. You can see all the `mongosniff` options by running it with `--help`.

BSONDUMP

Another useful command is `bsondump`, which allows you to examine raw BSON files. BSON files are generated by the `mongodump` command (discussed in section 13.3) and by replica set rollbacks.[17] For instance, let's say you've dumped a collection with a single document. If that collection ends up in a file called users.bson, then can examine the contents easily:

```
$ bsondump users.bson
{ "_id" : ObjectId( "4d82836dc3efdb9915012b91" ), "name" : "Kyle" }
```

As you can see, `bsondump` prints the BSON as JSON by default. If you're doing serious debugging, you'll want to see the real composition of BSON types and sizes. For that, run the command in debug mode:

```
$ bsondump --type=debug users.bson
--- new object ---
size : 37
_id
type:  7 size: 17
name
type:  2 size: 15
```

---

[17] MongoDB writes replica set rollback files to the rollback directory inside the data directory.

This gives you the total size of the object (37 bytes), the types of the two fields (7 and 2), and those fields' sizes.

THE WEB CONSOLE

Finally, MongoDB provides some access to statistics via a web interface and a REST server. As of v3.0, these systems are old and under active development. On top of that, they report the same information available via the other tools or database commands presented earlier. If you want to use these systems, be sure to look at the current documentation and carefully consider the security implications.

13.2.4 *MongoDB Monitoring Service*

MongoDB, Inc. provides MMS Monitoring for free, which not only allows you to view dashboards to help you understand your system, but also provides an easy way to share your system information with MongoDB support, which is indispensable if you ever need help with your system. MMS Monitoring can also be licensed as a self-hosted version for large enterprises with paid contracts. To get started, all you need to do is create an account on the MMS Monitoring website at https://mms.mongodb.com. Once you create an account, you'll see instructions to walk you through the process of setting up MMS, which we won't cover here.

13.2.5 *External monitoring applications*

Most serious deployments will require an external monitoring application. Nagios and Munin are two popular open source monitoring systems used to keep an eye on many MongoDB deployments. You can use each of these with MongoDB by installing a simple open source plug-in.

Writing a plug-in for any arbitrary monitoring application isn't difficult. It mostly involves running various statistics commands against a live MongoDB database. The `serverStatus`, `dbstats`, and `collstats` commands usually provide all the information you might need, and you can get all of them straight from the HTTP REST interface, avoiding the need for a driver.

Finally, don't forget the wealth of tools available for low-level system monitoring. For example, the `iostat` command can be helpful in diagnosing MongoDB performance issues. Most of the performance issues in MongoDB deployments can be traced to a single source: the hard disk.

In the following example, we use the `-x` option to show extended statistics and specify 2 to display those stats at two-second intervals:

```
$ iostat -x 2
Device:   rsec/s    wsec/s avgrq-sz avgqu-sz   await  svctm  %util
sdb         0.00   3101.12    10.09    32.83  101.39   1.34  29.36
Device:   rsec/s    wsec/s avgrq-sz avgqu-sz   await  svctm  %util
sdb         0.00   2933.93     9.87    23.72  125.23   1.47  34.13
```

For a detailed description of each of these fields, or for details on your specific version of iostat, consult your system's man[18] pages. For a quick diagnostic, you'll be most interested in two of the columns shown:

- The await column indicates the average time in milliseconds for serving I/O requests. This average includes time spent in the I/O queue and time spent actually servicing I/O requests.
- %util is the percentage of CPU during which I/O requests were issued to the device, which essentially translates to the bandwidth use of the device.

The preceding iostat snippet shows moderate disk usage. The average time waiting on I/O is around 100 ms (hint: that's a lot!), and the utilization is about 30%. If you were to investigate the MongoDB logs on this machine, you'd likely see numerous slow operations (queries, inserts, or otherwise). In fact, it's those slow operations that would initially alert you to a potential problem. The iostat output can help you confirm the problem. We've covered a lot of ways to diagnose and monitor a running system to keep it running smoothly, but now let's get into an unavoidable aspect of a production deployment: backups.

13.3 Backups

Part of running a production database deployment is being prepared for disasters. Backups play an important role in this. When disaster strikes, a good backup can save the day, and in these cases, you'll never regret having invested time and diligence in a regular backup policy. Yet some users still decide that they can live without backups. These users have only themselves to blame when they can't recover their databases. Don't be one of these users.

Three general strategies for backing up a MongoDB database are as follows:

- Using mongodump and mongorestore
- Copying the raw data files
- Using MMS Backups

We'll go over each of these strategies in the next three sections.

13.3.1 mongodump and mongorestore

mongodump writes the contents of a database as BSON files. mongorestore reads these files and restores them. These tools are useful for backing up individual collections and databases as well as the whole server. They can be run against a live server (you don't have to lock or shut down the server), or you can point them to a set of data files,

---

[18] The man pages, or "manual" pages, are the way many programs on Unix-based systems provide documentation. For example, type man iostat in a terminal to get the iostat man page.

but only when the server is locked or shut down. The simplest way to run mongodump is like this:[19]

```
$ mongodump -h localhost --port 27017
```

This will dump each database and collection from the server at localhost to a directory called dump.[20] The dump directory will include all the documents from each collection, including the system collections that define users and indexes. But significantly, the indexes themselves won't be included in the dump. This means that when you restore, any indexes will have to be rebuilt. If you have an especially large data set, or a large number of indexes, this will take time.

RESTORING BSON FILES
To restore BSON files, run mongorestore and point it at the dump folder:

```
$ mongorestore -h localhost --port 27017 dump
```

Note that when restoring, mongorestore won't drop data by default, so if you're restoring to an existing database, be sure to run with the --drop flag.

13.3.2 *Data file–based backups*

Most users opt for a file-based backup, where the raw data files are copied to a new location. This approach is often faster than mongodump because the backups and restorations require no transformation of the data.

The only potential problem with a file-based backup is that it requires locking the database, but generally you'll lock a secondary node and thus should be able to keep your application online for the duration of the backup.

COPYING THE DATA FILES
Users frequently make the mistake of copying the data files without first locking the database. Even if journaling is enabled, doing so will result in corruption of the copied files. This section will cover how to bring the data files to a consistent state by locking the database to allow for safe backups.

> **Snapshotting a live system**
>
> You may wonder why you have to lock the data files even when journaling is enabled. The answer is that journaling is only able to restore a database to a consistent state from a single point in time. If you're manually copying the data files, there may be some delay between copying each file, which means different data files may be from different points in time, and journaling can't deal with this.

---

[19] If you have secondary reads enabled, you can run this against the secondary of a replica set rather than the primary.

[20] If possible, this directory should be stored on a separate disk, both for performance and for extra defense against disk failure.

But if your filesystem, storage provider, or hosting provider explicitly supports "point-in-time" snapshots, you can use this feature to safely snapshot a live system without locking the data files. Note that everything has to be saved at exactly the same time, including the journal. This means that if your journal is on a separate disk (or you have journaling disabled), you're out of luck unless you have a system that supports point-in-time snapshots across multiple volumes.

To safely copy the data files, you first need to make sure that they're in a consistent state, so you either have to shut down the database or lock it. Because shutting down the database might be too involved for some deployments, most users opt for the locking approach. Here's the command for syncing and locking:

```
> use admin
> db.fsyncLock()
```

At this point, the database is locked against writes[21] and the data files are synced to disk. This means that it's now safe to copy the data files. If you're running on a filesystem or storage system that supports snapshots, it's best to take a snapshot and copy later. This allows you to unlock quickly.

If you can't run a snapshot, you'll have to keep the database locked while you copy the data files. If you're copying data files from a secondary node, be sure that the node is current with the primary and has enough oplog to remain offline for the duration of the backup.

Once you've finished making a snapshot or backing up, you can unlock the database. The somewhat arcane unlock command can be issued like this:

```
> db.fsyncUnlock()
```

Note that this is merely a request to unlock; the database may not unlock right away. Run the db.currentOp() method to verify that the database is no longer locked.

13.3.3 *MMS backups*

Once again, the MMS team at MongoDB has a solution for this problem. MMS Backups use the replication oplog to provide point-in-time backups for your entire cluster. This works for stand-alone replica sets as well as for entire sharded cluster. As we mentioned earlier, the MMS team is constantly adding new features, so check the up-to-date documentation for details.

---

[21] Any attempts to write will block behind this lock, and reads that come after those writes will also block. This unfortunately includes reads of authentication data, meaning that new connection attempts will also block on this lock when you're running with authentication, so keep your connections open when you're running the backup process. See https://docs.mongodb.org/manual/reference/method/db.fsyncLock/ for more details.

13.4 Security

Security is an extremely important, and often overlooked, aspect of deploying a production database. In this section, we'll cover the main types of security, including secure environments, network encryption, authentication, and authorization.

We'll end with a brief discussion of which security features are only available in the enterprise edition of MongoDB. Perhaps more than for any other topic, it's vital to stay up to date with the current security tools and best practices, so treat this section as an overview of what to consider when thinking about security, but consult the most recent documentation at https://docs.mongodb.org/manual/security when putting it into production.

13.4.1 Secure environments

MongoDB, like all databases, should be run in a secure environment. Production users of MongoDB must take advantage of the security features of modern operating systems to ensure the safety of their data. Probably the most important of these features is the firewall.

The only potential difficulty in using a firewall with MongoDB is knowing which machines need to communicate with each other. Fortunately, the communication rules are simple:

- With a replica set, each node must be able to reach every other node.
- All database clients must be able to connect with every replica set node that the client might conceivably talk to.
- All communication is done using the TCP protocol.
- For a node to be reachable, it means that it's reachable on the port that it was configured to listen on. For example, `mongod` listens on TCP port 27017 by default, so to be reachable it must be reachable on that port.

A shard cluster consists in part of replica sets. All the replica set rules apply; the client in the case of sharding is the `mongos` router. Additionally:

- All shards must be able to communicate directly with one another.
- Both the shards and the `mongos` routers must be able to talk to the config servers.

Figure 13.2 shows a simplified visualization of these connectivity rules, with the one addition that any arrow connecting to a boxed replica set or set of config servers means that the connectivity requirement applies to every individual server inside the box.

For the most part, running MongoDB in a secure environment is completely external to MongoDB and is a full topic on its own. But one option, `--bind_ip`, is relevant here.[22] By default, MongoDB will listen on all addresses on the machine, B=but you may want MongoDB to listen on one or more specific addresses instead. For this you

---

[22] Note that as of v2.6, the prebuilt packages for Linux include `--bind_ip` by default.

can start `mongod` and `mongos` with the `--bind_ip` option, which takes a list of one or more comma-separated IP addresses. For example, to listen on the loopback interface as well as on the internal IP address 10.4.1.55, you'd start `mongod` like this:

```
mongod --bind_ip 127.0.0.1,10.4.1.55
```

Note that data between machines will be sent in the clear unless you have SSL enabled, which we'll cover in the next section.

13.4.2 Network encryption

Perhaps the most fundamental aspect of securing your system is ensuring your network traffic is encrypted. Unless your system is completely isolated and no one you don't trust can even see your traffic (for example, if all your traffic is already encrypted over a virtual private network, or your network routing rules are set up such that no traffic can be sent to your machines from outside your trusted network[23]), you should probably use MongoDB with encryption. Fortunately, as of v2.4, MongoDB ships with a library that handles this encryption—called the Secure Sockets Layer (SSL)—built in.

To see why this is important, let's play the role of an eavesdropper using the Unix command `tcpdump`. First, use the `ifconfig` command to find the name of the loopback interface, or the interface that programs communicating from the local machine to the local machine use.

Here's what the beginning of the output looks like on our machine:

```
$ ifconfig
lo: flags=73<UP,LOOPBACK,RUNNING>  mtu 65536
        inet 127.0.0.1  netmask 255.0.0.0
        . . .
        . . .
```

For us, the loopback interface is `lo`. Now we can use the appropriate `tcpdump` command to dump all traffic on this interface:

```
$ sudo tcpdump -i lo -X
```

> **NOTE** Reading network traffic using `tcpdump` requires root permissions, so if you can't run this command, just read along with the example that follows.

In another terminal on the same machine, start a `mongod` server without SSL enabled (change the data path as appropriate):

```
$ mongod --dbpath /data/db/
```

---

[23] Many cloud hosting providers have tools to help with this, such as Virtual Private Clouds (VPCs), subnets, and security groups in AWS.

Then, connect to the database and insert a single document:

```
$ mongo
...
> db.test.insert({ "message" : "plaintext" })
> exit
bye
```

Now, if you look at the `tcpdump` output in the terminal, you'll see a number of packets output, one of which looks something like this:

```
16:05:10.507867 IP localhost.localdomain.50891 >
     ➡   localhost.localdomain.27017 ...
        0x0000:  4500 007f aa4a 4000 4006 922c 7f00 0001   E....J@.@..,....
        0x0010:  7f00 0001 c6cb 6989 cf17 1d67 d7e6 c88f   ......i....g....
        0x0020:  8018 0156 fe73 0000 0101 080a 0018 062e   ...V.s..........
        0x0030:  0017 b6f6 4b00 0000 0300 0000 ffff ffff   ....K..........
        0x0040:  d207 0000 0000 0000 7465 7374 2e74 6573   ........test.tes
        0x0050:  7400 2d00 0000 075f 6964 0054 7f7b 0649   t.-...._id.T.{.I
        0x0060:  45fa 2cfc 65c5 8402 6d65 7373 6167 6500   E.,.e...message.
        0x0070:  0a00 0000 706c 6169 6e74 6578 7400 00     ....plaintext..
```

Document **❶** sent in plaintext over the network

There's our message, right in the clear **❶**! This shows how important network encryption is. Now, let's run MongoDB with SSL and see what happens.

RUN MONGODB WITH SSL

First, generate the key for the server:

```
openssl req -newkey rsa:2048 -new -x509 -days 365 -nodes -out mongodb-
cert.crt -keyout mongodb-cert.key
cat mongodb-cert.key mongodb-cert.crt > mongodb.pem
```

Then, run the `mongod` server with SSL, using the `--sslPEMKeyFile` and `--sslMode` options:

```
$ mongod --sslMode requireSSL --sslPEMKeyFile mongodb.pem
```

Now, connect the client with SSL and do exactly the same operation:

```
$ mongo --ssl
...
> db.test.insert({ "message" : "plaintext" })
> exit
bye
```

If you now go back to the window with `tcpdump`, you'll see something completely incomprehensible where the message used to be:

```
16:09:26.269944 IP localhost.localdomain.50899 >
     ➡   localhost.localdomain.27017: ...
        0x0000:  4500 009c 52c3 4000 4006 e996 7f00 0001   E...R.@.@.......
        0x0010:  7f00 0001 c6d3 6989 c46a 4267 7ac5 5202   ......i..jBgz.R.
        0x0020:  8018 0173 fe90 0000 0101 080a 001b ed40   ...s...........@
```

Document ① sent over the network securely encrypted

```
0x0030:  001b 6c4c 1703 0300 637d b671 2e7b 499d  ..lL....c}.q.{I.
0x0040:  3fe8 b303 2933 d04b ff5c 3ccf fac2 023d  ?...)3.K.\<....=
0x0050:  b2a1 28a0 6d3f f215 54ea 4396 7f55 f8de  ..(.m?..T.C..U..
0x0060:  bb8d 2e20 0889 f3db 2229 1645 ceed 2d20  ........").E..-.
0x0070:  1593 e508 6b33 9ae1 edb5 f099 9801 55ae  ....k3........U.
0x0080:  d443 6a65 2345 019f 3121 c570 3d9d 31b4  .Cje#E..1!.p=.1.
0x0090:  bf80 ea12 e7ca 8c4e 777a 45dd            .......NwzE.
```

Success! Is our system secure now? Not quite. Proper encryption is only one aspect of securing your system. In the next section, we'll discuss how to verify the identity of services and users, and following that we'll talk about how to get fine-grained control of what each user is allowed to do.

SSL IN CLUSTERS

Now you know how to set up SSL between the mongo shell and a single mongod, which raises the obvious question of how this extends to an entire cluster. Fortunately this is fairly similar to the previous example. Simply start every node in the cluster with the `--sslMode requireSSL` option. If you're already running a cluster without SSL, there's an upgrade process to ensure that you can upgrade without losing connectivity between your nodes in the transition; see https://docs.mongodb.org/manual/tutorial/upgrade-cluster-to-ssl/.

> **Keep your keys safe!**
>
> Most of the security mechanisms in this chapter depend on the exchange of keys. Make sure to keep your keys safe (and stored using the proper permissions) and not share them between servers except when necessary.
>
> As an extreme example, if you use the same key across all machines, that means all an attacker has to do is compromise that single key to read all traffic on your network.
>
> If you're ever unsure about whether you should share a key, consult the official documentation either for MongoDB or the underlying mechanism.

13.4.3 Authentication

The next layer of security is authentication. What good is network encryption if anyone on the internet can pose as a legitimate user and do whatever they want with your system?

Authentication allows you to verify the identity of services and users in a secure way. First we'll discuss why and how to authenticate services and then users. We'll then briefly discuss how these concepts translate to replica sets and sharded clusters. As always, we'll cover the core concepts here, but you should consult the latest documentation for your version of MongoDB to ensure you're up-to-date (https://docs.mongodb.org/manual/core/authentication).

SERVICE AUTHENTICATION

The first stage of authentication is verifying that the program on the other end of the connection is trusted. Why is this important? The main attack that this is meant to prevent is the *man-in-the-middle attack*, where the attacker masquerades as both the client and the server to intercept all traffic between them. See figure 13.3 for an overview of this attack.

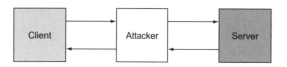

Figure 13.3   Man-in-the-middle attack

As you can see in the figure, a man-in-the-middle attack is exactly what it sounds like:

- A malicious attacker poses as a server, creating a connection with the client, and then poses as the client and creates a connection with the server.
- After that, it can not only decrypt and encrypt all the traffic between the client and server, but it can send arbitrary messages to both the client and the server.

Fortunately, there's hope. The SSL library that MongoDB uses not only provides encryption, but also provides something called *certificate authentication*, which consists of using a trusted third party not involved in the communication to verify the person sending the key is who they claim to be. In theory, the attacker hasn't compromised the third party.

Generating certificates and getting them signed by the trusted third party, known as the certificate authority (CA) for online communication, is outside the scope of this book. There are numerous options here, and each is a topic on its own. To get started, you can work with a CA directly, such as Symantec, Comodo SSL, GlobalSign, and others, or you can use tools that have been built to make this process easier, such as SSLMate.

Once you have a certificate, you can use it in MongoDB like this

```
mongod --clusterAuthMode x509 --sslMode requireSSL --sslPEMKeyFile server.pem
--sslCAFile ca.pem
mongo --ssl --sslPEMKeyFile client.pem
```

where `ca.pem` contains the root certificate chain from the CA and `client.pem` is signed by that CA. The server will use the contents of `ca.pem` to verify that `client.pem` was indeed signed by the CA and is therefore trusted.

Taking these steps will ensure that no malicious program can establish a connection to your database. In the next section, you'll see how to make this more fine-grained and authenticate individual users in a single database.

USER AUTHENTICATION

Although service authentication is great for preventing attackers from even creating a connection to your system, sometimes we want to grant or revoke access on the level of individual users.

NOTE This API changed dramatically from v2.4 to v2.6, and may change again in future versions, so be sure to read the documentation for your server version when you try to set this up. The examples here are for v2.6 and v3.0, which support role-based authentication.

In MongoDB a *role* is essentially a set of privileges, and a *privilege* is any operation that can be performed in MongoDB. The role is a useful concept because sometimes our logical idea of a user "role" doesn't map exactly to primitive database operations. For example, the built-in read role doesn't only allow a user to perform find queries; it also allows users to run certain commands that display statistics about the databases and collections for which they have the read role.

MongoDB has a convenient set of built-in roles, but it also supports user-defined roles if these aren't enough. We won't cover roles in detail here; this topic falls into the category of more advanced and specialized security features, so if you're in a situation where you know you need user-defined roles, we recommend that you consult the most up-to-date documentation for your system and version of MongoDB. For now, we'll jump straight into an example of how to set up basic authentication for a single mongod.

SETTING UP BASIC AUTHENTICATION

First, you should start a mongod node with auth enabled. Note that if this node is in a sharded cluster or a replica set, you also need to pass options to allow it to authenticate with other servers. But for a single node, enabling authentication requires only one flag:

```
$ mongod --auth
```

Now, the first time you connect to the server, you want to add an administrative user account:

```
> use admin
> db.createUser(
  {
    user: "boss",
    pwd: "supersecretpassword",
    roles: [ { role: "userAdminAnyDatabase", db: "admin" } ]
  }
)
```

In our example, we gave this user a role of userAdminAnyDatabase, which essentially gives the user complete access to the system, including the ability to add and remove new users, as well as change user privileges. This is essentially the superuser of MongoDB.

Now that we've created our admin user, we can log in as this user:

```
> use admin
> db.auth("boss", "supersecretpassword")
```

We can now create users for individual databases. Once again we use the `createUser` method. The main differences here are the roles:

```
> use stocks
> db.createUser(
  {
    user: "trader",
    pwd: "youlikemoneytoo",
    roles: [ { role: "readWrite", db: "stocks" } ]
  }
)
> db.createUser(
  {
    user: "read-only-trader",
    pwd: "weshouldtotallyhangout",
    roles: [ { role: "read", db: "stocks" } ]
  }
)
```

Now the `trader` user has the `readWrite` role on the `stocks` database, whereas the read-only-trader only has the `read` role. This essentially means that the first user can read and write stock data, and the second can only read it. Note that because we added these users to the `stocks` database, we need to authenticate using that database as well:

```
> use stocks
> db.auth("trader", "youlikemoneytoo")
```

REMOVING A USER
To remove a user, use the `dropUser` helper on the database it was added to:

```
> use stocks
> db.dropUser("trader")
```

This is a bit heavyweight, so note that you can also revoke user access without completely dropping them from the system using the `revokeRolesFromUser` helper, and grant them roles again using the `grantRolesToUser` helper.

To close the session you don't need to explicitly log out; terminating the connection (closing the shell) will accomplish that just fine. But there's a helper for logging out if you need it:

```
> db.logout()
```

Naturally, you can use all the authentication logic we've explored here using the drivers. Check your driver's API for the details.

> ### Localhost exception
>
> You may have noticed we were able to add a user before authenticating our connection. This may seem like a security vulnerability, but it's actually due to a convenience provided by MongoDB called the *localhost exception*.
>
> This means that if the server hasn't yet been configured, any connections from the local machine get full permissions. After you add your first user, unauthenticated connections don't have privileges, as you'd expect. You can pass `--setParameter enableLocalhostAuthBypass=0` on the command line to disable this behavior and set up your first admin user by first starting the server with authentication completely disabled, adding the user, and then restarting with authentication enabled.
>
> This approach isn't any more secure—during the same window where the localhost exception would've been a factor, anyone could've come into your system—but it's another option.

13.4.4 Replica set authentication

Replica sets support the same authentication API just described, but enabling authentication for a replica set requires extra configuration, because not only do clients need to be able to authenticate with the replica set, but replica set nodes also need to be able to authenticate with each other.

Internal replica set authentication can be done via two separate mechanisms:

- Key file authentication
- X509 authentication

In both cases, each replica set node authenticates itself with the others as a special internal user that has enough privileges to make replication work properly.

KEY FILE AUTHENTICATION

The simpler and less secure authentication mechanism is key file authentication. This essentially involves creating a "key file" for each node that contains the password that replica set node will use to authenticate with the other nodes in the replica set. The upside of this is that it's easy to set up, but the downside is that if an attacker compromises just one machine, you'll have to change the password for every node in the cluster, which unfortunately can't be done without downtime.

To start, create the file containing your secret. The contents of the file will serve as the password that each replica set member uses to authenticate with the others. As an example, you might create a file called secret.txt and fill it with the following (don't actually use this password in a real cluster):

```
tOps3cr3tpa55word
```

Place the file on each replica set member's machine and adjust the permissions so that it's accessible only by the owner:

```
sudo chmod 600 /home/mongodb/secret.txt
```

Finally, start each replica set member by specifying the location of the password file using the `--keyFile` option:

```
mongod --keyFile /home/mongodb/secret.txt
```

Authentication will now be enabled for the set. You'll want to create an admin user in advance, as you did in the previous section.

X509 AUTHENTICATION

X509 certificate authentication is built into OpenSSL, the library MongoDB uses to encrypt network traffic. As we mentioned earlier, obtaining signed certificates is outside the scope of this book. However, once you have them, you can start each node like this

```
mongod --replSet myReplSet --sslMode requireSSL --clusterAuthMode x509 --
sslClusterFile --sslPEMKeyFile server.pem --sslCAFile ca.pem
```

where `server.pem` is a key signed by the certificate authority that `ca.pem` corresponds to.

There's a way to upgrade a system using key file authentication to use X509 certificates with no downtime. See the MongoDB docs for the details on how to do this, or check in the latest MMS documentation to see whether support has been added to MMS automation.

13.4.5 *Sharding authentication*

Sharding authentication is an extension of replica set authentication. Each replica set in the cluster is secured as described in the previous section. In addition, all the config servers and every `mongos` instance can be set up to authenticate with the rest of the cluster in exactly the same way, using either a shared key file or using X509 certificate authentication. Once you've done this, the whole cluster can use authentication.

13.4.6 *Enterprise security features*

Some security features exist only in MongoDB's paid enterprise plug-in. For example, the authentication and authorization mechanisms that allow MongoDB to interact with Kerberos and LDAP are enterprise. In addition, the enterprise module adds auditing support so that security-related events get tracked and logged. The MongoDB docs will explicitly mention if a particular feature is enterprise only.

13.5 *Administrative tasks*

In this section, we'll cover some basic administrative tasks, including importing and exporting data, dealing with disk fragmentation, and upgrading your system.

13.5.1 *Data imports and exports*

If you're migrating an existing system to MongoDB, or if you need to seed the database with information from, something like a data warehouse, you'll need an efficient import method. You might also need a good export strategy, because you may have to export data from MongoDB to external processing jobs. For example, exporting data to Hadoop for batch processing has become a common practice.[24]

There are two ways to import and export data with MongoDB:

- Use the included tools, `mongoimport` and `mongoexport`.
- Write a simple program using one of the drivers.[25]

MONGOIMPORT AND MONGOEXPORT

Bundled with MongoDB are two utilities for importing and exporting data: `mongoimport` and `mongoexport`. You can use `mongoimport` to import JSON, CSV, and TSV files. This is frequently useful for loading data from relational databases into MongoDB:

```
$ mongoimport -d stocks -c values --type csv --headerline stocks.csv
```

In the example, you import a CSV file called stocks.csv into the `values` collection of the `stocks` database. The `--headerline` flag indicates that the first line of the CSV contains the field names. You can see all the import options by running `mongoimport --help`.

Use `mongoexport` to export all of a collection's data to a JSON or CSV file:

```
$ mongoexport -d stocks -c values -o stocks.csv
```

This command exports data to the file stocks.csv. As with its counterpart, you can see the rest of `mongoexport`'s command options by starting it with the `--help` flag.

CUSTOM IMPORT AND EXPORT SCRIPTS

You're likely to use MongoDB's import and export tools when the data you're dealing with is relatively flat; once you introduce subdocuments and arrays, the CSV format becomes awkward because it's not designed to represent nested data.

When you need to export a rich document to CSV or import a CSV to a rich MongoDB document, it may be easier to build a custom tool instead. You can do this using any of the drivers. For example, MongoDB users commonly write scripts that connect to a relational database and then combine the data from two tables into a single collection.

That's the tricky part about moving data in and out of MongoDB: the way the data is modeled may differ between systems. In these cases, be prepared to use the drivers as your conversion tools.

13.5.2 *Compaction and repair*

MongoDB includes a built-in tool for repairing a database. You can initiate it from the command line to repair all databases on the server:

```
$ mongod --repair
```

---

[24] There's also a Hadoop plug-in for MongoDB, sometimes known as the MongoDB Connector for Hadoop.

[25] You can also use a tool known as mongoconnector to keep a different storage system in sync with MongoDB.

Or you can run the `repairDatabase` command to repair a single database:

```
> use cloud-docs
> db.runCommand({repairDatabase: 1})
```

Repair is an offline operation. While it's running, the database will be locked against reads and writes. The repair process works by reading and rewriting all data files, discarding any corrupted documents in the process. It also rebuilds each index. This means that to repair a database, you need enough free disk space to store the rewrite of its data. To say repairs are expensive is an understatement, as repairing a large database can take days and impact traffic to other databases on the same node.

MongoDB's repair was originally used as a kind of last-ditch effort for recovering a corrupted database. In the event of an unclean shutdown, without journaling enabled, a repair is the only way to return the data files to a consistent state, and even then you may lose data. Fortunately, if you deploy with replication, run at least one server with journaling enabled, and perform regular off-site backups, you should never have to recover by running a repair. Relying on repair for recovery is foolish. Avoid it.

What, then, might a database repair be good for? Running a repair will compact the data files and rebuild the indexes. As of the v2.0 release, MongoDB doesn't have great support for data file compaction. If you perform lots of random deletes, and especially if you're deleting small documents (less than 4 KB), it's possible for total storage size to remain constant or grow despite these regularly occurring deletes. Compacting the data files is a good remedy for this excess use of space.[26]

If you don't have the time or resources to run a complete repair, you have two options, both of which operate on a single collection:

- Rebuilding indexes
- Compacting the collection

To rebuild indexes, use the `reIndex()` method:

```
> use cloud-docs
> db.spreadsheets.reIndex()
```

This might be useful, but generally speaking, index space is efficiently reused. The data file space is what can be a problem, so the `compact` command is usually a better choice.

`compact` will rewrite the data files and rebuild all indexes for one collection. Here's how you run it from the shell:

```
> db.runCommand({ compact: "spreadsheets" })
```

This command has been designed to be run on a live secondary, obviating the need for downtime. Once you've finished compacting all the secondaries in a replica set, you can step down the primary and then compact that node. If you must run the compact

---

[26] Compacting your data on disk may also result in more efficient use of space in RAM.

command on the primary, you can do so by adding {force: true} to the command object. Note that if you go this route, the command will write lock the system:

```
> db.runCommand({ compact: "spreadsheets", force: true })
```

On WiredTiger databases, the compact() command will release unneeded disk space to the operating system. Also note that the paddingFactor field, which is applicable for the MMAPv1 storage engine, has no effect when used with the WiredTiger storage engine.

13.5.3 *Upgrading*

As with any software project, you should keep your MongoDB deployment as up to date as possible, because newer versions contain many important bug fixes and improvements.

One of the core design principles behind MongoDB is to always ensure an upgrade is possible with no downtime. For a replica set, this means a rolling upgrade, and for a sharded cluster, this means that mongos routers can still function against mixed clusters.

You can take one of two paths when dealing with upgrades:

- First, you can choose to do the process manually. In this case you should check the release notes describing the upgrade process and read them carefully. Sometimes there are important caveats or steps that must be taken to ensure that the upgrade is safe. The advantage here is that you have complete control over the process and know exactly what's happening when.
- The second option is to again use the MongoDB Management Service. MMS Automation not only can be used to provision your nodes, but can also be used to upgrade them. Be sure to read the release notes for the version you're upgrading to as well as the MMS documentation to be sure you know what's happening under the hood.

13.6 *Performance troubleshooting*

Performance in MongoDB is a complicated issue that touches on nearly every other topic. It's nearly impossible to know exactly how your application will perform before you test it with your specific workload and environment. A node on the Joyent Cloud will have completely different performance characteristics than a node on EC2, which will again have completely different performance characteristics than a node that you installed in your own private datacenter.

In this section, we'll address some common issues that come up in MongoDB support, as least up through version 3.0, that are important to watch out for. First, we'll reintroduce the working set concept; then we'll cover two ways the working set can affect your system: the performance cliff and query interactions.

In the end, it's up to you to monitor your system closely and understand how it's behaving. Good monitoring could be the difference between quickly resolving, or even predicting and preventing performance issues, and having angry users be the first to tell you your systems have slowed to a crawl.

13.6.1 Working set

We've covered the idea of the working set in various parts of this book, but we'll define it here again with a focus on your production deployment.

Imagine you have a machine with 8 GB of RAM, running a database with an on-disk size of 16 GB, not including indexes. Your *working set* is how much data you're accessing in a specified time interval. In this example, if your queries are all full collection scans, your "working set" will be 16 GB because to answer those queries your entire database must be paged into memory.

But if your queries are properly indexed, and you're only querying for the most recent quarter of the data, most of your database can stay on disk, and only the 2 GB that you need, plus some extra space for indexes, needs to be in memory.

Figure 13.4 shows visually what this means for your disk use.

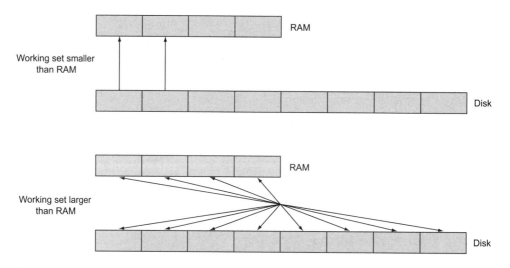

Figure 13.4 The impact on disk usage when the working set exceeds RAM

In the bottom row of the figure, when you're doing full table scans, you have a lot of *thrashing*, or moving blocks of data in and out of RAM, because you can't keep all 16 GB in your 8 GB of RAM at once.

In the top example, you can bring the 2 GB you need into memory, and then keep it there, answering all the queries with only minimal disk access. This illustrates not only why keeping your working set in RAM is extremely important, but also shows how a simple change, such as adding the right index, can completely change your performance characteristics.

13.6.2 *Performance cliff*

Closely related to the working set concept is an unfortunate artifact of the way MongoDB runs queries. As of 3.0, MongoDB doesn't limit the resources a single operation can use[27], nor does it explicitly push back on clients when it's starting to become overwhelmed. As long as you aren't approaching MongoDB's limits, this won't be a problem, but as you reach the limit, you may see a "performance cliff."

To see why this is the case, imagine you have a system with 8 GB of RAM, running a database that's 64 GB on disk. Most of the time, your working set is only 6 GB, and your application performs perfectly well. Now, fast-forward to Christmas Eve, when you see a traffic spike big enough to bring you to 8 GB. MongoDB will start to slow down, because the working set no longer fits in memory and will start thrashing to disk. Despite this, MongoDB will continue to accept new requests.

The combination of slowing down while still accepting new requests is disastrous for performance, and you may see a steep drop-off at this point. If you think this will be a concern for you, we strongly recommend that you understand exactly how much load your MongoDB deployment can handle, and if possible put some kind of load balancer in front of it that will ensure that you steer away from the edge of this precipice.

13.6.3 *Query interactions*

Another side effect of the fact that MongoDB doesn't enforce resource limits is that one badly behaving query can affect the performance of all other queries on the system.

It's the same drill as before. Assume you have a working set of 2 GB, with a 64 GB database. Everything may be going well, until someone runs a query that performs a full collection scan. This query will not only place a huge amount of load on the disk, but may also page out the data that was being used for the other queries on the system, causing slowdown there as well. Figure 13.4 from earlier illustrates this issue, where the top represents normal query load and the bottom represents the load after the bad query.

This is actually another reason why access controls are important. Even if you get everything else right, one table scan by an intern can hose your system. Make sure everyone who has the ability to query your database understands the consequences of a bad query.[28]

---

[27] A crude approximation is the `maxTimeMS` cursor option, which sets a maximum time limit for processing operations. This won't prevent one resource-hungry operation from interfering with others, but it will at least kill operations that run for longer than expected.

[28] You can mitigate this a bit by running your long-running queries on secondaries, but remember from chapter 11 that the secondary must have enough bandwidth to keep up with the primary, otherwise it will fall off the end of the oplog.

All about the indexes

When you discover a performance issue, indexes are the first place you should look. Unless your operation is insert only, indexes are a vital part of ensuring good performance.

Chapter 8 outlines a procedure for identifying and fixing slow operations that involves enabling the query profiler and then ensuring that every query and update uses an index efficiently. In general, this means each operation scans as few documents as possible.

It's also important to make sure there are no redundant indexes, because a redundant index will take up space on disk, require more RAM, and demand more work on each write. Chapter 8 mentions ways to eliminate these redundant indexes.

What then? After auditing your indexes and queries, you may discover inefficiencies that, when corrected, fix the performance problems altogether. You'll no longer see slow query warnings in the logs, and the `iostat` output will show reduced utilization. Adjusting indexes fixes performance issues more often than you might think; this should always be the first place you look when addressing a performance issue.

13.6.4 *Seek professional assistance*

The sources of performance degradations are manifold and frequently idiosyncratic. Anything from poor schema design to sneaky server bugs can negatively affect performance. If you think you've tried every possible remedy and still can't get results, consider allowing someone experienced in the ways of MongoDB to audit your system. A book can take you far, but an experienced human being can make all the difference in the world. When you're at a loss for ideas and in doubt, seek professional assistance. The solutions to performance issues are sometimes entirely unintuitive.

When or if you seek help, be sure to provide all the information you have about your system when the issue occurred. This is when the monitoring will pay off. The official standard used by MongoDB is MMS Monitoring, so if you're using MongoDB support, being set up with MMS Monitoring will speed up the process significantly.

13.7 *Deployment checklist*

We've covered a lot of topics in this chapter. It may seem overwhelming at first, but as long as you have the main areas covered, your system will keep running smoothly. This section is a quick reference for making sure you've got the important points covered:

- Hardware
  - *RAM*—Enough to handle the expected working set.
  - *Disk space*—Enough space to handle all your data, indexes, and MongoDB internal metadata.
  - *Disk speed*—Enough to satisfy your latency and throughput requirements. Consider this in conjunction with RAM—less RAM usually means more disk usage.

- *CPU*—Usually not the bottleneck for MongoDB, but if you're getting low disk utilization but low throughput, you may have a CPU bound workload. Check this as part of careful performance testing.
- *Network*—Make sure the network is fast and reliable enough to satisfy your performance requirements. MongoDB nodes communicate with each other internally, so be sure to test every connection, not just the ones from your clients to the mongos or mongod servers.

- Security
  - *Protection of network traffic*—Either run in a completely isolated environment or make sure your traffic is encrypted using MongoDB's built-in SSL support or some external method such as a VPN to prevent man-in-the-middle attacks.
  - *Access control*—Make sure only trusted users and clients programs can operate on the database. Make sure your interns don't have the "root" privilege.

- Monitoring
  - *Hardware usage (disks, CPU, network, RAM)*—Make sure you have some kind of monitoring setup for all your hardware resources that will not only keep track of the usage, but also alert you if it goes above a certain threshold.
  - *Health checks*—Periodically make sure your servers are up and responsive, and will alert you if anyone stops calling back.
  - *MMS Monitoring*—Monitor your services using MMS Monitoring. Not only does this provide monitoring, health checks, and alerts, but it's what the MongoDB support team will use to help you if you run into trouble. Historically it's been free to use, so don't hesitate to add this to your deployment.
  - *Client performance monitoring*—Periodically run automated end-to-end tests as a client to ensure that you're still performing as well as you expect. The last thing you want is for a client to be the first one to tell you that your application is slow.

- Disaster recovery
  - *Evaluate risk*—Imagine that you've lost all your data. How sad do you feel? In all seriousness, losing your data may be worse in some applications than others. If you're analyzing Twitter trends, losing your data may cost a week's worth of time, whereas if you're storing bank data, losing that may cost quite a bit more. When you do this evaluation, assume that a disaster of some kind will happen, and plan accordingly.
  - *Have a plan*—Create a concrete plan for how you'll recover in each failure case. Depending on how your system fails, you may react completely differently.
  - *Test your plan*—Be sure to test your plan. The biggest mistake people make with backups and disaster recovery is assuming that having a backup or a plan is enough. It's not enough. Maybe the backup is getting corrupted. Maybe it's in a format that's impossible to reimport into your production systems. As in a production system, many things can go wrong, so it's important to make sure your recovery strategy works.

- *Have a backup plan*—Your first disaster recovery plan might fail. When it does, have a last resort available. This doesn't have to be an appealing option, but you'll be happy it's there if you get desperate.

- Performance
    - *Load testing*—Make sure you load test your application with a realistic workload. In the end, this is the only way to be sure that your performance is what you expect.

13.8 Summary

This chapter has presented the most important considerations for deploying MongoDB in production. You should have the knowledge you need to select the right hardware for MongoDB, monitor your deployments, and maintain regular backups. In addition, you should have some idea about how to go about resolving performance issues. Ultimately, this knowledge will develop with experience. But MongoDB is predictable enough to be amenable to the simple heuristic presented here—except for when it isn't. MongoDB tries to make life simple, but databases and their interactions with live applications are frankly complex. The guidelines in this chapter can point you in the right direction, but in the end it's up to you to take an active role in understanding your system. Make sure you take full advantage of the resources available, from the MongoDB documentation all the way to the official and community support from MongoDB maintainers and users.

appendix A
Installation

In this appendix you'll learn how to install MongoDB on Linux, Mac OS X, and Windows, and you'll get at an overview of MongoDB's most commonly used configuration options. For developers, there are a few notes on compiling MongoDB from its source.

We'll conclude with some pointers on installing Ruby and RubyGems to aid those wanting to run the Ruby-based examples from the book.

A.1 Installation

Before we proceed to the installation instructions, a note on MongoDB versioning is in order. Briefly, you should run the latest stable version for your architecture. Stable releases of MongoDB are marked by an even minor version number. Thus, versions 1.8, 2.0, 2.2, 2.4, 2.6 and 3.0 are stable; 2.1, 2.3, and 2.5 are development versions and shouldn't be used in production. The downloads page at www.mongodb.org provides statically linked binaries compiled for 32- and 64-bit systems. But as of MongoDB v3.0, 32-bit binaries will no longer be supported. These binaries are available for the latest stable releases as well as for the development branches and nightly builds of the latest revision. The binaries provide an easy way to install MongoDB across most platforms, including Linux, Mac OS X, Windows, and Solaris, and they're the method we'll prefer here. If you run into trouble, you can find more information in the official MongoDB manual at http://docs.mongodb.org/manual/installation.

A.1.1 Production deployments

Using a package manager installation may be preferable for server deployments of MongoDB, because the package installation usually includes scripts to start and stop MongoDB when the machine restarts. In the precompiled binary installation described here, we demonstrate how to run MongoDB from the command line, which is perfect for learning and debugging but not ideal if you're running a server that other people are accessing. Each operating system distribution and package management system has small differences and idiosyncrasies, such as where MongoDB's log file is placed. If you plan on running MongoDB as a production service, you should understand MongoDB's configuration and think through error scenarios, such as what would happen if the server suddenly goes down. If you're just learning MongoDB or experimenting with it, any installation method is fine.

A.1.2   32-bit vs. 64-bit

You can download MongoDB binaries compiled for 32- or 64-bit architectures depending on the MongoDB version. If you're installing MongoDB on a 64-bit machine, we highly recommended that you use the 64-bit binaries because the 32-bit installation is limited to storing only 2 GB of data. Most machines nowadays are 64-bit, but if you're unsure you can check a Linux or Mac OS X machine by running the command

```
$ uname -a
```

which prints information about the operating system. If the OS version includes the text x86_64 (as opposed to i386), then you're running a 64-bit version. For Windows machines, check the documentation for how to determine which architecture your OS is running.

A.2   MongoDB on Linux

There are three ways to install MongoDB on Linux. You can download the precompiled binaries directly from the mongodb.org website, use a package manager, or compile manually from source. We'll discuss the first two in the next sections, and then provide a few notes on compiling later in the appendix.

A.2.1   Installing with precompiled binaries

First navigate to www.mongodb.org/downloads. There you'll see a grid with all the latest downloadable MongoDB binaries. Select the download URL for the latest stable version for your architecture. These examples use MongoDB v2.6 compiled for a 64-bit system.

Open a command line and download the archive using your web browser, the curl utility or the wget utility. (You should check on the downloads page for the most recent release.) Then expand the archive using tar:

```
$ curl http://downloads.mongodb.org/linux/mongodb-linux-x86_64-2.6.7.tgz >
mongo.tgz
$ tar xzvf mongo.tgz
```

To run MongoDB, you'll need a data directory. By default, the mongod daemon will store its data files in /data/db. Create that directory, and ensure that it has the proper permissions:

```
$ sudo mkdir -p /data/db/
$ sudo chown `id -u` /data/db
```

You're ready to start the server. Change to the MongoDB bin directory and launch the mongod executable:

```
cd mongodb-linux-x86_64-2.6.7/bin
./mongod
```

If all goes well, you should see something like the following abridged startup log. The first time you start the server it may allocate journal files, which takes several minutes, before being ready for connections. Note the last lines, confirming that the server is listening on the default port of 27017:

```
Thu Mar 10 11:28:51 [initandlisten] MongoDB starting :
  pid=1773 port=27017 dbpath=/data/db/ 64-bit host=iron
Thu Mar 10 11:28:51 [initandlisten] db version v2.6.7
...
Thu Mar 10 11:28:51 [websvr] web admin console waiting for connections on
➥    port 28017
Thu Mar 10 11:28:51 [initandlisten] waiting for connections on port 27017
```

You should now be able to connect to the MongoDB server using the JavaScript console by running ./mongo. If the server terminates unexpectedly, refer to section A.6.

At the time of writing this, the most recent MongoDB release is 3.0.6.

A.2.2   *Using a package manager*

Package managers can greatly simplify the installation of MongoDB. The only major downside is that package maintainers may not always keep up with the latest MongoDB releases. It's important to run the latest stable point release, so if you do choose to use a package manager, be sure that the version you're installing is a recent one.

If you happen to be running Debian, Ubuntu, CentOS, or Fedora, you'll always have access to the latest versions. This is because MongoDB, Inc. maintains and publishes its own packages for these platforms. You can find more information on installing these particular packages on the mongodb.org website. Instructions for Debian and Ubuntu can be found at http://mng.bz/ZffG. For CentOS and Fedora, see http://mng.bz/JSjC.

Packages are also available for FreeBSD and ArchLinux. See their respective package repositories for details. There may also be other package managers not listed here that include MongoDB. Check the downloads page at www.mongodb.org/downloads for more details.

A.3   *MongoDB on Mac OS X*

If you're using Mac OS X, you have three options for installing MongoDB. You can download the precompiled binaries directly from the mongodb.org website, use a package manager, or compile manually from source. We'll discuss the first two options in the next sections, and then provide a few notes on compiling later in the appendix.

A.3.1   *Precompiled binaries*

First navigate to www.mongodb.org/downloads. There you'll see a grid with all the latest downloadable MongoDB binaries. Select the download URL for the latest stable version for your architecture. The following example uses MongoDB v3.0.6 compiled for a 64-bit system.

Download the archive using your web browser or the `curl` utility. You should check on the downloads page for the most recent release. Then expand the archive using `tar`:

```
$ curl https://fastdl.mongodb.org/osx/mongodb-osx-x86_64-3.0.6.tgz >
mongo.tgz
$ tar xzvf mongo.tgz
```

To run MongoDB, you'll need a data directory. By default, the `mongod` daemon will store its data files in /data/db. Go ahead and create that directory:

```
$ sudo mkdir -p /data/db/
$ sudo chown `id -u` /data/db
```

You're now ready to start the server. Just change to the MongoDB bin directory and launch the `mongod` executable:

```
$ cd mongodb-osx-x86_64-3.0.6/bin
$ ./mongod
```

If all goes well, you should see something like the following abridged startup log. The first time you start the server it may allocate journal files, which takes several minutes, before being ready for connections. Note the last lines, confirming that the server is listening on the default port of 27017:

```
2015-09-19T08:51:40.214+0300 I CONTROL  [initandlisten] MongoDB starting :
    pid=41310 port=27017 dbpath=/data/db 64-bit host=iron.local
2015-09-19T08:51:40.214+0300 I CONTROL  [initandlisten] db version v3.0.6
...
2015-09-19T08:51:40.215+0300 I INDEX    [initandlisten] allocating new ns
    file /data/db/local.ns, filling with zeroes...
2015-09-19T08:51:40.240+0300 I STORAGE  [FileAllocator] allocating new
    datafile /data/db/local.0, filling with zeroes...
2015-09-19T08:51:40.240+0300 I STORAGE  [FileAllocator] creating directory /
    data/db/_tmp
2015-09-19T08:51:40.317+0300 I STORAGE  [FileAllocator] done allocating
    datafile /data/db/local.0, size: 64MB,  took 0.077 secs
2015-09-19T08:51:40.344+0300 I NETWORK  [initandlisten] waiting for
    connections on port 27017
```

You should now be able to connect to the MongoDB server using the JavaScript console by running `./mongo`. If the server terminates unexpectedly, refer to section A.6.

A.3.2   *Using a package manager*

MacPorts (http://macports.org) and Homebrew (http://brew.sh/) are two package managers for Mac OS X known to maintain up-to-date versions of MongoDB. To install via MacPorts, run the following:

```
sudo port install mongodb
```

Note that MacPorts will build MongoDB and all its dependencies from scratch. If you go this route, be prepared for a lengthy compile.

Homebrew, rather than compiling, merely downloads the latest binaries, so it's much faster than MacPorts. You can install MongoDB through Homebrew as follows:

```
$ brew update
$ brew install mongodb
```

After installing, Homebrew will provide instructions on how to start MongoDB using the Mac OS X launch agent.

A.4   *MongoDB on Windows*

If you're using Windows, you have two ways to install MongoDB. The easier, preferred way is to download the precompiled binaries directly from the mongodb.org website. You can also compile from source, but this option is recommended only for developers and advanced users. You can read about compiling from source in the next section.

A.4.1   *Precompiled binaries*

First navigate to www.mongodb.org/downloads. There you'll see a grid with all the latest downloadable MongoDB binaries. Select the download URL for the latest stable version for your architecture. Here we'll install MongoDB v2.6 compiled for 64-bit Windows.

Download the appropriate distribution and unzip it. You can do this from the Windows Explorer by locating the MongoDB ZIP file, right-clicking on it, and selecting Extract All. You'll then be able to choose the folder where the contents will be unzipped. Please keep in mind that because MongoDB v2.6, prebuilt MSIs are also available for download.

Alternatively, you can use the command line. First navigate to your Downloads directory. Then use the `unzip` utility to extract the archive:

```
C:\> cd \Users\kyle\Downloads
C:\> unzip mongodb-win32-x86_64-2.6.7.zip
```

To run MongoDB, you'll need a data folder. By default, the `mongod` daemon will store its data files in C:\data\db. Open the Windows command prompt and create the folder like this:

```
C:\> mkdir \data
C:\> mkdir \data\db
```

You're now ready to start the server. Change to the MongoDB bin directory and launch the `mongod` executable:

```
C:\> cd \Users\kyle\Downloads
C:\Users\kyle\Downloads> cd mongodb-win32-x86_64-2.6.7\bin
C:\Users\kyle\Downloads\mongodb-win32-x86_64-2.6.7\bin> mongod.exe
```

If all goes well, you should see something like the following abridged startup log. The first time you start the server it may allocate journal files, which takes several minutes, before being ready for connections. Note the last lines, confirming that the server is listening on the default port of 27017:

```
Thu Mar 10 11:28:51 [initandlisten] MongoDB starting :
  pid=1773 port=27017 dbpath=/data/db/ 64-bit host=iron
Thu Mar 10 11:28:51 [initandlisten] db version v2.6.7
...
Thu Mar 10 11:28:51 [websvr] web admin console waiting for connections on
➥    port 28017
Thu Mar 10 11:28:51 [initandlisten] waiting for connections on port 27017
```

If the server terminates unexpectedly, refer to section A.6.

Finally, you'll want to start the MongoDB shell. To do that, open a second terminal window, and then launch `mongo.exe`:

```
C:\> cd \Users\kyle\Downloads\mongodb-win32-x86_64-2.6.7\bin
C:\Users\kyle\Downloads\mongodb-win32-x86_64-2.6.7\bin> mongo.exe
```

A.5 *Compiling MongoDB from source*

Compiling MongoDB from source is recommended only for advanced users and developers. If all you want to do is operate on the bleeding edge, without having to compile, you can always download the nightly binaries for the latest revisions from the mongodb.org website.

That said, you may want to compile yourself. The trickiest part about compiling MongoDB is managing the various dependencies. The latest compilation instructions for each platform can be found at www.mongodb.org/about/contributors/tutorial/build-mongodb-from-source.

A.6 *Troubleshooting*

MongoDB is easy to install, but users occasionally experience minor problems. These usually manifest as error messages generated when trying to start the `mongod` daemon. Here we provide a list of the most common of these errors along with their resolutions.

A.6.1 *Wrong architecture*

If you try to run a binary compiled for a 64-bit system on a 32-bit machine, you'll see an error like the following:

```
bash: ./mongod: cannot execute binary file
```

On Windows 7, the message is more helpful:

```
This version of
C:\Users\kyle\Downloads\mongodb-win32-x86_64-2.6.7\bin\mongod.exe
is not compatible with the version of Windows you're running.
Check your computer's system information to see whether you need
a x86 (32-bit) or x64 (64-bit) version of the program, and then
contact the software publisher.
```

The solution in both cases is to download and then run the 32-bit binary instead. Binaries for both architectures are available on the MongoDB download site (www.mongodb .org/downloads).

A.6.2 *Nonexistent data directory*

MongoDB requires a directory for storing its data files. If the directory doesn't exist, you'll see an error like the following:

```
dbpath (/data/db/) does not exist, terminating
```

The solution is to create this directory. To see how, consult the preceding instructions for your OS.

A.6.3 *Lack of permissions*

If you're running on a Unix variant, you'll need to make sure that the user running the mongod executable has permissions to write to the data directory. Otherwise, you'll see this error

```
Permission denied: "/data/db/mongod.lock", terminating
```

or possibly this one:

```
Unable to acquire lock for lockfilepath: /data/db/mongod.lock, terminating
```

In either case, you can solve the problem by opening up permissions in the data directory using chmod or chown.

A.6.4   *Unable to bind to port*

MongoDB runs by default on port 27017. If another process, or another `mongod`, is bound to the same port, you'll see this error:

```
listen(): bind() failed errno:98
    Address already in use for socket: 0.0.0.0:27017
```

This issue has two possible solutions. The first is to find out what other process is running on port 27017 and then terminate it, provided that it isn't being used for some other purpose. One way of finding which process listens to port number 27017 is the following:

```
sudo lsof -i :27017
```

The output of the `lsof` command will also reveal the process ID of the process that listens to port number 27017, which can be used for killing the process using the `kill` command.

Alternatively, run `mongod` on a different port using the `--port` flag, which seems to be a better and easier solution. Here's how to run MongoDB on port 27018:

```
mongod --port 27018
```

A.7   *Basic configuration options*

Here's a brief overview of the flags most commonly used when running MongoDB:

- `--dbpath`—The path to the directory where the data files are to be stored. This defaults to /data/db and is useful if you want to store your MongoDB data elsewhere.
- `--logpath`—The path to the file where log output should be directed. Log output will be printed to standard output (`stdout`) by default.
- `--port`—The port that MongoDB listens on. If not specified, it's set to 27017.
- `--rest`—This flag enables a simple REST interface that enhances the server's default web console. The web console is always available 1000 port numbers above the port the server listens on. Thus if the server is listening at `localhost` on port 27017, then the web console will be available at http://localhost:28017. Spend some time exploring the web console and the commands it exposes; you can discover a lot about a live MongoDB server this way.
- `--fork`—Detaches the process to run as a daemon. Note that `fork` works only on Unix variants. Windows users seeking similar functionality should look at the instructions for running MongoDB as a proper Windows service. These are available at www.mongodb.org.

Those are the most important of the MongoDB startup flags. Here's an example of their use on the command line:

```
$ mongod --dbpath /var/local/mongodb --logpath /var/log/mongodb.log
--port 27018 --rest --fork
```

Note that it's also possible to specify all of these options in a config file. Create a new text file (we'll call it mongodb.conf) and you can specify the config file equivalent[1] of all the preceding options:

```
storage:
    dbPath: "/var/local/mongodb"
systemLog:
    destination: file
    path: "/var/log/mongodb.log"
net:
    port: 27018
    http:
        RESTInterfaceEnabled: true
processManagement:
    fork: true
```

You can then invoke mongod using the config file with the -f option:

```
$ mongod -f mongodb.conf
```

If you ever find yourself connected to a MongoDB and wondering which options were used at startup, you can get a list of them by running the getCmdLineOpts command:

```
> use admin
> db.runCommand({getCmdLineOpts: 1})
```

A.8   Installing Ruby

A number of the examples in this book are written in Ruby, so to run them yourself, you'll need a working Ruby installation. This means installing the Ruby interpreter as well as Ruby's package manager, RubyGems.

You should use a newer version of Ruby, such as 1.9.3 or preferably 2.2.3, which is the current stable version. Version 1.8.7 is still used by many people, and it works well with MongoDB, but the newer versions of Ruby offer advantages such as better character encoding that make it worthwhile to upgrade.

A.8.1   Linux and Mac OS X

Ruby comes installed by default on Max OS X and on a number of Linux distributions. You may want to check whether you have a recent version by running

```
ruby -v
```

If the command isn't found, or if you're running a version older than 1.8.7, you'll want to install or upgrade. There are detailed instructions for installing Ruby on Mac OS X as well as on a number of Unix variants at https://www.ruby-lang.org/en/downloads/

---

[1] As of 2.6, MongoDB uses a YAML config file format. See docs.mongodb.org/manual/reference/configuration-options for the current documentation on the available options.

(you may have to scroll down the page to see the instructions for the various plat-forms). Most package managers (such as MacPorts and Aptitude) also maintain a recent version of Ruby, and they're likely to be the easiest avenue for getting a work-ing Ruby installation.

In addition to the Ruby interpreter, you need the Ruby package manager, Ruby-Gems, to install the MongoDB Ruby driver. Find out whether RubyGems is installed by running the gem command:

```
gem -v
```

You can install RubyGems through a package manager, but most users download the latest version and use the included installer. You can find instructions for doing this at https://rubygems.org/pages/download.

A.8.2   *Windows*

By far, the easiest way to install Ruby and RubyGems on Windows is to use the Windows Ruby Installer. The installer can be found here: http://rubyinstaller.org/downloads. When you run the executable, a wizard will guide you through the installation of both Ruby and RubyGems.

In addition to installing Ruby, you can install the Ruby DevKit, which permits the easy compilation of Ruby C extensions. The MongoDB Ruby driver's BSON library may optionally use these extensions.

appendix B
Design patterns

The early chapters of this book implicitly advocate a certain set of design patterns. Here I'll summarize those patterns and augment them with a few patterns that fall outside the flow of the text.

B.1 Embed vs. reference

Suppose you're building a simple application in MongoDB that stores blog posts and comments. How do you represent this data? Do you embed the comments in their respective blog post documents? Or is it better to create two collections, one for posts and the other for comments, and then relate the comments to the posts with an object ID reference (_id)?

This is the problem of embedding versus referencing, and it's a common source of confusion for new users of MongoDB. Fortunately, there's a simple rule of thumb that works for most schema design scenarios: embed when the child objects never appear outside the context of their parent. Otherwise, store the child objects in a separate collection.

What does this mean for blog posts and comments? It depends on the application. If the comments always appear within a blog post, and if they don't need to be ordered in arbitrary ways (by post date, comment rank, and so on), then embedding is fine. But if, say, you want to be able to display the most recent comments, regardless of which post they appear on, then you'll want to reference. Embedding may provide a slight performance advantage, but referencing is far more flexible.

B.2 One-to-many

As stated in the previous section, you can represent a one-to-many relationship by either embedding or referencing. You should embed when the many object intrinsically belongs with its parent and rarely changes. The schema for a how-to application illustrates this well. The steps in each guide can be represented as an array of subdocuments because these steps are an intrinsic part of the guide and rarely change:

```
{ title: "How to soft-boil an egg",
        steps: [
        { desc: "Bring a pot of water to boil.",
          materials: ["water", "eggs"] },
        { desc: "Gently add the eggs a cook for four minutes.",
          materials: ["egg timer"]},
        { desc: "Cool the eggs under running water." },
        ]
}
```

Please note that if you want to guarantee the order of an array, you might need to add another attribute that will hold the order of the array elements, because some languages don't guarantee the order of an array.

When the two related entities will appear independently in the application, you'll want to relate them. Many articles on MongoDB suggest that embedding comments in blog posts is a good idea. But relating is far more flexible. For one thing, you can easily show users a list of all their comments—using sparse indexes might help here because sparse indexes only contain entries for documents that have the indexed field. You can also show all recent comments across all posts. These features, considered de rigueur for most sites, aren't possible with embedded documents at this time.[1] You typically relate documents using an object ID. Here's a sample post:

```
{ _id: ObjectId("4d650d4cf32639266022018d"),
  title: "Cultivating herbs",
  text: "Herbs require occasional watering..."
}
```

And here's a comment, related by the post_id field:

```
{ _id: ObjectId("4d650d4cf32639266022ac01"),
  post_id: ObjectId("4d650d4cf32639266022018d"),
  username: "zjones",
  text: "Indeed, basil is a hearty herb!"
}
```

The post and the comment live in their own collections, and it takes two queries to display a post with its comments. Because you'll query comments on their post_id field, you'll want an index there:

```
db.comments.createIndex({post_id: 1})
```

We used this one-to-many pattern extensively in chapters 4, 5, and 6; look there for more examples.

---

[1] There's a popular feature request for *virtual collections*, which could provide the best of both worlds. See http://jira.mongodb.org/browse/SERVER-142 to track this issue.

B.3 Many-to-many

In RDBMSs, you use a join table to represent many-to-many relationships; in MongoDB, you use array keys. You can see a clear example of this technique earlier in the book where we relate products and categories. Each product contains an array of category IDs, and both products and categories get their own collections. If you have two simple category documents

```
{ _id: ObjectId("4d6574baa6b804ea563c132a"),
  title: "Epiphytes"
}
{ _id: ObjectId("4d6574baa6b804ea563c459d"),
  title: "Greenhouse flowers"
}
```

then a product belonging to both categories will look like this:

```
{ _id: ObjectId("4d6574baa6b804ea563ca982"),
  name: "Dragon Orchid",
  category_ids: [ ObjectId("4d6574baa6b804ea563c132a"),
                  ObjectId("4d6574baa6b804ea563c459d") ]
}
```

For efficient queries, you should index the array of category IDs:

```
db.products.createIndex({category_ids: 1})
```

Then, to find all products in the Epiphytes category, match against the category_id field:

```
db.products.find({category_id: ObjectId("4d6574baa6b804ea563c132a")})
```

And to return all category documents related to the Dragon Orchid product, first get the list of that product's category IDs:

```
product = db.products.findOne({_id: ObjectId("4d6574baa6b804ea563c132a")})
```

Then query the categories collection using the $in operator:

```
db.categories.find({_id: {$in: product['category_ids']}})
```

You'll notice that finding the categories requires two queries, whereas the product search takes just one. This optimizes for the common case, as you're more likely to search for products in a category than the other way around.

B.4 Trees

Like MySQL, MongoDB has no built-in facility for tree representation and traversal—Oracle has CONNECT BY and PostgreSQL has WITH RECURSIVE for performing a tree traversal. Thus, if you need tree-like behavior in MongoDB, you've got to roll your own solution. I presented a solution to the category hierarchy problem in chapters 5 and 6.

The strategy there was to store a snapshot of the category's ancestors within each category document. This denormalization makes updates more complicated but greatly simplifies reads.

Alas, the denormalized ancestor approach isn't great for all problems. Another common tree scenario is the online forum, where hundreds of messages are frequently nested many levels deep. There's too much nesting, and too much data, for the ancestor approach to work well here. A good alternative is the *materialized path.*

Following the materialized path pattern, each node in the tree contains a `path` field. This field stores the concatenation of each of the node's ancestor's IDs, and root-level nodes have a null `path` because they have no ancestors. Let's flesh out an example to see how this works. First, look at the comment thread in figure B.1. This represents a few questions and answers in thread about Greek history.

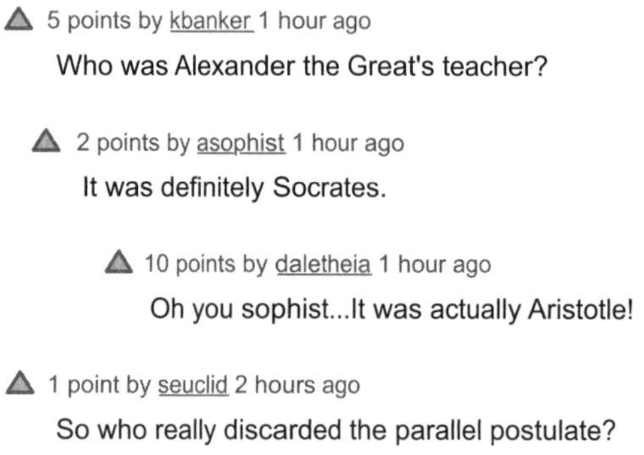

▲ 5 points by kbanker 1 hour ago

    Who was Alexander the Great's teacher?

  ▲ 2 points by asophist 1 hour ago

      It was definitely Socrates.

    ▲ 10 points by daletheia 1 hour ago

        Oh you sophist...It was actually Aristotle!

▲ 1 point by seuclid 2 hours ago

    So who really discarded the parallel postulate?

Figure B.1   Threaded comments in a forum

Let's see how these comments look as documents organized with a materialized path. The first is a root-level comment, so the `path` is `null`:

```
{  _id: ObjectId("4d692b5d59e212384d95001"),
   depth: 0,
   path: null,
   created: ISODate("2011-02-26T17:18:01.251Z"),
   username: "plotinus",
   body: "Who was Alexander the Great's teacher?",
   thread_id: ObjectId("4d692b5d59e212384d95223a")
}
```

The other root-level question, the one by user `seuclid`, will have the same structure. More illustrative are the follow-up comments to the question about Alexander the Great's teacher. Examine the first of these, and note that `path` contains the `_id` of the immediate parent:

```
{  _id: ObjectId("4d692b5d59e212384d951002"),
   depth: 1,
   path: "4d692b5d59e212384d95001",
```

```
    created: ISODate("2011-02-26T17:21:01.251Z"),
    username: "asophist",
    body: "It was definitely Socrates.",
    thread_id: ObjectId("4d692b5d59e212384d95223a")
}
```

The next deeper comment's path contains both the IDs of the original and immediate parents, in that order and separated by a colon:

```
{ _id: ObjectId("4d692b5d59e212384d95003"),
  depth: 2,
  path: "4d692b5d59e212384d95001:4d692b5d59e212384d951002",
  created: ISODate("2011-02-26T17:21:01.251Z"),
  username: "daletheia",
  body: "Oh you sophist...It was actually Aristotle!",
  thread_id: ObjectId("4d692b5d59e212384d95223a")
}
```

At a minimum, you'll want indexes on the thread_id and path fields, as you'll always query on exactly one of these fields:

```
db.comments.createIndex({thread_id: 1})
db.comments.createIndex({path: 1})
```

Now the question is how you go about querying and displaying the tree. One of the advantages of the materialized path pattern is that you query the database only once, whether you're displaying the entire comment thread or only a subtree within the thread. The query for the first of these is straightforward:

```
db.comments.find({thread_id: ObjectId("4d692b5d59e212384d95223a")})
```

The query for a particular subtree is subtler because it uses a prefix query (discussed in Chapter 5):

```
db.comments.find({path: /^4d692b5d59e212384d95001/})
```

This returns all comments with a path beginning with the specified string. This string represents the _id of the comment with the username plotinus, and if you examine the path field on each child comment, it's easy to see that they'll all satisfy the query. And they'll do so quickly because these prefix queries can use the index on path.

Getting the list of comments is easy—it only requires one database query. Displaying them is trickier because you need a list that preserves thread order. This requires a bit of client-side processing, which you can achieve with the following Ruby methods.[2]

---

[2] This book's source code includes a complete example of threaded comments with materialized paths using the display methods presented here.

The first method, `threaded_list`, builds a list of all root-level comments and a map that keys parent IDs to lists of child nodes:

```
def threaded_list(cursor, opts={})
  list      = []
  child_map = {}
  start_depth = opts[:start_depth] || 0
  cursor.each do |comment|
    if comment['depth'] == start_depth
      list.push(comment)
    else
      matches = comment['path'].match(/([d|w]+)$/)
      immediate_parent_id = matches[1]
      if immediate_parent_id
        child_map[immediate_parent_id] ||= []
        child_map[immediate_parent_id] << comment
      end
    end
  end
  assemble(list, child_map)
end
```

The `assemble` method takes the list of root nodes and the child map and then builds a new list in display order:

```
def assemble(comments, map)
  list = []
  comments.each do |comment|
    list.push(comment)
    child_comments = map[comment['_id'].to_s]
    if child_comments
      list.concat(assemble(child_comments, map))
    end
  end
  list
end
```

To print the comments, you merely iterate over the list, indenting appropriately for each comment's depth:

```
def print_threaded_list(cursor, opts={})
  threaded_list(cursor, opts).each do |item|
    indent = "  " * item['depth']
    puts indent + item['body'] + " #{item['path']}"
  end
end
```

Querying for the comments and printing them is then straightforward:

```
cursor = @comments.find.sort("created")
print_threaded_list(cursor)
```

B.5 Worker queues

You can implement worker queues in MongoDB using either standard or capped collections (discussed in chapter 4). In both cases, the findAndModify command will permit you to process queue entries atomically.

A queue entry requires a state and a timestamp plus any remaining fields to contain the payload. The state can be encoded as a string, but an integer is more space-efficient. We'll use 0 and 1 to indicate *processed* and *unprocessed*, respectively. The timestamp is the standard BSON date. And the payload here is a simple plaintext message but could be anything in principle:

```
{ state: 0,
  created: ISODate("2011-02-24T16:29:36.697Z"),
  message: "hello world" }
```

You'll need to declare an index that allows you to efficiently fetch the oldest unprocessed entry (FIFO). A compound index on state and created fits the bill:

```
db.queue.createIndex({state: 1, created: 1})
```

You then use findAndModify to return the next entry and mark it as processed:

```
q = {state: 0}
s = {created: 1}
u = {$set: {state: 1}}
db.queue.findAndModify({query: q, sort: s, update: u})
```

If you're using a standard collection, be sure to remove old queue entries. It's possible to remove them at processing time using findAndModify's {remove: true} option. But some applications may want to postpone removal for a later time, once the processing is complete.

Capped collections may also serve as the basis for a worker queue. Without the default index on _id, a capped collection has potentially faster insert speed, but the difference will be negligible for most applications. The other potential advantage is automatic deletion. But this feature is a double-edged sword: you'll have to make sure that the collection is large enough to prevent unprocessed entries from aging out. Thus if you do use a capped collection, make it extra-large. The ideal collection size will depend on your queue write throughput and the average payload size.

Once you've decided on the size of capped collection to use, the schema, index, and findAndModify will be identical to those of the standard collection just described.

B.6 Dynamic attributes

MongoDB's document data model is useful for representing entities whose attributes vary. Products are the canonical example of this, and you saw some ways of modeling these attributes earlier in the book. One viable way to model these attributes is to scope them to a subdocument. In a single `products` collection, you can then store disparate product types. You might store a set of headphones

```
{ _id: ObjectId("4d669c225d3a52568ce07646")
  sku: "ebd-123"
  name: "Hi-Fi Earbuds",
  type: "Headphone",
  attrs: { color: "silver",
           freq_low: 20,
           freq_hi: 22000,
           weight: 0.5
         }
}
```

and an SSD drive:

```
{ _id: ObjectId("4d669c225d3a52568ce07646")
  sku: "ssd-456"
  name: "Mini SSD Drive",
  type: "Hard Drive",
  attrs: { interface: "SATA",
           capacity: 1.2 * 1024 * 1024 * 1024,
           rotation: 7200,
           form_factor: 2.5
         }
}
```

If you need to frequently query on these attributes, you can create sparse indexes for them. For example, you can optimize for range queries in headphone frequency response:

```
db.products.createIndex({"attrs.freq_low": 1, "attrs.freq_hi": 1},
  {sparse: true})
```

You can also efficiently search hard disks by rotation speed with the following index:

```
db.products.createIndex({"attrs.rotation": 1}, {sparse: true})
```

The overall strategy here is to scope your attributes for readability and app discoverability and to use sparse indexes to keep null values out of the indexes.

If your attributes are completely unpredictable, you can't build a separate index for each one. You have to use a different strategy—in this case, arrays of name-value pairs—as illustrated by the following sample document:

```
{ _id: ObjectId("4d669c225d3a52568ce07646")
  sku: "ebd-123"
  name: "Hi-Fi Earbuds",
  type: "Headphone",
  attrs: [ {n: "color", v: "silver"},
           {n: "freq_low", v: 20},
           {n: "freq_hi", v: 22000},
           {n: "weight", v: 0.5}
         ]
}
```

Here `attrs` points to an array of subdocuments. Each of these documents has two values, `n` and `v`, corresponding to each dynamic attribute's name and value. This normalized representation allows you to index these attributes using a single compound index:

```
db.products.createIndex({"attrs.n": 1, "attrs.v": 1})
```

You can then query using these attributes, but to do that, you must use the `$elem-Match` query operator:

```
db.products.find({attrs: {$elemMatch: {n: "color", v: "silver"}}})
```

Note that this strategy incurs a lot of overhead because it requires storing the key names in the index. It'd be important to test this for performance on a representative data set before going into production.

B.7 Transactions

MongoDB doesn't provide ACID guarantees over a series of operations (however, individual operations are atomic), and no equivalent of RDBMSs' `BEGIN`, `COMMIT`, and `ROLLBACK` semantics exists. When you need these features, use a different database (either for the data that needs proper transactions or for the application as a whole) or a different design like executing a series of operations one by one. Still MongoDB supports atomic, durable updates on individual documents and consistent reads, and these features, though primitive, can be used to implement transaction-like behavior in an application.

You saw an extended example of this in chapter 6's treatments of order authorization and inventory management. And the worker queue implementation earlier in this appendix could easily be modified to support rollback. In both cases, the foundation for transaction-like behavior is the ever versatile `findAndModify` command, which is used to atomically manipulate a `state` field on one or more documents.

The transactional strategy used in all these cases can be described as *compensation-driven*.[3] The compensation process in abstract works like this:

1. Atomically modify a document's state.
2. Perform some unit of work, which may include atomically modifying other documents.
3. Ensure that the system as a whole (all documents involved) is in a valid state. If so, mark the transaction complete; otherwise, revert each document to its pre-transaction state.

---

[3] Two pieces of literature covering compensation-driven transactions are worth studying. The original is Garcia-Molina and Salem's "Sagas" paper (http://mng.bz/73is). The less formal but no less interesting "Your Coffee Shop Doesn't Use Two-Phase Commit" by Gregor Hohpe (http://mng.bz/kpAq) is also a great read.

It's worth noting that the compensation-driven strategy is all but necessary for long-running and multistep transactions. The whole process of authorizing, shipping, and canceling an order is one example. For these cases, even an RDBMS with full transactional semantics must implement a similar strategy.

There may be no getting around certain applications' requirements for multi-object ACID transactions. But with the right patterns, MongoDB can pull some transactional weight and might support the transactional semantic your application needs.

B.8 *Locality and precomputation*

MongoDB is frequently billed as an analytics database, and plenty of users store analytics data in MongoDB. A combination of atomic increments and rich documents seems to work best. For example, here's a document representing total page views for each day of the month along with the total for the month as a whole. For brevity, the following document contains totals only for the first five days of the month:

```
{ base: "org.mongodb", path: "/",
  total: 99234,
  days: {
    "1": 4500,
    "2": 4324,
    "3": 2700,
    "4": 2300,
    "5": 0
  }
}
```

You can update the totals for the day and month with a simple targeted update using the `$inc` operator:

```
use stats-2011
db.sites-nov.update({ base: "org.mongodb", path: "/" },
  $inc: {total: 1, "days.5": 1 });
```

Take a moment to notice the collection and database names. The collection, sites-nov, is scoped to a given month, and the database, stats-2011, to a particular year. This gives the application good locality. When you query for recent visits, you're always querying a single collection that's relatively small compared with the overall analytics history. If you need to delete data, you can drop a time-scoped collection rather than removing some subset of documents from a larger collection. That latter operation may result in on-disk fragmentation.

The other principle at work here is *precomputation*. Sometime near the beginning of the month, you insert a template document with zeroed values for each day of the month. As a result, the document will never change size as you increment the counters therein because you'll never actually add fields; you'll only change their values in place. This is important because it keeps the document from being relocated on disk as you write to it. Relocation is slow and often results in fragmentation.

B.9   Antipatterns

MongoDB lacks constraints, which can lead to poorly organized data. Here are a few issues commonly found in problematic production deployments.

B.9.1   Careless indexing

When users experience performance problems, it's not unusual to discover a whole slew of unused or inefficient indexes. The most efficient set of indexes for an application will always be based on an analysis of the queries being run. Be disciplined about the optimization methods presented in chapter 7.

Keep in mind that when you have unnecessary indexes, inserts and updates will take longer because the related indexes have to be updated. As a rule of thumb, you should periodically reexamine your indexes to make sure that you're using the right ones for the right job.

B.9.2   Motley types

Ensure that keys of the same name within a collection all share the same type. If you store a phone number, for instance, store it consistently, either as a string or an integer (but not as both). The mixing of types in a single key's value makes the application logic complex, and makes BSON documents difficult to parse in certain strongly typed languages.

B.9.3   Bucket collections

Collections should be used for one type of entity only; don't put products and users in the same collection. Because collections are cheap, each type within your application should get its own collection. As a side effect, this also has huge concurrency gains.

B.9.4   Large, deeply nested documents

There are two misunderstandings about MongoDB's document data model. One is that you should never build relationships between collections, but rather represent all relationships in the same document. This frequently degenerates into a mess, but users nevertheless sometimes try it. The second misunderstanding stems from an overly literal interpretation of the word *document*. A document, these users reason, is a single entity like a real-life document. This leads to large documents that are difficult to query and update, let alone comprehend.

The bottom line here is that you should keep documents small (well under 100 KB per document unless you're storing raw binary data) and that you shouldn't nest more than a few levels deep. A smaller size makes document updates cheaper because in the case where a document needs to be rewritten on disk completely, there's less to rewrite. The other advantage is that the documents remain comprehensible, which makes life easier for developers needing to understand the data model.

It's also a good practice to put raw binary data into a separate collection and reference it by `_id`. Appendix C will help you deal with binary data.

B.9.5 *One collection per user*

It's rarely a good idea to build out one collection per user. One problem with this is that the namespaces (indexes plus collections) max out at 24,000 by default. Once you grow beyond that, you have to allocate a new database. In addition, each collection and its indexes introduce extra overhead, making this strategy a waste of space.

B.9.6 *Unshardable collections*

If you expect a collection to grow large enough to merit sharding, be sure that you can eventually shard it. A collection is shardable if you can define an efficient shard key for that collection. Review the tips in chapter 12 on choosing a shard key.

appendix C
Binary data and GridFS

For storing images, thumbnails, audio, and other binary files, many applications rely on the filesystem only. Although filesystems provide fast access to files, filesystem storage can also lead to organizational chaos. Consider that most filesystems limit the number of files per directory. If you have millions of files to keep track of, you need to devise a strategy for organizing files into multiple directories. Another difficulty involves metadata. Because the file metadata is still stored in a database, performing an accurate backup of the files and their metadata can be incredibly complicated.

For certain use cases, it may make sense to store files in the database itself because doing so simplifies file organization and backup. In MongoDB, you can use the BSON binary type to store any kind of binary data. This data type corresponds to the RDBMS *BLOB* (*binary large object*) type, and it's the basis for two flavors of binary object storage provided by MongoDB.

The first uses one document per file and is best for smaller binary objects. If you need to catalog a large number of thumbnails or binary MD5s, using single-document binary storage can make life much easier. On the other hand, you might want to store large images or audio files. In this case, GridFS, a MongoDB API for storing binary objects of any size, would be a better choice. In the next two sections, you'll see complete examples of both storage techniques.

C.1 Simple binary storage

BSON includes a first-class type for binary data. You can use this type to store binary objects directly inside MongoDB documents. The only limit on object size is the document size limit itself, which is 16 MB since MongoDB v2.0. Because large documents like this can tax system resources, you're encouraged to use GridFS for any binary objects you want to store that are larger than 1 MB.

We'll look at two reasonable uses of binary object storage in single documents. First, you'll see how to store an image thumbnail. Then, you'll see how to store the accompanying MD5.

C.1.1 Storing a thumbnail

Imagine you need to store a collection of image thumbnails. The code is straightforward. First, you get the image's filename, canyon-thumb.jpg, and then read the data into a local variable. Next, you wrap the raw binary data as a BSON binary object using the Ruby driver's BSON::Binary constructor:

```
require 'rubygems'
require 'mongo'
image_filename = File.join(File.dirname(__FILE__), "canyon-thumb.jpg")
image_data = File.open(image_filename).read
bson_image_data = BSON::Binary.new(image_data)
```

All that remains is to build a simple document to contain the binary data and then insert it into the database:

```
doc = {"name" => "monument-thumb.jpg",
       "data" => bson_image_data }
@con = Mongo::Client.new(['localhost:27017'], :database => 'images')
@thumbnails = @con[:thumbnails]
result = @thumbnails.insert_one(doc)
```

To extract the binary data, fetch the document. In Ruby, the to_s method unpacks the data into a binary string, and you can use this to compare the saved data to the original:

```
@thumbnails.find({"name" => "monument-thumb-jpg"}).each do |doc|
  if image_data == doc["data"].to_s
    puts "Stored image is equal to the original file!"
  end
end
```

If you run the preceding script, you'll see a message indicating that the two files are indeed the same.

C.1.2 Storing an MD5

It's common to store a checksum as binary data, and this marks another potential use of the BSON binary type. Here's how you can generate an MD5 of the thumbnail and add it to the document just stored:

```
require 'md5'
md5 = Digest::MD5.file(image_filename).digest
bson_md5 = BSON::Binary.new(md5, :md5)
@thumbnails.update_one({:_id => @image_id}, {"$set" => {:md5 => bson_md5}})
```

Note that when creating the BSON binary object, you tag the data with :md5. The subtype is an extra field on the BSON binary type that indicates what kind of binary data is being stored. This field is entirely optional, though, and has no effect on how the database stores or interprets the data.[1]

It's easy to query for the document just stored, but do notice that you exclude the data field to keep the return document small and readable:

```
> use images
> db.thumbnails.findOne({}, {data: 0})
{
  "_id" : ObjectId("4d608614238d3b4ade000001"),
  "md5" : BinData(5,"K1ud3EUjT49wdMdkOGjbDg=="),
  "name" : "monument-thumb.jpg"
}
```

See that the MD5 field is clearly marked as binary data (briefly mentioned in Table 5.6) with the subtype and raw payload. Keep in mind that MongoDB sorts BinData first by the length or size of the data, second by the BSON one-byte subtype, and last by the data, performing a byte-by-byte comparison.

C.2 GridFS

GridFS is a convention for storing files of arbitrary size in MongoDB. The GridFS specification is implemented by all the official drivers and by MongoDB's mongofiles tool, ensuring consistent access across platforms. GridFS is useful for storing large binary objects in the database. It's frequently fast enough to serve these objects as well, and the storage method is conducive to streaming.

The term *GridFS* may lead to confusion, so two clarifications are worth making right off the bat. The first is that GridFS isn't an intrinsic feature of MongoDB. As mentioned, it's a *convention* that all the official drivers (and some tools) use to manage large binary objects in the database. Second, it's important to clarify that GridFS doesn't have the rich semantics of bona fide filesystems. For instance, there's no protocol for locking and concurrency, and this limits the GridFS interface to simple put, get, and delete operations. This means that if you want to update a file, you need to delete it and then put the new version.

GridFS works by dividing a large file into small, 255 KB chunks and then storing each chunk as a separate document—versions prior to MongoDB v2.4.10 use 256 KB chunks. By default, these chunks are stored in a collection called fs.chunks. Once the chunks are written, the file's metadata is stored in a single document in another collection called fs.files. Figure C.1 contains a simplistic illustration of this

---

[1] This wasn't always technically true. The deprecated default subtype of 2 indicated that the attached binary data also included four extra bytes to indicate the size, and this did affect a few database commands. The current default subtype is 0, and all subtypes now store the binary payload the same way. Subtype can therefore be seen as a kind of lightweight tag to be optionally used by application developers.

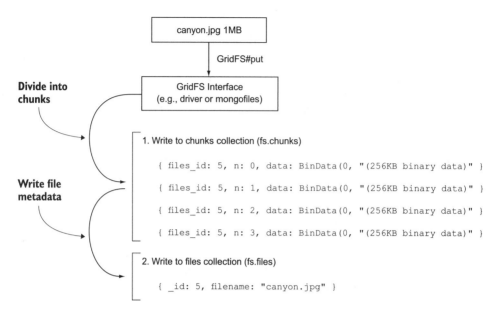

Figure C.1   Storing a file with GridFS using 256 KB chunks on a MongoDB server prior to v2.4.10

process applied to a theoretical 1 MB file called canyon.jpg. Note that the use of the term *chunks* in the context of GridFS isn't related to the use of the term *chunks* in the context of sharding.

That should be enough theory to use GridFS.[2] Next we'll see GridFS in practice through the Ruby GridFS API and the mongofiles utility.

C.2.1   *GridFS in Ruby*

Earlier you stored a small image thumbnail. The thumbnail took up only 10 KB and was thus ideal for keeping in a single document. The original image is almost 2 MB in size, and is therefore much more appropriate for GridFS storage. Here you'll store the original using Ruby's GridFS API. First, you connect to the database and then initialize a Grid object, which takes a reference to the database where the GridFS file will be stored.

Next, you open the original image file, canyon.jpg, for reading. The most basic GridFS interface uses methods to put and get a file. Here you use the Grid#put method, which takes either a string of binary data or an IO object, such as a file pointer. You pass in the file pointer and the data is written to the database.

---

[2] You can find more information about GridFS at http://docs.mongodb.org/manual/core/gridfs/ and at http://docs.mongodb.org/manual/reference/gridfs/.

The method returns the file's unique object ID using the latest Ruby MongoDB driver:

```
require 'rubygems'
require 'mongo'
include Mongo
$client = Mongo::Client.new([ '127.0.0.1:27017' ], :database => 'images')
fs = $client.database.fs
$file = File.open("canyon.jpg")
$file_id = fs.upload_from_stream("canyon.jpg", $file)
$file.close
```

As stated, GridFS uses two collections for storing file data. The first, normally called `fs.files`, keeps each file's metadata. The second collection, `fs.chunks`, stores one or more chunks of binary data for each file. Let's briefly examine these from the shell.

Switch to the `images` database, and query for the first entry in the `fs.files` collection. You'll see the metadata for the file you just stored:

```
> use images
> db.fs.files.find({filename: "canyon.jpg"}).pretty()
{
  "_id" : ObjectId("5612e19a530a6919ed000001"),
  "chunkSize" : 261120,
  "uploadDate" : ISODate("2015-10-05T20:46:18.849Z"),
  "contentType" : "binary/octet-stream",
  "filename" : "canyon.jpg",
  "length" : 281,
  "md5" : "597d619c415a4db144732aed24b6ff0b"
}
```

These are the minimum required attributes for every GridFS file. Most are self-explanatory. You can see that this file is about 2 MB and is divided into chunks 256 KB in size, which means that it was from a MongoDB server prior to v2.4.10. You'll also notice an MD5. The GridFS spec requires a checksum to ensure that the stored file is the same as the original.

Each chunk stores the object ID of its file in a field called `files_id`. Thus you can easily count the number of chunks this file uses:

```
> db.fs.chunks.count({"files_id" : ObjectId("4d606588238d3b4471000001")})
8
```

Given the chunk size and the total file size, eight chunks are exactly what you should expect. The contents of the chunks themselves are easy to see, too. As earlier, you'll want to exclude the data to keep the output readable. This query returns the first of the eight chunks, as indicated by the value of n:

```
> db.fs.chunks.findOne({files_id: ObjectId("4d606588238d3b4471000001")},
        {data: 0})
{
  "_id" : ObjectId("4d606588238d3b4471000002"),
```

```
  "n" : 0,
  "files_id" : ObjectId("4d606588238d3b4471000001")
}
```

Reading GridFS files is as easy as writing them. In the following example, you create a text file on-the-fly, give it a name, and store it using GridFS. You then find it in the database using a find_one() statement that returns a Mongo::Grid::File object. Then you have to get the file ID from the Mongo::Grid::File object to use it and retrieve the text file from the database, which is saved using the perfectCopy filename:

```
require 'rubygems'
require 'mongo'
include Mongo

$client = Mongo::Client.new([ '127.0.0.1:27017' ], :database => 'garden')
fs = $client.database.fs

# To create a text file with raw data
file = Mongo::Grid::File.new('I am a NEW file', :filename => 'aFile.txt')
$client.database.fs.insert_one(file)

# Select the file from scratch
$fileObj = $client.database.fs.find_one(:filename => 'aFile.txt')
$file_id = $fileObj.id

# And download it
$file_to_write = File.open('perfectCopy', 'w')
fs.download_to_stream($file_id, $file_to_write)
```

You can then verify for yourself that perfectCopy is a text file with the correct data in it:

```
$ cat perfectCopy
I am a NEW filei
```

That's the basics of reading and writing GridFS files from a driver. The various GridFS APIs vary slightly, but with the foregoing examples and the basic knowledge of how GridFS works, you should have no trouble making sense of your driver's docs. At the time of writing, the latest Ruby MongoDB Driver is v2.1.1.

C.2.2 *GridFS with mongofiles*

The MongoDB distribution includes a handy utility called mongofiles for listing, putting, getting, and deleting GridFS files using the command line. For example, you can list the GridFS files in the images database:

```
$ mongofiles -d images list
connected to: 127.0.0.1
canyon.jpg  2004828
```

You can also easily add files. Here's how you can add the copy of the image that you wrote with the Ruby script:

```
$ mongofiles -d images put canyon-copy.jpg
connected to: 127.0.0.1
added file: { _id: ObjectId('4d61783326758d4e6727228f'),
              filename: "canyon-copy.jpg",
              chunkSize: 262144, uploadDate: new Date(1298233395296),
              md5: "9725ad463b646ccbd287be87cb9b1f6e", length: 2004828 }
```

You can again list the files to verify that the copy was written:

```
$ mongofiles -d images list
connected to: 127.0.0.1
canyon.jpg  2004828
canyon-copy.jpg  2004828
```

mongofiles supports a number of options, and you can view them with the --help parameter:

```
$ mongofiles --help
Usage:
  mongofiles <options> <command> <filename or _id>

Manipulate gridfs files using the command line.

Possible commands include:
    list      - list all files; 'filename' is an optional prefix which listed
                filenames must begin with
    search    - search all files; 'filename' is a substring which listed
                filenames must contain
    put       - add a file with filename 'filename'
    get       - get a file with filename 'filename'
    get_id    - get a file with the given '_id'
    delete    - delete all files with filename 'filename'
    delete_id - delete a file with the given '_id'

See http://docs.mongodb.org/manual/reference/program/mongofiles/ for more
    information.

general options:
      --help                    print usage
      --version                 print the tool version and exit

verbosity options:
  -v, --verbose                 more detailed log output (include multiple times for more
                                verbosity, e.g. -vvvvv)
      --quiet                   hide all log output

connection options:
  -h, --host=                   mongodb host to connect to (setname/host1,host2 for
                                replica sets)
      --port=                   server port (can also use --host hostname:port)

authentication options:
  -u, --username=               username for authentication
  -p, --password=               password for authentication
```

```
     --authenticationDatabase=   database that holds the user's credentials
     --authenticationMechanism=  authentication mechanism to use

storage options:
  -d, --db=                      database to use (default is 'test')
  -l, --local=                   local filename for put|get
  -t, --type=                    content/MIME type for put (optional)
  -r, --replace                  remove other files with same name after put
      --prefix=                  GridFS prefix to use (default is 'fs')
      --writeConcern=      write concern options e.g. --writeConcern majority,
                           --writeConcern '{w: 3, wtimeout: 500, fsync: true, j:
                           true}' (defaults to 'majority')
```

index

Symbols

. (dot operator), with queries
  108–109
. character 88, 93
@tweets variable 67
$** field 257
$ character 57, 93, 193
=> character 55
> character 32

Numerics

-9 command-line option 387
10gen, subscription services 5–6
32-bit integer type 116
64-bit integer type 116

A

ad hoc queries 10
$add function 142
additionalOptions object 147
address already in use (error message)
  418
address_length field 112
addshard command 371
addShard() method 346
add_to_cart function 168–169, 175–177
$addToSet operator 137–138, 159–160,
  180, 185, 193
administrative tasks 402–405
  compaction and repair 403–405
  data imports and exports 402–403
  upgrading 405
aggregate() function 147, 252, 267

aggregation framework
  operators
    $sort 138
    $unwind 139
  overview 121
  pipeline performance 146
    aggregation cursor option 151
    allowDiskUse option 151
    explain() function 147
    options 147
  reshaping documents 140
    arithmetic functions 142
    date functions 142
    logical functions 143
    miscellaneous functions 145
    set operators 144
    string functions 141
  See also e-commerce aggregation example
agile development 22–23
AGPL (GNU-Affero General Public
  License) 15
$all operator 105–106
$allElementsTrue function 144
allowDiskUse option 147, 151
allPlans key 240
allPlansExecution mode 238
Amazon EC2 336
analytics 22–23
ancestor_list array 164
ancestors attribute 164
$and operator 106–107, 143
antipatterns 431–432
  bucket collections 431
  careless indexing 431
  large, deeply nested documents 431
  motley types 431

antipatterns *(continued)*
  one collection per user 432
  unshardable collections 432
$anyElementTrue function 144
Apache license 17
AppEngine 5
application data, storage of 337–338
arbiterOnly option 302, 316–317
arbiters 300
architecture
  hardware 379–380
  installation problems and 417
ArchLinux 413
arithmetic functions 142
Array type 116
arrays 110–112
  querying for, by size 112
  update operators for 183–187
atime, disabling 382
atomic document processing 171–179
  inventory management 174–179
    failure 178–179
    inventory fetcher 175–176
    inventory management 176–178
  order state transitions 172–174
    finishing order 173–174
    preparing order for checkout 172–173
    verifying order and authorization 173
attributes, dynamic 427–429
authentication 397–400
  basic, setting up 399–400
  removing user 400
  service authentication 398
  user authentication 398–399
authors field 254
average product ratings 162–163
average review, calculating 126
$avg function 127, 137

B

background indexing 215
backups 391–393
  data file-based backups 392–393
  for sharded clusters 373
  indexes 216
  MMS backups 393
  mongodump and mongorestore 391–392
balancer 373
BasicCursor 223, 240
Bayer, Rudolf 292
binary data, simple binary storage 433–435
  storing an MD5 434–435
  storing thumbnails 434
Binary JSON. *See* BSON

Binary type 116
–bind_ip option 394
$bit operator 186, 193
BLOB (binary large object) type 433
book index example 198–201
  compound index 199–201
  indexing rules 201
  simple index 198–199
books collection 255–256, 268
Boolean operators 106–107
Bostic, Keith 276
BSON (Binary JSON) 7
BSON files, restoring 392
bson gem 54
BSON types, min key and max key 351
BSON::Binary constructor 434
bsondump tool 18, 314, 389–390
bson_ext gem 54
BSON::OrderedHash class 109
BtreeCursor 225
B-trees 205–206
  estimating storage size 206
  maximum key size 206
  node structure 206
bucket collections 431
buildIndexes option 318

C

caching 23
Cahill, Michael 276
capacity planning 369
capped collections 88–90
careless indexing 431
case-insensitive search 246
Cassandra database 19
categorical failures 321
categories collection 99, 423
categories field 254
category hierarchy 163–166
category_id field 423
category_ids field 79–80
CentOS 413
certificate authentication 398
changelog collection 354
chmod 417
chown 417
chunks
  as data unit 339, 341
  collection storing chunk ranges 350
  counting 350
  pre-splitting for faster distribution 370
  problem when too large to split 365
  splitting and migrating of 342
clean failures 321

clocks 383
close field 224
cluster topology 377
$cmd collection 48
coarse granularity 362
collectionConfig.blockCompressor option 277
collections 7, 87–92
  as data unit 339
  automatic creation of 31
  capped collections 88–90
  drop() method 38
  listing 46
  managing collections 87–88
  sharding existing 369
  sharding within 341–342
  stats 47
  system collections 91–92
  time-to-live (TTL) collections 90–91
  See also system collections
collstats command 48, 390
command method 58
command shell 16
command-line options 418–419
commands 48
  implementation of 48
  runCommand() method 48
  running from MongoDB Ruby driver 58–59
Comma-Separated Values. *See* CSV (Comma-Separated Values)
commits 314
compact command 216, 404
compaction and repair 403–405
compensation-driven mechanisms 429
compiling MongoDB, from source 416
compound-key indexes 199–203, 242
$concat function 141–142
$cond function 143–144
config database 350
config servers 337–338
  deployment of 367
  two-phase commit and 338
config variable 63, 316
configdb option 346
configsvr option 346
configuration, basic options 418–419
connecting MongoDB Ruby driver 53–54
core server 15–16
CouchDB (Apache document-based data store) 22
count command 32
count field 125
count function 163
.count() function 153
count() command 40
countsByCategory collection 131

countsByRating variable 127
covering indexes, query patterns and 204, 242–243
CPU, performance issues and 380
createIndex() command 43, 211
createUser method 400
CSV (Comma-Separated Values) 18
curl utility 414
currentOp() command 214, 371
cursor field 223, 225
cursor option 147
cursor.explain() function 243
cursor.forEach() function 152
cursor.hasNext() function 152
cursor.itcount() function 152
cursor.map() function 152
cursor.next() function 152
cursor.pretty() function 37, 152
cursors
  BtreeCursor (explain output) 225
  MongoDB Ruby driver 56–57
cursor.toArray() function 152
custom import and export scripts 403

D

data centers, multiple with sharding 368
data directory 413
data imports and exports 402–403
database commands, running from MongoDB Ruby driver 58–59
database drivers 17
databases 84–87
  allocating initial data files 32
  as data unit 339
  automatic creation of 31
  creating 31
  data files and allocation 85–87
  document databases 22
  listing 46
  managing 84–85
  MongoDB shell and 31–32
  others vs. MongoDB 19–22
    document databases 22
    relational databases 21
    simple key-value stores 19–20
    sophisticated key-value stores 20–21
  relational databases 21
  stats 47
dataSize field 87
date functions 142
Date type 116
$dayOfMonth function 143
$dayOfWeek function 143
$dayOfYear function 143

db.collection.stats( ) function 335
db.currentOp() method 388, 393
db.currentOp(true) command 388
db.getReplicationInfo() method 310, 322
db.help() method 49
db.isMaster() method 95, 302
dbpath does not exit (error message) 417
dbPath option 277
–dbpath option 335
dbpath option 418
db.runCommand({top:1}) command 388
db.serverStatus() command 387
db.spreadsheets.createIndex() command 357
dbstats command 48, 390
db.stats() command 335, 388
Debian 413
dedicated text search engines, vs. text search 250–253
deeply nested documents 431
defragmenting, indexes 216
DELETE command 38
deleteIndexes command 212
deletes 57–58, 189
denormalizing data model 128
deployment environment 378–385
    architecture 379–380
    clocks 383
    CPU 380
    disks 380–381
    file descriptors 382–383
    filesystems 382
    journaling 383–385
    locks 381–382
    RAM 380
description field 77, 80
design patterns 421–432
    antipatterns 431–432
        bucket collections 431
        careless indexing 431
        large, deeply nested documents 431
        motley types 431
        one collection per user 432
        unshardable collections 432
    dynamic attributes 427–429
    embedding vs. referencing 421
    locality 430
    many-to-many relationships 423
    one-to-many relationships 421–422
    precomputation 430
    transactions 429–430
    trees 423–426
    worker queues 427
details attribute 78, 108

diagnostics
    commands 387–388
    tools 388–390
        bsondump 389–390
        mongosniff 389
        mongostat 388
        mongotop 388–389
        web console 390
    See also monitoring
dictionary (Python primitive) 17
–directoryperdb flag 381
disks, performance issues and 380–381
.distinct( ) function 153
$divide function 142
document data model 5–9
document databases 22
document updates 158–162
    modifying by operator 159–162
    modifying by replacement 159–162
document-oriented data 73–97
    bulk inserts 96
    collections 87–92
        capped 88–90
        managing 87–88
        system collections 91–92
        time-to-live (TTL) collections 90–91
    databases 84–87
        data files and allocation 85–87
        managing 84–85
    documents
        limits on 95–96
        serialization 92, 96
    numeric types 93–94
    schema design principles 74–75
    string values 93
    virtual types 95
    See also e-commerce data model, designing
documents 15
    advantages of 5, 8
    as data unit 339
    example social news site entry 6
    inserting in Ruby 55–56
    lack of enforced schema 8
    limits on 95–96
    nested 78–79
    relation to agile development 8
    reshaping 140
        arithmetic functions 142
        date functions 142
        logical functions 143
        miscellaneous functions 145
        set operators 144
        string functions 141
    serialization 92–96
dollar sign ($) 125

Double type 116
drivers 17
  how they work 59–61
  replication and 324–332
    connections and failover 324–326
    read scaling 328–330
    tagging 330
    write concern 327–328
  See also MongoDB Ruby driver
–drop flag 392
drop() method 38, 58
drop_collection method 59
dropDatabase() method 85
dropDups option 207–208
dropIndex() function 212, 257
dump directory 392
duplicate key error 207
durability 12–13
dynamic attributes 427–429
dynamic queries 10
Dynamo 20

E

each iterator 57
$each operator 183, 185, 193
e-commerce 9
e-commerce aggregation example 123
  product information summaries 125
    calculating average review 126
    counting reviews by rating 127
    joining collections 128
    $out operator 129
    $project operator 129
    $unwind operator 130
  user and order summaries 132
    finding best Manhattan customers 133
    summarizing sales by year and month 132
e-commerce data model, designing 75–84
  product reviews 83
  schema basics 76–80
    many-to-many relationships 79
    nested documents 78–79
    one-to-many relationships 79
    relationship structure 79–80
    slugs 78
  users and orders 82, 84
e-commerce queries 99–103
  findone vs. find queries 99–100
  partial match queries in users 102
  products, categories, and reviews 99–101
  querying specific ranges 102–103
  skip, limit, and sort query options 100–101
  users and orders 101–103

e-commerce updates 162–171
  average product ratings 162–163
  category hierarchy 163–166
  orders 168–171
  reviews 167–168
Elasticsearch in Action (Gheorghe, Hinman and Russo) 245
$elemMatch operator 110, 112, 429
email attribute 159
embedding, vs. referencing 421
emit() function 154
enablesharding command 347
engine option 277
engineConfig.cacheSize option 277
engineConfig.journalCompressor option 277
ensureIndex() function 43, 211–212
enterprise security features 402
entity-attribute-value pattern 9
$eq function 143
error messages 416
eventual consistency 19
executionStats keyword 41, 224, 243
$exists operator 106–107
expireAfterSeconds setting 91
explain() function 39, 44, 110, 147, 149–150, 222–224, 228, 230, 357–359
  output of 222
  viewing attempted query plans 238
exports, data. *See* data imports and exports

F

-f option 419
facets 250
failover 306, 313–322
Fedora 413
fields option 189
file descriptors 382–383
files_id field 437
fileSize field 87
filesystems 382
find method 17, 56, 99
find queries, vs. findone queries 99–100
find() command 258, 260–261, 263
findAndModify command 158, 171–173, 177–178, 188–189, 429
  for implementing a queue 427
  implementing transactional semantics with 174
findmnt command 382
findOne method 99
find_one method 99
findone queries, vs. find queries 99–100
findOne() function 129, 253
find_one() function 438
$first function 137

force option 323
forEach function 129
–fork option 344
fork option 418
FreeBSD 413
FROM command 123
from_mongo method 95
fs.chunks collection 435
fs.files collection 435, 437

G

gem command 420
generate_ancestors() method 165
generation_time method 61
$geoNear operator 122, 135
geospatial indexes 211
getCmdLineOpts command 419
getIndexes() method 43, 47, 348
getIndexKeys() function 232
getIndexSpecs() method 212
getLastError command 326–327, 331
getLastErrorDefaults option 319
getLastErrorModes 331
getLastErrorModes option 320
getSiblingDB() method 347
global queries 355
GNU-Affero General Public License. See AGPL
grantRolesToUser helper 400
granularity, coarse 362
greater than ($gte) operator 102–103
grep command 218
Grid object 436
Grid#put method 436
GridFS 435–440
  in Ruby 436–438
  with mongofiles 438–440
GROUP BY clause, SQL 122
GROUP BY command 123
$group operator 122–123, 125–126, 133, 135–136, 152
$gt (greater than) operator 41, 103, 107, 143
$gte (greater than or equal) operator 102–103

H

halted replication 312
hash (Ruby primitive) 17
hashed indexes 209–211
hashed shard keys 361
HAVING command 123
Hazard pointers 276
–headerline flag 403
heartbeat 313
–help flag 403

help() method 49
hidden option 318
hint() function 238, 240, 260
history of MongoDB 5–6, 25–27
  version 1.8.x 25
  version 2.0.x 25
  version 2.2.x 26
  version 2.4.x 26
  version 2.6.x 26–27
  version 3.0.x 27
Homebrew 415
horizontal scaling 14
–host option 388
host option 317
hotspots 360–362
$hour function 143

I

/i modifier 115
i regex flag 114
_id field 17, 59, 64, 79–80, 100, 117, 137, 342, 357, 360–361
ifconfig command 395
$ifNull function 143
imbalanced writes 360–362
imports, data. See data imports and exports
$in operator 104–107, 423
$inc operator 161, 163, 167, 169–170, 181, 191, 193, 430
IN_CART state 176, 179
index locality 364
indexBounds field 225
indexConfig.prefixCompression option 277
indexes 10–11
  administration of 211–216
  background indexing 215
  backing up 216
  book example 198–201
  B-trees 205–206
  building 213–215
  caution about building online 213
  compaction of 216
  compound-key indexes 203, 242
  cookbook analogy 11, 198, 201
  core concepts 201–205
    compound-key indexes 202–203
    index efficiency 203–205
    single-key indexes 201
  covering indexes 242–243
  creating and deleting 211–212
  defragmenting 216
  efficiency issues 203, 205
  ensureIndex() method 43
  getIndexes() method 43

indexes *(continued)*
  in sharded cluster 356–357
  maximum key size 206
  multikey indexes 211
  offline 215
  ordering of keys 203
  performance cost 203
  RAM requirements 204
  sharding and 356–357, 359
  single-key 201, 241–242
  sparse 209
  text search indexes 255–257
    assigning index name 256–257
    text index size 255–256
  types of 207–211
    geospatial indexes 211
    hashed indexes 209–211
    multikey indexes 209
    sparse indexes 208–209
    unique indexes 207
  unique indexes 207
  when to declare them 213
  write lock when building 215
indexOnly field 243
indexSizes field 256
infix notation 160
initialize method 63
injection attacks 113
insert() method 50, 56
insert_one function 84
inserts, MongoDB shell and 32–34
installation 411
  basic configuration options
    418–419
  MongoDB on Linux 412–413
    installing with precompiled binaries
      412–413
    using package manager 413
  MongoDB on Mac OS X 414–415
    precompiled binaries 414–415
    using package manager 415
  MongoDB on Windows 415–416
  MongoDB Ruby driver 53–54
  MongoDB versioning and 411–412
  on Linux 412–413
  on OS X 414–415
  on Windows 415–416
  Ruby 419
  troubleshooting 416–418
    lack of permissions 417
    nonexistent data directory 417
    unable to bind to port 418
    wrong architecture 417
  with Linux package managers 413
  with OS X package managers 415

inventory management 174–179
  failure 178–179
  inventory fetcher 175–176
InventoryFetcher 177
InventoryFetchFailure exception 178
iostat command 390
irb shell 55
isbn field 254
isMaster command 317–318, 324–326, 389
ISODate object 115
$isolated operator 190–191
it command 40
itcount() function 152
items array 177

J

j option 327
JavaScript Object Notation. *See* JSON
JavaScript query operators 112–113
JavaScript shell. *See* MongoDB shell
JavaScript type 116
JOIN command 123
joins, complexity of 4, 10
journal.enabled option 277
journaling 13, 383–385
JSON (JavaScript Object Notation) 4, 31

K

key features of MongoDB 6–15
  ad hoc queries 10
  document data model 6–9
  indexes 10–11
  replication 11–12
  scaling 14–15
  speed and durability 12–13
key file authentication 401–402
–keyFile option 402
key-value stores 19
  query model 10
  simple 19–20
  sophisticated 20–21
  use cases 20
kill command 387, 418
KVEngine 291–292
KVStorageEngine class 290

L

languages, text search 267–272
  available languages 271
  specifying in document 269
  specifying in index 267–268
  specifying in search 269–271

large, deeply nested documents 431
$last function 137
less than ($lt) operator 102–103
$let function 145–146
licensing, core server 15
$limit operator 122, 135
limit query option 100–101, 118
Linux
    installing MongoDB on
        installing with precompiled binaries
            412–413
        using package manager 413
    installing Ruby on 419
listDatabases command 58
listshards command 347
$literal function 145–146
load distribution 335–336
localhost exception 401
locality 430
:local_threshold option 329
locking 294, 381–382
locks element 215
–logappend option 387
logging 23, 217
logical functions 143
–logpath option 387
logpath option 344, 418
logrotate command 387
long polling 311
longDescription field 254, 266
ls command 62
LSM (log-structured merge-trees) 11, 289
lsof command 418
$lt (less than) operator 41, 102–103, 143
$lte (less than or equal) operator 103, 143, 160

M

Mac OS X
    installing MongoDB on 414–415
        precompiled binaries 414–415
        using package manager 415
    installing Ruby on 419
MacPorts 415
mainCategorySummary collection 129–130
man-in-the-middle attacks 398
many-to-many relationships 79, 423
$map function 145–146
map-reduce function 132, 153–154
master-slave replication 297, 311
$match operator 121–123, 126–127, 133, 135, 139,
    146, 156, 264
materialized views 140
$max function 137
max parameter 90

maxBsonObjectSize field 95
maxElement 225
$maxElement field 225
$maxKey 351, 361
Maxkey type 116
McCreight, Ed 292
:md5 435
MD5, storing 434–435
Memcached 19
$meta function 145
$meta:"textScore" field 263
metadata, storage of 338
method chaining 100
migration rounds 353
millis field 222
$millisecond function 143
$min function 137
$minElement field 225
$minKey 351
Minkey type 116
$minute function 143
mmap() function 204
MMAPv1, WiredTiger compared with 278–289
    benchmark conclusion 288–289
    configuration files 279–281
    insertion benchmark results 283–284
    insertion script and benchmark script 281–283
    read performance results 286–288
    read performance scripts 285–286
MMAPV1DatabaseCatalogEntry class 291
MMAPV1Engine class 290
MMS Automation 386
MMS Monitoring 390, 409
$mod operator 115, 142
modifying document updates
    by operator 159
    by replacement 159–162
mongo (executable) 16, 30
mongo gem 54, 62
Mongo::Client constructor 328
mongoconnector tool 403
mongod (executable) 16
MongoDB
    additional resources 27–28
    core server 15–16
    definition of 4
    design philosophy 18
    document-oriented data model 6
    history of 5–6, 25–27
        version 1.8.x 25
        version 2.0.x 25
        version 2.2.x 26
        version 2.4.x 26
        version 2.6.x 26–27
        version 3.0.x 27

MongoDB *(continued)*
　　installing on Linux
　　　　installing with precompiled binaries 412–413
　　　　using package manager 413
　　installing on Mac OS X 414–415
　　　　precompiled binaries 414–415
　　　　using package manager 415
　　installing on Windows 415–416
　　key features of 6–15
　　　　ad hoc queries 10
　　　　document data model 6–9
　　　　indexes 10–11
　　　　replication 11–12
　　　　scaling 14–15
　　　　speed and durability 12–13
　　open source status 6
　　operating system support 15
　　reasons for using 18–23
　　tips and limitations 24–25
　　tools
　　　　command-line tools 18
　　　　database drivers 17
　　　　JavaScript shell 16–17
　　uniqueness of data model 4
　　use cases and production deployments 22–23
　　　　agile development 22–23
　　　　analytics and logging 23
　　　　caching 23
　　　　variable schemas 23
　　　　web applications 22
　　user's manual 27
　　vs. other databases 19–22
　　　　document databases 22
　　　　relational databases 21
　　　　simple key-value stores 19–20
　　　　sophisticated key-value stores 20–21
　　with object-oriented languages 5
　　See also MongoDB shell
Mongo::DB class 84
MongoDB Management System Automation. *See*
　　MMS Automation
MongoDB Monitoring Service 390
MongoDB Ruby driver 53–59
　　database commands 58–59
　　inserting documents in Ruby 55–56
　　installing and connecting 53–54
　　queries and cursors 56–57
　　updates and deletes 57–58
MongoDB shell 30–39
　　administration 46–49
　　　　commands 48–49
　　　　getting database information 46–48
　　collections 31–32
　　databases 31–32
　　deleting data 38

documents 31–32
help 49
indexes 39–41
　　explain( ) method 41–46
　　range queries 41
inserts and queries 32–34
　　_id fields in MongoDB 32
　　pass query predicate 33–34
other shell features 38–39
starting 30
updating documents 34–38
　　advanced updates 37–38
　　operator update 34–35
　　replacement update 35
　　updating complex data 35–37
MongoDB user groups 28
mongod.lock file 417
mongodump command 389
mongodump utility 18, 216, 391–392
mongoexport utility 403
mongofiles utility 435–436, 438–440
Mongo::Grid::File object 438
mongoimport utility 23, 403
Mongo::OperationFailure exception 178
mongooplog utility 18
mongoperf utility 18
mongorestore utility 18, 216, 391–392
mongos routers 337
mongosniff utility 18, 389
mongostat utility 18, 386, 388
mongotop utility 18, 388–389
monitoring
　　external applications for 390–391
　　logging 387
　　MongoDB Monitoring Service 390
　　See also diagnostics
$month function 133, 143
motley types 431
movechunk command 370–371
moveprimary command 372
msg field 215
multi parameter 166
multi: true parameter 180
multidocument updates 180
multikey indexes 209
$multiply function 142
Munin monitoring system 390
MySQL 13, 19, 21

N

n integer 89
Nagios monitoring system 390
name attribute 166
name field 77, 80

name parameter 212
namespaces 256, 340
NASDAQ (example data set) 217
$natural operator 219
$ne (not equal to) operator 106, 144
nearest setting, MongoDB driver 328
nested documents 78–79
network encryption 395–397
   running MongoDB with SSL
      396–397
   SSL in clusters 397
new option 189
next() function 126
$nin (not in) operator 105–106
noatime directive 382
–nojournal flag 384
nonexistent data directory 417
–noprealloc option 86
$nor operator 106–107
normalization 3, 7
NoSQL 5
not equal to ($ne) operator 106, 144
$not function 144
not in ($nin) operator 105
$not operator 106
nReturned 230
nscanned 230–232, 240–241
–nssize option 86
NTP (Network Time Protocol) 383
ntpd daemon 383
Null type 116
null value 208
num key 43
num_1 field 44
NumberInt() function 187
numbers collection 39, 43, 94
numeric types 93–94

O

object IDs, generation of 59–61
Object type 116
offline indexing 215
one collection per user 432
one-to-many relationships 79, 421–422
op field 309
operations, router of 338
operators 181–188
   aggregation framework operators 135
      $group 136
      $limit 138
      $match 138
      $out 139
      $project 136
      $skip 138

      $sort 138
      $unwind 139
   array update operators 183–187
   modifying document updates by 159
   positional updates 187–188
   standard update operators 181–183
oplog, querying manually 308
oplog.rs collection 92, 308
–oplogSize option, mongod 313
optimistic locking 161
$options operator 114
$or operator 105–107, 144
Oracle database 19
order state transitions 172–174
   finishing order 173–174
   preparing order for checkout 172–173
   verifying order and authorization 173
orders 168–171
$out operator 122, 131, 135, 139–140

P

p method, Ruby 56
padding factor 192
paddingFactor field 405
page faults 204
pageCount field 254
pagination 100
parent_id attribute 164
partial match queries in users 102
path field 424–425
pattern matching, vs. text search 246–247
patterns, design. *See* design patterns
PCRE (Perl Compatible Regular Expressions) 114
Percona 290
performance troubleshooting 405–408
   performance cliff 407
   query interactions 407–408
   seeking professional assistance 408
   working set 406
Perl Compatible Regular Expressions. *See* PCRE
permission denied (error message) 417
permissions, lack of 417
pluggable storage engines
   classes to deal with storage modules 290–292
   data structure 292–294
   examples of 289–290
   locking 294
   storage engine API 273–275
poor targeting 360, 362–363
$pop operator 185–186, 193
–port flag 418
port option 418
ports, inability to bind to 418
positional updates 187–188

PostgreSQL 19
post_id field 7, 422
precomputation 430
prefix notation 160
pretty() function 37, 152
primary key field. *See* _id fields
primary setting, MongoDB driver 328
primaryPreferred setting, MongoDB driver 328
priority option 317
privileges 399
product information summaries 125
    calculating average review 126
    counting reviews by rating 127
    joining collections 128
    $out operator 129
    $project operator 129
    $unwind operator 130
product reviews. *See* reviews, product
product_id field 101
production deployments. *See* use cases and production deployments
products collection 169, 252
programs, writing 52–69
    building simple application 61–69
        gathering data 62–65
        setting up 61–62
        viewing archive 65
    how drivers work 59–61
    MongoDB Ruby driver 53–59
        database commands 58–59
        inserting documents in Ruby 55–56
        installing and connecting 53–54
        queries and cursors 56–57
        updates and deletes 57–58
$project operator 121, 123, 130–131, 135, 264, 266
Project Voldemort 19
projections 117–118
provisioning 385–386
    cloud and 385–386
    Management System (MMS) Automation 386
ps command 387
publishedDate field 254
$pull operator 187, 193
$pullAll operator 179, 187, 193
$push operator 137–138, 167, 183, 185, 191, 193
$pushAll operator 183, 193

Q

queries 33, 98–119
    e-commerce queries 99–103
        findone vs. find queries 99–100
        partial match queries in users 102
        products, categories, and reviews 99–101
        querying specific ranges 102–103

        skip, limit, and sort query options 100–101
        users and orders 101–103
    explain() method 41
    _id lookups 99
    matching sub-documents 108
    MongoDB Ruby driver 56–57
    MongoDB shell and 32–34
        _id fields in MongoDB 32
        pass query predicate 33–34
    object id reference lookups 99
    range 41
    ranges 103
    vs. updates 159
query language, MongoDB's 103–119
    query criteria and selectors 103–117
        arrays 110, 112
        Boolean operators 106–107
        JavaScript query operators 112–113
        matching subdocuments 108–109
        miscellaneous query operators 115, 117
        querying for an array by size 112
        querying for document with specific key 107–108
        ranges 103–104
        regular expressions 113, 115
        selector matching 103
        set operators 104, 106
    query options 117, 119
        projections 117–118
        skip and limit 118
        sorting 118
    See also queries
query optimization 216, 243
    common query patterns and indexes for 243
    query patterns 241–243
        compound-key indexes and 242
        covering indexes and 242–243
        single-key indexes and 241–242
    slow queries
        adding index and retrying 224–227
        explain( ) method 222–224
        identifying 217–221
        indexed key use 227–230
        MongoDB's query optimizer 230–238
        query plan cache 240–241
        showing query plans 238–240
    with compound-key indexes 242
    with single-key indexes 242
query optimizer
    caching and expiring query plans 240–241
    internal 230, 241
    running queries in parallel 232
query selectors 33, 103
queryPlanner mode 238
queues, implementing 427

R

RAM
  in-memory databases 12
  page size 204
  performance issues and 380
range queries, optimizing indexes for 242
ranges 103–104
rating field 163
ratingSummary variable 127
:read parameter 324–325
read role 400
read scaling 328–330
readWrite role 400
RecordStore class 291
recovery, from network partitions 321
$redact operator 122, 135
reduce() function 154
referencing, vs. embedding 421
$regex operator 114
Regex type 116
regular expressions 113–115
reIndex command 216
reIndex() method 404
rejectedPlans list 240
relational databases 21
relationships
  many-to-many 79, 423
  one-to-many 79
  structure of 79–80
releases 15, 411
remove method 38, 57, 189
remove option 189
removeshard command 372
$rename operator 182, 193
renameCollection method 88
repairDatabase command 404
replacement, modifying document updates
    by 159–162
replica sets 300–324
  administration 314–324
    configuration details 315–320
    deployment strategies 322–324
    failover and recovery 321–322
    replica set status 320
  and automated failover 12
  authentication 401–402
    key file authentication 401–402
    X509 authentication 402
  commits and rollback 314
  connecting to 324
  halted replication 312
  heartbeat and failover 313
  how failover works 313
  oplog capped collection 307

  overview 377
  setup 300–307
  sizing replication oplog 312–313
  tagging 330
replication 11–12, 296–332
  drivers and 324–332
    connections and failover 324–326
    read scaling 328–330
    tagging 330
    write concern 327–328
  failure modes it protects against 297
  importance of 297–298
  overview 297–300
  use cases and limitations 298–300
  See also replica sets
–replSet flag 323
replSetGetStatus command 320
replSetInitiate command 316
replset.minvalid 308
replSetReconfig command 316
reshaping documents 140
  arithmetic functions 142
  date functions 142
  logical functions 143
  miscellaneous functions 145
  set operators 144
  string functions 141
REST interface 418
rest option 418
reviewing update operators 192–193
reviews, product 167–168
  average review, calculating 126
  counting by rating 127
revokeRolesFromUser helper 400
Riak 19
roles 399
rollback 314
rs.add() function 302, 315–316
rs.conf() method 316
rs.help() command 316
rs.initiate() command 302, 315–316, 345
rs.reconfig() command 316, 321
rs.slaveOk() function 306
rs.status() command 303–304, 313, 320, 322, 345
Ruby
  GridFS in 436–438
  installing 419
Ruby driver. See MongoDB Ruby driver
runCommand() method 48–49

S

–s option 382
save() method 50, 64
save_tweets_for method 64

scalability, as original design goal 6
scaling 14–15
  See also read scaling; sharding
scanAndOrder field 223, 225, 230
scatter/gather queries 355
schema design, principles of 74–75
schema-less model, advantages of 8–9
schemas, variable 23
Scoped JavaScript type 116
score attribute 264
$search parameter 258
secondary indexes 11
secondary setting, MongoDB driver 328
secondaryPreferred setting, MongoDB driver 328
Secure Sockets Layer. *See* SSL
security 394–402
  authentication 397–400
    basic, setting up 399–400
    removing user 400
    service authentication 398
    user authentication 398–399
  enterprise security features 402
  network encryption 395–397
    running MongoDB with SSL 396–397
    SSL in clusters 397
  replica set authentication 401–402
    key file authentication 401–402
    X509 authentication 402
  secure environments 394–395
  sharding authentication 402
SELECT command 123
selectors, query 103–117
  arrays 110, 112
  Boolean operators 106–107
  JavaScript query operators 112–113
  matching subdocuments 108–109
  miscellaneous query operators 115, 117
  querying for an array by size 112
  querying for document with specific
    key 107–108
  ranges 103–104
  regular expressions 113, 115
  selector matching 103
  set operators 104, 106
sequential vs. random writes 13
serialize method 92
serverStatus command 371, 388, 390
service authentication 398
$set operator 159, 163, 180–181, 193
$setDifference function 144
$setEquals function 144
$setIntersection function 144
$setIsSubset function 144
$setOnInsert operator 182–183, 193
setProfilingLevel command 219

$setUnion function 144
sh helper object 346
sh.addShard() command 346
shard clusters
  backing up 373
  checking chunk distribution 352
  failover and recovery of 375
  querying and indexing 355, 359
  unsharding a collection 373
shard keys, examples of 347
shardcollection command 347
sharding 14, 333, 366–375
  across data centers 368
  authentication 402
  building sample shard cluster 343–355
    sharding collections 347–349
    starting mongod and mongos servers
      343–347
    writing to sharded cluster 349–355
  checking which collections are sharded 348
  choosing shard key 359–365
    ideal shard keys 363
    imbalanced writes 360–362
    inherent design trade-offs 364–365
    poor targeting 362–363
    unsplittable chunks 362
  components of 336–338
    Mongos router 338
    shards 337–338
    storage of metadata 338
  distributing data in sharded cluster 339–342
    distributing databases to shards 341
    methods of 340–341
    sharding within collections 341–342
  estimating cluster size 369
  how it works 342
  in production 365–375
    deployment 369–370
    maintenance 370–375
    provisioning 366–369
  overview 334–336
  problem definition 334
  processes required 343
  production deployment techniques 375
  query types 355
  querying and indexing shard cluster 355–359
    aggregation in sharded cluster 359
    explain() tool in sharded cluster 357–359
    indexing in sharded cluster 356–357
    query routing 355–356
  sample deployment topologies 367–368
  when to use 335–336
    load distribution 335–336
    storage distribution 335
shardsvr option 344

shell. *See* MongoDB shell
sh.enableSharding() method 347
sh.help() function 346
sh.moveChunk() method 370
shortDescription field 254, 266
sh.shardCollection() method 347
sh.splitAt() method 370
sh.status() method 347, 352–353
sh.stopBalancer() function 374
siblings 101
simple index 198–199
simple key-value stores 19–20
sinatra gem 62
single nodes 377
single point of failure. *See* SPOF
single-key indexes 201, 241–242
$size operator 110, 112, 145–146
$skip operator 122, 135
skip option 100–101, 118
sku field 77, 208
slaveDelay option 318
slaves collection 327
Sleepycat Software 276
$slice operator 117–118, 183–184, 193
slow queries
    adding index and retrying 224–227
    explain( ) method 222–224
    identifying 217–221
    indexed key use 227–230
    MongoDB's query optimizer 230–238
    query plan cache 240–241
    showing query plans 238–240
slowms flag 218
slug field 80
slugs 78
–smallfiles option 86
snappy compression algorithm 279
snapshotting live systems 393
sophisticated key-value stores 20–21
$sort operator 122, 133, 135, 146, 185, 193, 264
sort option 100–101, 189
sort() function 133
sorting, optimizing indexes for 100, 118, 241–242
sparse indexes 208–209
sparse option 209
speed 12–13
split command 370–371
SPOF (single point of failure) 15
SQL 10, 103
SSL (Secure Sockets Layer) 395
    in clusters 397
    running MongoDB with 396–397
–sslMode option 396–397
–sslPEMKeyFile option 396

Stack Overflow 27
standard update operators 181–183
state field 111, 429
state machines 172
stateStr field 305
stats() command 47–48, 86, 205, 255
status field 254
stemming 247, 250, 267
Stirman, Kelly 245
stop words 255
storage distribution 335
storage engines. *See* pluggable storage engines
storage, binary 433–435
    storing an MD5 434–435
    storing thumbnails 434
StorageEngine class 290
storageSize field 87
$strcasecmp function 141
String (UTF-8) type 116
string functions 141
string values 93
StringIO class 93
subdocuments, matching in queries 108–109
$substr function 141–142
$subtract function 142
$sum function 125, 127, 137
Symbol type 116
symlink (symbolic link) 384
synonym libraries 250
system collections 91–92
system.indexes collection 47, 92, 211
system.namespaces collection 92
system.profile collection 219
system.replset collection 308, 316

T

table scans. *See* collection scans
tagging replica sets 330
tags field 110
tags option 319
targeted queries 355
targetedCustomers collection 139–140
tcpdump command 395
test database 31
$text operator 115, 258, 264
text search 244–272
    aggregation framework text search 263–267
    basic 257–259
    book catalog data download 253–254
    complex 259–261
        excluding documents with specific words or phrases 260
        specifications 260–261
    costs vs. benefits 251–252

text search *(continued)*
   defining indexes 255–257
      assigning index name 256–257
      indexing all text fields in collection 256–257
      text index size 255–256
   languages 267–272
      available languages 271
      specifying in document 269
      specifying in index 267–268
      specifying in search 269–271
   scores 261–263
   simple example 252–253
   vs. dedicated text search engines 250–253
   vs. pattern matching 246–247
   vs. web page searches 247–249
textSearchScore 263
this keyword 112, 154
thrashing 204, 406
thread_id field 425
thumbnails, storing 434
thumbnailUrl field 254
Time object 61, 94
time_field 91
Timestamp type 116
title field 254
toArray() method 152
TokuFT key-value store 289
TokuMXse Pluggable Storage API 290
$toLower function 141
to_mongo method 95
tools
   command-line tools 18
   database drivers 17
   JavaScript shell 16–17
tools tag 186
to_s method 434
totalDocsExamined 230, 243
$toUpper function 141–142
transaction logging. *See* journaling
transactions 429–430
transition_state method 177, 179
trees 423–426
   category hierarchy example 163
   denormalized ancestor pattern 424
   representing threaded comments with 424
troubleshooting, installation problems 416–418
   lack of permissions 417
   nonexistent data directory 417
   unable to bind to port 418
   wrong architecture 417
   See also performance troubleshooting
ts field 309
TTL (time-to-live) collections 90–91
TweetArchiver class 62
TWEETS constant 66

tweets.erb file 67
twitter gem 62
Twitter, storing tweets 23
$type operator 115
types
   numeric types 93–94
   string values 93
   virtual types 95

U

Ubuntu 413
ulimit comman 383
unique indexes 207
unique key 348
$unset operator 35, 182, 193
unshardable collections 432
unsplittable chunks 360
$unwind operator 122–123, 129–131, 135
unzip utility 415
update() method 34, 50, 62, 64, 159, 189
update_many method 57
updates
   atomicity 190–191
   by replacement vs. by operator 162
   concurrency 190–191
   findAndModify command 188–189
   isolation 190–191
   MongoDB Ruby driver 57–58
   operators 181–188
      array update operators 183–187
      positional updates 187–188
      standard update operators 181–183
   performance notes 191–192
   types and options 179–181
      multidocument updates 180
      upserts 180–181
   vs. queries 159
   See also document updates
upgrading 405
upsert option 189
upsert: true parameter 180
upserts 168, 180–181
use cases and production deployments 22–23
   agile development 22–23
   analytics and logging 23
   caching 23
   variable schemas 23
   web applications 22
use command 347
user authentication 398–399
user groups, MongoDB 28
user's manual, MongoDB 27
user_actions collection 89
userAdminAnyDatabase 399

user_id attribute 81
user_id field 101, 113, 208
username field 33, 117, 342, 356, 362–363
users collection 32, 36, 54, 102, 159, 206–207

V

variable schemas 23
versioning 15, 411
   See also releases
versions of MongoDB
   version 1.8.x 25
   version 2.0.x 25
   version 2.2.x 26
   version 2.4.x 26
   version 2.6.x 26–27
   version 3.0.x 27
vertical scaling 14
virtual types 95
votes setting 317
-vvvvv option 387

W

w parameter 327
web applications 3, 22
web console tool 390
web page searches, vs. text search 247–249
$week function 143
weight, for fields 262
wget utility 412
WHERE command 123
$where operator 112, 139
wildcard field name 257
Windows, installing MongoDB on 415–416

WiredTiger 275–278
   migrating database to 277–278
   MMAPv1 compared with 278–289
      benchmark conclusion 288–289
      configuration files 279–281
      insertion benchmark results 283–284
      insertion script and benchmark script 281–283
      read performance results 286–288
      read performance scripts 285–286
   switching to 276–277
wiredTiger option, MongoDB configuration file 277
WiredTigerFactory class 291
WiredTigerKVEngine class 291
WiredTigerRecordStore class 291
wiredtiger-snappy.conf file 280
worker queues 427
working data set 205
write concern 327–328
write speed 12
wtimeout parameter 327

X

-x option 390
X509 authentication 402

Y

$year function 133, 143

Z

Zlib compression algorithm 279